PRINCIPLES
OF
PRODUCTS LIABILITY

By

Michael I. Krauss
Professor of Law
George Mason University School of Law

CONCISE HORNBOOK SERIES®

A Thomson Reuters business

Mat #40590527

Concise Hornbook Series and Westlaw are trademarks registered in the U.S. Patent and Trademark Office.

© 2011 Thomson Reuters

 610 Opperman Drive
 St. Paul, MN 55123
 1–800–313–9378

Printed in the United States of America

ISBN: 978–0–314–18039–1

Dedication

*To my son Joshua (U.S.M.C., 2LT) and my daughter
Rebecca (Judicial Clerk to the United States Court
of Appeals and the United States Supreme Court):
two more defenders of our safety and of the Rule of Law.*

Preface

Products liability is perhaps the most contested and confused area of American private law. It affects every American who purchases or uses any product, domestic or imported. Who hasn't heard of the hot coffee burn case? Who hasn't grown weary reading interminable warnings on the seemingly simple products? Products liability is the object of late-night talk show jokes and politicians' stump speeches.

Yet, like many subjects discussed by politicians and TV stars, products liability is arguably more subtle and multi-layered than they make it appear. This book is designed to "unpack" these subtleties and to allow the reader to understand current American products liability doctrine, and to intelligently participate in debates about proposed reforms. The book is chock full of summaries of theoretical positions as well as advice for practitioners.

By the time the reader has finished this book, she or he will understand a lot about automobiles, pharmaceuticals and workplace technology! Indeed, the practical knowledge imparted by an understanding of products liability is a powerful fringe benefit of practicing this area of the law.

Two innovations characterize this book. First, care has been taken to include and discuss hundreds of important cases, all the "classics" as well other illustrative cases applying the laws of all fifty states, the District of Columbia, and even Guam. In this way the book is meant to be useful to law students and to practitioners nationwide. Second, one recent Florida case has been extensively researched and is employed as a case study. This case is discussed in every chapter, allowing the reader to see how disparate doctrinal points can come together in the practical handling of a single products liability case. The idea behind both of these innovations is to impart to the reader a "feel" for the depth of current debates and for the somewhat different approaches of different courts. Finally, footnotes in each chapter provide suggestions for further reading, for those interested in exploring some chapters' themes at greater length.

I enjoyed writing this book and hope readers find it both informative and, yes, interesting to read. I look forward to receiving comments.

Several people deserve thanks for helping this project along, none more than my wife Cynthia Conner–Krauss, whose love and patience (not to mention her legal editing skills!) are unmatched. Thanks also to Princeton University's James Madison Program, whose generous offer of a sabbatical semester at that glorious institution made it possible for me to write this book in an ideal setting. Two research assistants deserve thanks: Ms. Carroll Chancellor for providing valuable advice in organizing the material and in choosing the case study, and Ms. Lindsey Champlin for excellent bluebooking and editing. Last but not least, everlasting thanks are due to twenty years' worth of products liability students at George Mason University School of Law, for posing the hard questions to which this Book tries to provide answers. My students educate their teacher every day.

MICHAEL I. KRAUSS
George Mason University
School of Law
mkrauss@gmu.edu

June 2010

Summary of Contents

Table of Contents

ix

PART TWO.   ANALYSIS OF PRODUCTS LIABILITY LAW

PRINCIPLES
OF
PRODUCTS LIABILITY

INTRODUCTION

Wreckage of the "loaner" Lexus E350 driven by California Highway
Patrol Officer Mark Sayler, killed along with three family members when the
vehicle accelerated out of control and crashed into a ravine.

February 24, 2010 was an important day in American automo-
tive history. Toyota Chairman Akio Toyoda testified before the
House of Representatives' Committee investigating thirty-four
deaths allegedly resulting from the uncontrolled acceleration of
Toyota and Lexus vehicles. The previous day, the *Wall Street
Journal* published two columns in its *Opinion* section dealing with
Mr. Toyoda's impending testimony. Here they are. When reading
them, try to imagine how Toyota attorneys likely briefed Mr.
Toyoda concerning the implications of his testimony. Consider the
legal régime that Mr. Jenkins, the author of the first op-ed, would
prefer to see in the United States. Much of this book will deal with
the universe Mr. Toyoda fears and that Messrs Robinson and
Calcagnie praise, and a bit will deal with the universe Mr. Jenkins
hopes for.

"My Sudden Acceleration Nightmare"

Reading the mind of Akio Toyoda as he faces Washington's grand inquistors.

By HOLMAN W. JENKINS, JR.

Secret National Security Agency transcript of CEO Akio Toyoda's inner monologue as he prepares to testify in today's congressional hearing into the Toyota recall crisis:

Oh what a feeling. I wonder what Hank Paulson does for the dry heaves?

How I envy Ford-san. At least the Firestone mess[1] involved a real defect, a tire spec unsuitable for Americans accustomed to cruising all day in hot weather at 80 mph on underinflated tires.

Toyota is battling a "defect" it can't find and may not exist. Our crisis management has not been the best, but . . . oy vey.

I wouldn't be here if not for an accident fluky and bizarre even by unintended-acceleration standards. A San Diego Lexus dealer installed an unapproved and ill-fitting floor mat in a loaner car. The mat was placed in the car upside-down and wasn't fastened down. The dealer ignored a previous customer's complaint that the mat interfered with the gas pedal. The next borrower didn't . . . shift into neutral when the pedal jammed. Four people died in a horrible crash.

Before the accident, Toyota issued recalls and service bulletins related to floor mats. How is this not the dealer's fault? Not a single incident of runaway speeding has been traced to the sticky pedals Toyota subsequently recalled. No electronic defect has been found.

I should have listened to the Germans. They racked up billions of miles on their vehicle electronics before bringing them to lawyer-happy America. They installed a brake-override so a foot on the brake would always shut the throttle.

To think, if we had adopted the same kludge, our runaway-vehicle complaints would probably be in line with those of our competitors. It's the fix that fixes whether the problem is pedal blockage, electronic glitch or a driver's foot on gas and brake at the same time. The only problem it doesn't fix is a driver mistakenly stomping on the gas—the actual source of most unintended acceleration.

I wonder if Dr. Richard Restak is in his office today? Years ago, the George Washington University neurologist coined the term "neuro-

---

1. In 2000, both Ford Motor Company and Firestone Tire Co. were sued after dozens of reports of tire failures in Ford SUV's. Victims had been driving at high speed, on very hot days, on grossly underinflated tires, when the tires exploded and rollover typically ensued. A Ford rollover injury constitutes the case study with which we will introduce most of the subsequent material in this book: see Chapter 1, *infra*.

behaviorally impaired" for such drivers: "He or she acts too fast or not fast enough; steps on the accelerator when the intention is to put on the brake; slips the gear into reverse instead of forward; comes to a full stop when the sign merely indicates 'yield.' In all cases, the response is almost but not quite appropriate to the situation ... [and] leaves a wake of dented fenders, sore necks and inflamed tempers."

Great quote, but I can't afford to blame our customers.

No such inhibitions trouble the National Transportation Safety Board (the folks who investigate plane crashes). Last fall, they issued a special report on four school-bus accidents and a fire-truck crash, fingering "pedal misapplication" in every case: "In all five, the drivers either reported a loss of braking or were observed by vehicle occupants to be unsuccessfully attempting to stop the vehicles, though no evidence of braking system failure was found." And these were professional drivers!

I wonder how many congressmen were around for the industry-wide crisis kicked off years ago by Audi. In 1987, the feds received 2,500 complaints of "unintended acceleration," more than in the previous 20 years combined. "The defect, which involves almost all makes of cars, causes them to accelerate without warning.... Sophisticated electronic controls are now believed to play a role in the problem," concluded the New York Times, citing (who else?) Clarence Ditlow, the trial lawyer handmaiden who will be testifying against me today.

Two years later, the National Highway Traffic Safety Administration issued its own exhaustive report on the post-Audi fury: "pedal misapplication."

Far be it from me to suggest a defect is never to blame—say, a poorly designed gas pedal and floor mat. But what a shocker that even our San Diego dealer now has hired a lawyer to float a theory that an electronic bug was behind a crash that every investigation has attributed to floor mats?

Trial lawyers love the electronic gremlin theory because it's impossible to disprove in any individual case. But we're here to talk about a *pattern* of cases. That's what Congressman Henry Waxman, who accuses Toyota and NHTSA of "resisting" evidence of an electronic fault, doesn't understand.

What can "resist" possibly mean in a context where only data and analysis can establish an answer? Eight of the 34 deaths the plaintiffs' bar insists are due to runaway Toyotas are accounted for by just two crashes—the San Diego crash (floor mats) and a Texas crash in which an epileptic drove into a lake. What was the average age of drivers in the remaining unexplained (i.e., non-floor mat) incidents? What, if anything, did drivers have in common? Were they new to the vehicle?

Electronic bugs should occur at random. Here's guessing that once we and the feds agree on a database of incidents and examine them in detail, we'll be able to say conclusively whether there's a "trend" that indicates an electronic defect.

Of course, a competent investigator wouldn't pronounce without data—but who ever said Congress was a competent investigator?

Holman Jenkins is an editorial writer for the Wall Street Journal.

Copyright 2009 Holman Jenkins. Reproduced with permission

"Why We Need Trial Lawyers"

Toyota is only the latest example of lethal defects gone unaddressed by regulators.

By MARK ROBINSON AND KEVIN CALCAGNIE

The alleged need for "tort reform" has become a refrain in American political life. Yet for all the demonizing of trial lawyers, the reality is that product-liability litigation has become an ever more important means of keeping consumers safe.

Case in point: the current Toyota Motor Corp. recalls, with their attendant revelations of corporate obfuscation. This is only the most recent situation in which lethal defects have gone uncorrected for years at least in part because of insufficient government oversight.

In model after model, as we've now learned, car owner complaints were either minimized or ignored altogether by Toyota and by the regulatory agencies that were supposed to police the company. In one review of federal records, the Los Angeles Times found 2,600 complaints of sudden acceleration from 2000 to 2010 by Toyota and Lexus owners. And according to CBS, recently released internal company documents indicate that as far back as 2005 Toyota was tracing its sudden acceleration problem to its software—not to floor mats.

Yet for nearly a decade, neither Toyota nor federal regulators aggressively addressed the problem. Toyota is now likely to face a rising tide of class action lawsuits as consumers look to their historic fallback: the courts.

Regulation is crucial to the creation of a level playing field for consumers, particularly in this era of growing corporate power. But regulation alone has never been enough. Federal agencies such as the Food and Drug Administration (FDA), the Consumer Product Safety Commission and the National Highway Traffic Safety Administration have long been swamped by large work loads. And lobbyists are adept at weakening and fending off regulations.

The laissez-faire policies of the Bush administration only further weakened regulatory agencies by cutting funding and personnel, since such agencies were viewed as an impediment to private-sector growth. Government watchdogs soon found themselves so overwhelmed and undermanned that they could scarcely do their jobs.

Consider the FDA. By the mid–2000s, the FDA's caseload extended to more than 11,000 existing drugs, some 100 new drugs a year, and a breadth of products from food to vaccines to medical devices that comprise approximately 25 percent of all consumer spending.

Resources were stretched so thin that a 2006 report on drug safety by the Institute of Medicine of the National Academies found that the FDA simply couldn't ensure the safety of new prescription drugs. The reasons given? Inadequate funds, cultural and structural problems, and "unclear and insufficient regulatory authorities."

The FDA is just one example. Until April 2009, federal motor vehicle safety standards were so weak that many vehicles could comply and still sustain severe roof collapse from a force equivalent to a 5 mph parking lot collision. Similarly, drivers and passengers are far too frequently ejected in rear-end collisions because the minimum standard for automobile seatback strength is so low that many folding lawn chairs can pass the test.

The recession threatens to further starve the agencies responsible for consumer safety, even as the tough economic climate subjects manufacturers to brutal competition and discourages them from investing in product safety on their own.

As a result, consumers are increasingly left with the courts not only to compensate them when the regulatory system fails to protect them, but also to deter manufacturers from cutting corners in the future.

Product liability lawsuits have played a crucial role in ensuring public safety, encouraging—and sometimes compelling—manufacturers to put safety first. A 1988 survey of 264 CEO's of manufacturing companies found that a third had improved their product lines as a result of the threat of litigation, 35% had improved product safety, and 47% had improved warnings to consumers.

At the same time, such lawsuits have provided important assistance to agencies overseeing product safety. Litigation involving defective products has increased access by regulators and the public to critical safety information about particular products. This has resulted in stronger regulations, safer new products, and the removal of dangerous products from the market. Just last year, in *Wyeth v.*

Levine, the Supreme Court noted that state tort suits "can serve as a catalyst" for regulatory action.

Litigation has not only advanced public safety, but has encouraged improvement in products almost too numerous to mention: airbags, seat belts, child safety seats, tires, minivan doors, hot water vaporizers, children's pajamas, farm machinery, firearms, building materials, tobacco products, intra-uterine contraceptive devices, tampons, sleeping pills, anti-depressants, pain medication, appetite suppressants and many more. Toyota is just another sign of how much work remains to be done.

Strong product liability laws remain vital to public health and safety—no matter how passionate the political debate on tort reform.

Mr. Robinson, managing partner at Robinson, Calcagnie & Robinson in Newport Beach, Calif., has represented plaintiffs in the Ford Pinto, Vioxx, major tobacco and other cases. Mr. Calcagnie is a senior partner at the firm.

Copyright 2009 Messrs Robinson and Calcaigne. Used with permission

Organization of this book

These two op-eds reflect radically different visions of American products liability law. This book provides a thorough overview of products liability, explaining the evolution and impact of these two visions.

Perhaps both visions might concede these background facts:

1. Life in America is manifestly safer than it has ever been. We live longer than ever: life expectancy for a female born in the United States in 1900 was under forty-nine years,[2] while females born in 2003 had a life expectancy of over eighty years.[3] Safety and health are being enhanced at an increasing rate; more than half of all people born in the United States in 2010 will live to the year 2100.[4]

2. A longer life means more chances to have an accident. When our hypothetical 1900 female died in 1949 of "consumption," her death was "natural:" there was no one to sue. But longer life today is made possible in large part

---

2. This means that *if mortality conditions existing in 1900 did not change,* baby girls born at that time would have lived, on average, until they were forty-nine.

3. Again, this assumes that mortality conditions of 2003 are frozen. Laura B. Shrestha, Congressional Research Service, Life Expectancy in the United States 6, *available at http://aging.senate. gov/crs/aging1.pdf.*

4. Kaare Christensen, Gabriele Doblhammer, Roland Rau & James W Vaupel, *Ageing populations: the challenges ahead,* 374 The Lancet 1196, 1208 (2009).

because we can use complex machinery (cars get us to work; nuclear-sourced gas-electric furnaces keep us warm; high-tech vaccines and prescription drugs ward off disease and chronic illness, etc.). We interact with so many *things*; some of these interactions may not be positive ones.

3. When a horse gets lame, the rider feels it immediately, usually in time to avoid injury. She dismounts from the horse and she typically chalks the lameness up to "nature." But when brakes fail, we tend to attribute these complex system failures to human agency, and we may not discover the problem until it is too late unless redundancy is built in to the design. Even redundancy can't prevent all failures. As William Langewiesche showed in his brilliant description of the 1996 crash of ValuJet 592 in Florida's Everglades, in extremely complex systems stochastic (random, periodic) accidents may be "normal."[5] Insisting on preventing all product failures could make our lives both more dangerous and more primitive.

Accidents involving ever more complex goods designed and produced by man are increasingly the source of products liability suits. It is hard to believe that in 1950, manufacturers' CGL (Commercial General Liability) policies covered products liability at no significant cost.[6] Today premiums for these same policies amount to billions of dollars, less than half of which actually reaches injured consumers.[7]

This book describes the rapid evolution of products liability law. The book is divided into three distinct parts:

- *Part I* describes the seminal events in the history of modern products liability law, the different theories of liability underlying this history, and the role of insurance theory in explaining the emergence of the dominant theory of products liability: "strict liability." Part I also introduces Julian Felipe's case, a real products liability dispute from Florida. This case will be adapted in each chapter of the book to draw attention to the practical implications of each doctrinal area of the law.

---

5. *The Lessons of ValuJet 592*, THE ATLANTIC MONTHLY, March 1998, *available at* http://www.theatlantic.com/doc/199803/valujet-crash.

6. Manufacturers were not even charged separate premiums for their products liability exposure, much as today one's home insurance covers tort liability as well as fire insurance.

7. *See* COMMITTEE FOR ECONOMIC DEVELOPMENT, WHO SHOULD BE LIABLE? 53 (1989) (estimating that 35–45 percent of all products liability premiums eventually compensate victims); STEPHEN D. SUGARMAN, DOING AWAY WITH TORT LAW 23–24 (1989) (citing estimates of 37–40 percent).

- *Part II* analyzes the nuts and bolts of products liability law. The notion of "defect" that underlies current law will be unpacked in an effort to determine whether "strict liability" does and should prevail. Products liability causation issues (both "but-for" and "proximate") as well as problems involved in the determination of recoverable damages are also examined in this part of the book. Each chapter in Part II continues to rely on Julian Felipe's case to illustrate specific concepts. Make an effort to answer the questions the book poses about the Felipe case: your effort will enhance your understanding of the material.

- *Part III* discusses the special situations created by toxic products, also often known as "mass torts." This Part will examine alternative approaches to products liability, whether proposed in current literature prevailing internationally.

Two more organizational comments are in order.

- An Appendix provides a primer in the simple economics of various Products Liability rules. Two illustrations, one of a design defect and one of a manufacturing defect, are developed. *The Appendix is most usefully read before beginning Part II of the book.* It will facilitate the understanding of the analytical chapters.

- Thousands of articles and hundreds of books about products liability have been written. Each chapter's first footnote, and to a lesser extent subsequent footnotes, contain suggestions for additional reading. If readers find the material in a chapter to be of particular interest, chances are that the suggested readings will be particularly valuable.

My hope is that the dividend for reading and thinking about this book will be an understanding of both the theory and the caselaw in this extremely important, controversial and fluid area of American law. I look forward to having you join the debate begun on page 1!

Part One

HISTORY AND BASIC STRUC-
TURE OF PRODUCTS
LIABILITY LAW

Chapter 1

JULIAN FELIPE'S CASE

The 1993 Ford Aerostar driven by Mrs. Mirtha Felipe, after
its crash in Lee County, Florida, August 3, 2002.[1]*

On August 3, 2002, twenty-two year old Julian Felipe was a passenger in the family van, which his mother Mirtha was driving from their home in Hialeah, Florida to a family reunion in Sarasota, some 225 miles away. The van was a 1993 Ford Aerostar, which Mirtha Felipe had purchased in 1999 from Seagate Auto Brokers, a used car dealer in Hallandale, Florida, fifteen miles from Hialeah. Almost the entire route between Hialeah and Sarasota is on Interstate 75.

About 80 miles from their destination, on a clear day and on a flat and well-paved highway, the Felipe van's right front tire exploded. It is unclear why the tire blew, how old the tire was, what brand the tire was, how often Mrs. Felipe checked the air pressure in the tire, or whether there had been any forewarning of a blowout. Also unknown is the speed of the Aerostar at the moment of the blowout.

1. Source: Channel 10 Fort Lauderdale News, July 26, 2007, *available at* http://www.youtube.com/watch?v=0r50 TKK3nfg. [last consulted March 18, 2010]

* Courtesy of JustNews.com.

Mrs. Felipe lost control of the Aerostar. She jerked the steering wheel, and the van rolled over onto the right (passenger) side. During the rollover the van's roof deformed downward on this side. The deforming roof did not touch the diminutive Mrs. Felipe on the driver's side. But the roof did strike Julian's head on the passenger side.

Paramedics extracted Julian from the vehicle and airlifted him to hospital in nearby Ft. Myers, where he received competent treatment. Ultimately he was transferred to a different hospital in Miami for full-time care and therapy. Julian's spinal cord was damaged. After a period in which he was confined to a wheelchair, he regained the ability to walk with a cane and a brace on his right leg. Julian also suffered damage to the nerves controlling his right arm and hand, and can no longer use the fingers on that hand.

Julian Felipe sued Ford Motor Company and Seagate Auto Brokers, in Florida State Court,[2] to receive compensation for these injuries. He did not sue the tire manufacturer, or the tire seller, or his mother.

Questions About Julian Felipe's Case

- At this early juncture in your reading, what kind of claim do you be believe the Felipes' attorney should make against Ford? Against Seagate?

- Why do you think Felipes' attorney chose not to sue the tire manufacturer or the tire retailer? Why did Julian's attorney not sue Felipe's mother (assume that she had automobile insurance and would not have been forced to pay out of pocket)?

- If you were Ford Motor Co.'s attorney, what kind of defense do you think you would you mount?

- If you were Seagate Auto Broker's attorney, would you be surprised to be sued three years after you sold a six-year-old van to the Felipes? Assume the van was sold "as is" with no warranty, and that Seagate committed no fraud.

2. Federal diversity jurisdiction under 28 U.S.C. § 1332 (2006), requires "complete" diversity, which means all plaintiffs must be from different states than all defendants. *See, e.g.,* Exxon Mobil Corp. v. Allapattah Servs., Inc., 545 U.S. 546, 553–554 (2005) (explaining that although "the complete diversity requirement is not mandated by the Constitution . . . the presence of parties from the same State on both sides of a case" eliminates the principal reason for § 1332 jurisdiction: "state courts . . . favoring[] home-state litigants.") In the Felipe case complete diversity did not exist because Felipe was a Florida resident and Seagate a Florida corporation.

Chapter 2

FROM OLD TO NEW: A PRIMER ON THE RISE OF PRODUCTS LIABILITY[1]

1. Introduction

People have been injured using "tools" for as long as there have been people and tools. From time immemorial, tools didn't always work as they should. The horse-drawn buggy "fails" when the horse goes suddenly lame, injuring the driver. The musket blows up in the hand of the hunter shooting the deer. The boat suddenly springs a leak and sinks.

Even when tools worked as designed they weren't foolproof. The driver of the buggy loses control when a rattlesnake spooks the horse that is pulling it. The gun fires straight, straight into the foot of the distracted shooter. The well-built boat is struck by lightning.

Sometimes a component part of the tool fails, causing what today would be called a "system failure." The poorly-made horse-shoe infects the horse, which collapses while being ridden. The bullet ill-fits the chamber of the gun, with dire consequences for the shooter. The substandard lot of glue purchased by the unsuspecting boat manufacturer holds only for five months.

When people are injured while using tools, should they have recourse against those who made the tool? Against those who re-sold it? Against those who made or re-sold a component of the tool? Against all of these people? Should one's answers to these questions depend on whether the tool was "natural" (the horse bred by the horse dealer) or man-made (the car sold by the car dealer)? Should it matter if the victim herself, horseback rider or shooter or sailer, "brought on" the accident through their want of care? Should *caveat emptor* apply?[2] After all, we all know that horses go lame

---

1. In this and every chapter, I provide, in alphabetical order by author, suggestions for Additional Reading: RICHARD A. EPSTEIN, MODERN PRODUCTS LIABILITY LAW 1980; George L. Priest, *The Current Insurance Crisis and Modern Tort Law*, 96 YALE L.J. 1521 (1987); William L. Prosser, *The Assault Upon The Citadel (Strict Liability to the Consum-* er), 69 YALE L.J. 1099 (1960); Gary T. Schwartz, Forward: *Understanding Products Liability*, 67 CAL. L. REV. 435 (1979).

2. Under the common law doctrine of "buyer beware," the buyer could not recover from the seller for defects of the property that rendered it unfit for ordinary purposes. The only exception was if

occasionally and suddenly, and that rubber tires inflated to high pressure can puncture and blow up, don't we? Should this doctrine only apply some of the time? Never? Should a products liability suit always be seen as a suit for breach of contract? It was pretty clear in our contract that the bullet in the gun I bought from you would travel forward, not backward. It was understood that the car I bought from you would stop when I applied the brakes, right?

When someone is injured while using a tool, the facts can be perplexing because one cannot blame a tool—for a tool has no moral agency. If one has made the tool oneself, one has only oneself to blame, for one knows the tool better than anyone else. In the pre-modern world, that is, in a world in which one makes or finds almost all of one's tools, one would never consider blaming anyone else. Products liability law is unintelligible in a pre-modern society.

However, to the extent people in a legal system use tools made by and purchased from others, that system has to answer questions like those put in the preceding paragraphs. Indeed, as specialization gave rise to the industrial revolution, freedom might be defined in part by one's ability to self-determine, making only as many tools as one wants.[3] Specialization "alienates" (in Marxian terminology) people from their tools. I likely do not understand the workings of my gun, or my car, or my industrial press to the extent it has been engineered and fabricated by others. And I am more likely to be surprised when my tool injures me if I don't understand it intimately. But sometimes the effects of a modern malfunction can be both unexpected and devastating. Consider this report from the *Wall St. Journal*:[4]

"This isn't my face. I used to be real pretty."

Roblyn Ruggles is weeping. "This isn't my face," she says. "I used to be real pretty."

Eight oral-surgery operations have left her disfigured, without jaw joints, her mouth permanently agape. She can't bite into a sandwich. She can't purse her lips for a kiss.

And alone at night, she can hardly bear the muscle spasms and the pain. "It never goes away; it's God-awful pain," says the onetime nurse, who lives in Cuyahoga Falls, Ohio. "I have to pretend it's something else to hold onto my sanity."

Ms. Ruggles, 37 years old, is a victim of biomaterials engineering gone awry, caught

the seller actively concealed latent defects or made material misrepresentations amounting to fraud.

3. Albania became a near-"autarky" in 1976, when Communist Party dictator Enver Hoxha instituted a policy of "self-reliance." North Korea may be the most autarkical state extant today—

most every contract is with a state agency. It is hard to imagine how primitive such societies were and are. Products liability law requires private ordering and specialization.

4. Bruce Ingersoll and Rose Gutfeld, "*Surgical Merry–Go–Round,*" WALL ST. J., Aug. 31, 1993.

up in a medical catastrophe that is claiming new casualties almost every day. The cause of her pain and disfigurement: synthetic jaw implants aggressively marketed by Charles Homsy, founder of Vitek Inc., without adequate premarket testing. Hundreds of oral surgeons embraced the so-called interpositional implants as a breakthrough of sorts in the 1980s. One prominent surgeon, John Kent, lent his name to Vitek products and served as Dr. Homsy's clinical consultant.

More than 25,000 patients afflicted with the same jaw disorder as Ms. Ruggles—temporomandibular joint syndrome, or TMJ—received Vitek implants before liability-insurance problems forced the small Houston company to take them off the market in mid-1988. In 1990 the Food and Drug Administration forced the company to issue a safety alert and eventually seized its products.

But for thousands of patients, the implant affair is far from over. Medical experts now expect a high percentage, if not all, of the implants to break up into microscopic fragments and beget a biochemical reaction in patients that erodes jaw bone, creating many other painful complications. Says Larry Wolford, a Dallas oral surgeon: "This is the worst disaster our specialty has ever faced."

. . .

TMJ disorders can produce arthritis, jaw and facial pain, headaches, earaches, clicking sounds in the jaw, and restricted jaw movement. The temporo-mandibular joint is terribly complicated: It lets the lower jaw, or mandible, move up and down, side to side, forward and back, and in many combinations as a person speaks, bites, chews, swallows, smiles, laughs, grimaces. It is an exquisite network of nerves and muscles, and it isn't well understood. No one knows, for instance, why TMJ disorders afflict women more than men; 90% of the Vitek implant recipients are women.

Treatment of TMJ disorders has long occupied a medical gray area. Orthopedic surgeons have stayed away from it, fearful of slipping up in an area so close to the brain, ear and facial nerves. But oral and maxillo-facial surgeons have been more aggressive in treating TMJ, and when the Vitek implant came on the market, many turned to it enthusiastically.

. . .

Dr. Homsy, a chemical engineer who was president and majority owner of now-defunct Vitek, blames surgeons for putting his products in the wrong patients or for botching the procedure. The implants, he asserts, "weren't at fault; poor surgical judgment and technique were." If there were any gaps in testing, he says, it is the fault of Dr. Kent.

Dr. Kent, head of oral and maxillofacial surgery at Louisiana State University, blames Dr. Homsy for inadequate testing. "The ultimate responsibility for testing is the manufacturer's," says Dr. Kent. Counters his erstwhile friend, who contends that he urged Dr. Kent to conduct the appropriate tests: "I'm a scientist. I can't operate on animals."

Ms. Ruggles, for one, has been on a "surgical merry-go-round" ever since her implants came out in June 1989. Doctors have tried just about every option—a dermal tissue implant, a silicone rubber implant, a pair of Vitek total-joint implants—without any success. Her surgery bills to date total $280,000, only partly covered by her husband's medical insurance.

In Tucson, Ariz., oral surgeon Stephen Harkins is treating 100 implant patients, 20 of whom he says are suicidal. "They are barely functional, under heavy pain medication and antidepressants," he says. "They have had significant damage to the bones and muscles of the face and nerve damage." Some have had to have their jaws rebuilt with ribs and cartilage from their own bodies or from cadavers, with mixed results. "These people aren't kooks," says Dr. Harkins. "They look like they've spent 10 years in Auschwitz."

Thousands of patients already have had their failed implants removed, and thousands more will have to have theirs "explanted" as well. While many aren't showing any overt symptoms of failure, X-rays and CT scans reveal the onset of bone loss. Deborah Zeitler, an associate professor of oral surgery at the University of Iowa, says more than 90% of her patients with implants already have had them out. Douglas Morgan, a surgeon in La Crescenta, Calif., reports finding an implant had eroded a hole into a patient's brain. Other surgical implants have failed, of course, but few so completely. Silicone-gel breast implants are failing at a rate of about 1%. But it now looks as if the failure rate of the interpositional implant, or IPI, ultimately "could be 100%," says Daniel Laskin, editor in chief of the Journal of Oral and Maxillofacial Surgery.

The IPI, Vitek's main product, was widely used to replace an oval disk of cartilage that acts as shock absorber between the temporal and mandibular bones. The disk can easily be dislocated by a blow to the jaw or irreparably damaged by too much grinding or clenching of the teeth.

The IPI was nothing more than two layers of plastic laminated together—a super-thin sheath of Teflon FEP, which is a smooth DuPont Co. polymer, and a wafer of highly porous Proplast, which is a biomaterial concocted by Dr. Homsy out of another DuPont polymer, Teflon PTFE, and carbon or aluminum oxide. A fundamental flaw doomed the tiny implant: It simply couldn't withstand the wear and tear of the lower jaw sliding on its Teflon surface. In some cases, it disintegrated within a few months.

The IPI fiasco has been ruinous for everybody involved. Vitek was forced into bankruptcy; Dr. Homsy is in professional exile in Switzerland. DuPont, Vitek's Teflon supplier and the only deep-pocketed entity in reach, has been ensnared in litigation, despite a disclaimer it sent Dr. Homsy in 1967 warning about medical complications caused by implanted Teflonlike polymers.

Dr. Homsy is one of bioengineering's pioneers. After earning a Ph.D. in chemical engineering at Massachusetts Institute of Technology, he spent seven years at DuPont in sales and as a Teflon researcher. In 1968 he developed Proplast, which gained wide use in plastic surgery, including chin and cheek implants.

In 1974, Dr. Kent began cutting implants out of sheets of laminated Proplast/Teflon (then being sold by Vitek for plastic surgery) and using them to cover the tips of jawbones in TMJ patients. Other surgeons followed his lead with good results, and some began using the sheeting to replace perforated disks.

By 1979, sponge-like Proplast was being touted by the American Association of Oral and Maxillofacial Surgeons as the "living implant" because human tissue could grow into its pores. At the group's annual meeting that year, Dr. Kent reported on the results of 50 jaw implants, saying that virtually all of the patients showed "marked pain relief and restoration of jaw movement," according to a press release.

At a major meeting of TMJ specialists three years later, Dr. Kent sensed booming demand for Proplast/Teflon. "We anticipate numbers of procedures to rise to 10,000 or more annually easily within the next year," he wrote to Dr. Homsy in March 1982. In the letter, he suggested producing precut disks in an "ovoid shape" so surgeons wouldn't have to do the cutting at the operating table.

One year later, Vitek had the go-ahead from the FDA to market a precut disk, the IPI. To obtain FDA approval, Dr. Homsy merely had to persuade a bureaucrat that a Proplast/Teflon device was "substantially equivalent" to a product already on the market before the enactment of a 1976 law regulating medical devices. In this case, the product was an implant

made of Silastic, or silicone rubber. Silastic implants have failed, too, but the consequences generally have been less severe.

Once approved, the IPI took off commercially, thanks largely to a timely boost from a trio of Tucson surgeons, one of whom had been taught by Dr. Kent how to use Proplast/Teflon in the TMJ. At an oral-surgery meeting in Berlin, Tucson surgeon Theodore Kiersch reported a 93% success rate—high for this kind of procedure.

This helped touch off what Dr. Kent later called "a stampede" among oral and maxillofacial surgeons to implant the IPI in TMJ patients. For them, it was a bona fide business opportunity, a chance to do more than wisdom-tooth extractions and root canals. "It became the fashion," says John Westine, a Delray Beach, Fla., oral surgeon. "Guys were putting them in and having success, and so people were jumping on the bandwagon."

The 1983 class of implant recipients included Betty Jean Meyer, a onetime real-estate broker in Tucson who readily agreed to have an IPI put in for headache relief. She says her surgeon told her, "We'll slip this little disk in, and you'll be out of the hospital in two to three days." The attending surgeon was Dr. Kiersch. It was the first of four major operations for Ms. Meyer, all unsuccessful, including a 1985 procedure by Dr. Kent, who replaced two IPIs with Vitek-made jaw joints.

Yet another surgeon has since removed those joints and rebuilt her eroded jaw bones with grafts from her rib cage, leaving her in perpetual pain. "There are days when my jaws are so swollen and blue I can't open my mouth," she says. "I have to pack my face in ice and stay in bed, with the curtains drawn and the door closed. I need the quiet. I need darkness."

Dr. Kiersch, looking back, feels betrayed by the implant's makers. "My duty was to find the best material possible," he says. "I'm a clinician; I'm not a research person. We were told the material had been released by the FDA. We assumed it had been tested in the animal joint."

Today, many medical devices undergo lab tests, animal experiments and human trials involving groups of closely monitored patients. In those days, however, such testing generally wasn't required of medical devices. Vitek never tested the IPI in animal jaws before marketing it. Vitek took the position that there was no way to reproduce in a lab animal what happens in the human TMJ.

The company didn't do any human trials, either. It relied on the early success that Dr. Kent and others had in implanting Proplast/Teflon in TMJ patients. While such limited, unstructured testing would never pass FDA muster as a clinical trial, Dr. Homsy contends it was an "effective" one.

Vitek did run tests on a mechanical simulator that imitates the human jaw. But the company never did the most obvious test of all: testing Proplast and Teflon together, as a laminated product, to determine how long the IPI would withstand the stresses from biting and chewing.

Fontenot, a bioengineer who once consulted with Vitek on a physical-therapy device and who has done research with Dr. Kent, three years ago did such a test using a simulator patterned after Vitek's. He found that the machine, in sliding back and forth over the IPI with 20 pounds of force, wore through the Teflon surface into the underlying Proplast 100 to 200 times faster than the wear-rate reported by Dr. Homsy. It fractured the thin Teflon layer, scattered microscopic Teflon particles all about and ate into the underlying Proplast. At that rate, according to a scientific paper Dr. Fontenot published last year with Dr. Kent, the IPI would have a "service life" of only one to three years.

How did Dr. Homsy err so badly? His wear-testing was of Teflon with a metal backing that didn't give way under the 20-pound load, Dr. Fontenot says. Had he tested laminated Teflon/Proplast, it would have been obvious that highly porous Proplast isn't solid enough.

"It's like paper backed by a sponge," says Dr. Fontenot. "You can take a pencil and punch a hole in the Teflon surface. Almost anything would have been better than Proplast, even 'papier-mache'."

Dr. Homsy says Dr. Fontenot's simulator test isn't representative because the implant was supposed to gain strength after implantation as body tissue grew into the pores of the Proplast. In most cases, however, "you don't get in-growth," says Barry Sands, a biomedical engineer and former FDA investigator who did a risk evaluation of the Vitek implants. Once implanted, he says, the IPI gets repeatedly compressed between the upper and lower jaws "like a carpet that binds up under a door," and the pores in the Proplast "get closed off."

Only after reports of IPI failure began rumbling in around 1984 were animal studies done. In 1984, a colleague of Dr. Kent's implanted IPIs in dogs. The results were "essentially catastrophic," according to a 1990 deposition that Dr. Kent gave in an Arizona court case against Vitek in Tucson. After just a few months, the Teflon layer was "completely worn" and Teflon particles had triggered bone erosion in the dogs. To Drs. Kent and Homsy, however, the test showed mainly that the dog wasn't a good test animal to use.

The dog study wasn't the only one to be disregarded. In May 1986, Mohamed El Deeb, a professor at the University of Minnesota dental school, had Dr. Homsy come to Minneapolis to see the results of his experiments on monkeys. Both Proplast/Teflon and Silastic implants began to fragment after a year, causing "severe degenerative joint changes," but the reaction was more pronounced with Proplast/Teflon, says Dr. El Deeb.

He says Dr. Homsy made no comment. Asked about the study today, Dr. Homsy says that monkeys weren't a good model.

Reports of Vitek implant failures continued to crop up. The most alarming, published in 1986, involved a 37-year-old woman who had an IPI put in after having her jaw broken by her abusive husband. Teflon debris from the worn implant had migrated through her lymphatic vessels into lymph nodes in her neck, causing painful inflammations, according to researchers in Chicago. The IPI failed, they concluded, because it "couldn't withstand the loads generated" by chewing.

For Dr. Kent, this case was something of a turning point. Besides bringing it to Dr. Homsy's attention, he says he began "blowing the whistle" on the IPI, albeit indirectly. As chairman of scientific sessions at the Oral Surgeons association's national meeting in 1986, he gave IPI critics a chance to present papers.

In October of that year, Vitek had no choice but to notify every member of the association about the increasingly obvious complications. Among other things, it said the prognosis for the IPI's success beyond three years was unknown. But Vitek blunted the letter's warning by also trumpeting the results of an oral-surgeon survey: 91.5% of 5,070 implant cases showed "satisfactory" results, it said, without defining "satisfactory."

By 1987, malpractice lawsuits against surgeons and product-liability suits against Vitek were mounting. Nonetheless, in July of that year, a Memphis surgeon suggested to Marcie Grossberg, a school librarian who had been hit in the jaw by a student, that she get IPIs.

"The only Teflon I knew about was in my skillet," says Ms. Grossberg, 40, who says she trusted the doctor's assurances that the IPI was "state-of-the-art" treatment.

She shouldn't have. Within a few months, her implants were disintegrating and her chin was receding. "I couldn't get my teeth together," she says. "Food would fall out of my mouth." In October 1988, she found another surgeon to extract the implants. Now she suffers from immune-system disorders that doctors believe may be caused by unremoved Teflon particles.

Today, Drs. Homsy and Kent are squabbling over the testing issue. In a February 1990 letter, Dr. Kent says Dr. Homsy didn't do the "appropriate" animal tests "in spite of my suggestion in the early 1980s that they be performed." The next month, Dr. Homsy retorted: "You have repeatedly informed us that there were no appropriate animal models and that testing performed by you and LSU substantiated that conclusion."

Dr. Kent, nationally known as an innovator in reconstructive and oral surgery, is trying to distance himself from the entire catastrophe. "My role in the IPI was essentially nothing," he asserts, even though he advised Dr. Homsy on the implant's shape. Dr. Kent also owned a 1% stake in Vitek, and from 1984 on he got a 4% royalty on every TMJ product sold—about $50,000 a year, he says (Dr. Homsy pegs it closer to $100,000 some years). He got additional royalties on Proplast facial implants of his design.

As for Dr. Homsy, he sees the entire affair as a "holocaust" for himself, his family and his company, as well as for bioengineering and the medical-device industry. But he doesn't concede that the IPI was a misapplication of his beloved invention, Proplast, or that, as designed, it was inherently flawed. "Unfortunately," he says, "the implant is a set piece for scapegoating."

Instead, he blames not only surgeons but also patients, for failing to follow their surgeons' post-operative admonitions against opening their jaws wide or eating solid food until they are fully healed.

Throughout all this, the FDA seems to have missed several opportunities to intervene and head off the IPI disaster. The initial inspections of Vitek's plants after the IPI was approved in 1983 were limited and failed to uncover any significant problems. It wasn't until July 1988—one month after the company pulled the product off the market—that the agency conducted a comprehensive inspection of Vitek's plant. That inspection, which included checking quality controls and other manufacturing practices, turned up numerous violations.

FDA officials say Vitek wasn't relaying all of the reports it was receiving of problems with the devices, as it was required to do. But the FDA also was unaware of or failed to act on several other signs that something was seriously amiss, including the company's 1986 letter to surgeons and a 1987 report from the U.S. Air Force about implant failures, severe pain and bone erosion. Complaints from air bases prompted a notice to every branch of the armed services cautioning surgeons against using the IPI. But the government didn't recall the product until December 1990. Says Henry Wall, a Norcross, Ga., oral surgeon: "The FDA was asleep at the switch."

FDA officials contend that the agency acted as soon as the problems came to the agency's attention.

. . .

Arlen Huber, 35, suffers from facial swelling and severe headaches and wants the IPI he received after a farming accident taken out. The lowest surgeon's estimate the Fingal, N.D., farmer can get for doing so is $25,000, not counting anesthesia or hospitalization. But under a 1989 state law, insurance carriers can limit lifetime coverage for surgical treatment of TMJ disorders to $8,000.

Mr. Huber says he has appealed to state officials in Bismarck for help, but "they can't do anything for me."

©Wall St. Journal reproduced under license.

Questions

- In your opinion, who is to blame for what has happened to Vitek® jaw implant patients?
- Drs. Homsy and Kent are insolvent. Did anyone else misbehave?
- Should anyone, apart from the victims themselves, pay for the devastating losses they have suffered? If so, how if at all should

the people you wish to hold liable recoup their payments? Should they be able to charge consumers? Should they impoverish their stockholders? Should taxpayers foot the ultimate bill?

- Should misbehavior have anything to do with the duty to compensate an innocent victim like Ms. Ruggles? If not, why not?

As the Vitek® tragedy indicates, products liability is an increasingly important problem in modern, hyper-specialized, advanced societies where tools exist of which one would not have dreamt one generation earlier. Part of the huge increase in products liability suits, in other words, is a reflection of the progress of modern life.

That said, on the road from the era of self-made tools to modern products liability law, there have been a number of significant judicial mileposts. Here are several of importance to American products liability law:

2. Seminal Early Cases

A. Winterbottom v. Wright[5]

Wright, a coach maker, had supplied the Postmaster–General with a defective coach. The Postmaster–General then provided this coach to Winterbottom, a mailman, who was injured while delivering the mail. Winterbottom had no claim against his employer (who had done no wrong and who benefitted from sovereign immunity), so he sued Wright. Winterbottom's suit was dismissed on demurrer, the court holding that he had no claim against Wright. In relevant part Lord Abinger's opinion reads as follows:

> "There is no privity of contract between these parties; and if the plaintiff can sue, every passenger, or even any person passing along the road who was injured by the upsetting of the coach, might bring a similar action."[6]

If *Winterbottom* stands for the proposition that X, in performing a contract for Y, cannot commit a tort against Z, the case is manifestly absurd. The Common Law has never supported that premise. If you hire me to hunt rabbits on your land, and I do so while inebriated and shoot Smith, I may not invoke my contract with you to avoid tort liability to Smith. Tort liability does not require privity of contract![7] Rather, in the *Winterbottom* case, it is likely that the decision stands for the proposition that coachmakers (unlike hunters, for example) do not directly harm anyone other

---

5. Winterbottom v. Wright, 152 Eng. Rep. 402, 10 M. & W. 109 (Ex. 1842).

6. 10 M. & W. 109, at 114.

7. Labatt, *Negligence in Relation to Privity of Contract*, 16 L.Q.R. 168 (1900).

than their contracting party.[8] The hunter's bullet enters the neighbor's body, while the inartful carriage doesn't actively strike anyone. Is this distinction appropriate? *Winterbottom* declined to elaborate. In any case *Winterbottom*'s half-life would be brief.

B. Thomas v. Winchester[9]

A narrow view of *Winterbottom* was impliedly accepted in a leading New York case, *Thomas v. Winchester*. A supplier had negligently mislabeled the deadly poison belladonna as "extract of dandelion," which is a diuretic. A druggist received the mislabeled poison and sold it to a customer, whose wife was injured when she consumed it. The court held that the supplier breached a duty *to the eventual user* when he sold a product that was not what it purported to be. It became quickly accepted on both sides of the Atlantic[10] that when one supplies tools meant to be used by others, and likely to cause injury if negligently supplied, one is liable for injuries sustained by the users as a result of that negligence.

C. MacPherson v. Buick[11]

The facts of this famous case are best stated in the words of Judge Cardozo:

> The defendant is a manufacturer of automobiles. It sold an automobile to a retail dealer. The retail dealer resold to the plaintiff. While the plaintiff was in the car, it suddenly collapsed. He was thrown out and injured. One of the wheels was made of defective wood, and its spokes crumbled into fragments. The wheel was not made by the defendant; it was bought from another manufacturer. There is evidence, however, that its defects could have been discovered by reasonable inspection, and that inspection was omitted. There is no claim that the defendant knew of the defect and willfully concealed it... The charge is one, not of fraud, but of negligence. The question to be determined is whether the defendant owed a duty of care and vigilance to any one but the immediate purchaser.[12]

MacPherson is a reiteration of *Thomas* and *Heaven*, and a recognition (notwithstanding the thoughtlessness of *Winterbottom* on this count) that if one negligently unleashes a dangerous instru-

---

8. Vernon Palmer, *Why Privity Entered Tort—An Historical Reexamination of* Winterbottom v. Wright, 27 AM. J. LEG. HIST. 85 (1983).

9. Thomas v. Winchester, 6 N.Y. 397 (1852).

10. *See, e.g.,* Heaven v. Pender, (1883) 11 Q.B.D. 503 (C.A.).

11. MacPherson v. Buick, 217 N.Y. 382, 111 N.E. 1050 (1916).

12. *Id.* at 384–385, 111 N.E. 1050 at 1051. Judge Cardozo answered the question in the affirmative, with the court upholding the lower court's verdict against the defendant manufacturer.

ment one has violated a (tort) duty to the person whom the instrument directly injures.

There are several questions not answered by this line of cases, which continue to resonate in current products liability law. Here are two such questions:

- In *Thomas*, had the druggist (and not the supplier) been sued, would he have been held liable?

- In *MacPherson*, had Buick been able to establish that it was not negligent for failing to check the wheel (imagine that it had used all available quality control, and that the wheel maker had an impeccable reputation), would it still have been held liable?

Notwithstanding these unanswered questions, the basic structure of 19th-Century products liability law that emerged from the early cases is clear and instructive:

1. In each case the defendant sold a product that was *defective*, i.e., materially different, in a bad way, from the product he purported to be selling; and this danger was both *serious* and *hidden*.

2. In each case there was no misfeasance on the part of the user of the product.[13]

In each of these seminal cases, in other words, the defendant crucially and dangerously misrepresented his product, and in each case liability of this defendant would not lead to "moral hazard," i.e., to a reward to a careless user. In other words, early cases did *not* bundle a compulsory injury insurance policy with the sale of every product. Such insurance would have to be paid for by every consumer as a fixed "premium" added on to the sale price of the good. If all were forced to buy this insurance, low-risk (for example very careful) users might be unwilling to pay this premium. This would lead to increasingly higher premiums on remaining users, more of whom would decline to purchase, until perhaps the entire purchasing pool for the product unraveled. This unraveling is known as "adverse selection."[14] The phenomena of moral hazard and adverse selection are "market failures" for insurance markets. But early products liability did not result in market failure, for it declined to impliedly bundle a general injury insurance policy with the sale of every product.

---

13. Indeed, the best explanation for *Winterbottom* might be that the injured party was not a passerby but the employee of the buyer, who likely had forewarning of the breakdown and was arguably contributorily negligent.

14. Richard A. Epstein, *Products Liability as an Insurance Market*, 14 J. LEGAL STUD. 645 (1985).

3. Eliminating Privity: From Implied Warranty to Strict Liability

A. Implied Warranty and Tort Liability

I might conceivably invent a tool with the sole intention of using it myself. If the tool is defective and I injure someone while using it, I could be liable for that injury. For example, I might manufacture a hatchet, but do such a sloppy job of attaching the tip to the handle that the first time I swing the hatchet back to split a log the tip flies off and strikes a passerby. In that scenario my liability would be determined using basic principles of negligence—I am liable when my careless splitting of logs proximately harms another just as I am liable when my careless driving of a car proximately harms another.

As the Introduction indicated, today's products are manufactured not for personal use but with the desire to introduce them to the stream of commerce. Tools, i.e., products, are designed and made for ultimate sale to end-users. When a manufactured product is sold under these circumstances, *what* exactly is sold?

Suppose for instance that I make and sell a hatchet. When I sell this hatchet, I need not draft a "complete contract" specifying in excruciating detail everything this hatchet can and cannot be expected to do. Such a contract would be so expensive to negotiate and draft that the transaction costs would likely absorb all of the joint economic surplus that would result from the purchase and sale.[15] Rather, my sale of the hatchet to you implies that it is suitable for certain uses. It might well imply, for example, that the hatchet is suitable for cutting down a sapling. If, a buyer tried to (non-negligently) use it for its implied purpose and the handle separated from the tip, which flew into the air and struck a passerby, should that passerby have a claim against me, the maker of the hatchet? Note that the passerby has no claim against the user, who was not negligent.

Winterbottom's apparent ruling (that the maker of a deceptively rotten coach wheel breached a duty only to the purchaser of the coach) seemed to make implied warranty a contract doctrine invocable only by the "promisee" (i.e., the purchaser of the hatchet). But as cases prior and subsequent to *Winterbottom* clearly saw, implied warranty is perfectly compatible with the tort of *misrepresentation*.[16] When a seller (impliedly) promises that his hatchet will cut down a sapling, he is *warranting* that this is the case. It is wrongful to warrant a falsehood. The seller didn't have to warrant

---

15. Oliver Hart & John Moore, *Incomplete Contracts and Renegotiation*, 56 Econometrica 755 (1988).

16. William L. Prosser, *The Implied Warranty of Merchantability*, 27 Minn. L. Rev. 117 (1943).

that the hatchet could cut down a sapling. Instead, he might have explicitly warned "I have not tried this hatchet; it might not work the way it looks it will work. Try it in a safe place before relying on it." Had he done so, and had the purchaser received the disclaimer and nonetheless tried out the hatchet for the first time in a congested public location, this would arguably constitute user negligence toward any third party struck by the loose hatchet tip. In this case, the user would be liable for wrongdoing.

Realistically, of course, a hatchet seller who disclaims the implied warranty of fitness could not receive a very high price for his hatchet, which might (for all the purchaser knows) only be a toy. The placing of the hatchet in the stream of commerce implies the warranty of fitness, or merchantability. If the hatchet is marketed as a useful tool, the implied warranty that it would work with saplings has not been waived. If this promise turns out to have been a false one, i.e., if the hatchet will not in fact cut down a sapling because the tip will quickly separate from the handle in normal use, then the warranty was wrongfully given. When this wrongfully delivered warranty is reasonably relied on by the purchaser and results in injury to the purchaser or to a third party, then that injury is proximately caused by the seller's wrongdoing. In this instance, all the elements of tort liability are present: wrongdoing, causation and damages.[17] The basis for recovery does not depend solely on the existence of some imperfection in the product, but rather depends on the false representation.

One person can quite reasonably rely on another's warranty, even if the relier is not in privity with the warrantor. If I were to warrant (impliedly or explicitly) that the book I have printed may be opened without danger, then I have committed a wrong to the non-purchaser (perhaps the recipient of a gift from the unsuspecting purchaser) who opens the book only to suffer injury from the poisonous ink I have used to compose it. My liability is not necessarily based on negligence or fraud (I may not have known I was using poisonous ink) but on misrepresentation. Professor Karl Llewellyn analyzed over one hundred cases from 1850 to 1937 and found a constant trend to impose tort liability in such cases.[18]

Is this liability "strict"? That is, is it liability without regard to fault? In a way it is a combination of the doctrines of *misrepresentation* and of *estoppel*; it is liability for misrepresenting a product, whether or not the misrepresentation was *negligent*. In other words, when representing a product as embodying certain characteristics, the warrantor is waiving the right to invoke his innocent

---

17. Michael I. Krauss, *Tort Law and Private Ordering*, 35 St. Louis U. L.J. 623 (1992).

18. Karl N. Llewellyn, *On Warranty of Quality, and Society: II*, 37 Colum. L. Rev. 341, 404 (1937).

mistake if it turns out that this representation was both false and reasonably relied on. The Buick manufacturer did not claim, "we think this car will run, we've checked it a bit and we think so, but we really don't know." Rather, the manufacturer marketed the car as being driveable. Buick is estopped from subsequently denying responsibility for the direct consequences of its misrepresentation.

Questions About Julian Felipe's Case

- Do you believe that Ford Motor company misrepresented the 1993 Aerostar? If so, in what way?
- What about Seagate Auto Brokers?

B. The Road to Strict Liability

1). *Escola v. Coca–Cola Bottling Co. of Fresno*[19]

Several cases of Coca Cola were delivered to a restaurant, where they remained for thirty-six hours. A waitress picked up the top case of bottles. She then proceeded to take the bottles from the case with her right hand, one at a time, and put them into the refrigerator. She testified that after she had placed three bottles in the refrigerator and moved the fourth bottle about 18 inches from the case "it exploded in my hand." The bottle broke into two jagged pieces and inflicted a five-inch cut, severing blood vessels, nerves and muscles of the thumb and palm of the waitress's hand.

The broken bottle was not produced at trial, the pieces having been thrown away by other employees shortly after the accident. The waitress described the broken pieces, and a diagram of the bottle was made showing the location of the 'fracture line' where the bottle broke in two. The victim sued the local bottler for negligence, relying on the doctrine of *res ipsa loquitur* to presume negligent handling from the fact that the bottle shattered. A jury found for plaintiff, and the defendant appealed on the grounds that in fact plaintiff had produced no evidence of poor handling. The California Supreme Court noted that the manufacturer of the bottle had implemented virtually infallible pressure tests for each bottle, but that the bottler re-used bottles without re-subjecting them to these pressure tests. Justice Gibson, writing for the court, opined,

> "Obviously, if such defects do occur in used bottles there is a duty upon the bottler to make appropriate tests before they are refilled, and if such tests are not commercially practicable the bottles should not be re-used. This would seem to be particularly true where a charged liquid is placed in the bottle. It follows that a defect which would make the bottle unsound could be discovered by reasonable and practicable tests.

19. Escola v. Coca–Cola Bottling Co., 150 P.2d 436 (Cal. 1944).

"Although it is not clear in this case whether the explosion was caused by an excessive charge or a defect in the glass there is a sufficient showing that neither cause would ordinarily have been present if due care had been used. Further, defendant had exclusive control over both the charging and inspection of the bottles. Accordingly, all the requirements necessary to entitle plaintiff to rely on the doctrine of *res ipsa loquitur* to supply an inference of negligence are present."[20]

The bottler had presented evidence that it was not negligent, but Justice Gibson noted that the jury had presumably weighed that evidence and found it wanting. Justice Traynor, however, felt the need to concur separately. He wrote that, "It should now be recognized that a manufacturer incurs an absolute liability when an article that he has placed on the market, knowing that it is to be used without inspection, proves to have a defect that causes injury to human beings."[21]

Provided that the defect is hidden, Justice Traynor could be understood to hold that the bottle was misrepresented to the restaurant by the bottler as being sound, and that this misrepresentation was a direct cause of the damage to the waitress. Justice Traynor rightly objected to the façade of invoking the *negligence*, in practice irrefutably presumed via *res ipsa loquitur*, when in fact it is of a dangerous *misrepresentation* that the defendant is guilty.

Justice Traynor's concurrence percolated silently in California for nineteen years, until...

2). *Greenman v. Yuba Power Products*[22]

A hobbyist sued both the retailer and the manufacturer of the *Shopsmith*®, a combination power tool that could be used as a saw, drill, and lathe. The plaintiff had seen a *Shopsmith*® demonstrated by the retailer and studied a brochure prepared by the manufacturer. He decided he wanted one for his home workshop, and his wife bought one for Christmas in 1955. In 1957 he bought additional attachments to use the *Shopsmith*® as a lathe for turning a large piece of wood he wished to make into a chalice. After he had worked on the piece of wood several times without difficulty, it suddenly flew out of the machine and struck him on the forehead, inflicting serious injury. About ten and a half months later, he gave the retailer and the manufacturer written notice of claimed breaches of implied and express warranties, and sued both on these grounds and on grounds of negligence. Plaintiff's expert witness testified that flimsy screws were used to hold the machine together, so that normal vibration caused the tailstock of the lathe to move

---

20. *Id.* at 439–440.
21. *Id.* at 440.

22. Greenman v. Yuba Power Prods., 377 P.2d 897 (Cal. 1963).

away from the piece of wood being turned, permitting it to fly out of the lathe. The experts also testified that there were other ways of fastening the parts of such a machine together, the use of which would have clearly prevented the accident.

Question

- Are there any significant differences between the plaintiffs' claims in *Escola* and in *Greenman*?

After a jury trial, the court ruled that plaintiff had presented no evidence that the retailer was negligent[23] or had breached any express warranty, and that the manufacturer was not liable for breach of implied warranty because of lack of privity. Accordingly, the judge submitted to the jury only the suit for breach of implied warranty against the retailer, and for negligence and breach of express warranty against the manufacturer. The jury returned a verdict for the retailer and against the manufacturer. The manufacturer appealed on the ground that there was no evidence of either its negligence or of any express warranty.[24]

The California Supreme Court saw possible evidence of both negligence and breach of express warranty. However, the manufacturer noted that plaintiff did not give it notice of breach of express warranty within the reasonable time required by California's Civil Code. In addition, it was unclear whether the jury had found the manufacturer liable for express warranty or for negligence. Thus, the manufacturer, claimed, the entire judgment against it was vitiated.

This unusual procedural posture was the occasion for one of American tort law's most famous rulings. Justice Traynor, this time writing for a unanimous court, wrote that "[a] manufacturer is strictly liable in tort when an article he places on the market, knowing that it is to be used without inspection for defects, proves to have a defect that causes injury to a human being,"[25] and that "the liability is not one governed by the law of contract warranties but by the law of strict liability in tort."[26] Ratifying the idea of dangerous misrepresentation that has been sketched above, Justice Traynor observed,

---

23. This seems obviously correct: the retailer had no opportunity to inspect the Shopsmith and no knowledge of its alleged design defect.

24. The following two statements appeared in the manufacturer's brochure. (1) "WHEN SHOPSMITH IS IN HORIZONTAL POSITION Rugged construction of frame provides rigid support

from end to end. Heavy centerless-ground steel tubing ensuers perfect alignment of components." (2) "SHOPSMITH maintains its accuracy because every component has positive locks that hold adjustments through rough or precision work."

25. *Greenman*, 377 P.2d at 900.

26. *Id*. at 901.

"Implicit in the machine's presence on the market, however, was a representation that it would safely do the jobs for which it was built. Under these circumstances, it should not be controlling whether plaintiff selected the machine because of the statements in the brochure, or because of the machine's own appearance of excellence that belied the defect lurking beneath the surface, or because he merely assumed that it would safely do the jobs it was built to do."[27]

Is it liability *without wrongdoing* when one deliberately markets a product that cannot safely do what it purports to be able to do? In any case, it is evident that *Greenman* created a "paradigm shift."[28] In 1964 the influential American Law Institute approved § 402A of the *Restatement (Second) of Torts*:

(1) One who sells any product in a defective condition unreasonably dangerous to the user or consumer or to his property is subject to liability for physical harm thereby caused to the ultimate user or consumer, or to his property, if

(a) the seller is engaged in the business of selling such a product, and

(b) it is expected to and does reach the user or consumer without substantial change in the condition in which it is sold.

(2) The rule stated in Subsection (1) applies although

(a) the seller has exercised all possible care in the preparation and sale of his product, and

(b) the user or consumer has not bought the product from or entered into any contractual relation with the seller.[29]

By 1976, virtually every state in the union had adopted either § 402A, liability for implied warranty with no privity requirement (which is virtually the same thing[30]), or (same result, though arguably less honest, as Justice Traynor indicated) an irrefutable negligence presumption via *res ipsa loquitur*.[31]

C. How "Strict" Is Strict Liability?

Cases seen thus far involve dangerous misrepresentation of products put into the stream of commerce. Such misrepresentation

---

27. *Id.*

28. Thomas Kuhn, The Structure of Scientific Revolutions (3d ed. 1996).

29. RESTATEMENT (SECOND) OF TORTS § 402A (1977).

30. In Comment m to § 402A, the authors recognize that the strict liability promoted by the ALI is in fact tort liability for breach of implied warranty of merchantability. *Id.* § 402A cmt. m.

31. *See* David G. Owen, *Defectiveness Restated: Exploding the "Strict" Products Liability Myth*, U. ILL. L. REV. 743, 743 (1996) (referring to section 402A as "the most often cited Restatement section in history").

(or, if you will, breach of the implied warranty that these products perform normally), seen as a tort and not merely as a contract breach, allow recovery of damages against a manufacturer by a directly injured person not in privity with that manufacturer. If it is "wrong" to profit from a product one has misrepresented, then this is not liability without wrongdoing.[32]

So is liability for the sale of a defective product truly without regard to wrongdoing? The question is not merely semantic: it affects the way parties will approach product liability litigation. Consider the following case:

1). *Pulley v. Pacific Coca–Cola Bottling Co.*[33]

Lamont and Dorothy Pulley together purchased a carton of six "king-size" bottles of Coca–Cola from retailer Lucky Stores, Inc., in May of 1962. In the court's words, here is what happened next:

> "The respondents went home immediately and placed the six-pack carton on its side in the family refrigerator. On the following day, Mrs. Pulley removed an apparently sealed bottle from the refrigerator, uncapped it, and took a swallow. She noted that the beverage seemed to have an odd taste, but she took a second swallow. At the trial Mrs. Pulley described her reactions as follows:
>
> > 'Immediately thought this tasted like, it didn't taste like coke, it tasted like tobacco or tobacco smoke, and it was bitter, and it was a little slimy.'
>
> Mrs. Pulley examined the remaining contents of the bottle. She noticed a cigarette and floating bits of loose tobacco. Immediately thereafter, she became violently ill. During the course of her ensuing three-day period of intermittent regurgitation and nausea, she unfortunately lost her dentures in the commode."[34]

Question

- Should Mrs. Pulley's behavior be seen as distinguishable from the plaintiff's behavior in *Escola?* From the plaintiff's behavior in *Greenman?*

The two plaintiffs sued Lucky Stores and Pacific Coca–Cola Bottling Co., on a theory of breach of an implied warranty of fitness for human consumption (as Washington's strict products liability was then known). The bottler's interests were clearly divergent

---

32. For a discussion of the subtleties involved in caselaw's (often careless) use of the term strict liability, see Douglas N. Husak, *Varieties of Strict Liability,* [1995] CAN. J.L. & JURIS. 189.

33. Pulley v. Pacific Coca–Cola Bottling Co., 415 P.2d 636 (Wash. 1966).

34. 415 P.2d 636, at 638.

from the retailer's—for if the bottler could establish that the bottle left its premises properly sealed *sans* cigarette, they would not have misrepresented the product they sold to Lucky Stores. In that case, only the retailer would be in breach of "implied warranty."

Of course, one way to "prove a negative" (to prove that an adulterated bottle did not become adulterated on one's premises) is to show that the proposition is well-nigh impossible. If for instance Pacific Coca–Cola Bottling Co. could prove that it had never produced any Coca–Cola, it could never have produced a bottle with a cigarette inside. But the bottler could not show that contamination was *impossible*. Why should it have to prove to a certainty that the cigarette originated elsewhere, since in civil adjudication a mere preponderance of the evidence is all that need be produced?[35] So the bottler tried to show how *unlikely* it was that the cigarette originated in its premises, as opposed to on the premises of Lucky Stores, where an interloper could have easily un-capped and re-capped the bottle in the store's refrigerator. Pacific proffered testimony relating to the methods it utilized in processing and bottling its product. It offered evidence that it didn't allow cigarettes beyond the employees' dressing room; that it obliged employees to wear uniforms with no pockets (in which cigarettes might be concealed); that it had several levels of inspection for each bottle as it passed through the plant; etc.

The bottler's attempts to produce this evidence were met with a constant objection by the plaintiffs. Their contention was a simple one: if Pacific Coca–Cola Bottling Co. were allowed to show that it managed its plant safely and effectively (thus making it unlikely that it was the source of the contamination), it would essentially be proving its lack of negligence. Since Washington had abandoned negligence in favor of "strict liability," Pacific's evidence was inadmissible.

The judge sustained Pulley's objections, precluding the submission of exculpatory evidence by the bottler. Washington's Supreme Court agreed:

> "The proffered testimony as to the bottling methods employed would obviously be admissible if the question was whether or not Pacific Coca–Cola Bottling Company exercised due care in the manufacturing of its product. But the question is not whether Pacific Coca–Cola Bottling Company was negligent, but whether or not it and Lucky Stores, Inc., breached an implied warranty that the Coca–Cola was fit for human consumption. ... An assertion of breach of warranty by a consum-

---

35. *See* James Brook, *Inevitable Errors: The Preponderance of the Evidence Standard in Civil Litigation*, 18 Tulsa L.J. 79 (1982), for a nice essay on the meaning of the term "preponderance."

er-plaintiff, that he or she was harmed by the presence of some foreign object in food or drink, in practical effect thrusts a burden upon the defendant manufacturer and the defendant retailer to show who contaminated the particular food product—and will not permit a showing by indirect and circumstantial evidence that it was improbable or even impossible that the defendants were responsible for the presence of the harmful object.... It is thus our view, under the existing authorities, that the trial court properly excluded the proffered evidence as to the bottling methods utilized by the defendant bottling company."[36]

Questions

- Has the bottler become the insurer of the drink?

- If so, is this the same result reached in *Escola*? In *Greenman*?

- Did the bottler ever impliedly warrant that no one would ever tamper with the bottle after it left its premises?

- Does strict liability mean "insurance?"

As *Pulley* illustrates, one's characterization of the modern rule is crucial. If the rule is that one must not produce a product that dangerously misrepresents itself, then the defendant's evidence in *Pulley* seems admissible—for Pacific was in fact trying to prove (by a preponderance of evidence) that the Coca–Cola bottle it produced was as represented.[37] If on the other hand the modern rule is truly one of strict liability, precluding the manufacturer from defending itself by demonstrating that its behavior was reasonable, then the Washington Supreme Court is correct.

Questions About Julian Felipe's Case

- Should Ford Motor Co. be allowed to produce evidence establishing that its design protocol for the roof structure of its 1993 Aerostar vans was reasonable, or should such evidence be ruled irrelevant because of Strict Liability?

- Would it matter to your answer if Ford claims that an exploding tire was the "proximate cause" of plaintiff's injuries (assume Ford is not liable for any tire defects)?

- Would it matter to your answer if Ford claimed that the structure of this particular Aerostar had been weakened by some event that occurred in the nine years of use of the van?

---

36. *Pulley*, 415 P.2d at 640.

37. This was the view in Brown v. General Foods Corp., 117 Ariz. 530, 573 P.2d 930 (Ariz. App. 1978) (disagreeing explicitly with *Pulley*).

Chapter 3

THRESHOLD ISSUES FOR MODERN PRODUCTS LIABILITY[1]

As seen in Chapter 2, products liability law gradually (until 1964) then quickly (from 1964 through 1976) recognized that liability for injuries proximately caused by defective products was tort-based. This liability was deemed "strict" by the *Restatement (Second)*—distinguishing products liability law from the rest of tort, where liability explicitly requires wrongdoing.

This chapter considers threshold issues for this new legal regime. Since only "products" give rise to liability "without wrongdoing," for instance, it is important to know what counts as a product. What are the policy rationales behind the creation of this ground for liability? What is the relationship between products liability and insurance?

1. What Is the "Sale of a Product?"

The American Law Institute specifies that "One who sells any product in a defective condition" will be strictly liable in certain circumstances. Which contracts involve the sale of a product? Several jurisdictions have legislatively defined "product," though in ways perhaps that are less than theoretically satisfying. In Washington, for example, "product" means,

> "any object possessing intrinsic value, capable of delivery either as an assembled whole or as a component part or parts, and produced for introduction into trade or commerce. Human tissue and organs, including human blood and its components, are excluded from this term."[2]

Why exclude human blood as a product? Isn't tainted blood much more dangerous, and much harder for the end-user to inspect, than almost any other human product?

Many other jurisdictions left definitions to evolving Common law. Consider the following problems confronted by the cases:

---

1. <u>Additional Readings</u>: Charles E. Cantu, *The Illusive Meaning of the Term "Product" Under Section 402A of the Restatement (Second) of Torts*, 44 Okla. L. Rev. 635 (1991); Alan Schwartz, "Proposals for Products Liability Reform: A Theoretical Synthesis", 97 Yale L.J. 353 (1988).

2. *See, e.g.*, Wash. Rev. Code Ann. § 7.72.010(3) (2010).

- What if the contract is for *sale and installation* of a product? What if most of the cost of the product is for installation, not sale? Is the seller-installer still subject to strict liability? In *Brandt v. Sarah Bush Lincoln Health Center,* for instance, a hospital was not held strictly liable for the installation of a defective implant, since the implant surgery was "principally a service" and only secondarily a sale.[3] The manufacturer of the defective implant would be strictly liable, but the hospital could only be liable if negligent, the court held. Why? If the hospital's bill itemizes the cost of the implant, why isn't this a sale? If the court's answer is that it does not wish to wastefully increase the cost of medical care, does this constitute an admission that strict liability wastefully increases the cost of sold products?

- As seen above, some states have legislatively declared that blood is not a product,[4] so that distributors are not strictly liable for the damages caused by HIV and other blood-borne diseases. Why not define blood as a "product?" If the answer is that blood sellers, such as the Red Cross, are often not-for-profit corporations, does this imply that products liability should only apply to for-profit firms?

- Is real property a "product?" *Calloway v. City of Reno* held that a townhouse is not a product for purposes of strict liability.[5] But this holding was subsequently superseded by statute.[6] Is there any theoretical reason why real and personal property should be subject to different liability rules?

- Is human sperm a "product?" If so, who is its end-user? In *D.D. v. Idant Laboratories,*[7] a woman was artificially inseminated with sperm from an anonymous donor. The daughter conceived from this insemination was determined to be a carrier of "Fragile X premutation."[8] Her mother contended that Fragile X was the cause of her daughter's "trouble sleeping, tantrums, and anxiety as well as developmental delays." The Third Circuit upheld the

---

3. Brandt v. Sarah Bush Lincoln Health Ct., 771 N.E.2d 470 (Ill. App. 2002), *declining to follow* Garcia v. Edgewater Hosp., 613 N.E.2d 1243 (Ill. App. 1993).

4. *See* note 2 *supra. See also e.g.,* Va. Code. Ann. § 32.1–297 ("No action for implied warranty shall lie" for procurement or transfusion of blood. [Virginia's strict liability is nominally one of "implied warranty."]).

5. Calloway v. City of Reno, 993 P.2d 1259 (Nev. 2000).

6. *See* Olson v. Richard, 89 P.3d 31, 33 (Nev. 2004).

7. D.D. v. Idant Laboratories, 2010 WL 1257705 (3d Cir. 2010) (Pa. applying NY law).

8. According to the Eastern District of Pennsylvania, Fragile X premutation is "a genetic syndrome which results in a spectrum of physical, intellectual, emotional and behavioral characteristics which range from severe to mild in manifestation ... the gene responsible for "Fragile X" was first discovered in 1991; there is no known cure." *Id.* No. 09–3460, slip op. at 1, n.1 (quoting Donovan v. Idant Laboratories, Corp., 625 F. Supp. 2d 256, 263 (E.D. Pa. 2009)).

trial court's dismissal of the daughter's products liability suit on the grounds that sperm could not be dangerous to the person it created, since that person's nonexistence (had the sperm not been used) is not comparable to existence as a learning-disabled individual.[9]

A book is surely a product, isn't it? Consider however this decision.

Winter v. G.P. Putnam's Sons[10]

The Encyclopedia of Mushrooms was a reference guide to the habitat, collection, and cooking of mushrooms. It was written by two British authors, and originally published by a British publisher. Defendant, an American publisher, purchased U.S. rights to the book, then purchased copies of the book from the British publisher and distributed them in the United States. Putnam neither wrote nor edited the book. Two California residents each purchased a copy of the encyclopedia. In 1988, plaintiffs went mushroom hunting and relied on the descriptions in the book to determine which mushrooms were safe to eat. It turns out, however, that on one page of the book a copy editor had made a mistake, inverting two photographs, one of a safe mushroom and one of an extremely poisonous variety. Relying on the book, plaintiffs collected the type of mushroom represented as fit for consumption. After cooking and eating their harvest, plaintiffs became critically ill. Each required a liver transplant. They sued defendant for their damages. The trial court granted summary judgment to the publisher, on the grounds that defendant had not been negligent, and that strict products liability did not apply in this case.

The Ninth Circuit Court of Appeals affirmed the summary judgment. It noted that "[p]roducts liability law is geared to the tangible world."[11] Here the tangible product, ink and paper, did not harm the plaintiffs. Rather, they were harmed by an intangible, the intellectual property communicated by the book. The court noted that the American Law Institute had specified that,

> "The rule stated in this Section is not limited to the sale of food for human consumption, or other products for intimate bodily use, although it will obviously include them. It extends to any product sold in the condition, or substantially the same condition, in which it is expected to reach the ultimate user or consumer. Thus the rule stated applies to an automobile, a tire,

---

9. D.D. v. Idant Laboratories, 2010 WL 1257705 (3d Cir. 2010) (explaining that " 'a cause of action may not be maintained on behalf of an infant plaintiff based on a claim of wrongful life' " (quoting Sheppard–Mobley v. King, 830 N.E.2d 301 (N.Y. 2005))).

10. Winter v. G.P. Putnam's Sons, 938 F.2d 1033 (9th Cir. 1991) (applying California law).

11. *Id.* at 1034.

an airplane, a grinding wheel, a water heater, a gas stove, a power tool, a riveting machine, a chair, and an insecticide. It applies also to products which, if they are defective, may be expected to and do cause only "physical harm" in the form of damage to the user's land or chattels, as in the case of animal food or a herbicide."[12]

All these examples were tangible goods, and the court concluded that the purposes of products liability law would not be met if strict liability were extended to intangibles. Interestingly, several cases, some under California law, had previously held that the producers and resellers of incorrect aeronautical charts were strictly liable if airplanes crashed because the pilots relied on them (e.g., if they specified too low of an altitude for mountains, etc.).[13] The court was unimpressed with these precedents, which it distinguished as follows:

"Aeronautical charts are highly technical tools. They are graphic depictions of technical, mechanical data. The best analogy to an aeronautical chart is a compass. Both may be used to guide an individual who is engaged in an activity requiring certain knowledge of natural features. Computer software that fails to yield the result for which it was designed may be another. In contrast, The Encyclopedia of Mushrooms is like a book on how to use a compass or an aeronautical chart. The chart itself is like a physical "product" while the "How to Use" book is pure thought and expression."[14]

The court also approved of the dismissal of the negligence suit:

In order for negligence to be actionable, there must be a legal duty to exercise due care.... The plaintiffs urge this court that the publisher had a duty to investigate the accuracy of *The Encyclopedia of Mushrooms'* contents. We conclude that the defendants have no duty to investigate the accuracy of the contents of the books it publishes. A publisher may of course assume such a burden, but there is nothing inherent in the role of publisher or the surrounding legal doctrines to suggest that such a duty should be imposed on publishers. Indeed the cases uniformly refuse to impose such a duty. Were we tempted to create this duty, the gentle tug of the First Amendment and

12. RESTATEMENT (SECOND) OF TORTS § 402A Comment d (1965).

13. *See* Brocklesby v. United States, 767 F.2d 1288, 1294–95 (9th Cir.1985) (applying Restatement for the purpose of California law), *cert. denied,* 474 U.S. 1101 (1986); Saloomey v. Jeppesen & Co., 707 F.2d 671, 676–77 (2d Cir.1983)

(applying Restatement for the purpose of Colorado Law); Aetna Cas. & Sur. Co. v. Jeppesen & Co., 642 F.2d 339, 342–43 (9th Cir.1981) (applying Nevada law); Fluor Corp. v. Jeppesen & Co., 170 Cal. App.3d 468, 475 (1985) (applying California law).

14. *Winter,* 938 F.2d at 1036.

the values embodied therein would remind us of the social costs."[15]

Questions

- Do you find the court's reasoning persuasive? How are aeronautical charts different from mushroom encyclopedias? Aren't both tangible products containing information? Is the court's analogy to a compass persuasive? Can an erroneous compass reading ever directly harm anyone, or is it not the intangible information, if relied on, that causes the harm?

- If your answer is that damages from an incorrect aeronautical chart are higher than damages from an incorrect mushroom photo, does this signify that strict liability should apply only if potential damages exceed a certain threshold? Anyway, what's so minor about a liver transplant?

- If the stated ground for liability had not been strict liability but "dangerous misrepresentation," or "implied warranty," would the defendant have been found liable? If not, why not? Wasn't the book clearly and dangerously misrepresenting itself as being a reliable guide to mushrooms? Wasn't it impliedly warranting that the pictured mushroom could be eaten?

Cases like *Winter* highlight the importance both of defining terms rigorously (is liability "strict" or does it result from "dangerous misrepresentation"?) and of clarifying the policy reasons for the historical shift sketched in Chapter 2.

2. Safety v. Insurance: Justice Traynor's Reasons for Enacting Strict Liability

Escola v. Coca–Cola of Fresno, the pathbreaking 1944 case containing Justice Traynor's famous concurrence, offers a convenient portal for this analysis. Recall that Traynor objected to the dishonest use of an irrebutable *res ipsa loquitur* presumption of negligence, preferring in its stead "absolute liability" for placing in the marketplace a dangerously defective item whose defect proximately causes harm. Traynor announced the rationale for his proposal in this passage:

"Even if there is no negligence, however, public policy demands that responsibility be fixed wherever it will most effectively reduce the hazards to life and health inherent in defective products that reach the market. It is evident that the manufacturer can anticipate some hazards and guard against the recurrence of others, as the public cannot. Those who suffer injury from defective products are unprepared to meet its consequences. The cost of an injury and the loss of time or health may be an overwhelming misfortune to the person injured, and

---

15. 938 F.2d 1033, at 1037 (footnotes omitted).

a needless one, for the risk of injury can be insured by the manufacturer and distributed among the public as a cost of doing business. It is to the public interest to discourage the marketing of products having defects that are a menace to the public. If such products nevertheless find their way into the market it is to the public interest to place the responsibility for whatever injury they may cause upon the manufacturer, who, even if he is not negligent in the manufacture of the product, is responsible for its reaching the market. However intermittently such injuries may occur and however haphazardly they may strike, the risk of their occurrence is a constant risk and a general one. Against such a risk there should be general and constant protection and the manufacturer is best situated to afford such protection."[16]

Traynor seems to be making the following points, each of which deserves careful consideration.

1. **Accidents will be reduced** if liability is placed on the manufacturer without regard to its wrongdoing. [(Strict liability) "will most effectively reduce the hazards to life and health inherent in defective products that reach the market."]. The belief that strict liability increases the care taken by manufacturers and sellers is widespread, but it has been challenged for years by basic economic analysis.[17] As the exercises in the Appendix show, if a negligence rule is applied correctly it deters all reasonably avoidable products accidents. Strict liability merely shifts the cost of the "residual" accidents (those not reasonably avoidable) from the injured party to the manufacturer and sellers. Strictly liable manufacturers will *not* take additional care beyond what is cost-justified, which they are already motivated to take under a negligence rule, because it will be cheaper for them to simply pay liability awards than to take this inefficient care.

2. **Consumers, many of them poor, cannot anticipate accidents, while manufacturers, who are "rich," can. Strict liability will therefore help the poor.** ["It is evident that the manufacturer can anticipate some hazards and guard against the recurrence of others, as the public cannot."] This statement is puzzling. If the "hazards" of which Justice Traynor

16. Escola v. Coca–Cola Bottling Co., 150 P.2d 436, 440–41 (Cal. 1944).

17. *See, e.g.,* A. Mitchell Polinsky, *Strict Liability vs. Negligence in a Mar-*ket Setting, 70 AMERICAN ECONOMIC REVIEW: PAPERS AND PROCEEDINGS (1980). *See also* ch. 5 and the Appendix, *infra.*

writes should have been guarded against, it was negligent not to do so, and strict liability is not needed. But if these hazards are not efficiently and reasonably avoidable, they can be "anticipated" by consumers through the first-party insurance, which consumers may purchase for particular risks (flight insurance) as well as general ones (life insurance, health insurance, etc.). Perhaps Justice Traynor believes that consumers should not have to purchase such insurance for damages caused by products; perhaps he wishes to require that such insurance be provided "for free" by manufacturers. And indeed manufactures can bundle an insurance policy with their product.[18] But such insurance will assuredly not be "free" for poor consumers. Given that rich consumers, if injured, suffer greater damages than do poor consumers,[19] it follows that if all purchasers of a product pay the same "residual risk insurance premium" as part of the purchase price of a product, the poor will be subsidizing the rich under strict liability.

3. **Manufacturers can spread losses better than can consumers.** ["Those who suffer injury from defective products are unprepared to meet its consequences. The cost of an injury and the loss of time or health may be an overwhelming misfortune to the person injured, and a needless one, for the risk of injury can be insured by the manufacturer and distributed among the public as a cost of doing business."]. Again, Justice Traynor's is perhaps a common understanding, but it is almost surely incorrect. Traynor correctly understands that a manufacturer can either purchase third-party (i.e., liability) insurance to cover possible liability for its products, or can self-insure. Either way the costs require building an implied third party insurance premium into the price charged for the product. Without such liability for damages incurred by residual defects (recall that a negligence rule would already protect against efficiently preventable defects), consumers would be obliged to purchase first-party insurance if they wished to protect themselves against residual risks. In other words,

18. Thomas Schelling, *An Economist Looks at Risk and Liability*, in Risk, Compensation, and Liability: The Policy Choices 53 (1986).

19. One who makes $200,000 per year has greater lost income than one who makes $15,000 per year. One who drives a 2010 Jaguar suffers greater harm if his car explodes than does one who drives a 1995 Chevy.

the "paradigm shift" proposed in *Escola* substitutes third-party for first-party insurance. Only if third-party insurance is cheaper than first-party insurance would it be the case that manufacturers (as opposed to consumers) are the "cheaper" spreaders of residual risk. But:

a. **Third-party insurance payouts are much higher than first-party payouts.** In part because of the payment of pain and suffering awards, and in part because of the inaccuracy of jury determinations of damages, it has been estimated that third-party insurance payouts are over twice as high as the amount that consumers wish to pay for.[20] Yet consumers do indeed "pay for" this third party insurance in the form of higher prices.

b. **For any given coverage, the intrinsic characteristics of third-party insurance require much higher premiums than does first-party insurance.** "Loading," or administrative, costs of third-party insurance exceed those of first-party insurance by as much as 575 percent.[21] This is in part because third-party coverage requires a tort adjudication (hiring of lawyers, deposing of witnesses, massive "discovery," hiring of experts, etc.) while first-party coverage is contractual and typically involves much less "friction." But the difference between third-party and first-party premiums is exacerbated further by the fact that the third-party insurance is provided in a way that makes it very difficult for the "insurer" to segregate low-risk from high-risk "insureds." In first-party coverage, an insurer can ask questions designed to determine the risk presented by the insured. This enables the insurer to charge a premium that corresponds to the insured's *ex ante* risk. Drivers who drive 5000 miles per year will not pay as much for "collision coverage" as those who drive 30,000 miles per year, etc. But for third-party insurance, bundled into the price of a product, the person receiving the eventual payment is not the person paying the premium.

20. For the basic insight, *see, e.g.* George Priest, *The Current Insurance Crisis and Modern Tort Law*, 96 YALE L.J. 1521, 1555 (1987); Patricia Danzon, *Tort Reform and the Role of Government in Private Insurance*, 13 J. LEGAL STUD. 3 (1984).

21. Priest, 96 YALE L.J. at 1560.

Often the risk presented by purchasers will be heterogeneous. For instance, purchasers of a chainsaw may vary from the neophyte to the professional, and from the homeowner to the daily user. Both pay the same price for their chainsaw, and thus the same implied insurance premium, since a manufacturer will be unable to "price discriminate."[22] Obviously, in any insurance pool, the premium must be set according to the average level of risk created the pool. The wider the range of risks, i.e., the more heterogeneous the pool, the more likely low-risk members are to drop out of the pool (that is, decline to purchase the product) because they find the insurance too expensive. This increases the average risk level, requiring additional price increases and entailing additional drop-outs from the pool. Ultimately, a product market may unravel due to this "adverse selection."[23]

The policy rationales provided by Justice Traynor for the move to strict liability are stubbornly persistent. Since manufacturers are typically wealthier than victims of product accidents, increasing payments from the former to the latter appears to be a "progressive" redistribution from the rich to the poor. Economic theory, however, leads to the conclusion that manufacturers' liability, if it becomes "insurance" (that is, if liability is truly independent of any wrongdoing), will tend to produce the following results:

- Higher priced products[24];
- Subsidization of rich consumers by poor consumers in some cases;
- Choice by some consumers (disproportionately the poor and low-risk) of some products (e.g., ladders, up to 25 percent of the price of which is apparently a "product liability insurance" premium[25]) to decline to purchase

22. If a seller tried to charge different prices for the same product to different types of purchasers, he would encounter two obstacles. First, "arbitrage" would occur (lower-price purchasers would resell to higher-price purchasers). Second, the seller would run afoul of consumer protection laws such as the *Robinson–Patman Act*, 15 U.S.C. § 13(a)–(f) (1988) and its state equivalents.

23. *See* George L. Priest, *Puzzles of the Tort Crisis*, 48 Ohio St. L.J. 497, 500 (1987).

24. This may even affect competitiveness, to the extent that American manufacturers cannot price discriminate in their sales to foreign purchasers governed by a less "strict" regime. *See* Randolph J. Stayin, *The U.S. Product Liability System: A Competitive Advantage to Foreign Manufacturers*, 14 Can.-U.S. L.J. 193 (1988).

25. W. Kip Viscusi, *Product and Occupational Liability*, 5 J. of Econ. Perspectives 71 (1991).

the product, and to possibly continue using their old (potentially more dangerous) product. This could actually increase the accident rate.

These counter-intuitive consequences might be minimized if some of the following limitations of liability (perhaps implied by Justice Traynor) were enforced:

- No liability unless the defect is *hidden*;

- No liability if the consumer has *misused* the product (this is the "moral hazard" of insurance)[26];

These limitations would return an element of wrongdoing to products liability law—for as has been shown above, it is wrong to commercially misrepresent a dangerously defective product.

Questions About Julian Felipe's Case

- Based on your reading so far, how strong do you believe a roof should be on a Ford Aerostar? Strong enough to withstand any impact of any kind? Strong enough to withstand the weight of a collapsing bridge, for instance? Should it matter how much strengthening the roof would cost, and how impacts of different kinds occur? If your answer to the last question was "yes," are you evaluating Ford's design decision under a "negligence" rule instead of "strict liability? If your answer was "no" because of the strict liability standard, does Ford become an insurer of passengers in its automobiles?

- Who should have authority to decide these questions? Ford? Federal regulators? Juries?

26. James Garven, *Moral Hazard, Adverse Selection and Tort Liability*, 28 J. OF INS. ISSUES 1 (2005).

Chapter 4

"NON–STRICT" THEORIES OF PRODUCTS LIABILITY[1]

A modern products liability suit may include a number of different legal claims that justify recovery of financial compensation from the manufacturer or seller of a product that has caused injury. In the United States, the types of claims associated with products liability are negligence, strict liability, breach of warranty, tortious misrepresentation and various consumer protection claims. Because complaints are written before discovery, products liability complaints typically allege many of these legal grounds, even though at trial the experienced plaintiff's attorney will focus on theories most likely to be successful in the case at hand.

1. Negligence

Despite the rise of strict liability described in chapter 3, negligence has retained a persistent toehold in American products liability law. In subsequent chapters the thesis that negligence is the *only* viable rule for design and information defects will be examined. In this chapter, it is sufficient to note that even if strict liability is a viable grounding for products liability, negligence principles will continue to be invoked. There are at least three reasons for this:

- First, lawyers are accustomed to invoking negligence in every other area of unintentional torts. The analytical concepts of duty and breach are familiar to lawyers and judges, and it is quite natural that these concepts would continue to be used, even if the nominally applicable rule is one of strict liability. Thus, in *Phillips v. Kimwood Machinery Co.* the Oregon Supreme Court ruled that a manufacturer would not be strictly liable for design defect (strict liability requires that a product be "defective and unreasonably dangerous"), if its product was not "unreasonably dangerous." A product would not be unreasonably dangerous, the court continued, if

1. Additional Readings: Richard C. Ausness, *Product Liability's Parallel Universe: Fault–Based Liability Theories And Modern Products Liability Law*, 74 Brook. L. Rev. 635 (2009); Richard L. Cupp Jr., *The Rhetoric Of Strict Products Liability Versus Negligence: An Empirical Analysis*, 77 N.Y.U. L. Rev. 874 (2002).

"a reasonably prudent manufacturer would have so designed and sold the article in question had he known of the risk involved."[2] This of course is explicit negligence language.

- Second, every plaintiff's products liability attorney will admit that whenever possible, they will structure their trial rhetoric around negligence principles, not strict liability. The ubiquity of wrongdoing as a moral grounding for tort is such that juries are perceived to be much less likely to find a product defective, or proximately causal of a plaintiff's injuries, if they cannot find any wrongdoing on the part of the defendant.

- Finally, although it has not yet been widely adopted by state courts, the use of the terminology of negligence by the *Restatement (Third) for Products Liability's* (to be discussed *infra*) will certainly expand negligence's grip.[3]

A basic negligence claim consists of proof of:

- a duty owed on the part of the manufacturer;

- a breach of that duty,

- a causal link between this breach and a legally cognizable injury to the plaintiff.

A products liability negligence claim usually falls into one of three possible types:

- Suits claiming that a manufacturer used unreasonably shoddy quality control, thereby allowing a "lemon" that should have been caught at the factory to be marketed;[4]

- Suits claiming that the manufacturer carelessly forgot to warn of a non-obvious danger in the use of the product, which danger could easily have been avoided by the plaintiff had she only received the warning, the communication of which would have been quite inexpensive on the part of the manufacturer;

- Suits claiming that of several possible designs for the product, the manufacturer carelessly chose a very dangerous design, despite the fact that a much safer design would have been cost efficient.[5]

All three types of negligence suits parallel the three strict liability suits (for manufacturing defect, informational defect and design defect, respectively) discussed in Part II of this book. But the

---

2. Phillips v. Kimwood Machinery Co., 525 P.2d 1033, 1037 (Or. 1974).

3. This was recognized well before the *Restatement (Third)* was adopted. *See, e.g.*, John F. Vargo, *Caveat Emptor:*

Will the ALI Erode Strict Liability in the Restatement (Third) for Products Liability? 10 TOURO L. REV. 21 (1993).

4. See Appendix, Section 2, *infra*.

5. See Appendix, Section 1, *infra*.

choice of grounding is of more than semantic importance. To take one obvious example, is the cigarette butt found in the Coke bottle in *Pulley*[6] the source of a negligence suit (the cigarette might be seen as *res ipsa loquitur* evidence of the bottler's negligence) or of a strict liability suit? If the former, the defendant is allowed to rebut the inference by showing that its bottling procedure was "state of the art"; if the latter, as was seen above, such evidence may be deemed inadmissible.

The *Pulley* court's refusal to characterize the plaintiff's suit as a negligence suit essentially deprived Pacific Coca–Cola of any feasible defense. For only if detectives followed each bottle until it was consumed could Pacific Coca–Cola establish where in the chain of distribution the cigarette entered the bottle—and the cost of detectives is too high to allow Pacific to sell bottles profitably. All the bottler can practically do is prove that it was likely not the source of the contamination. Perhaps the retailer hired delinquent employees, perhaps the victim's friends pulled a prank. The bottler had no way of economically producing evidence of such possibilities: it could only defend itself by offering evidence of its own practices. Since this was not allowed, the bottler essentially became the plaintiff's insurer, with the unintended consequences discussed in Chapter 3.

A. Salient Characteristics of a Negligence Suit

Because negligence is often an essential component of a products liability suit, it is useful to review the characteristics of a negligence products claim.

1). No Privity Is Needed

Negligence suits are obviously tort suits. Therefore no contractual privity is required between plaintiff and defendant.

2). Plaintiff's Conduct Is Relevant

Because a negligence suit is a tort suit, the victim's negligence will be assessed as either contributory or comparative, depending on the substantive rule in the jurisdiction. Product misuse, for example, might constitute plaintiff's negligence—and in a contributory negligence jurisdiction[7] this might bar recovery automatically. Other tort defenses, including assumption of risk, also clearly apply.

3). A Presumption Of Negligence Is Possible

The doctrine of *res ipsa loquitur* facilitates plaintiff's task when direct evidence of negligence is not possible. Circumstantial

---

6. Pulley v. Pacific Coca–Cola, see Chapter 2 *supra*.

7. Alabama, Maryland, Virginia, District of Columbia, and North Carolina.

evidence, i.e., the product defect itself (whether it be a manufacturing defect, a failure to warn, or a design flaw) might give rise to a presumption of negligence *if* the defect arose while the product was in the defendant's possession, and if most such defects arise as a result of negligence.[8]

4). No Punitive Damages

Punitive damages are essentially limited to intentional tort cases, to cases of gross negligence, and to intentional breach of contract cases.[9] Therefore, in principle, there are no punitive damages in negligence-based products liability suits.

2. Tortious Misrepresentation

A product may be defective and dangerous because of false or misleading information conveyed by the manufacturer or seller of a product. A person who reasonably relies on the information conveyed by the seller and who is harmed by such reliance may recover for the misrepresentation. This basis for recovery does not depend on a defect in the product, but rather depends on the false or inaccurate communication.

A. Types of Misrepresentation Suits

Previous chapters introduced the thesis that all modern products liability suits, including those filed under a strict liability theory, can be seen as implicit misrepresentation cases. However, some suits are explicitly based on misrepresentation.

1). Fraud[10]

This intentional tort (giving rise to the possibility of punitive damages) requires a showing of *scienter*, i.e., that the defendant knew his representation was false and would be relied on. These suits are infrequent but not unheard of. Thus, in *St. Joseph Hospital v. Corbetta Construction Co.*,[11] defendant General Electric, through one of its agents, wrote the following letter providing a quote for the installation of one of its products, the Batten Panel System, in a Chicago hospital setting:

> "Further at this time I wish to point out that our Batten Panel System does not carry a flame spread rating of any kind... We can supply a U–L flame spread rated panel, but not under the

---

8. Richard Epstein, *Products Liability: The Search for the Middle Ground*, 56 N.C.L. Rev. 643, 651 (1978).

9. Michael I. Krauss, *Punitive Damages and the Supreme Court: A Tragedy in Five Acts*, 4:2 Engage (2008).

10. Known in some states as the tort of "Deceit."

11. St. Joseph Hosp. v. Corbetta Construction Co., 316 N.E.2d 51 (Ill. App. 1974).

terms and drawings submitted in conjunction with the contract."[12]

In fact, the agent knew that the Batten Panel System *had* been flame tested, scoring a horrible 1700 percent of the flammability allowed for hospitals under the building Code. The court found General Electric liable for fraud after Chicago required costly disassembly by the hospital before issuing an occupancy permit. The court noted that, "[i]t is well established that a statement which is technically true as far as it goes may nevertheless be fraudulent..."[13]

Note that the damages in *St. Joseph Hospital* were not traditional products liability damages (no one had been injured in a fire spread by the panel system), but the costs incurred to *remove* the walls without any fire damage. As the award in this case illustrates, many fraud cases are for "loss of bargain," rather than for personal injury.

Fraud suits are difficult to prosecute, in part because of the difficulty of proving *scienter* and detrimental reliance. In addition, many jurisdictions require "clear and convincing evidence" of fraud.[14] The tort of fraud does not require privity—a consumer can sue in fraud if she relied on a fraudulent claim by a manufacturer.

2). *Misrepresentation*

Many negligent misrepresentation cases involve retailers who are not strictly liable for a product's defects, because a particular state's statutes have derogated from the *Restatement*. Moreover, sometimes the negligent misrepresentation is itself the only "defect" in the product. Need the misrepresentation be negligent to create liability in such cases? Consider *Crocker v. Winthrop Laboratories.*[15]

In *Crocker*, the plaintiff had suffered a double hernia and frostbite in two fingers while working as a carpenter in a cold storage vault. His hernia was successfully repaired, but it was necessary to amputate part of his thumb and middle finger. Prior to these amputations, the several doctors who had treated Crocker had prescribed both Demerol® (a narcotic) and Talwin® for pain relief, and never observed any symptom of addiction to either drug. Crocker told the surgeon who amputated his fingers that he liked the relief he received from Talwin®. The surgeon responded that this was fortunate, as Talwin® had no addictive side effect. That physician continued to prescribe Talwin® for him following the

---

12. *Id.* at 70.

13. *Id.* at 70.

14. *See, e.g.,* Idaho Code I.C. § 6–1604(1).

15. Crocker v. Winthrop Laboratories, Division of Sterling Drug, Inc., 514 S.W.2d 429 (Tex. 1974).

amputation. But in fact Crocker did become addicted to Talwin®. He travelled to nearby Mexico to obtain additional supplies of the drug. He was hospitalized in early June 1968 by a psychiatrist, for treatment of his drug dependency. After undergoing withdrawal treatment for six days, Crocker walked out of the hospital and went home. He proceeded to threaten his wife, who called another physician who, on June 10, came to the Crocker home and gave Mr. Crocker an injection of Demerol®. Crocker died shortly thereafter. The wrongful death products liability suit against the manufacturer of Talwin® claimed that had Crocker known about Talwin's addictive qualities he would not have become dependant on it, and therefore would not have died during detoxification.

Winthrop Laboratories had, in fact, no reason to believe that Talwin® was addictive: none of the research that had preceded FDA approval for the drug revealed any potential for addiction. However, for unusually susceptible patients, it turns out that Talwin® is in fact an addictive pain-killer. The jury specifically found that Winthrop Laboratories could not have reasonably foreseen Crocker's addiction because of his unusual susceptibility and the state of medical knowledge when the drug was marketed.

The trial court dismissed Crocker's suit for this reason, but the Texas Supreme Court reversed. Winthrop was *not* liable for failing to warn of Talwin®'s addictiveness, for it could not have known about that risk at the time,[16] the court ruled. Rather, the drug manufacturer was liable for falsely representing that the drug was not addictive. Citing § 402B of the *Restatement (Second)*,[17] the court insisted that if a misrepresentation causes reliance, products liability ensues.[18]

As has been suggested earlier, this form of representational misfeasance arguably underlies all products liability. Did *Crocker* break new ground? Not really. In another case, *thirty years before the strict liability revolution*, it was held that a non-negligent

---

16. *See infra*, Chapter 8. Liability for failure to warn, though nominally "strict," is in fact arguably indistinguishable from negligence liability.

17. "One engaged in the business of selling chattels who, by advertising, labels, or otherwise, makes to the public a misrepresentation of a material fact concerning the character or quality of a chattel sold by him is subject to liability for physical harm to a consumer of the chattel caused by justifiable reliance upon the misrepresentation, even though

(a) it is not made fraudulently or negligently, and

(b) the consumer has not bought the chattel from or entered into any contractual relation with the seller." Restatement (Second) of Torts § 402B (1965).

18. "Whatever the danger and state of medical knowledge, and however rare the susceptibility of the user, when the drug company positively and specifically represents its product to be free and safe from all dangers of addiction, and when the treating physician relies upon that representation, the drug company is liable when the representation proves to be false and harm results." *Crocker*, 514 S.W.2d at 433.

misrepresentation would give rise to liability if it was relied on and injury resulted.[19]

Questions

- Would the outcome of the *Crocker* case have been different if Winthrop Laboratories had not marketed Talwin® as non-addictive, but had marketed it with the indication that no addictive tendencies had been thus far been found in any testing (assume that testing continued after FDA approval and that the indication was changed as soon as the potential for addiction in a tiny percentage of the population was discovered)?

- If Crocker had proved that he would have taken another (non-addictive) painkiller had he learned that few studies of Talwin® had taken place, would this enhance his chance of recovery?

- If Winthrop Laboratories had proved that Crocker would have taken some other (addictive) pain-killer had he not been able to take Talwin®, what impact should this proof have had on the case?

3.   Breach of Warranty

In many misrepresentation cases no guarantee is offered. Rather, the product is mischaracterized to the user's ultimate detriment. What if the manufacturer or seller goes further, and actually warrants a result? Warranty breach cases are acute examples of misrepresentation; the boundary between the two causes of action is sometimes difficult to define. Should a warranty claim sound in contract and not in tort? In other words, should privity (a contract doctrine) of the parties be required?

A.   Express Warranty

The easiest kind of warranty to understand is the express warranty, defined in the law of sales by the Uniform Commercial Code[20] (UCC) and applied without a privity requirement in products

---

19. Baxter v. Ford Motor Co., 12 P.2d 409 (Wash. 1932) (windshield represented as "shatterproof" could in fact shatter under unusual conditions).

20. § 2–313. Express Warranties by Affirmation, Promise, Description, Sample.

(1) Express warranties by the seller are created as follows:

(a) Any affirmation of fact or promise made by the seller to the buyer which relates to the goods and becomes part of the basis of the bargain creates an express warranty that the goods shall conform to the affirmation or promise.

(b) Any description of the goods which is made part of the basis of the bargain creates an express warranty that the goods shall conform to the description.

(c) Any sample or model which is made part of the basis of the bargain creates an express warranty that the whole of the goods shall conform to the sample or model.

(2) It is not necessary to the creation of an express warranty that the seller use formal words such as "warrant" or "guarantee" or that he have a specific intention to make a warranty, but an affirmation merely of the value of the goods or a statement purporting to be

liability cases under § 402(B) of the *Restatement (Second)*. If a manufacturer warrants that its sleeping bag will allow a winter camper to survive temperatures of -30°F, and if the user relying on this warranty suffers frostbite after using the bag properly at -20°F, a clear case of liability has been made out. The fact that no other sleeping bag made would have protected the victim any better is irrelevant in this case—the manufacturer promised plaintiff that this one would protect her.[21] In that sense the detrimental reliance required when suing for misrepresentation is narrowed when suing for breach of warranty. Here are two other examples, from before and after the strict liability revolution described in Chapter 2:

1. *Lane v. C.A. Swanson & Sons*:[22] Plaintiff purchased Swanson "Boned Chicken," after reading an advertisement that said "All luscious white and dark meat. *No bones.* No waste..." Plaintiff was injured when a small bone lodged in his throat. On appeal, it was held that "[T]he label on the can, coupled with... ads that the contents contained no bones, constituted an express warranty... If there could be a doubt as to the meaning of 'boned chicken', it was removed by the statement that it contained no bones."[23]

2. *Hauter v. Zogarts*:[24] The plaintiff's father purchased "Golfing Gizmo" (essentially a golf ball tethered to an elasticized cord) to teach his son to drive a golf ball. The packaging declared that the "Gizmo" could not result in the golf ball returning and striking the student golfer. This is exactly what happened. Holding the manufacturer liable, the court indicated that it was not necessary to prove that the boy or even his father had actually read the statement on the package. Once made, such warranties are part of the basis of the bargain and may be invoked without privity in a products liability suit.

Note that express warranties don't have to be explicitly labeled "guarantee," or "warranty" or "promise," under § 2–313(2) of the UCC. Advertising a purported feature of a product could create a warranty; on the other hand, enunciating an opinion might be "puffing" without legal effect. To illustrate, if a tire is advertised as "puncture-proof," that arguably constitutes a warranty. If pepper spray is marketed as capable of "effecting *instantaneous incapaci-*

---

merely the seller's opinion or commendation of the goods does not create a warranty. U.C.C. § 2–313 (2001).

21. *See, e.g., Baxter*, 12 P.2d at 412. It mattered not that no manufacturer had shatter proof glass. Ford promised the user that this glass *was* shatterproof and is therefore liable for the damages caused by the shattering.

22. Lane v. C.A. Swanson & Sons, 278 P.2d 723 (Cal. App. 1955).

23. *Id.* at 726. Emphasis in original text.

24. Hauter v. Zogarts, 534 P.2d 377 (Cal. 1975).

tation . . . an attacker is *subdued—instantly,*" that is also a warranty.[25] "This is a great car" is puffing, but portraying a used car as "mechanically A–1," was ruled a warranty that the vehicle was capable of at least getting the buyer home from the dealership.[26]

B.   Implied Warranty of Merchantability

Making express every implied term of a contract would greatly increase the costs of transacting. Implied contract terms, including warranties, have been relied on from time immemorial.[27] Automobile tires, fitted on the wheels at the factory, need not be expressly warranted to be able to be able to carry an automobile's weight when properly inflated. A new tire that does not meet this standard would be deemed defective, and would incur liability of the tire manufacturer and all sellers regardless of privity.[28] Even the few jurisdictions that purport *not* to follow strict liability recognize the implied warranty of merchantability, with results that appear indistinguishable from those reached in strict liability jurisdictions.[29]

Utterly non-merchantable items clearly breach the implied warranty of merchantability, but for other goods the notion of implied warranty is rather vague. *How* strong should the roof of a Ford Aerostar be? How weak must it be for the vehicle to be non-merchantable? Do the concepts of defect (in products liability law) and of merchantability (in the UCC) overlap when personal injury occurs? It is very hard to argue the contrary.

On the other hand, it is difficult to argue that any warranty is implied if all warranties are expressly excluded. Under the provisions of the UCC, the liability of a manufacturer or seller for personal injury, death, or property damage caused by a defective product, predicated on breach of an express or implied warranty, may be "disclaimed" in whole or in part in the manner prescribed by UCC § 2–316.[30] Selling someone an old tire, for use solely as a

25. Klages v. General Ordinance Equip. Corp., 367 A.2d 304 (Pa. Super. Ct. 1976).

26. Jones v. Kellner, 451 N.E.2d 548 (Ohio App. 1982).

27. *See, e.g.,* Gardiner v. Gray, 171 Eng. Rep. 46 (1815).

28. U.C.C., § 2–318 (2001).

29. These jurisdictions retain "warranty" language for products liability: Delaware, Massachusetts, Michigan, North Carolina, and Virginia. AMERICAN LAW OF PRODUCTS LIABILITY § 16:14 (3d ed. 2009). "Anti-privity" rules (*see, e.g.,* Va. Code Ann. § 8.2–318) accompany the warranty language, thereby making the apparent contract doctrine indistinguishable from tort.

30. § 2–316. Exclusion or Modification of Warranties.

(1) Words or conduct relevant to the creation of an express warranty and words or conduct tending to negate or limit warranty shall be construed wherever reasonable as consistent with each other; but subject to the provisions of this Article on parol or extrinsic evidence . . . negation or limitation is inoperative to the extent that such construction is unreasonable.

(2) Subject to subsection (3), to exclude or modify the implied warranty of merchantability or any part of it the language must mention merchantability and in case of a writing must be conspic-

swing, might entail disclaiming the implied warranty of merchantability of this tire for purposes of automobile travel. On the other hand, if marketing efforts tout the product as being able to accomplish certain tasks, a seller may not "talk out of both sides of his mouth" by then burying a disclaimer of all warranties in the small print of the sales contract. This important point was emphasized in the following seminal case:

- **1).** *Henningsen v. Bloomfield Motors*:[31]

A man purchased a new Plymouth. Ten days later his wife was driving the car, with 469 miles on the odometer, when it lost all steering function and smashed into a brick wall, injuring her and "totaling" the vehicle. Chrysler and the dealership were sued by the victim (for her bodily injuries) and her husband (for the value of the vehicle). Both defendants invoked the following language from the contract:

"7. *It is expressly agreed that there are no warranties, express or implied*, made by either the dealer or the manufacturer on the motor vehicle, chassis, of parts furnished hereunder except as follows.

The manufacturer warrants each new motor vehicle (including original equipment placed thereon by the manufacturer except tires), chassis or parts manufactured by it to be free from defects in material or workmanship under normal use and service. Its obligation under this warranty being limited to making good at its factory any part or parts thereof which shall, within ninety (90) days after delivery of such vehicle To the original purchaser or before such vehicle has been driven 4,000 miles, whichever event shall first occur, be returned to it with transportation charges prepaid and which its examination shall disclose to its satisfaction to have been thus defective; *This warranty*

---

uous, and to exclude or modify any implied warranty of fitness the exclusion must be by a writing and conspicuous. Language to exclude all implied warranties of fitness is sufficient if it states, for example, that "There are no warranties which extend beyond the description on the face hereof."

(3) Notwithstanding subsection (2)

(a) unless the circumstances indicate otherwise, all implied warranties are excluded by expressions like "as is", "with all faults" or other language which in common understanding calls the buyer's attention to the exclusion of warranties and makes plain that there is no implied warranty; and

(b) when the buyer before entering into the contract has examined the goods or the sample or model as fully as he desired or has refused to examine the goods there is no implied warranty with regard to defects which an examination ought in the circumstances to have revealed to him; and

(c) an implied warranty can also be excluded or modified by course of dealing or course of performance or usage of trade. U.C.C. § 2–316 (2001).

31. Henningsen v. Bloomfield Motors, 161 A.2d 69 (N.J. 1960).

being expressly in lieu of all other warranties expressed or implied, and all other obligations or liabilities on its part, and it neither assumes nor authorizes any other person to assume for it any other liability in connection with the sale of its vehicles."

The New Jersey Supreme Court refused to enforce this disclaimer. Its opinion is replete with assertions about monopolization and bargaining power, which certainly do not prevail today in the automobile industry. But the essence of its decision is fully applicable today: a reasonable purchaser of a new automobile is entitled to assume that the steering will not fail while the car is brand new. If stipulations to the contrary, buried in the fine print of a sales contract, contradict the assurances conveyed through the marketing of the vehicle, such a disclaimer is *per se* unreasonable and unenforceable under § 2–316 (1). The essence of this and similar[32] refusals to countenance disclaimers is *estoppel*: manufacturers and sellers may not simultaneously impliedly warrant their product in their marketing and then exclude that warranty in the fine print. Disclaimers are theoretically possible,[33] but they must be unequivocal to avoid misrepresentation. Even in jurisdictions[34] that insist on the right of manufacturers to disclaim the implied warranty of merchantability, "unreasonable" disclaimers and limitations remain unenforceable.[35]

Today, of course, in most states a products liability suit is styled as one of "strict liability," not one of "implied warranty," so the UCC provisions will not be dispositive. As noted earlier, the grounds for recovery on either theory are virtually identical.[36]

C.   Implied Warranty of Fitness for a Particular Purpose

What if a buyer has a *non*-ordinary purpose in mind for the product she is purchasing? If the seller knows of this particular purpose, and does not dispel the buyer's belief that the product is suited to it, then a warranty of fitness for this particular purpose will be implied.[37] If a furniture retailer sells a chair to a morbidly obese man, who is subsequently injured after the chair collapses

---

32. *See also* Dorman v. Internationalal Harvester, 120 Cal.Rptr. 516 (Cal. App. 1975); Manheim v. Ford Motor Co., 201 So.2d 440 (Fla. 1967); McCarty v. E.J. Korvette, 347 A.2d 253 (Md. App. 1975); Berg v. Stromme, 484 P.2d 380 (Wash. 1971).

33. U.C.C. § 2–316, 2–719 (2001).

34. *See, e.g.,* Ford Motor Co. v. Moulton, 511 S.W.2d 690 (Tenn. 1974), *cert. denied,* 419 U.S. 870.

35. *See, e.g.,* McCullough v. General Motors Corp., 577 F.Supp. 41 (W.D. Tenn. 1982).

36. *See, e.g.,* Larsen v. Pacesetter Systems, Inc., 837 P.2d 1273, 1284–85 (Haw. 1992).

37. U.C.C. § 2–315.

under his weight, the retailer will not be allowed to claim that the man's heft was such that the chair was not impliedly warranted to withstand it. Reliance by the buyer on this implied warranty is of the essence here.[38]

Question About Julian Felipe's Case

- Was there any express warranty concerning the strength of the roof of the Felipes' Ford Aerostar? Any implied warranty of merchantability?

- If the latter, is it understood how strong a roof must be in case of rollover? Is it implied that the roof will never weaken or crumple in case of rollover? If this is your view, would it matter if no minivans possess roofs of such strength?

---

38. *See, e.g.*, Peters v. Lyons, 168 N.W.2d 759 (Iowa 1969) (Buyer asked for a dog chain strong enough to restrain his 120–lb. German shepherd— the chain offered by the salesman did not do the job, and injury to the buyer ensued. Held, liability.)

Part Two

ANALYSIS OF PRODUCTS LIABILITY LAW

Chapter 5

"STRICT" LIABILITY: WHO MAY SUE WHOM?[1]

Plaintiffs in products liability suits typically invoke negligence, misrepresentation and breach of warranty as causes of action, for reasons described in Chapter 4. In some jurisdictions "breach of warranty" is the term used for the cause of action styled as strict liability in most jurisdictions, and embodied in § 402A of the *Restatement (Second)*. In this chapter, the basic parameters of strict liability are explored:

- Who is Strictly Liable?
- How does Worker's Compensation mesh with Strict Liability?
- Who may sue under Strict Liability?

1. Who Is Strictly Liable?

The "paradigmatic" defendant in a lawsuit based on strict liability for product defect is, of course, the manufacturer of the product. If X makes a widget with a hidden defect, which causes it to blow up in the face of an unsuspecting Y, basic tort principles discussed in Chapter 3 dictate that X will be liable to Y.

But there are many "non-paradigmatic" cases. Consider the following questions:

- What if X makes a defective component of a product, which Z assembles along with other components to make a finished product Z then sells?[2] Should both X and Z be strictly liable if Y is injured because of this defect? If so, should one defendant, if forced to compensate Y for her injury, be indemnified by the other?

- If X, the manufacturer, packages a product and sells it to wholesaler Z, who in turn sells it to retailer A, and if neither intermediary has the right or even the ability to inspect it,[3] should Z and A be strictly liable to the injured party Y?

---

1. Additional Reading: George L. Priest, *The Invention of Enterprise Liability: A Critical History of the Intellectual Foundations of Modern Tort Law*, 14 J. LEGAL STUD. 461 (1985); Paul Weiler, *Workers' Compensation And Product Liability: The Interaction Of A Tort And A* *Non–Tort Regime*, 50 OHIO ST. L.J. 825 (1989).

2. This is *MacPherson v. Buick*, discussed in Chapter 2.

3. Think of a box of laundry detergent—if opened by an intermediary seller it loses all resale value.

- What if X makes a defective product and sells it to Z, a service provider who subsequently serves Y, bundling the product incidentally with this service? Should X and Z be strictly liable?

- If X is a wholly owned subsidiary of Z, should Z be strictly liable? What if Z is one of several owners of X? What if X merges with Z, or sells all its assets to Z, subsequent to the production of the defective product?

- If X sells a defective product to Z, who *rents* or *leases* it to Y, is Z strictly liable when Y is injured?

- If Z, a retailer, sells a *used* product to Y, and that product turns out to be defective and unreasonably dangerous, injuring Y, should Z be strictly liable?

- If X or the purchaser is Y's employer, shielded from liability by Workers' Compensation laws, should this shield give way to strict liability?

A. Component Manufacturers

The authors of the *Restatement (Second)* provide little information about component parts,[4] though the *Restatement (Third)* has elaborated.[5] The basic theory of strict liability sketched out in earlier chapters does allow us to draw a few general conclusions:

4. § 402A, Comment q, reads as follows: "*q. Component parts.* The same problem arises in cases of the sale of a component part of a product to be assembled by another, as for example a tire to be placed on a new automobile, a brake cylinder for the same purpose, or an instrument for the panel of an airplane. Again the question arises, whether the responsibility is not shifted to the assembler. It is no doubt to be expected that where there is no change in the component part itself, but it is merely incorporated into something larger, the strict liability will be found to carry through to the ultimate user or consumer. But in the absence of a sufficient number of decisions on the matter to justify a conclusion, the Institute expresses no opinion on the matter." RESTATEMENT (SECOND) OF TORTS § 402A (1965).

5. § 5. Liability Of Commercial Seller Or Distributor Of Product Components For Harm Caused By Products Into Which Components Are Integrated.

One engaged in the business of selling or otherwise distributing product components who sells or distributes a component is subject to liability for harm to persons or property caused by a product into which the component is integrated if:

(a) the component is defective in itself, as defined in this Chapter, and the defect causes the harm; or

(b)(1) the seller or distributor of the component substantially participates in the integration of the component into the design of the product; and

(b)(2) the integration of the component causes the product to be defective, as defined in this Chapter; and

(b)(3) the defect in the product causes the harm.

RESTATEMENT (THIRD) OF TORTS, PRODUCTS LIABILITY § 5 (1998).

1. If X makes a component part that is defective, and which causes injury to Y,[6] then both X and Z (the final manufacturer) are liable to Y.[7] Note here that the liability of Z (who may have reasonably relied on X's competence) is somewhat vicarious, like an employer's liability for the negligence of its employee. Even if Z had no opportunity to inspect X's work, Z would be liable for having sold a defective and unreasonably dangerous car that proximately injured Y. Z may have an indemnity suit against X, unless Z waived the right to indemnity in its contract with X.[8]

2. If Z makes a component part that is not defective, but that is used by X to make a defective and unreasonably dangerous product not endorsed or authorized by Z, and if Y is injured by this product, then only X is liable to Y. There is no liability on the part of the component part manufacturer unless the latter "substantially participates in the integration of the component into the design of the product," which integration causes the product to be defective.[9]

3. If Z makes a component part of a product assembled by X, and that product is defective and unreasonably dangerous because of a failure to warn of a condition created by the finished product, which condition injures Y, only X is liable to Y. Z would also be liable if its component part created this dangerous condition *and* if it did not transmit a warning to X.[10]

B. Downstream Sellers

Manufacturers "own" their defective and unreasonably dangerous product, but what of a downstream wholesaler or retailer who has no opportunity to inspect it before resale? Products liability law holds these resellers liable as well.[11] This liability is, again, somewhat vicarious; resellers will generally benefit from an indemnity suit against the manufacturer of the defective product.[12]

Manufacturers are often located out-of-state, while retailers are situated near the residence of the injured buyer. Local retailers are

---

6. Think of a manufacturing defect in a steering wheel assembly, which is hypothetically sold as a sealed unit by Company Z to X Motor Co.

7. *See, e.g.,* Wagner v. General Motors Corp., 258 S.W.3d 749 (Ark. 2007).

8. *See, e.g.,* General Motors Corp. v. Hudiburg Chevrolet, Inc., 199 S.W.3d 249 (Tex. 2006).

9. *See, e.g.,* Apperson v. E.I. Du Pont de Nemours & Co., 41 F.3d 1103

(7th Cir. 1994) (Teflon used to manufacture jaw implant, but Teflon not suited for this use.).

10. *See, e.g.,* Buonanno v. Colmar Belting Co., 733 A.2d 712 (R.I. 1999).

11. The seminal case is Vandermark v. Ford Motor Co., 391 P.2d 168 (Cal. 1964).

12. *See, e.g.,* Godoy v. Abamaster of Miami, Inc., 754 N.Y.S.2d 301 (N.Y. App. Div. 2d Dept. 2003).

a powerful lobbying force. Legislation adopted in several states has eliminated resellers' common law strict liability in cases where both of the following conditions obtain: (1) the manufacturer can be sued in courts in the state of plaintiff's domicile; and (2) the manufacturer is not, nor is likely to become, insolvent.[13]

C. Service Providers

What if X supplies defective and poisonous dry cleaning fluid to an unsuspecting dry cleaner (Z), injuring Z's customer, Y? What if X makes a toxic dental implant, which is inserted into Y's mouth by unsuspecting oral surgeon Z? What if ophthalmologist Z performs laser eye surgery on Y, using a machine made by X that malfunctions and causes injury? In cases such as these, should Z be strictly liable to Y (subject to a right of indemnity against X) or should Y have the burden of proving that Z was negligent? Should it matter to these questions whether or not X is insolvent?

§ 402A provides strict liability for "one who sells" the defective and unreasonably dangerous product. The dry cleaner and the surgeon do not sell goods; rather, they provide a service.[14] The dry cleaner does not typically advertise the solvent fluid he uses. Health care providers, however, do frequently market the "advanced" prostheses and medical machines they use. Should this marketing determine whether strict liability applies?

Generally, neither billing nor marketing is seen as crucial in the caselaw. Medical service providers are typically held *not* to be strictly liable for dangerous defects in machinery they use or in equipment they transmit to their patients, whether they use the equipment in their marketing or not. Typical is *Cafazzo v. Central Medical Health Services, Inc.*,[15] where it was held that a physician who had inserted the Vitek® jaw implant discussed in Chapter 2 was not strictly liable for the devastating harm suffered by his patient.[16] Similarly, many statutes make clear that blood transfusions constitute services, not sales, making transfusers liable only for negligence.[17]

What about non-professional services? If a beautician uses a defective permanent wave solution on a client, injuring her, is the beautician strictly liable? Here, some courts trend in a different

---

13. RESTATEMENT (THIRD) OF TORTS, PRODUCTS LIABILITY § 1 cmt. e (1998).

14. Though the dental surgeon's bill will likely itemize the implant—should this fact be relevant?

15. Cafazzo v. Central Med. Health Servs., Inc., 668 A.2d 521 (Pa. 1995).

16. A Missouri appellate decision reached the opposite conclusion in Mulli-

gan v. Truman Med. Ctr., 950 S.W.2d 576 (Mo. App. 1997). But that case was overruled by statute a few years later, as was confirmed in Budding v. SSM Healthcare Sys., 19 S.W.3d 678 (Mo. 2000).

17. *See, e.g.*, McDaniel v. Baptist Mem'l Hosp., 469 F.2d 230 (6th Cir. 1972) (applying Tennessee law).

direction. The New Jersey Supreme Court has ruled that non-professional service providers could be strictly liable, distinguishing professionals who spend "years of study and preparation" from those "engaged in a commercial enterprise."[18] Washington state employed a similar line of reasoning, holding a restaurant strictly liable after a client was injured when a wine glass broke in her hand—though surely the restaurant did not sell the glass.[19] Presumably these courts feel that the physician's labor adds more economic value to a product than do the beautician and the waiter—but why should this imply that only the latter, not the former, impliedly warrants her product? Presumably a LASIK® surgeon profits from the reputation of the machine he uses more than the wine bar markets the brand of glass in which the wine is served.

Meanwhile, intermediate categories abound. Are pharmacists, when filling prescriptions (with defective drugs), more like surgeons or more like hardware stores? California's Supreme Court shielded the pharmacist in such a case,[20] though not without a dissent that was revolted by the "elitist distinctions" of the majority.[21]

D.   Owners of Subsidiaries; Successor Corporations

Almost all product liability manufacturers are corporations, legal entities whose shares are owned by people or other legal entities. Limited liability is the quintessence of the corporate form, shielding the personal assets of shareholders from any liability for the debts of the corporation. Thus, in principle no shareholder, whether that shareholder be another corporation or an individual, may be held liable for the debts of a corporation in which the shareholder is an investor.

Of course, there are exceptions to this rule.

1).   *Where the Shareholder Is the Apparent Manufacturer*

Under basic agency rules, a principal is liable in cases of apparent agency. The corporation which, through its labeling or advertising, causes the public to believe that it is the manufacturer is estopped from subsequently claiming that in fact a subsidiary (or even an unrelated firm[22]) produced the defective product.[23]

---

18. Newmark v. Gimbel's Inc., 258 A.2d 697 (N.J. 1969).

19. Shaffer v. Victoria Station, Inc., 588 P.2d 233 (Wash. 1978).

20. Murphy v. E. R. Squibb & Sons, Inc., 710 P.2d 247 (Cal. 1985).

21. *Id.* at 258 (Bird, C.J., dissenting).

22. Murray v. Wilson Oak Flooring Co., Inc., 475 F.2d 129, 130 (7th Cir. 1973) (product bore the label of defen-dant, for whom the adhesive was manu-factured on a private label basis by a third party).

23. RESTATEMENT (THIRD) OF TORTS, PRODUCTS LIABILITY § 14 (1998); Mello v. K–Mart Corp., 604 F.Supp. 769 (D. Mass. 1985); Hebel v. Sherman Equip., 442 N.E.2d 199 (Ill. 1982); Lopez v. Chi-cago Bridge & Iron Co., 546 So.2d 291 (La. Ct. App.1989); Haymore v. Thew Shovel Co., 446 S.E.2d 865 (N.C. Ct.

2). *Where a Shareholder Is So Closely Related To the Manufacturer Corporation as To Be Its Alter Ego*

Courts are generally loathe to pierce the corporate veil, but will do so when the two entities (shareholder and manufacturing corporation) in fact act as one. This is especially likely to occur if the manufacturer is undercapitalized[24] or hard to reach. Thus, in *Torres v. Goodyear Tire & Rubber Co.*,[25] the defective tire was manufactured by Goodyear Great Britain, which was licensed by the defendant Goodyear Tire to use the Goodyear trademark. The Arizona Supreme Court held the defendant strictly liable:

> "[T]he facts set forth in this opinion show that Goodyear is anything but a mere licensor. On the present record before us, the undisputed facts certainly could support a finding that Goodyear participated significantly in the design, manufacture, promotion, and sale that resulted in the product reaching the consumer."[26]

3). *Where Defendant Has Purchased the Shares Or the Assets of the Manufacturer*

If Corporation X, which manufactured a defective widget that harmed Y, ultimately merges with Corporation Z, or has its shares purchased by Corporation Z with the result that the survivor corporation is Corporation Z, clearly all of Y's obligations are now Z's obligations. This is a fundamental principle of corporate law—corporations are immortal (unless and until they are dissolved by a sovereign act), and a successor corporation assumes its predecessor's obligations.

What if, however, Corporation X survives but sells assets (not shares) to Corporation Z? What if these assets include the production facilities for the previously produced widget that harmed Y? Here the same principles of corporate law dictate the opposite result: the acquirer of assets is not liable for injuries caused by products derived from these assets prior to the acquisition, unless of course he assumed such obligations when he purchased the assets[27] or unless the "purchase" is a *de facto* merger. The only significant exception to this rule is the case where the transaction is entered into fraudulently to escape legal obligations (as evidenced, for example, by underpayment of the market price for the assets, leaving the seller under capitalized).[28] Even if the buyer-

---

App. 1994); Sears, Roebuck & Co. v. Black, 708 S.W.2d 925 (Tex.App. 1986).

24. *See, e.g.*, North Am. Van Lines, Inc. v. Emmons, 50 S.W.3d 103 (Tex. App. 2001).

25. Torres v. Goodyear Tire & Rubber Co., 786 P.2d 939 (Ariz. 1990).

26. *Torres*, 786 P.2d at 945.

27. This would of course affect the purchase price of the assets.

28. *See, e.g.*, Schumacher v. Richards Shear Co., Inc., 451 N.E.2d 195 (N.Y. 1983). The *Restatement (Third) of*

corporation that acquires the assets uses them to produce the same product line, and benefits from the goodwill attached to the brand name, liability for units made by the seller-corporation does not usually follow,[29] except in the growing number of states that adopt California's "product line exception."[30]

E. Lessors

Sellers are strictly liable for harm caused by their defective and unreasonably dangerous products. What about *renters* of such products? In *Cintrone v. Hertz Truck Leasing and Rental Service,*[31] Hertz was held liable for damages caused to a third party by its defective truck just as a dealer would have been, despite the lack of any sale. The New Jersey Supreme Court noted that Hertz impliedly represented all of its vehicles as being roadworthy.[32] The court's reasoning is that companies like Hertz effectively "sell" their vehicles a little bit at a time.

Similar rulings have affected ski equipment lessors.[33] Like sellers, these lessors are typically within the chain of distribution and profit by placing their product in the stream of commerce. On these grounds laundromats have been held strictly liable for harm caused by a hidden defect in a washing machine or dryer,[34] and supermarkets for defective shopping carts.[35] The opposite result was, interestingly, reached (by a trial court) as regards a health club and a defective piece of exercise equipment.[36]

Not all leases are identical. In some cases a lease is essentially a financing mechanism, and the lessor is not in the chain of distribution of the product. In such cases courts are much less likely to find the lessor strictly liable.[37] Most such cases correspond well to the misrepresentation thesis sketched in the early chapters of this book. A financier makes no implied representation about the

Torts: Products Liability § 12(c) enshrines this rule.

29. *See, e.g.,* Semenetz v. Sherling & Walden, 851 N.E.2d 1170 (N.Y. 2006).

30. Ray v. Alad Corp., 560 P.2d 3 (Cal. 1977). California's product line exception holds strictly liable in tort a party that acquires a manufacturing business and continues the output of its line of products using the same assets and "holding itself out to customers and the public as a continuation of the same enterprise." *Id.* at 11.

31. Cintrone v. Hertz Truck Leasing and Rental Service, 212 A.2d 769 (N.J. 1965).

32. But doesn't the LASIK® opthalmologist represent his machine as being safe?

33. *See, e.g.,* Westlye v. Look Sports, 22 Cal.Rptr.2d 781 (Cal. App. 1993).

34. *See, e.g.,* Garcia v. Halsett, 82 Cal.Rptr. 420 (Cal. App. 1970).

35. Keen v. Dominick's Finer Foods, Inc., 364 N.E.2d 502 (Ill. App. 1977).

36. Nickerson v. Nautilus Plus, II, Inc., 1993 WL 818703 (Mass. Super. 1993).

37. *See, e.g.,* AgriStor Leasing v. Meuli, 634 F.Supp. 1208, 1216 (D. Kan. 1986) ("A distinction is drawn ... between commercial lessors and finance lessors, with strict liability being imposed on the former but not the latter.").

characteristics of the object being purchased with the money he is lending.

F. Franchisors and Trademark Licensors

One who authorizes that a product bear his name as manufacturer (even if the product is actually manufactured by another) is treated, for products liability purposes, as the real manufacturer (though the real manufacturer may also be sued).[38] This doctrine affects the liability of parent corporations for defective products produced by subsidiaries, and can be extended to trademark and franchise situations. Two examples may prove useful:

- In *Torres v. Goodyear Tire & Rubber Co., Inc.,*[39] plaintiffs claimed to have been injured in an accident caused by the tread separation of a defective Goodyear tire installed on their Triumph Spitfire. During discovery, plaintiffs learned that the tire had not been manufactured by defendant Goodyear Tire & Rubber Co., Inc. (Goodyear); rather, it had been produced in England by a different corporation, Goodyear Tyre & Rubber (Great Britain), Ltd (Goodyear GB). A third company, Goodyear International Technical Center (GITC), itself a fully owned subsidiary of a fourth company, Goodyear SA of Luxembourg (Goodyear Luxembourg), designed the tire. Goodyear controlled the other three companies, and the court found that,

  > "Goodyear and Goodyear GB have entered into a licensing contract that permits Goodyear GB to manufacture Goodyear tires. The licensing agreement provides that tires will be manufactured in accordance with formulas, specifications, and directions given by Goodyear, and produced from materials approved by Goodyear. Goodyear GB is also required to comply with Goodyear's instructions on labeling, marketing, packaging, and advertising the tires."

The court found Goodyear strictly liable under these circumstances.

- In *Harris v. Aluminum Co. of America,*[40] plaintiff was blinded in one eye when the twist-off aluminum cap on a plastic bottle of Coca–Cola blew off the bottle and struck her in the eye as she removed it. She sued Coca–Cola (franchisor of the finished product), Alcoa (manufacturer of the cap), Wometco Bottling Company (franchisee and manufacturer of the finished product) and Winn–Dixie (retail seller). Plaintiff of-

---

38. RESTATEMENT (SECOND) OF TORTS § 400 (1965).

39. Torres v. Goodyear Tire & Rubber Co., Inc., 786 P.2d 939 (Ariz. 1990).

40. Harris v. Aluminum Co. of Am., 550 F.Supp. 1024 (W.D. Va. 1982).

fered that the bottle cap in question had imprinted on it the following words: "Bottled under the authority of The Coca-Cola Company . . ." The court held all four defendants strictly liable, and as regards Coca–Cola it ruled that,

> "if a soft drink package was unreasonably dangerous for its ordinary use, and that unreasonably dangerous condition existed when the bottling requirements of the soft drink package were under the franchisor's control, then implied warranty liability [Virginia's version of strict liability for manufacturing defects] would lie against the franchisor."[41]

G. Sellers of Used Products

When one sells a new product, one implies it will "work"—even a hidden "as is" clause buried in the fine print will not legally countermand the implied warranty created by the new car marketing.[42] What of commercial sellers of used products, though? Do they represent their inventory as being non-defective? If the answer is "not always," then should strict liability always attach to the used car seller, for example? Should it matter whether the car is marketed as "good as new," "refurbished," or "handyman's special—sold as is?" Note that, unlike the new product retailer, the used product dealer is unlikely to have an indemnity suit against the manufacturer (because it is unlikely the defect existed when the product was manufactured). Should this affect the used product seller's liability to a retail purchaser?

Consider the following decisions:

- In *Harrison v. Bill Cairns Pontiac of Marlow Heights, Inc.,*[43] a consumer purchased a four-year-old Mercury with 58,000 miles on the odometer from a Pontiac dealer, with no express warranty. Eleven months after the purchase, a fire ignited behind the instrument panel of the vehicle. The car hit a tree and the driver was injured. The Maryland appeals court affirmed the summary judgment granted at trial to the used car dealer, holding that only a defect *introduced by* the dealer (as opposed to a defect that existed when the dealer sold the used car) could lead to the dealer's strict liability.

- In *Turner v. International Harvester,*[44] a New Jersey court reached the opposite conclusion, holding a used truck dealer who sold a truck "as is" liable for a defect on the following

---

41. *Harris*, 550 F.Supp. at 1028.

42. *See Henningsen, supra.*

43. Harrison v. Bill Cairns Pontiac of Marlow Heights, Inc., 549 A.2d 385 (Md. 1988).

44. Turner v. International Harvester, 336 A.2d 62 (N.J. Super. Ct. Law Div. 1975).

grounds: "Sellers of used goods may ... distribute [among all their buyers] the costs of doing business...."[45] This rationale makes the used car seller an insurer, as discussed in Chapter 2—it has nothing to do with implied misrepresentation.

- This distinction was understood by the Oregon Supreme Court in *Tillman v. Vance Equipment*,[46] where a plaintiff injured by a defect in a used crane sought recovery from the dealer that sold him the machine. The court denied the strict liability cause of action, noting that it had never adopted strict liability as a method of insurance, but for other reasons, including to enforce implied representations of safety.

Question

- If *Turner* is sound, why shouldn't a doctor be strictly liable if his implant is defective?

Clearly, these disparities in the caselaw flow from different understandings of the basis for strict liability. The *Restatement (Third)* takes an unequivocal stand here, holding the commercial used goods seller strictly liable only if the dealer has sold a "remanufactured" good, or if the marketing of the product would have caused a reasonable buyer to believe that the used good was no more likely to be defective than a new good.[47] The *Restatement* uses the following revealing illustrations:

- A commercial used-product seller sells a six-month-old used clothes dryer to plaintiff, who is injured when a manufacturing defect in the dryer causes a fire. The seller is strictly liable, since a reasonable buyer might have believed the dryer was no more risky than a new dryer (assuming this belief was not dispelled by the seller).

- A used product is sold with a specific disclaimer by the dealer of any warranty. The disclaimer is relevant to the plaintiff's claim that she reasonably assumed the used product was as safe as a new product, especially "when disclaimer language either reminds the buyer that the product is used or warns the buyer of the increased risk of defect."[48]

Questions About Julian Felipe's Case

- Assuming for the purpose of this question that the Aerostar's roof was defectively weak, should the used car dealer that sold the van to Mrs. Felipe be strictly liable for Julian's damages?

---

45. *Id.* at 69.

46. Tillman v. Vance Equip., 596 P.2d 1299 (Or. 1979).

47. RESTATEMENT (THIRD) OF TORTS, PRODUCTS LIABILITY § 8(b), (c) (1998).

48. *Id.* § 8, cmt. k.

- Should it matter to your answer that the roof had not been altered (no previous rollover, etc.) since its manufacture?

- Should it matter if the van was sold to Mrs. Felipe "as is"? If so, should the disclaimer be valid as against Julian, who is a third party to the contract of sale?

H. Certifiers and Endorsers

Imagine that *Consumers Reports* recommends a particular product it identifies as the best in a ranking of similar products. What if a product received the *Good Housekeeping Seal of Approval®* or was touted in marketing as having been inspected by Underwriters' Laboratories? What if an avid football fan purchased the product after a successful football player endorsed it in an ad in which he declared it to be "very safe?"

In one or more of these situations, should the certifier or endorser be liable to the purchaser of the widget, if it is subsequently found to have been defective and unreasonably dangerous?

A large number of private agencies test, endorse and certify consumer products and their components. Many are print-based; an increasing number use electronic media. These agencies may be classified as:

(1) Those who require the manufacturer to advertise the approved product in their periodical (e.g., the *Good Housekeeping Seal of Approval*, etc.);

(2) Those who depend primarily on the manufacturer to make the public aware of approvals or endorsements, through the manufacturer's use of their seals and labels on products and in the manufacturer's marketing. These agencies do not solicit or publish advertising for the products they review (e.g., Underwriters' Laboratories, Inc. (UL));

(3) Those who test and grade products for the edification of the consumer, and who publish magazines or other periodicals for public distribution containing summaries of the results of their testing and grading procedures (e.g., *Consumer Reports*, etc.);

(4) Those who, for compensation, lend their fame to a product by endorsing it (e.g., Bob Vila, etc.).

Should any of these agencies be strictly liable if the product they certify, rate, or endorse turns out to be defective and unreasonably dangerous? In *Hanberry v. Hearst Corp.*[49] plaintiff alleged that she had purchased defective (because too slippery) shoes because they had received the *Good Housekeeping* seal.[50] While

---

49. Hanberry v. Hearst Corp., 81 Cal.Rptr. 519 (Cal. Ct. App. 1969).

50. The certification by the magazine read as follows: "We satisfy our-

wearing these shoes she slipped on her vinyl kitchen floor and was injured. She sued the *Good Housekeeping's* publisher, alleging both manufacturing and design defects. The trial court granted defendant's demurrer, but on appeal it was held that the complaint had competently alleged that the magazine purported to have tested the product when in fact it merely received advertising funds and issued the certification. If true, the magazine would liable for *negligent* misrepresentation. The court rejected any strict liability suit against the publisher, however, finding that in no way was it a seller of the product. Practically, this means Hearst Corp. could not be liable for any manufacturing defect (as there was clearly no representation by the magazine that it had inspected and tested the particular pair of shoes purchased by plaintiff). Note that if a magazine tests a car and deems it to be "dependable," there is no negligent misrepresentation if the exact unit purchased by the consumer falls apart and injures her. Finally, of course, publishing an advertisement in one's magazine in no way constitutes an endorsement of a product.[51]

The rule in *Hanberry* has been generally applied to certifying agencies[52] and endorsers. On the other hand, rules examined earlier might apply. If a defective driver that comes apart, injuring a golfer, was marketed as "the Michael Krauss driver" (assume, absurdly, that Krauss is a Masters' Champion lending his name to the product), Krauss might conceivably appear to be the manufacturer of the product. If it is clear on the packaging that Krauss is merely a trademark licensor, plaintiff must show that Krauss had some involvement in distribution or manufacturing in order to be held strictly liable.[53] Otherwise liability could only be for negligent misrepresentation. If the author of this book were the aforementioned Krauss, he would prudently ensure that an indemnity agreement by a solvent manufacturer was part of his endorsement contract for the golf club.

I.　Workplace Accidents and Products Liability

In all fifty states, workers' compensation statutes require employers to provide insurance for their employees against losses suffered (according to the typical statutory language) "out of and in the course of employment." Such insurance must be issued either from approved carriers or through the employer's own resources, as certified by a state agency.

selves that the products and services advertised in Good Housekeeping are good ones, and that the claims made for them in our magazine are truthful."

51. *See, e.g.,* Walters v. Seventeen Magazine, 241 Cal.Rptr. 101 (Cal. Ct. App. 1987).

52. *See, e.g.,* Hempstead v. General Fire Extinguisher Corp., 269 F.Supp. 109 (D. Del. 1967) (Virginia law applied).

53. Harrison v. ITT Corp., 603 N.Y.S.2d 826 (App. 1993).

An employee's work-related accident is compensable by the employer or his insurance company even if the accident was no one's fault, indeed even if (as is often the case) the only party at fault was the injured employee herself. Employees typically recover medical costs and a percentage of their income, with the amount of recovery varying according to the degree of permanent disability suffered. The lack of full compensation (there is no recovery for non-economic damages, also known as "pain and suffering," for example) reduces the "moral hazard" that might lead employees to take less than optimal care at work, knowing that injuries are covered.

In return for this insurance, nominally paid for by the employer,[54] workers' compensation statutes deprive employees of the right to sue their employers in tort. But workers do not lose the right to sue third parties. If X, who is neither the employer nor a fellow employee, drops a banana peel on a factory floor, where employee Y trips and falls, Y can sue X. Against X, Y can recover the full panoply of tort damages (including pain and suffering).

Rare are the trespassers who throw down banana peels on factory floors. Much less rare are workplace injuries involving machinery. Often an injured employee was poorly trained to operate a machine. But this negligent training may not be transformed into tort liability, because of the immunity the employer receives as consideration for the provision of workers' compensation insurance. This immunity redirects lawsuits onto the only available defendants: the manufacturer and the distributor of the machine, the only available targets without immunity.

The interaction of workers' compensation insurance and products liability is potentially toxic. A United States Department of Commerce Interagency Task Force on Product Liability, covering claims from mid–1976 into early 1977, found that at least 10 percent of all products liability claims arose from workplace accidents.[55] Because machines tend to be involved in the most serious workplace injuries (for less serious injuries, workers are typically quite content with workers' compensation payouts), the 10 percent figure in fact vastly understates the problem. Reliable estimates are that *40* percent of all dollars paid in products liability damages are in fact for workplace injuries.[56] The development of the doctrine of

---

54. The insurance is of course not "free" for employees. The greater the likelihood of injury, the more expensive the insurance, and the less, *ceteris paribus*, an employer will be willing to pay in wages.

55. W. Kip Viscusi, *The Interaction Between Product Liability and Workers'* *Compensation* as *Ex Post Remedies for Workplace Injuries*, 5 J. L. ECON. & ORGANIZATION 185, 188–95 (1989).

56. Jonathan M. Weisgall, *Product Liability in the Workplace: The Effect of Workers' Compensation on the Rights and Liabilities of Third Parties*, 1977 WIS. L. REV. 1035, 1038–39.

strict liability for defective products (including industrial machines) facilitates the task of an injured worker—if she can plausibly assert that the machine was "defective" (see Chapter 6), she may recover many multiples of what she has recouped in workers' compensation.[57]

The pressure exerted on products liability by employers' tort immunity is exacerbated by the fact that even employees who misuse a machine may recover from product manufacturers if their misuse of a defective machine was "foreseeable." A considerable scholarship has been critical of products liability suits in the workplace.[58] The proposal of many authors is to extend to product sellers and manufacturers the immunity granted employers. But this proposal has had no traction in legislation or caselaw.

The nexus between products liability and workers' compensation produces two additional complications.

1).　The Employer Is Sued for Contribution by the Product Manufacturer.

Is a negligent employer liable to the manufacturer of a defective workplace product? This problem was nicely illustrated by a New York case, *Dole v. Dow*.[59] In *Dole*, a woman sued the manufacturer of a chemical fumigant alleged to have caused the workplace death of her husband. The decedent's employer used the poisonous fumigant to control mice and insects in a grain storage bin. The manufacturer was sued for failure to sufficiently warn the deceased employee of the dangers of the fumigant. The defendant responded to the suit by filing a third-party complaint, alleging that the employer was guilty of "active and primary" negligence by not taking proper precautions in fumigating, by using untrained personnel, and by failing to test or aerate the bin before permitting the decedent to enter. The New York courts found that the employer was immune (because of workers' compensation) to suit by the plaintiff for wrongful death, but could nonetheless be sued for contribution by the product manufacturer. This allowed the manufacturer to recoup the lion's share of the damages, for which the employer had been deemed comparatively responsible by the jury.

The *Dole* decision gave rise to the anomalous situation where an employer remains totally immune if his negligence is the only proximate cause of the employee's injury, but loses all protection if he is "99 percent negligent" and a jury can find some minuscule

---

57. Paul Weiler, *Workers' Compensation And Product Liability: The Interaction Of A Tort And A Non–Tort Regime*, 50 OHIO ST. L.J. 825, 829 (1989).

58. *See, e.g.,* Philip Oliver, *Once is Enough: A Proposed Bar of the Injured Employee's Cause of Action Against a Third Party*, 58 FORDHAM L. REV. 117 (1989).

59. Dole v. Dow, 282 N.E.2d 288 (N.Y. 1972).

defect in a workplace product. For in that situation the manufacturer, held liable, could recoup 99 percent of its payment from the employer.

Dole has not been followed in other states,[60] and was substantially repealed by statute in New York.[61] Preserving the integrity of the workers' compensation immunity, of course, comes at the expense of holding liable (with no right of contribution from the employer) a manufacturer whose defective product may be barely responsible for the employee's injury, to the benefit of possibly negligent employers and employees. Even if a manufacturer has provided a product to a customer according to the precise specifications of that customer, if the customer's employee is injured by the product and sues the manufacturer there is no right of indemnity against the employer.[62]

As one author has noted, "[i]t is difficult to imagine that, if society were starting anew, any disinterested observer would recommend the present system for compensating injured employees."[63] One approach advanced by another author[64] would preserve the employer's immunity while holding the manufacturer only severally liable for its share of wrongdoing. But the manufacturer is deemed liable *irrespective* of wrongdoing, so calculating shares might be insuperably difficult. Another flaw of this proposal is that the manufacturer would have the incentive to claim that the employer was greatly at fault (as this would lower his liability to the employee), while the employer (who remains immune to liability) has no reciprocal incentive to claim lack of fault.

Other possible solutions to this problem have been proposed,[65] but none are capable of "squaring the circle" by fully reconciling an insurance mechanism with one based on tort.

---

60. Illinois had also adopted the *Dole v. Dow* solution, but abandoned it in Kotecki v. Cyclops Welding Corp., 585 N.E.2d 1023 (Ill. 1991), which limits an employer's liability to its exposure under workers' compensation. Essentially, a negligent employer will be denied subrogation, but will not be further liable.

61. *See* Omnibus Workers' Compensation Reform Act of 1996, L.1996, ch. 635, § 2; *see also* N.Y. Workers' Compensation Law § 11 (McKinney 2010). The 1996 Amendment to the § 11 Alternative Remedy provision of New York's Workers' Compensation Law was intended to limit the reach of *Dole v. Dow*. Johnson v. Space Saver Corp., 656 N.Y.S.2d 715, 716 (1997). Section 11 now limits contribution by an employer already paying worker compensation to

situations where a "third person proves through competent medical evidence that such employee has sustained a 'grave injury'". *Id.* at 717 (quoting N.Y. Workers' Compensation Law § 11); *see also* Mustafa v. Halkin Tool, Ltd., 2004 WL 2011384 (E.D.N.Y. 2004).

62. *See* Unique Equipment Co., Inc. v. TRW Vehicle Safety Systems, Inc., 3 P.3d 970 (Ariz. App. 1999).

63. Oliver, *supra* note 48, at 124.

64. Paul Weiler, *Workers' Compensation And Product Liability: The Interaction Of A Tort And A Non–Tort Regime*, 50 OHIO ST. L. J. 825, 845 (1989).

65. *See* Thomas Eaton, *Revisiting the Intersection of Workers' Compensation and Product Liability*, 64 TENN. L. REV. 881 (1997).

2). The Employer Is the Manufacturer or Seller of the Product that Injured Its Worker

If an employee of Goodyear Tire is injured on the job while driving a truck equipped with defective and exploding Firestone tires, he can receive workers' compensation benefits from Goodyear and sue Firestone for products liability, as discussed above. What if the truck were equipped with defective and exploding Goodyear tires? Some courts, relying on what they called the "dual capacity" doctrine, have held that an employee may sue her employer in tort (even if she has already recovered workers' compensation payments) if the employer was the manufacturer or seller of the defective product that caused the injury. Such was the case in *Bell v. Industrial Vangas, Inc.*[66] Noting that workers' compensation predated strict liability for defective products, California's Supreme Court found nothing in the workers' compensation laws to shield a manufacturer from strict liability when its defective product injures an employee. As happened in Ohio, where the dual capacity doctrine was also invoked,[67] the legislature quickly intervened to reaffirm workers' compensation immunity.[68]

Obviously, an employee injured in the course of her *personal* life by a defective product her employer manufactures has a products liability remedy against the employer. There is no need to invoke the dual-capacity doctrine here. The Pepsi–Cola worker injured by an exploding Pepsi bottle she is drinking at home is treated like any other consumer. What if the Pepsi bottle exploded after it was purchased from a factory floor vending machine during a coffee break? Typical of results in this type of case is *Schump v. Firestone Tire & Rubber Co.*[69] In *Schump* the plaintiff worked as a truck driver for Firestone Tire, driving a truck equipped with Firestone tires. During one of his trips, an allegedly defective tire exploded, causing injuries to the plaintiff, who sued Firestone in Ohio, which was a state that recognized the dual capacity doctrine. The Court rejected the suit, since the employee was in fact on the job when the accident occurred:

> "The decisive dual-capacity test is not concerned with how separate or different the second function of the employer is from the first, but whether the second function generates obligations unrelated to those flowing from that of employer. This means that the employer must step outside the boundaries of the employer-employee relationship, creating separate

66. *See, e.g.,* Bell v. Industrial Vangas, Inc., 637 P.2d 266 (Cal. 1981).

67. Mercer v. Uniroyal, Inc., 361 N.E.2d 492 (Ohio App. 1976).

68. Cal. Labor Code § 3602; *see* Behrens v. Fayette Manufacturing Co., 7 Cal.Rptr.2d 264, 267 (Cal.App. 3 Dist. 1992).

69. Schump v. Firestone Tire & Rubber Co., 541 N.E.2d 1040 (Ohio 1989).

and distinct duties to the employee; the fact of injury must be incidental to the employment relationship."[70]

Under this rationale the Pepsi-drinking worker *could* sue her bottler-employer if she was drinking a Pepsi during a coffee break but not if she was hit by an exploding Pepsi bottle that she was inspecting. Only when the injury happens as part of the work itself (illustrated by the facts of *Schump*) is the dual capacity doctrine clearly rejected by caselaw

2. Who Can Sue?

The purchaser of a defective and unreasonably dangerous product could have sued her direct seller under traditional contract doctrine to recover damages for personal injuries proximately caused by the defect. The grounding of products liability in tort in lieu of contract law doctrine (as per *Baxter v. Ford Motor Co.*[71]) has also allowed third parties (for example, a bystander injured by a shard of glass when a defective Coca–Cola bottle explodes) to sue the seller and all to sue the manufacturer. In some states, the purchaser and his family members must sue for breach of implied warranty, while third parties must invoke strict liability.[72]

In order to sue, the plaintiff must claim cognizable damages. The determination of what constitutes cognizable damages raises issues common to other tort cases and not considered in this book.[73]

Questions About Julian Felipe's Case

If Julian Felipe is allowed to sue Ford Motor Co., are the following people allowed to sue as well?

- Shareholders of Ford Motor Co., who claim that the value of their shares dropped as a result both of expected liability outlays for Aerostars and of loss of general reputation for the quality of Ford products?

70. *Id.* at 152.

71. The tort of deceit, rather than contract, grounds the liability of a manufacturer that misrepresents its product. *See supra* ch. 4.

72. The linguistic hoop through which third party plaintiffs must jump is due to the fact that Uniform Commercial Code § 2–318 ("Third party beneficiaries of Warranties Express or Implied") was proposed in three variants. "Variant A" covered only the buyer and "any natural person who is in the family or household" of said buyer. Some state courts resolved the problem by simply ignoring the language of the statute that

had adopted Variant A: *See, e.g.,* Lukwinski v. Stone Container Corp., 726 N.E.2d 665 (Ill. App. 2000). Courts in other states that had adopted Variant A have a linguistic obstacle to warranty suits by third parties—but no such obstacle bars a substantively identical strict liability suit. Finally, in states such as Virginia, which purports never to have adopted strict liability (relying solely on implied warranty), "anti-privity" statutes have neutralized the argument derived from § 2–318.

73. For example, may loved ones of injured parties sue for loss of consortium?

- Ford dealers, whose lost sales affect the capital value of their franchise?

Chapter 6

THE PLAINTIFF'S CASE: STRICT LIABILITY FOR MANUFAC- TURING DEFECTS[1]

1. Introduction

Previous chapters provided an overview of the history of modern products liability law. They portrayed the law as capable of being understood as based on the notion that a defective product is a misrepresented product. The language of misrepresentation, however, is not typically used in products cases. Rather, the rhetorical thrust of the bulk of caselaw from *Greenman*[2] until the *Restatement (Third)*[3] employs strict liability as product liability's central organizing idea.[4]

Strict liability almost always requires a finding that the impugned product is *defective* and *unreasonably dangerous* in order to distinguish itself from insurance. "My car ran out of gas because the gauge is inaccurate: it showed I still had 1/8 of a tank. As a result, I missed an appointment and lost $1000 in business. Can I successfully sue the manufacturer to get this money back?" The answer to this question is, in a word, "No." The victim's economic damages are themselves problematic, to be sure,[5] but even more damaging to her claim is the fact that the mildly inaccurate gas gauge is likely not a defect that makes the car unreasonably dangerous. If the inaccurate gauge were on a helicopter, however, the plaintiff would have both a stronger case and, alas, different damages.[6]

---

1. Additional Reading: David G. Owen, *Manufacturing Defects*, 53 S.C.L. REV. 851 (2002).

2. Greenman v. Yuba Power Prods., 377 P.2d 897 (Cal. 1963). See *supra* Ch. 2 Section 3.B.2.

3. The *Restatement of the law Third, Torts: Products Liability*, § 1, no longer uses strict liability to characterize manufacturer and seller obligations: "One engaged in the business of selling or otherwise distributing products who sells or distributes a defective product is subject to *liability* for harm to persons or property caused by the defect." RE- STATEMENT (THIRD) OF TORTS, PRODUCTS LIA- BILITY § 1 (1998) (emphasis added). Most courts insist that they still comply with the *Restatement (Second)*.

4. As already seen, though jurisdictions speak of implied warranty, and victims' lawyers still have a strong incentive to prove negligence in every case.

5. *See* Chapter 13, *infra*.

6. *See* McLennan v. American Eu- rocopter Corp., Inc., 245 F.3d 403 (5th Cir. 2001) (applying Texas law).

Caselaw conceives of three kinds of product defects. This chapter explores manufacturing defects. A manufacturing defect is *a physical departure from a product's intended design*.[7] The importance of misrepresentation in manufacturing defect cases should be pellucidly clear. The manufacturer and the seller have made and marketed their product as corresponding to given performance parameters. It is supposed to do certain things in a certain way. It turns out that the unit purchased by the end user was a "lemon" that doesn't fit that bill. Manufacturers and sellers have therefore sold something other than what they purported to sell. When this misrepresentation causes injury, products liability follows in arguably its clearest form.

2. Negligence or Strict Liability?

Mr. Henningsen's automobile was designed to turn when the steering wheel was rotated.[8] Boilers are designed to heat, not to blow up, when properly maintained and fueled. Coca Cola bottles are designed to safely hold their contents when uncapped. If these products don't measure up to their design parameters, then in each case the imagined manufacturing defect is:

- *Hidden*: Allowing recovery creates no "moral hazard," i.e., does not encourage users to proceed to use a product that obviously does not work as designed; and

- *Serious*: This particular product defect is potentially dangerous.

In Chapter 7, this book discusses cases where these two conditions are not satisfied. Should there be liability if the manufacturing defect is *open and obvious*? What if the defect is a minor one, which does not prevent the product from being safely used?[9]

A. Breakdowns v. Defects v. Negligence

In many cases, manufacturing defects are caused by the manufacturer's negligence. Reasonable and prudent quality control catches many "lemons" that would otherwise pose a threat to safety.[10] It might seem that the new car that crashes, or the boiler or Coke bottle that blows up, is itself evidence of negligence. In this sense, strict liability for manufacturing defects might be viewed as performing a function similar to the doctrine of *res ipsa loquitur* in negligence law—and as Chapter 2 showed, *res ipsa* was a preferred doctrine before the shift to strict liability occurred.

---

7. RESTATEMENT (THIRD) OF TORTS, PRODUCTS LIABILITY § 2(a) (1998).

8. *See* Henningsen v. Bloomfield Motors, 161 A.2d 69 (N.J. 1960).

9. See *infra* Section B of this Chapter.

10. See the Appendix, Part 2, for a demonstration.

But strict liability is not always *res ipsa* in disguise. Not all "lemons" are uncovered by efficient quality control. Man is not perfect, and some "lemons" get through even the most thorough and painstaking examination. The woman injured by a "residual" lemon is injured by a product that is not what she was led to believe she was buying. This is why misrepresentation, not negligence, underlies liability for manufacturing defect. All would likely agree that it is not right to pass something off falsely in this way. It is this wrongdoing that underlies "strict liability" for manufacturing defects.

Strict liability enables the victim of such wrongdoing to be compensated by the manufacturer, instead of by the victim's own insurer. But strict liability does not create a safer world. As the second exercise in the Appendix illustrates, strict liability for manufacturing defects will NOT incentivize product manufacturers to catch all lemons. It is cheaper to pay "residual" liability costs than to spend exorbitant amounts to perfect the manufacturing process. The Appendix also shows that consumers are not willing to pay for perfect quality control.[11]

When the car crashes, or the bottle or boiler explodes, should strict liability be invoked? In other words, should the breakdown or malfunction be evidence of defect? If so, is it conclusive or merely rebuttable evidence of defect? If it is conclusive evidence of defect, is the manufacturer an insurer with the unfortunate consequences that were clarified in Chapter 3? Consider the following illustrations:

1. *Pulley v. Pacific Coca–Cola Bottling Co.*[12] A Coke bottle contains a cigarette. It was held that the presence of the cigarette was evidence of a manufacturing defect, *and* that the bottler may not expound in detail on its quality control standards in an effort to persuade the jury that the cigarette was inserted after the bottle left its plant. Strict

---

11. At some level safety measures have increasing marginal costs and diminishing marginal returns. Part 2 of the Appendix illustrates this phenomenon, but a simple example is in order here. Imagine that "one unit" of quality control costs $10 and will prevent $1000 in accidents. A "second unit" costs $100 and will prevent $500 in accidents. A "third unit" costs $300 and will prevent $200 in accidents. A "fourth unit" costs $2000 and will prevent $50 in accidents. Only two units of quality control are required by a negligence rule. *See* United States v. Carroll Towing, Co., 159 F.2d 169, 173–74 (2d Cir. 1947). Wheth-

er a manufacturer that has purchased two units of quality control is held ("strictly") liable for "residual" accidents or not, it will not have the incentive to invest in the third and fourth units of quality control, as those investments will be more costly than liability costs. This exercise shows that strict liability leads to no fewer manufacturing defects than does a negligence rule, if courts calculate liability and damages correctly.

12. Pulley v. Pacific Coca–Cola Bottling Co., 415 P.2d 636 (Wash. 1966), discussed in Chapter 2, *supra*.

liability, the court held, focuses solely on the product, and this makes the manufacturer's conduct irrelevant.[13]

2. *Myrlak v. Port Auth. of N.Y. and N.J.*[14] A 325–lb man is sitting in a chair at work, when suddenly the chair cracks and collapses, injuring the worker. The New Jersey Supreme Court held that the collapse was sufficient evidence of a manufacturing defect in the chair.[15] Plaintiff need not identify the specific cause of the defect: the breakdown suffices. The burden of proof is then shifted to the manufacturer to show that the defect was introduced after the chair left its control. As seen in *Pulley*, satisfying this burden is certainly difficult and perhaps impossible.

3. *Pouncey v. Ford Motor Co.*[16] The plaintiff purchased a used car with 62,000 miles on the odometer. While putting antifreeze in the car, he activated the throttle assembly to accelerate the engine. A blade broke off the radiator fan and struck him in the face, causing injury. Plaintiff's expert inspected the metal used in the blade and found that it had "inclusions," or imperfections. No steel is free of inclusions, but the greater the number of inclusions the more likely that with over time the blade will break. Ford produced evidence that the level of inclusions in this particular blade conformed to standards of the Society of Automotive Engineers. The trial court and appellate courts both held that the jury had sufficient evidence to find that there was a manufacturing defect in the fan blade.

These cases highlight an important difficulty for defendants in manufacturing defect cases. In the typical tort suit (for instance, an automobile accident) both parties witness the incident and each can testify as to the behavior of the other. But the breakdown of a product almost always occurs outside the presence of the defendant. The manufacturing defendant typically has no access to evidence of the care taken by the plaintiff, by her loved ones,[17] by retailers and by prior users. The manufacturer does have access to evidence about its own measures designed to minimize defects, but (as in *Pulley*) it may not be allowed to produce such evidence, and even

13. The reader might believe that a Coke bottle is defective if it is capable of being tampered with by others. That is a design defect claim, not the manufacturing defect claim pursued by plaintiff.

14. Myrlak v. Port Auth. of N.Y. and N.J., 723 A.2d 45 (N.J. 1999).

15. Had the chair only been "designed for lightweights," the plaintiff would have sued for design defect, claiming that this hidden design characteristic made the chair unreasonably dangerous for him.

16. Pouncey v. Ford Motor Co., 464 F.2d 957 (5th Cir. 1972) (applying Alabama law).

17. Was the cigarette in *Pulley* a practical joke that backfired?

when produced (as in *Pouncey*) this will not take the case from the jury.[18]

B. Why Must the Defective Product Be "Unreasonably Dangerous?"

What if a manufacturing defect is, in the scheme of things, minor? If a highly unusual accident occurs and the "minor" defect causes injury, should strict liability ensue? Recall that the *Restatement (Second)* entails strict liability for damages caused by a "defective condition unreasonably dangerous." Most jurisdictions have retained the "unreasonably dangerous" requirement, but some have not. These two cases highlight the debate.

- In *Ford Motor Co. v. Zahn,*[19] plaintiff was a passenger in the front seat of an automobile driven by his friend. Both had been drinking. Plaintiff, who was smoking a cigarette, dropped it onto the carpet, which began to smolder. Plaintiff bent down to retrieve the cigarette. At that very moment the driver suddenly and forcefully applied the brakes. Plaintiff's face was near the car's floor, and it smashed into the edge of the car's open ashtray. The edge was jagged (it had not been properly beveled at the factory), and the plaintiff lost the use of his eye when it struck the jagged edge. He sued Ford to recover these damages. The court, finding negligence on the part of the manufacturer,[20] concluded that it was irrelevant to its finding of negligence that the jagged edge of an ashtray would typically not result in more harm than a scratched finger.

- In *Cronin v. J.B.E. Olson Corp.,*[21] a hasp in a rack installed on a bakery truck was welded with poor materials. During an emergency braking maneuver the hasp slid forward and hit the driver, causing injuries. The trial judge instructed the jury that they should find for the plaintiff if the truck was "defective," but declined to require that the jury also find that the defect made the truck "unreasonably dangerous." The California Supreme Court affirmed on the ground that adding an "unreasonably dangerous" requirement would import notions of wrongdoing into products liability law,

---

18. As has been mentioned, jurors are almost always citizens of the same state as the victim; manufacturers are usually out-of-state corporations. *See* Michael I. Krauss, *Federalism and Product Liability: One More Trip to the Choice-of-Law Well,* 2002 B.Y.U.L. Rev. 759.

19. Ford Motor Co. v. Zahn, 265 F.2d 729 (8th Cir. 1959) (applying Minnesota law).

20. This case arose before the national move to strict liability sketched in Chapter 2.

21. Cronin v. J.B.E. Olson Corp., 501 P.2d 1153 (Cal. 1972).

diluting the strict liability adopted in *Greenman* and making it too difficult for injured plaintiffs to recover.

Questions

- How long should a fan blade last? Is *Pouncey* really a manufacturing defect case, or is it rather a disguised design defect case (the design defect being the decision not to guard the fan assembly with a shroud or a housing that would catch a breakaway blade)?

- As a prelude to Chapter 7, consider whether it should matter to this hypothetical design defect claim that 99.999 percent of the time a motor is running, the hood will be closed and therefore no human body part will be exposed if a fan blade breaks, but that servicing the blade will be much more expensive if it is shrouded. Does this affect your view of *Pouncey*?

- Your author knows of no study (and of no way to conduct a study) to determine the percentage of "foreign" substances in food products that is introduced after the product has left the "manufacturer." What if somehow it could be shown that a majority of food defects are the result of tampering (whether by the plaintiff or by third parties)? Should that result in a different decision in *Pulley*?

3. Special Case: Food and Drink and the "Foreign–Natural" Debate

Some foods (arguably, McDonald's Chicken McNuggets®. . .) are "manufactured" in the sense that they are substantially processed. But many food products are items already substantially found in nature. A packaged salad containing a rusty nail is surely a product with a manufacturing (i.e., contamination) defect.[22] What of a packaged salad containing an olive with a pit, however? What of a can of chicken soup containing a small chicken bone?

In *Kolarik v. Cory International Corp.*,[23] plaintiff prepared a salad using a jar of defendant's "minced pimento stuffed Spanish Olives." He bit down on an olive that had its pit still intact, fracturing a tooth. The court refused to allow his strict liability suit for manufacturing defect to reach the jury. The same fate was meted out to his warranty claim, as the court found that "minced pimento stuffed Spanish Olives" was not a guarantee that each and every olive was stuffed. There was an implied warranty that the olives contained no *foreign* matter (such as a rusty nail), but no implied warranty that the olives were free from naturally occurring

---

22. *See*, e.g., Hickman v. Wm. Wrigley, Jr. Co. Inc., 768 So.2d 812 (La. App. 2000) (screw in stick of chewing gum; strict liability).

23. Kolarik v. Cory Int'l Corp., 721 N.W.2d 159 (Iowa 2006).

pits. Finally, the court found no evidence of negligence, dismissing plaintiff's third cause of action.[24]

A "foreign-natural test" is often applied in cases of food and drink—holding that there is no defect for naturally occurring dangers.[25] *Kolarik* declined to endorse this test, instead relying on a similar but distinguishable provision of the *Restatement (Third)*. This provision[26] creates a "reasonable consumer expectations" test about the content of food products. Those expectations might consider some "natural" substances to be so unusual as to constitute a defect.[27] The crucial question therefore became whether a reasonable consumer expects that a pit might be found inside a "minced pimento stuffed Spanish Olive."

With respect for the *Kolarik* court, it is hard to see how the *Restatement (Third)* (unlike the foreign-natural distinction) can keep this kind of case from the jury, whose members are presumably representative of the "reasonable consumer." In other words, is there any law to the "reasonable consumer expectation" rule, or are juries always sovereign here (much to the dread of manufacturers)? Consider these decisions from neighboring courts:

- In *Yong Cha Hong v. Marriott Corp.*,[28] plaintiff was eating a piece of fried chicken when she bit into something she thought was a worm.

     "She suffered, it is alleged, great physical and emotional upset from her encounter with this item, including permanent injuries, in consequence of which she prays damages in the amount of $500,000.00."

  It turned out, however, that the item plaintiff bit into was not a worm at all, but "either one of the chicken's major blood vessels or its trachea."[29] This case would have been dismissed under the "foreign-natural" rule, but the court chose to send it to the jury with a "reasonable consumer expectations" instruction. Accordingly, the jury did find that the chicken was defective.

- On the other hand, in *Clime v. Dewey Beach Enterprises, Inc.*,[30] plaintiff consumed clams at defendant's restaurant. The claims contained "*vibrio vulnificus*, an organism occa-

---

24. The plaintiff also sued for failure to warn, see Chapter 8 *infra*. Summary judgment on that cause of action was properly denied.

25. *See*, e.g., Allen v. Grafton, 164 N.E.2d 167 (Ohio 1960) (piece of oyster shell in fried oysters).

26. RESTATEMENT (THIRD) OF TORTS, PRODUCTS LIABILITY § 7 cmt. b (1998).

27. The comment alludes to a "one-inch chicken bone" hypothetically found inside a chicken enchilada as likely failing this test.

28. Yong Cha Hong v. Marriott Corp., 656 F.Supp. 445 (D. Md. 1987).

29. *Id.* at 447.

30. Clime v. Dewey Beach Enters., Inc., 831 F.Supp. 341 (D. Del. 1993).

sionally contained in raw shellfish,"[31] Most people suffer vomiting, diarrhea, severe abdominal pain and dermatitis from this bacterium, but plaintiff was an alcoholic suffering from cirrhosis of the liver. As a result, his body could not destroy the bacterium, and he contracted sepsis (a potentially fatal whole-body inflammatory condition). He sued the restaurant for his damages. The court rejected the "foreign-natural" test (which would have exonerated defendant) in favor of the "reasonable consumer expectation" rule, but nonetheless refused to submit the plaintiff's strict liability claim to the jury on the ground that no reasonable consumer could expect all "wild" clams to be free from bacteria.[32]

In both cases the foods contained a "natural" but undesirable substance. In *Yong Cha Hong* (where there was no physical injury) the jury was allowed to find the food "defective," while in *Clime* (where there was severe physical damage) it was not. Is it relevant that in the former case chicken was served "cooked," while in the latter clams were served raw? Should the "foreign-natural" test have been conserved?

Question

Consider this excerpt from an article in the *New York Times*:[33]

"In June 1993, an elderly man in Tacoma, Wash., claimed to have found a syringe in his Diet Pepsi. It turned out to have been deposited innocently by a diabetic relative. But within a week, there were more than 60 copycats, daily front-page headlines and a national scare.

Pepsi put together a video showing its canning plants, to demonstrate it was most likely not responsible. It also caught a huge break when a woman in the Denver area was caught on videotape at a grocery store, planting a syringe in her soda.

Within the week, federal investigators exonerated Pepsi. Still, the company continued to fight after the investigation was closed. A week later, it took out full-page ads in newspapers nationwide, noting that it had done nothing wrong and thanking customers for their support.

Becky Madeira, senior vice president for corporate affairs at Pepsi-Co, said the ads were part of an underlying strategy of giving consumers a new story to replace the one created during the crisis. "You have to replace one picture with another, one idea with another," she said.

31. *Id.* at 342.

32. For the opposite result, see Cain v. Sheraton Perimeter Park South Hotel, 592 So.2d 218 (Ala. 1991).

33. Matt Richtel, *Wendy's gets a break in the case of the finger in the chili, but it still has work ahead of it,* N.Y. TIMES, April 29, 2005, C4.

To that end, she said she had one factor in her favor that Wendy's does not. Pepsi was able to discover how the syringe got into the can—and to show, vividly, that the other claims were hoaxes, thus giving consumers a sense of resolution.

"It helps to be able to provide a complete story to the consumer," she said."[34]

- Pepsi "caught a huge break," according to the reporter. If it had not "caught this break," would it have been found liable in all sixty cases? Is there any way to keep such cases from the jury?

Question About Julian Felipe's Case

- Imagine that, upon examination of the Felipes' Aerostar, it became clear that the van's roof had been previously weakened by impact with a large solid object. Evidently, someone had repaired and repainted the roof after this impact. When Mrs. Felipe purchased the van she had it inspected by a mechanic, but such inspections do not routinely examine roof structure. After the accident the Felipes' attorney retained an automotive engineer, who has concluded that the impact might have happened at the assembly factory, or subsequently. Under these circumstances, should the trial judge allow Julian Felipe's suit against Ford to reach the jury?

---

34. *Id.* The article alluded to a gruesome case in which a Wendy's customer found a severed finger in her chili. Wendy's was unable to discover the provenance of the finger.

Chapter 7

THE PLAINTIFF'S CASE: STRICT LIABILITY FOR DESIGN DEFECTS[1]

1. Introduction

Manufacturers and retailers are *much* more fearful of design defect claims than they are of manufacturing defect claims. The Coke bottle with a cigarette, or even the automobile with defective steering, is an anomaly, a "one-in-a-million" event possibly not efficiently preventable. Paying damages for such occurrences is a regrettable cost of doing business, "manageable" through outside insurance or self-insurance.

But in a design defect claim, the plaintiff's argument is that *every single item produced* is defective. Though some supposed manufacturing defect cases produce dangerous copycat frauds at times (see Chapter 6), design defect cases almost always spawn class actions (see Chapter 14). They are extremely difficult to "manage"—litigating them may be a "bet-the-company" proposition. Corporate executives are often tempted to settle these cases even when they are convinced their design is not defective. This perverse managerial incentive has been recognized since the beginning of the products liability revolution.[2]

Not only are design defect suits riskier for defendants, they also present more challenges for courts, as the central legal question is much harder to establish with confidence. In manufacturing defects, the impugned product does not correspond to its own design. But in a design defect case, the product is just as the manufacturer intended. Rather, the plaintiff insists that what the manufacturer intended was just not good enough, because it injured her.

Therein lies the rub. The simple fact that a person sustains injury while using a product has never been sufficient grounds for

---

1. Additional Reading: James A. Henderson & Aaron D. Twerski, *Achieving Consensus on Defective Product Design*, 83 CORNELL L. REV. 867 (1998); David Owen, *Defectiveness Redefined: Exploding the Myth of 'Strict' Products Liability*, 1996 U. ILL. L. REV. 743.

2. *See, e.g.*, HENRY J. FRIENDLY, FEDERAL JURISDICTION: A GENERAL VIEW (J.S. Carpenter Lecture) 120 (1973) (discussing "blackmail settlements").

products liability. 37,261 Americans were killed in automobile crashes in 2008,[3] but very few of their survivors have a good products liability case against the manufacturer of the automobile in which they were seated. Under both versions of the *Restatement*, being injured or killed is not grounds for liability. One must be injured (or killed) *because of a defect* in order to recover from the manufacturer and commercial sellers. So, what makes a product defective in design? That question is the focus of this chapter.

Consider first, as the late Aaron Wildavsky proposed, the design of the "rational potato."

> "Like all growing things, it could not survive the process of evolution unless it was able to ward off predators. Unable to run away or fight directly, the homely potato has evolved chemical defenses. When mother told us that the potato's vitamins were concentrated in the jacket [i.e., the skin], she was right. What she did not know, however, was that the poisons the potato uses to ward off predators also were in the jacket."[4]

Wildavsky's point is that the very thing that is good about the potato is also (somewhat) dangerous. Product attributes, in other words, also have costs. Tradeoffs apply for all things, both "natural" articles (such as potatoes) and human artifacts. The sharp knife is useful because it is sharp, but watch out when slicing that barely thawed bagel! The car without an engine is a useless hunk of metal; with an engine it's a 3000–lb. killing machine. The aspirin that stops the heart attack can also kill you, and not only if you're allergic to aspirin.[5] Acetaminophen, a leading substitute for aspirin as a pain reliever, is also the leading cause of liver failure. Every vaccine ever made has had side effects we cannot prevent. Nothing ever made has been "totally safe," whatever that means.

The design of every product involves trade-offs. Consider the 5 mph bumper. It could instead have been a 2.5 mph bumper.[6] The "safer" 5 mph bumper costs more, but at the margin this cost and others like it may lead a consumer to keep his dangerous old clunker instead of paying for the safer new car. The safer bumper

---

3. Fatality Analysis Reporting System, NHTSA, http://www-fars.nhtsa.dot.gov/Main/index.aspx. (Last consulted March 16, 2010.)

4. Aaron B. Wildavsky, Searching for Safety 4 (1988).

5. Aspirin can cause ulcerations in the digestive system and may harm kidneys.

6. Indeed, the National Highway Traffic Safety Administration (NHTSA)

reduced the minimum standards in 1982. The agency concluded that reducing the impact speed from 5 mph to 2.5 front and rear impact speed best satisfied the statutory criteria that the bumper standard "seek to obtain maximum feasible reduction in costs to the public and to the consumer." The agency also concluded that reducing the impact speed to 2.5 mph would not have an adverse effect on safety.

also weighs more (consuming more gasoline, costing more to produce, etc.) and costs *much* more to repair after a 6 mph crash (depleting resources that could be spent on other safety items, for example). A Rolls Royce is chock-full of safety features unavailable on less expensive vehicles. Safety is a "good," which means we want it, which means it has a positive cost and a "downward sloping demand curve."[7]

How is products liability law to determine when a design is safe enough and when it is defective? Recall that the *Restatement (Second)*, adopted *de jure* or *de facto* in almost every state, provides that liability for design defect is "strict." If this is true, then evidence from a manufacturer or a seller that the design is *nonnegligent* would not be admissible. But is this workable? If a design is defective and *unreasonably* dangerous (recall, that is a part of the *Restatement (Second)*'s proviso accepted in almost every state), isn't it negligent to produce a product so designed?

The *Restatement (Third)*, to the contrary, seems to reject strict liability for design defect. Here are its provisions dealing with manufacturing and design defects:

> A product:
>
> (a) contains a manufacturing defect when the product departs from its intended design even though all possible care was exercised in the preparation and marketing of the product;
>
> (b) is defective in design when the foreseeable risks of harm posed by the product could have been reduced or avoided by the adoption of a reasonable alternative design by the seller or other distributor, or a predecessor in the commercial chain of distribution, and the omission of the alternative design renders the product not reasonably safe;[8]

2. Tests for Design Defect

A. Negligence

A consumer is in a furniture store shopping for a *chaise longue*[9] for his patio. He decides to test a chair made by Acme, Inc. While sitting in the chair, he lays his right hand on the arm of the chair and starts reclining. The fingers of his right hand curl around the round the end of the arm of the chair. As the chair reclines the

---

7. In lay terms, this simply means that for any individual safety item, more of it will be purchased, the lower the price. Since the price cannot be zero, those with more money will be willing to pay for more safety than will those with less money.

8. RESTATEMENT (THIRD) OF TORTS, PRODUCTS LIABILITY § 2(a)–(b) (1998) (emphasis added).

9. Also known as a "chaise lounge" or "lounge chair."

moving parts of the chair cleanly shear off the middle finger of his right hand.

Does this story appear unrealistic? It is a real case.[10] The case resulted in the manufacturer's liability long before strict liability swept the nation, and despite the lack of privity between plaintiff and defendant (indeed, plaintiff was in privity with no one—he was a shopper, and (obviously) never purchased the finger-guillotine chair from the retailer). The Florida Supreme Court observed that "[n]o one would suspect that such a dangerous device would be concealed in such an innocent looking instrumentality."[11]

As in the "textbook" manufacturing defeat case discussed in Chapter 6, this design defect has the following characteristics, which make it an "easy case" for product liability:

- The design defect was *hidden* (eliminating moral hazard, and minimizing the likelihood that the consumer recognized the danger and traded it off against a lower price for the product).

- The defect was *serious*.

In easy cases such as this one, and as noted in Chapter 4, plaintiffs find it advantageous to ground their design defect suit against the manufacturer in negligence.[12] Against the retailer, the suit is typically based not on negligence but on breach of implied warranty: buying a chair equipped with a hidden finger-guillotine is buying something other than was bargained for.

Most design defect cases are not as clear as that of the finger-guillotine chair. In more difficult cases, tort law has searched for the proper test of design defect. After a question about Julian Felipe's case, the two rival "strict liability" design defect tests that have been pitted against each other are described.

Question About Julian Felipe's Case

- Julian Felipe sued Ford for design defect (an insufficiently solid roof structure) under both negligence and strict liability theories. At the start of trial, though, his attorney formally withdrew the strict liability claim and announced that he would proceed solely under a negligence theory. Why did he do this?

B. The Consumer Expectations Test

Chapter 6 revealed that the test for the existence of a *manufacturing* defect in food has morphed from a "foreign-natural" test to a "consumer expectations" test in some jurisdictions. If "reason-

---

10. *See* Matthews v. Lawnlite Co., 88 So.2d 299 (Fla. 1956).

11. *Id.* at 301.

12. See Gary T. Schwartz, *The Vitality of Negligence and the Ethics of Strict Liability*, 15 GA. L. REV. 963 (1981).

able consumers" expect the food item not to contain a particular ingredient, the food is defective if it contains that ingredient.

Should the same test determine the existence of a design defect? In some states this test has been incorporated by statute.[13] Many other states adopted it through caselaw.[14]

One argument for the consumers' expectation test is that it seems to reflect the theme of misrepresentation that this book presents as being the implicit grounding for products liability. Simply put, if consumers reasonably expect a certain level of safety from their product, and if the manufacturer does not disabuse them of this notion (for example, by warning them of a non-obvious and dangerous design characteristic), then the product they have purchased or used has in a significant way been misrepresented to them. If conceptually clear, however, the consumers expectations test is fraught with practical vagueness. How safe do consumers "expect" a product to be? Consumers surely expect to be able to recline in a chaise lounge without amputating their finger. But do they have any expectations about the results of a rollover at 70 mph in their minivan? If consumers "expect" a level of safety that is lacking in the impugned product, should its design be deemed defective for this reason alone? What if consumers have *unrealistic* expectations? What if they have no expectations at all?

The following examples, taken from cases and news reports, highlight the difficulties of the consumer expectations test.

1). *If the design's danger is* obvious, *can a reasonable consumer "expect" safety?*

- "As dangerous as the meat grinder may have been without a feed pan guard, it was clearly 'not dangerous beyond that which would be contemplated by the ordinary user.' "[15]

2). *Whose expectations count, the purchaser's or an injured bystander's?*

- The *Restatement (Second)* provides that the expectations of the "ultimate consumer" are key. Therefore a pedestrian struck by a truck cannot claim that she expected the truck to offer better visibility to its driver.[16] A blind

13. *See* Paugh v. R.J. Reynolds Tobacco Co., 834 F.Supp. 228 (N.D. Ohio 1993); Dewey v. R.J. Reynolds Tobacco Co., 577 A.2d 1239 (N.J. 1990); McCathern v. Toyota Motor Corp., 23 P.3d 320 (Or. 2001).

14. RESTATEMENT (SECOND) OF TORTS § 402A (1965). Comment i provides that a product as designed is defective "if the product is dangerous to an extent beyond that which would be contemplated by the ordinary consumer who either purchases it or uses it with the ordinary knowledge common to the community as to the product's characteristics." *Id.*

15. Chaney v. Hobart, 54 F. Supp. 2d 677, 681 (E.D. La. 1999).

16. Ewen v. McLean Trucking, 706 P.2d 929 (Or. 1985).

person who jaywalks and is struck by a silent "hybrid" car she couldn't hear may not invoke the consumer expectations test.[17]

3). When is the consumer expectations test invincibly indeterminate?

- A six-inch thick rock strikes a wheel of a Ford pickup truck while it is being driven at highway speed. The driver does not pull over to check for damage, but continues to drive for thirty minutes. At that time the wheel detaches from the truck, leading to injury. The driver sues Ford for design defect, since the truck did not perform to his expectations.[18] The Oregon Supreme Court confirms that the driver may reach the jury with his claim.

- On the other hand, a Kansas court refused to allow plaintiff to argue that consumers expect trousers not to catch fire when exposed to open flames.[19]

- A Wisconsin plaintiff was allowed to reach the jury with the argument that she reasonably expected not to be among the 5 percent of the population allergic to latex gloves, which were therefore defective in design.[20]

- Many courts have simply refused to apply the consumer expectations test in technical cases where the ordinary consumer has no idea how a product should perform. Thus, in *Soule v. General Motors Corp.*[21] it was held that the consumer expectations test was irrelevant to a design defect suit when a high-speed crash had caused the left front wheel to break free, collapse rearward, and smash the floorboard into the driver's feet. On the other hand, the same court held, in *Campbell v. General Motors Corp.*,[22] that the layout of a city bus (containing one side-facing row of seats at the front that had no available "grab bar") could be tested using the consumer expectations test (therefore requiring no expert witnesses), when a passenger was thrown from that seat after the driver made a sudden and violent driving maneuver.

17. Ben Nuckols, *Blind People: Hybrid Cars Pose Hazard*, USA Today Online, March 3, 2007, http://www.usatoday.com/money/economy/2007-10-03-2698183585_x.htm, (last visited on March 17, 2010).

18. Heaton v. Ford Motor Co., 435 P.2d 806 (Or. 1967).

19. Miller v. Lee Apparel Co., Inc., 881 P.2d 576 (Kan. App. 1994).

20. Green v. Smith & Nephew AHP, Inc., 629 N.W.2d 727 (Wis. 2001).

21. Soule v. General Motors Corp., 882 P.2d 298 (Cal. 1994).

22. Campbell v. General Motors Corp., 649 P.2d 224 (Cal. 1982).

- "The [consumer expectations] test can be utilized to explain most any result that a court or jury chooses to reach. The application of such a vague concept in many situations does not provide much guidance for a jury."[23]

Questions About Julian Felipe's Case

- Do consumers expect vans not to roll over when a tire violently blows out while the van is traveling at high speed?

- Do they expect the roof will not compress when rollovers occur?

- If they do have these expectations, is reliance on them to determine the existence of a design defect within the spirit of the representational view of products liability, or is it the equivalent of exposing manufacturers to insurance-style liability?[24]

C. The Risk–Utility Test

Discontent with the consumer expectation test is widespread. Especially when a product's danger is obvious, many resist the idea that a jury should be allowed to find that this danger was contrary to expectations. A diametrically opposed criticism is also leveled; that the consumer expectations test is unfair to plaintiffs because on occasion courts have ruled as a matter of law that an obvious danger could not possibly be a design defect.[25] Dean John Wade, the American Law Institute's Reporter for the *Restatement (Second)*, drew this conclusion:[26]

"The time has now come to be forthright in using a tort way of thinking and tort terminology (in cases of strict liability in tort). There are several ways of doing it, and it is not difficult. The simplest and easiest way, it would seem, is to assume that the defendant knew of the dangerous condition of the product and ask whether he was then negligent in putting it on the market or supplying it to someone else. In other words, the *scienter* is supplied as a matter of law, and there is no need for the plaintiff to prove its existence as a matter of fact. Once given this notice of the dangerous condition of the chattel, the question then becomes whether the defendant was negligent to people who might be harmed by that condition if they came into contact with it or were in the vicinity of it. *Another way of saying this is to ask whether the magnitude of the risk created*

---

23. W. Page Keeton, Dan B. Dobbs, Robert E. Keeton & David G. Owen, Prosser & Keeton on Torts 699 (5th ed. 1984).

24. Victor E. Schwartz & Rochelle M. Tedesco, *The Re-emergence of 'Super-Strict' Liability*, 71 U. Cin. L. Rev. 917 (2003).

25. *See, e.g.*, Sperry–New Holland v. Prestage, 617 So.2d 248 (Miss. 1993).

26. John Wade, *On The Nature Of Strict Tort Liability For Products*, 44 Miss. L.J. 825, 834–835 (1973).

by the dangerous condition of the product was outweighed by the social utility attained by putting it out in this fashion."

Dean Wade listed seven factors that, in his opinion, would help determine whether a given design passes the risk-utility test he advocated. These factors are cited quite frequently in the caselaw, so they are listed here *verbatim*:

(1) The usefulness and desirability of the product—its utility to the user and to the public as a whole.

(2) The safety aspects of the product—the likelihood that it will cause injury, and the probable seriousness of the injury.

(3) The availability of a substitute product which would meet the same need and not be as unsafe.

(4) The manufacturer's ability to eliminate the unsafe character of the product without impairing its usefulness or making it too expensive to maintain its utility.

(5) The user's ability to avoid danger by the exercise of care in the use of the product.

(6) The user's anticipated awareness of the dangers inherent in the product and their avoidability, because of general public knowledge of the obvious condition of the product, or of the existence of suitable warnings or instructions.

(7) The feasibility, on the part of the manufacturer, of spreading the loss by setting the price of the product or carrying liability insurance.[27]

With the exception of factor (7), which constitutes a sudden and surprising endorsement of products liability as insurance,[28] these factors generally apply cost-benefit analysis. Cost-benefit analysis has been intrinsic to the calculation of reasonable versus negligent behavior, so the risk-utility test appears to be a departure from the nominal strict liability of the *Restatement (Second)*.[29] Many courts have understood this implication. As one court put it,

"[A] growing number of courts and commentators have found that, in cases in which the plaintiff's injury is caused by an alleged defect in the design of a product, there is no practical difference between theories of negligence and strict liability."[30]

27. *Id.*, at 837–38.

28. See Chapter 3, *supra* for a discussion of the implications of seeing products liability as insurance.

29. *See, e.g.,* Michael Green, *The Schizophrenia of Risk–Benefit Analysis* *in Design Defect Litigation*, 48 VAND. L. REV. 609 (1995).

30. Ackerman v. American Cyanamid, 586 N.W.2d 208, 220 (Iowa 1998).

The move to risk-utility design analysis of product design has itself been criticized. Should the test apply to open and obvious design features or only to latent dangers? If the former, the risk-utility test may create moral hazard; a jury might find that a product fails this test even if the user knew of the risks involved in using the product.[31] The adoption of risk-utility to obvious dangers would therefore constitute a departure from the representational theory of products liability. This could lead to a situation where juries interfere with freely accepted risks, if they feel those risks are somehow not "optimal."

This tendency was illustrated by the New Jersey Supreme Court in *O'Brien v. Muskin Corp.*[32] O'Brien trespassed at a neighbor's home and dived into their above-ground, four-feet-deep pool. He struck his head on the bottom of the pool, sustaining serious injuries. He thereupon sued the manufacturer of the pool, alleging that it was liable for his injuries because it had manufactured and marketed a defectively designed pool. The alleged defect was that the liner was inappropriate for diving—the manufacturer's claim that the liner was the only feasible model for above-ground pools led to the plaintiff's subsequent claim that above-ground pools themselves were as a whole defective and unreasonably dangerous. The court held that this suit could go to the jury, which could measure the risks and benefits of above-ground pools as compared with in-ground pools.

O'Brien was ultimately superseded in New Jersey by a statutory provision that scaled back the risk-utility test when dangers were obvious.[33] Should juries be allowed to decide, for example, whether motorcycles are defective because they do not have protective cages surrounding the rider?

On the other hand, defenders of strict liability object to the risk-utility test because it gives manufacturers a chance to defend dangerous designs by introducing evidence of the costs of safer designs. As Dean Wade noted, this is essentially negligence analysis. Those who criticize this position submit that products liability should provide insurance for consumers injured by products—as long as some safer design was possible, manufacturers should "internalize" the cost of their design choices.[34]

---

31. Richard Epstein, *The Risks of Risk/Utility*, 48 Ohio St. L. Rev. 469 (1987).

32. O'Brien v. Muskin Corp., 463 A.2d 298 (N.J. 1983).

33. N.J.S.A. 2A:58C–3a(2).

34. *See, e.g.,* Howard Klemme, *The Enterprise Liability Theory of Torts*, 47 U. Colo. L. Rev. 153 (1976).

D. Two–Pronged Standards

In *Barker v. Lull Engineering Co.*,[35] the California Supreme Court attempted to merge the consumer expectations and risk-utility tests. The defendant had sold a front-end loader to an employer. The model sold was intended for use on level ground, and was therefore not equipped with the optional outriggers or rollover protective structure (ROPS) offered as an option for use on uneven surfaces or slopes. Having purchased the loader equipped for level ground use, the employer proceeded to use it on rough terrain. Indeed, the regular operator of the loader testified that he called in sick on the day of the accident because he knew the loader was not designed to make the lifts that had been scheduled for that day, and was too frightened to operate the loader in the area where the accident occurred. That employee testified that he informed the supervisor that a crane, rather than a high-lift loader, was required for lifts on such sloping ground, but that the supervisor declined to rent a crane. The plaintiff, a worker who took the regular operator's place, was injured, and as he could not sue his employer[36] he sued the manufacturer of the loader.

Recall that in *Cronin*,[37] the California Supreme Court determined that a manufacturing defect could result in liability even if it did not make the product "unreasonably dangerous." The *Cronin* court was particularly averse to importing negligence analysis into products liability. In *Barker*, California refused to implement risk-utility in design defect cases for the same reason. Instead, it developed a "hybrid test." A California design defect plaintiff now has an option. She may choose to establish that a product is defective because it did not perform as safely as an ordinary consumer would expect when used in its intended (or any other foreseeable) manner. Alternatively, she may simply show that the design feature (even an obvious design feature) caused her injury—if she chooses that option the *defendant* may attempt to show that the benefits of the chosen design outweigh its dangers.[38]

This burden shifting is arguably more onerous for defendants than the risk-utility test. How, for instance, is a motorcycle manufacturer to establish that its "design" (two wheels, no roll cage) passes the risk-utility test, when 98 percent of the vehicles on the road have four wheels and a cage? In *Ray v. BIC Corp.*, the Tennessee Supreme Court termed the shifting of the burden of proof on risk-utility an "aberrant move."[39] *Cronin* has not been widely followed.

35. Barker v. Lull Engineering Co., 573 P.2d 443 (Cal. 1978).

36. See Chapter 5 *supra* for the workers' compensation discussion.

37. Cronin v. J.B.E. Olson Corp., 501 P.2d 1153 (Cal. 1972). See Chapter 6 *supra*.

38. *Barker*, 573 P.2d at 457–58.

39. Ray v. BIC Corp., 925 S.W.2d 527, 532 (Tenn. 1996).

Question About Julian Felipe's Case

● At trial plaintiff presented video clips of a Volvo station wagon rolling over repeatedly during a controlled manufacturer's test. The roof withstood the rollovers with virtually no compression.[40] Recall that the Felipes' Aerostar's roof compressed by 11 inches on the passenger side when it rolled over. Of course, the Aerostar's higher center of gravity makes rollover more likely than in a Volvo station wagon. Under those facts, does Ford have any defense in a design defect suit?

E. The *Restatement (Third)*'s Design Defect Test

Arguably the most controversial section of the *Restatement (Third)* is § 2(b):

"A product is defective in design when the foreseeable risks of harm posed by the product could have been reduced by the adoption of a reasonable alternative design by the seller or a predecessor in the commercial chain of distribution and the omission of the alternative design renders the product not reasonably safe."

This subsection clearly adopts negligence-like reasoning. Nowhere are consumer expectations mentioned. Nor is a causal connection between the impugned design and the plaintiff's injury sufficient to reach a jury. Rather, plaintiff must posit an alternate design, which would have avoided or minimized the injury. This alternate design must, in essence, be "reasonable," *and* its omission in the impugned product must have been "unreasonable."

The Iowa Supreme Court ratified § 2(b) in *Parish v. Jumpking, Inc.*[41] Delbert Parish (plaintiff's brother) had purchased a Jumpking® fourteen-foot trampoline for use in his backyard. While plaintiff was visiting his brother, he attempted to do a back somersault on the trampoline, but landed on his head and was rendered a quadriplegic. The court dismissed his design defect suit, as the plaintiff failed to show that there was a feasible alternative design available for the trampoline.[42]

As will be discussed immediately below, however, many jurisdictions do not impose upon plaintiffs the requirement to prove

---

40. The reader can view the video about half-way through the plaintiff's closing argument: http://www.youtube.com/user/colsonhickseidson p/u/2/ntMo-YPdXEx8 (last consulted on March 18, 2010).

41. Parish v. Jumpking, Inc., 719 N.W.2d 540 (Iowa 2006).

42. Plaintiff had attempted to rely on Comment e to § 2(b), which exempts plaintiffs from the requirement of prov-

ing an alternate design if the design is "manifestly unreasonable." The court rejected this claim, observing that "approximately fourteen million people use them. Even data produced by the plaintiff in his resistance to summary judgment showed that in 2002 only 2.1 percent of trampolines were associated with injuries, and only one-half of one percent of jumpers were injured." *Id.* at 545.

feasible alternative design, notwithstanding the language of the *Restatement (Third)*.

3. Proof of Design Defect

Except in jurisdictions where the burden of proof of design defect is shifted under the *Barker v. Lull* rationale, plaintiff must establish (as the *Restatement (Third)* requires) that a product's design is defective. The principal caselaw debate is whether plaintiff must produce evidence of an alternative reasonable design, or whether showing that the existing design is dangerous is sufficient.

The permutations of this question are numerous. Here is a representative sample:

What if there is an alternative design, available as an extra-cost option?

Some cars have ten airbags, others only four. Does this make a four-bag car defective in design? In general, the answer to this question is "no"—the alternative would indirectly compel consumers to purchase the high-end model for every good manufactured. Thus, in *Vax v. Albany Lawn and Garden Center*, plaintiff sued after her lawn mower "reared up" and she fell, injuring her leg. Her design defect claim was that, unlike higher-end mowers, her mower was not equipped with a "deadman control." The appellate court dismissed this claim and affirmed the summary judgment granted at trial, noting that "[t]he law does not require, however, that a manufacturer produce or sell only the safest products it is capable of making."[43]

What if Plaintiff proposes an alternate design, which is not available in the marketplace?

In *Troja v. Black & Decker Mfg. Co.*,[44] plaintiff accidentally amputated his thumb while operating a radial arm saw manufactured by defendant. He sued, claiming the saw was defective in design because it lacked a system that would prevent the saw from operating unless the guide fence was in place. In *Troja*, plaintiff had borrowed the saw from another man, who had hired plaintiff to build a bar in the client's basement. Plaintiff and the saw's owner had removed the saw from its metal base and stand so that it could be carried to the work site. The guide fence and metal base were left behind at the original location.

At trial, plaintiff attempted to produce an expert in the field of "machine guarding safety systems" to testify that a radial saw design, which incorporated a safety device to prevent use without

---

43. Vax v. Albany Lawn and Garden Center, 433 S.E.2d 364, 366 (Ga. App. 1993).

44. Troja v. Black & Decker Mfg. Co., 488 A.2d 516 (Md. 1985).

the guide fence, could have been developed in 1976. The expert testified at *voir dire*[45] that he had taken courses in machine guarding and industrial safety. He said that he had been employed as a "safety engineer" and a "loss-control inspector." He acknowledged that he had no experience in radial arm saw design. He was unable to furnish a design demonstrating the actual placement of such a system, or to explain how it could be integrated in the saw without interfering with the functions for which the fence would normally not be employed. His conclusion that this "safety interlock device" could be implemented without great cost to the manufacturer was not supported by data regarding the cost of the materials necessary to include such a feature or the feature's actual utility. The trial judge excluded his testimony and granted defendant summary judgment, which was confirmed on appeal.

What if the manufacturer modified its design subsequent to plaintiff's injury, adding a safety device that would have prevented it. Is this modification proof of a reasonable alternate design?

If a case is heard in federal court, Fed. R. Evid. 407 provides in part as follows:

> "When, after an injury or harm allegedly caused by an event, measures are taken that, if taken previously, would have made the injury or harm less likely to occur, evidence of the subsequent measures is not admissible to prove negligence, culpable conduct, a defect in a product, a defect in a product's design, or a need for a warning or instruction."[46]

The idea, obviously, is not to discourage innovation by imposing a "tax" of retroactive design defect liability. New designs marketed after the manufacture of the impugned product but before plaintiff's injury are, curiously, not "protected" from being used as evidence of the prior design defect in federal court.

In state courts, the situation is less clear. In *Ault v. International Harvester Co.*,[47] the California Supreme Court refused to apply the federal "subsequent repair" rule to strict liability cases, because that rule sounded in negligence, not strict liability. However, as this chapter has shown, the idea of "strict design defect liability" is troublesome. Rule 407 was clarified in 1997, and it appears that most states today follow the federal rule.[48]

---

45. *Voir dire* refers to the process by which expert witnesses are questioned about their backgrounds and qualifications, in order to potentially give an expert opinion in court testimony.

46. Fed. R. Evid. 407.

47. Ault v. International Harvester Co., 528 P.2d 1148 (Cal. 1974).

48. *See* Paul Carver, *Subsequent Remedial Measures 2000 and Beyond*, 27 WM. MITCHELL L. REV. 583 (2000).

Must plaintiff produce an expert witness to support his claim that an alternate design is feasible?

Caselaw does not require expert witnesses when the design defect is obvious (as in the finger-guillotine chaise longue). In such instances the market typically provides alternate designs in any case. If experts are produced by plaintiff, they must be deemed qualified if their opinion is to be admissible. In *Kumho Tire Co., Ltd. v. Carmichael*,[49] the Supreme Court ruled that Fed. R. Evid. 702, adopted in 2000, codifies the holding in *Daubert v. Merrell Dow Pharmaceuticals*[50] and applies it to all technical or specialized expert testimony. A Note accompanying Rule 702 indicates that, in addition to the five *Daubert* guidelines for witness admissibility (testability of opinion, error rate, control standards, peer review of publication, and general acceptance), the following criteria are relevant:

1. Whether the proposed expert has conducted research independent of the litigation;

2. Whether the proposed expert's conclusion follows acceptably from his premises;

3. Whether the proposed expert has considered alternative views;

4. Whether the proposed expert "is being as careful as he would be in his regular professional work" when issuing his opinion;

5. Whether the proposed expert's field of expertise is reliable in the area in which the proposed expert would testify.[51]

Trial judges have considerable discretion in admitting experts.[52] Here are two representative instances illustrating why trial courts might reach different decisions on reliability of expert witnesses in design defect cases:

- After the death of a 14–year old girl using a "Jet Ski," an expert's proffered testimony relating to the safety of the watercraft throttle compared to alternative designs was rejected as unreliable. The expert had no education or experience in product design of watercraft or accelerating mechanisms, nor did he provide scientific, statistical or other

---

49. Kumho Tire Co., Ltd. v. Carmichael, 526 U.S. 137 (1999).

50. Daubert v. Merrell Dow Pharms., 509 U.S. 579 (1993).

51. Notes of Advisory Committee on Rules (2000 Amendment), Rule 702, *available at* http://federalevidence.com/ advisory-committee-notes (last consulted March 18, 2010).

52. General Electric Co. v. Joiner, 522 U.S. 136 (1997).

evidence evaluating the relative safety of actual watercraft models or their accelerating mechanisms.[53]

- An expert's opinion that the manufacturer of a hay baler should have equipped it with an emergency stop system was held to be "reliable" and admissible in an injured farm worker's design defect suit. The expert was an experienced professional engineer who had studied and written about emergency stop systems, and had designed and built at least ten emergency stop systems for various types of hay balers.[54]

4. Special Case: Automobiles

America's love affair with the automobile is universally known. More than in any other nation, Americans disparage collective transportation and define themselves in part by what they drive (or ride[55]). According to a 2007 federal study, there were 254,403,082 registered passenger (non-commercial) vehicles in the country,[56] or .85 vehicles for every human being.[57]

Automobiles are complicated machines, assemblages of thousands of parts made by dozens of manufacturers. The in-car entertainment systems of many models pack more processing power than the flight management system of the first space shuttle. We drive these vehicles in rain, sleet, snow and hail, while talking on our cell phones or to our passengers. Often we maintain them poorly. Yet every year these travelling explosive projectiles cause us fewer deaths per mile driven. The federal Department of Transportation announced on March 11, 2010 that the 2009 fatality count dropped 8.9 percent to 33,963, its lowest level since 1954, despite constant increases in the number of vehicles registered and the number of miles driven.

But accidents happen. Most accidents (even most of the 2010 Toyota "sudden acceleration" incidents[58] discussed in the Introduction to this Book) are the result of driver error. In some cases, however, injuries result from or are exacerbated by manufacturing defects (from airbags that don't deploy[59] to transmissions that slip into reverse gear by themselves[60]).

---

53. Calhoun v. Yamaha Motor Corp., 350 F.3d 316 (3d Cir. 2003) (applying Pennsylvania law).

54. Blevins v. New Holland N. Am., Inc., 128 F. Supp. 2d 952 (W.D. Va. 2001).

55. Full disclosure: the author of this book is an avid motorcyclist.

56. Research and Innovative Technology Administration (RITA), U.S. Dep't of Transportation (US DOT), *available* *at* http://www.bts.gov/publications/national_transportation_statistics (last consulted March 18, 2010).

57. The US population in 2007 was officially recorded as 299,398,000. U.S. Bureau of the Census.

58. Mike Ramsey and Kate Linebaugh, *Crash Data Suggest Driver Error in Toyota Accidents*, WALL ST. J., Jul. 13 2010.

59. Harris v. General Motors Corp., 201 F.3d 800 (6th Cir. 2000) (applying Ohio law); Estep v. Mike Ferrell Ford Lincoln–Mercury, Inc., 672 S.E.2d 345 (W. Va. 2008).

60. General Motors Corp. v. Sanchez, 997 S.W.2d 584 (Tex. 1999).

It is as regards design defects that automobile litigation presents more acute problems. Automotive design cases, like manufacturing defect auto cases, are of two different sorts. One kind of case features design flaws that allegedly caused a collision. Suzuki Samurai mini-SUV's were alleged to be defective in design in that they rolled over during normal driving.[61] Corvair sports cars were attacked as being "unsafe at any speed."[62] Sometimes an allegedly defective design is obvious to the buyer. Is a convertible defective if it is not equipped with a roll bar? Is a car defective if it is not equipped with antilock brakes, which the purchaser declined to select as an option? The presence of both roll bars and ABS is detectable from the inside of the vehicle.

A second kind of automobile design defect case alleges that a design flaw *exacerbated the injuries resulting from a collision caused by human error.*[63] Early caselaw held that, since smashing into things was not an intended use of automobiles, they needn't be designed to be safe in case of collision.[64] In *Larsen v. General Motors Corp.,*[65] however, it was famously held that "[n]o rational basis exists for limiting recovery to situations where the defect in design or manufacture was the causative factor of the accident, as the accident and the resulting injury ... all are foreseeable."[66] Today "crashworthiness" is a major factor in design liability.

In crashworthiness cases the burden of proof is hotly debated. One branch of caselaw requires the plaintiff to produce "some method of establishing the extent of enhanced injuries attributable to the defective design."[67] If the plaintiff cannot produce an expert who identifies what portion of the injury occurred as a result of the design defect, the enhanced injury claim fails. Under a second line of cases, the plaintiff need prove only that the product defect was a "substantial factor" in creating damage greater than that attributable solely to the underlying accident. The burden will then be on defendant to establish what the exacerbated portion was, failing which defendant will be liable for the entirety of damages.[68] Section

---

61. Consumer Group Asks Recall of Suzuki Samurai as Unsafe, N.Y. Times, June 3, 1988.

62. Ralph Nader, Unsafe at Any Speed: The Designed–In Dangers of the American Automobile (1965).

63. This is a complicating factor in that it creates the possibility of moral hazard. See *supra* Chapter 3.

64. *See, e.g.*, Evans v. General Motors Corp., 359 F.2d 822, 825 (7th Cir. 1966).

65. Larsen v. General Motors Corp., 391 F.2d 495 (8th Cir. 1968).

66. *Id.* at 502.

67. Huddell v. Levin, 537 F.2d 726, 737–38 (3d Cir. 1976).

68. *See* Mitchell v. Volkswagenwerk, AG, 669 F.2d 1199, 1206 (8th Cir. 1982); Fox v. Ford Motor Co., 575 F.2d 774, 787 (10th Cir. 1978).

16 of the *Restatement (Third)* seems to adopt the latter interpretation[69] in its treatment of this controversy:

(a) When a product is defective at the time of commercial sale
or other distribution and the defect is a substantial factor in
increasing the plaintiff's harm beyond that which would have
resulted from other causes, the product seller is subject to
liability for the increased harm.

(b) If proof supports a determination of the harm that would
have resulted from other causes in the absence of the product
defect, the product seller's liability is limited to the increased
harm attributable solely to the product defect.

(c) *If proof does not support a determination under Subsection
(b) of the harm that would have resulted in the absence of the
product defect, the product seller is liable for all of the plaintiff's harm attributable to the defect and other causes.*

(d) A seller of a defective product that is held liable for part of
the harm suffered by the plaintiff under Subsection (b), or all
of the harm suffered by plaintiff under Subsection (c), is jointly
and severally liable or severally liable with other parties who
bear legal responsibility for causing the harm, determined by
the applicable rules of joint and several liability.[70]

Question

● Is a car with seat belts but no (or "not enough") airbags, driven
by a drunk driver who crashes into a wall and is killed, defective
in design?[71]

The typical auto design defect case involves extensive expert
testimony about the costs and benefits of feasible alternate designs,
and highly technical "he said, she said" disputes, about how the
plaintiff's injuries were caused and what would (counterfactually)
have happened had the car been designed differently. What would
have happened to plaintiff had her car's gasoline tank been placed
two inches further from the passenger compartment? Recall that all
design choices are tradeoffs. Might the design changes proposed by
plaintiff have caused deaths to others even if they would have saved
the plaintiff? The exact circumstances of a fatal crash can often

---

69. According to the Reporter's
Note for § 16(c), "if the plaintiff has
established that the product defect increased the harm over and above that
which the plaintiff would have suffered
had the product been nondefective, and
if, at the close of the case, proof does not
support a determination of the harm

that would have resulted in the absence
of the product defect, then the defendant is liable for all the harm suffered
by the plaintiff." RESTATEMENT (THIRD) OF
TORTS, PRODUCTS LIABILITY § 16 (1998).

70. *Id.*

71. Geier v. American Honda Motor
Co., 529 U.S. 861 (2000).

only be approximated. Jurors are typically asked to parse conflicting auto design expert testimony after trials that often last for months.

Some problems render the determination of automobile design defect uniquely difficult:

- A variety of safety design is available "vertically." That is, one may at any moment purchase cars from many different model years. Each year's model may be slightly improved (including slightly safer) than the preceding year's model. Yet both manufacturers and car dealers continue to liquidate unsold stock, selling new cars that are no longer "state of the art."

- A variety of safety design is available "horizontally." That is, for any given model year there are cars available with vastly different safety features. There are tiny cars, which will be more dangerous than large cars, *ceteris paribus*, until the laws of physics are repealed.[72] There are cars with and without traction control and stability management. Some convertibles have roll bars while others do not. There are cars that issue a warning if the driver swerves into an adjacent lane, and cars that don't. Since 1998, when federal law mandated airbags in new cars, the number and location of airbags in different model of cars has varied widely. Some models have two airbags, while others have side airbags, knee airbags, and curtain airbags. One model of motorcycle offers an optional airbag. When does the availability of a safety device make cars without such devices obsolete, a.k.a. defective in design?

- Automobiles are heavily regulated by the National Highway Traffic Safety Administration (NHTSA), a division of the Department of Transportation. No automobile may be sold in the United States until NHTSA has approved the model's design features. Federal Motor Vehicle Safety Standards (FMVSS) create minimal safety standards that all manufacturers must meet. If a manufacturer meets FMVSS, should it be immune to a products liability suit that claims its product is defective for not having met a higher standard? If a particular design defect is latent (non-apparent) and unregulated,[73] how is a jury to determine what the non-defective level of safety is? Is an obliviousness to the cost of additional

---

72. INSURANCE INSTITUTE FOR HIGHWAY SAFETY, New crash tests demonstrate the influence of vehicle size and weight on safety in crashes; results are relevant to fuel economy policies, April 14, 2009, http://www.iihs.org/news/rss/pr041409.html (last consulted March 18, 2010).

73. For instance, the strength of the frame of different vehicles varies tremendously.

safety features the natural result of letting design defect automobile cases get to juries? If new cars are made prohibitively expensive in part because of fears of products liability suits, are motorists likely at the margin to stick with their comparatively dangerous clunkers?

Shipler v. General Motors Corp. highlights several of these issues.[74] In September 1997, Penny Shipler was a passenger in a 1996 Chevrolet S–10 Blazer SUV driven by Kenneth Long. Both individuals had apparently consumed significant quantities of alcohol before embarking on their journey. In addition, Ms. Shipler was carrying her infant son on her lap, with the passenger seatbelt improperly fastened over both of them. Eventually Kenneth Long's inebriation caused him to lose control of the SUV at high speed, and the vehicle rolled over at least four times. Shipler's infant was ejected from the vehicle. Shipler was rendered quadriplegic after the roof collapsed on her head during the rollover. Shipler sued General Motors. The trial lasted six weeks. The jury deliberated for six days before reaching a verdict. General Motors was condemned to pay $18,583,900.00 to Penny Shipler. The Nebraska Supreme Court affirmed this verdict.

Among the questions to ponder following this case (this book will deal with many of them in subsequent chapters) are these:

- How did the *Shipler* jury determine that the Blazer's roof was too weak? Note that the decision implies that every Blazer's roof is too weak, exposing General Motors to liability in every Blazer rollover crash.

- Should Kenneth Long's negligent driving affect General Motors' liability to Penny Shipler?[75]

- Should Penny Shipler's decision to consume alcohol and ride with a drunken driver affect General Motors' liability?[76]

- Should Penny Shipler's decision not to use her seatbelt properly affect General Motors' liability?[77]

- What is the cost (lawyers' fees, expert witnesses, lost income to jurors, court officials' salary, etc.) of trying a case for six weeks? $1 million? More? What do you think discovery cost before trial? How many cars must General Motors sell to

74. Shipler v. General Motors Corp., 710 N.W.2d 807 (Neb. 2006).

75. The jury and the judge decided that it did not—the inherent nature of the design defect suit is that the vehicle should withstand crashes, caused for any reason, thus the reason for the crash is irrelevant to the manufacturer's liability.

76. The jury and the judge decided that it did not, for the same reason.

77. Under a Nebraska statute that the court applied in this case, the award against GM was reduced by 5 percent for this reason.

earn \$19 million in profits? To earn the amounts needed to pay other victims of Blazer rollovers?

- General Motors and Chrysler each declared bankruptcy in 2009. Chrysler took advantage of its bankruptcy proceeding to discharge all products liability claims for cars manufactured pre-bankruptcy. This meant that existing products liability claims, along with any future claims for Chrysler vehicles purchased before the bankruptcy, would become unsecured debts, leaving plaintiffs with a limited likelihood of recovering anything from the firm known as the "new Chrysler." Consumers who purchased Chrysler vehicles before June 10, 2009, and who in the future want to allege that their car suffers from a design or manufacturing defect, would have almost no chance of recovering for their injuries. In the GM bankruptcy, the original plan was to do the same, but in this case objections lodged by consumer groups and state attorneys general were voiced. GM (mostly owned by the federal government) then reversed course and agreed to allow the "new GM" to be subject to products liability claims for vehicles manufactured before the bankruptcy. Chrysler had a change of heart in August 2009, perhaps under pressure from dealers who feared losing goodwill once the differential impact of the two bankruptcies became known. Was it appropriate for the bankruptcy court to approve Chrysler's original petition to discharge all current products liability exposure? Should products liability claimants be treated differently from other creditors of a bankrupt company?

Questions About Julian Felipe's Case

- Read this news report from *ConsumerAffairs.com*. Try to imagine its possible implications for plaintiff's and defendant's attorneys in the *Felipe* case. Note that the Felipe trial did not take place until 2007, after the *Consumer Affairs* report was published. To what extent should the information the article contains be relevant to a 2002 crash of a 1993 Ford?

"GM to Offer Rollover Airbags, Ford to Strengthen Roofs[78]

By Joe Benton
December 6, 2006

General Motors Corp. plans to make rollover-enabled airbags standard on all retail vehicles by 2012. The world's largest automaker now installs the rollover airbag systems in 43 percent of the light trucks and SUVs the company

---

78. Joe Benton, *GM to Offer Rollover Airbags, Ford to Strengthen Roofs,* CONSUMER AFFAIRS.COM, http://www. consumeraffairs.com/news04/2006/12/ gm_rollovers.html (last consulted March 18, 2010).

manufactures. A leading safety advocate said the announcement shows automakers are moving ahead of safety regulators.

Ford, meanwhile, said it would build stronger roofs on many of its vehicles, exceeding federal safety standards.

GM said it plans to perform 150 rollover tests in 2007 at a new company testing facility in a effort to understand the dynamics of rollover crashes. Despite the seriousness of rollover accidents, there are not many rollover crash tests because events that occur in a rollover are difficult to repeat.

Joan Claybrook[79], president of Public Citizen, said it was a "positive sign that GM acknowledges the need for new vehicle designs to protect people in rollover crashes."

Rollover crashes kill 10,800 and injure more than 16,000 people annually.

In 2005, rollovers accounted for about 4 percent of all crashes but 33 percent of highway fatalities. Nearly 60 percent of SUV fatalities are the result of rollovers and the driver is twice as likely to die in an SUV rollover as in a car rollover.

GM will use the testing to look for ways to keep people from being ejected in rollovers and develop sensors for rollover-enabled airbags, which can help reduce injuries and prevent ejections. Rollover-enabled airbags stay open for five seconds compared with the basic head curtain airbag, which offers protection for about three-tenths of a second.

For more than 30 years, GM has conducted rollover tests using a dolly system. Vehicles are pulled sideways on a platform at a 23–degree angle. The new GM facility has the capacity to conduct additional types of rollover tests that simulate crashes experienced by drivers on the highway.

Claybrook said GM's announcement shows automakers are prepared to move ahead even without a strong push from government regulators.

"Today's announcement makes it clear that the industry is well prepared to do the kind of testing necessary under a government dynamic test standard," Claybrook said. "The Volvo XC–90 SUV manufactured since 2003 is an example of a vehicle that protects passengers in rollover crashes. It was designed using dynamic testing."

---

79. Joan Claybrook was administrator of NHTSA from 1977–1981.

Not to be left out, Ford Motor Co. plans to improve the roof strength of many of its larger vehicles beyond the new standards that federal regulators at the National Highway Traffic Safety Administration (NHTSA) have proposed.

Ford, which is facing more than $250 million in lawsuits involving SUV rollovers since 2004, told NHTSA that some versions of 11 models of its vehicles will have roofs 20 percent stronger than required.

NHTSA has proposed a new roof strength standard that would require a vehicle roof to survive a force equal to 2.5 times the vehicle's weight, an increase from the current 1.5 times. The new standard requires the roof to maintain sufficient head room for a buckled-in average size adult male to avoid being struck by a crushed roof. A final rule won't be in place until late next year at the earliest; automakers will have until at least 2011 to build the stronger roofs.

The Ford Expedition and the Lincoln Navigator would exceed the new standards as would some of Ford's F–250 series trucks and E–Series vans, according to Ford.

Ford also has installed rollover safety canopies in 1 million vehicles now and predicts that figure will jump to 1.5 million by 2007.

Ford has a string of losses in rollover lawsuits and court decisions. While the company is appealing all of the verdicts, Ford has also fought to keep its internal roof strength documents secret.

GM neglected to say whether the information gleaned from this facility will be released to inform the public of vehicle performance. GM does mention the importance of seat belts but does not say whether it will offer rollover pretensioned seat belts (those that have been locked in place) in all its vehicles. Although there is no existing safety standard for seat belts in rollover crashes, the strength of the roof and the performance of the belts are the most critical safety protections in these crashes. Until these deficiencies are also addressed, drivers and passengers will continue to be put at risk of death or serious injury on our highways."[80]

- The base price of a 2003 Volvo XC 90 station wagon (mentioned in the report) was $33,350.[81] The base price of a 1993 Ford

---

80. *Id.*
81. Ford Aerostar Specs, CarsDi-
RECT, http://www.carsdirect.com/2003/

volvo/xc90/specs (last consulted March 18, 2010).

Aerostar was $14,321, which is the equivalent of $18,044 in 2003 dollars.[82] Should these figures be relevant to the Felipe lawsuit?

• In 1968 Mr. J.R. Weaver of the Ford Automotive Safety Research Office produced a "Roof Strength Study." A memo summarizing this study was produced at the Felipe trial. The study noted that many rollovers struck the roof with a load of twice the vehicle's weight. A strength-to-weight ratio (SWR) of 2 was attainable without altering basic roof design, the memo claimed. It continued,

> "It is obvious that occupants that are restrained in upright positions are more susceptible to injury from a collapsing roof than unrestrained occupants who are free to tumble about the interior of the vehicle. It seems unjust to penalize people wearing effective restraint systems by exposing them to more severe rollover injuries than they might expect with no restraints."[83]

NHTSA finally issued its roof strength standard in 1973.[84] That standard required an SWR of 1.5. The Aerostar met that legal standard. Should the Weaver memo be relevant to the disposition of the Felipe case? Should the federal standard be relevant? Should it be relevant that the SWR was increased to 2.5 in 2006, before the Felipe trial occurred?[85]

• What SWR would have prevented or mitigated Julian Felipe's injury?

82. Ford Aerostar Specs, CARSDI-RECT, http://www.carsdirect.com/1993/ford/aerostar/specs (last consulted March 18, 2010). Inflation calculation based on tables at http://www.westegg.com/inflation/.

83. Memorandum from J.R. Weaver to H.G. Brilmyer, Roof Strength Study, Ford Automotive Safety Office (July 8, 1968).

84. Federal Motor Vehicle Standards, FMVSS 216, *available at* http://www.crash-network.com/Regulations/FMVSS/fmvss.html.

85. When consumers demand a feature, industry does tend to respond. On March 24, 2009 the Insurance Institute for Highway Safety (IIHS), a private research institute funded by automobile insurers, released findings with roof crush results for 12 small SUVs. The IIHS test is more stringent than NHTSA's. The poorest performer (Kia Sportage and its sister vehicle, Hyundai Tucson) withstood 2.5 SWR before reaching five inches of deformation. The best performer was the Volkswagen Tiguan at almost 6 SWR. After the test, the Tiguan looked scratched after withstanding a force of 15,000 pounds. For 2010, the IIHS plans to remove its Top Safety Pick status for vehicles with an SWR of less than 4.0, fully twice the NHTSA rating. The IIHS findings may be found at http://www.iihs.org/news/rss/pr032409.html (last reviewed on March 18, 2010).

Chapter 8

THE PLAINTIFF'S CASE: STRICT LIABILITY FOR INFORMA-TIONAL DEFECTS[1]

1. Introduction

This book has argued that manufacturing defects are best understood as cases of strict liability for misrepresentation of a product by its seller, while the concept of design defect is likely best described as being virtually unintelligible absent negligence. Case-law has created a third type of products liability, styled "failure to warn." This book calls this cause of action liability for "informational defect."

As a threshold matter, consider whether informational defects should even be considered as a separate category of liability. Ultimately, every product is designed to be some combination of physical and informational output. For some products (tennis balls, pencils) the physical output represents virtually 100 percent of the object sold: if one doesn't know how to use a pencil properly one has not been to kindergarten. Imagine a plaintiff who sharpens a pencil, sticks it into her eye, and complains that the pencil was not sold with a warning against doing this. There is no jurisdiction in the country where a failure to warn lawsuit against the pencil's manufacturer would survive demurrer.

Not only are warnings not needed on pencils—they are also not feasible. It would be difficult to put an effective warning on a pencil without altering its physical design. But there are some products whose physical configuration enables the insertion of inane warnings.

- The following warning is found on the Axius® "Sno–Off" automobile windshield cover: *"Caution: Never drive with the cover on your windshield."* Presumably either Axius has been sued by a crazy driver or one of the firm's attorneys decided to preempt any such driver's suit by adding this easy-to-insert warning.

---

1. Additional Reading: James A. Henderson, Jr. & Aaron D. Twerski, *Doctrinal Collapse In Products Liability:* *The Empty Shell Of Failure To Warn*, 65 N.Y.U.L. REV. 265 (1990).

- It's hard to believe that this warning on an EAD® Ultradisc 2000 CD Player was preemptive—for how could it have been imagined: *"Do not use the Ultradisc 2000 as a projectile in a catapult."*

- What of this internationally curious warning on a packet of juggling balls—*"This product contains small granules under 3 millimeters. Not suitable for children under the age of 14 years in Europe or 8 years in the USA"*?

- Butane lighters present a smaller surface on which to place a warning than do CD players or car covers. Nevertheless one lighter manufacturer found the space to glue: *"Warning: Flame may cause fire."*[2]

- Finally, some warnings are simply bewildering head-scratchers. What to make of the following remark in the manual of a chainsaw: *"Do not attempt to stop the blade with your hand?"* Or of this engraving on the barrel of a .22 caliber rifle: *"Warning: Misuse may cause injury or death?"*[3]

Imagine that you were in-house counsel for the manufacturer of that rifle. Would it make good business sense to market your product without *any* engraved or appended (in a manual) informational content (a.k.a. warning), the way a tennis ball is marketed? To ask this question is to answer it. If, for example, purchasers of the rifle do not know what caliber ammunition to purchase, a dangerous misfire might occur. If the precise location and method of operation of the rifle's safety (trigger lock) are not known, unintended firings or ineffectiveness in an emergency might result. On the other hand, if the product is so complex that reading and understanding a 1000 page manual is needed for safe operation, perhaps the physical design itself needs to be rethought.[4]

Clearly, for a large number of products, *some* information is required in order to ensure optimally safe use. Few products are as self-explanatory as tennis balls. From this realization at least four questions arise that must be considered by counsel:

    1. *How much* information is needed to make the product's design *safe enough* (recall, "total safety" is either unattainable or unintelligible)? Should small cars come with warnings that they are more dangerous in case of collision than large cars? Should room air conditioners

---

2. Warning taken from Joey Green, Tony Dierckins, & Tim Nyberg, The Warning Label Book (1998), *available at* http://www.octanecreative.com/warning/ (last consulted March 22, 2010).

3. Warning taken from *Wacky Warning Labels*, COMMON GOOD, http://

commongood.org/society–45.html (last consulted March 22, 2010).

4. Perhaps, but not necessarily. If the product is an F–35 fighter, extensive informational content likely makes a lot of sense.

come with warnings that they might fall or be dropped out of windows and injure people below? Since one can endlessly add information,[5] every unexpected product-related injury can conceivably result in a "failure to warn" suit.

2. *Where in the chain of the product's distribution* should the information originate? For some products (e.g., industrial presses used in many different applications in different kinds of factory settings), warnings might best be tailored (by the retail seller? by the employer?) to the individual user. For other products (rifles?), a uniform warning (engraved on the stock? appended in a manual that will be lost?) to all users might be most effective.

3. Can information rectify (what would otherwise be) a design defect? To some extent, information and design are interchangeable. Every product is a combination of some physical attributes and some information. One can design a car with anti-lock brakes, or with non-ABS brakes and a *"Modulate brakes in panic stops or on snow"* warning. One can build a car with an automatic transmission, or one can design it with a manual transmission and perhaps a warning that failure to shift will "blow" the engine.

    On the other hand, there are surely some design dangers that are so egregious that no warning can legally neutralize them. Imagine that a furniture manufacturer creates a bar chair that is, in functional reality, a stool; the back of this piece of furniture is purely decorative and does not support weight. It will collapse if a user reclines, almost certainly causing a dangerous fall. Should an adhesive sticker (*Chair's back will not support weight and is for decorative purposes only!*) make the design legally palatable, or does the chair's design invite users to "lean on me," leading them to ignore the sticker's message?

4. Finally, what can "strict liability for failure to warn"[6] possibly mean? If strict liability requires only causation, not wrongdoing, does a manufacturer have to

---

5. Your author's automobile's owner's manual is so voluminous and heavy that it does not fit inside the car's glove compartment. The author has not and never will read it, and because of its size he doesn't carry it with him in case of a breakdown, either.

6. RESTATEMENT (SECOND) OF TORTS § 402A cmt. J (1965) (providing that a seller must provide a warning "if he has knowledge, or by the application of reasonable, developed human skill and foresight should have knowledge of the presence of the . . . danger).

anticipate and warn against every danger in use of the product, regardless of how unlikely it might be? Should the *artiste* who dons a Superman costume thinking it will help him fly recover damages from its manufacturer who has not warned against this use of its product?[7] Must a perfume manufacturer warn that the perfume (whose listed ingredients include alcohol as the principal component) will combust if used to scent candles?[8] Similarly, how "big" is "big enough" for a warning if strict liability is the standard? In General Motors v. Saenz,[9] General Motors had provided a label indicating the gross vehicle weight and warning against overloading.[10] Plaintiff complained that these warnings were not prominent enough to catch his attention.[11] Any warning can be made bigger and bolder, of course—until they are all big and bold, at which point none of them are "prominent" any more. Should General Motors be allowed to claim its warning was *reasonable*, if liability for inadequate warning is *strict*?

2. Negligence or Strict Liability?

If liability for failure to warn is negligence-based, then a plaintiff will have to prove either that her injuries were caused by a risk that *should* have been the object of a warning or that the warning for that particular risk should have been more aggressive, all things considered. The costs and benefits *ex ante* of making the allegedly needed warning must be considered. If, on the other hand, liability for failure to warn is truly strict, plaintiff need merely prove that the risk that injured her *could* have been warned of (or warned of more stringently). So long as the jury believes that a hypothetical warning (or a hypothetical stronger warning) would

7. J. M. Broder, Warning: A Batman cape won't help you fly, N.Y. TIMES, March 5, 1997, at A1.

8. Moran v. Fabergé, Inc., 332 A.2d 11 (Md. 1975).

9. General Motors v. Saenz, 873 S.W.2d 353 (Tex. 1993).

10. The truck's Gross Vehicle Weight Rating was imprinted on a metal plate that GM attached to the doorjamb, in conformity with federal regulations, on the driver's side at eye level. The plate stated that overloading could void the warranty and referenced the owner's manual for additional information. Page two of the owner's manual was captioned, in large block letters, "IMPORTANT INFORMATION ON VEHICLE LOADING." The text stated, in part: "OVERLOADING SAFETY CAUTION: . . . Overloading can create serious potential safety hazards and can also shorten the service life of your vehicle." *Id.* at 354.

11. Plaintiffs argued that a sticker should have been affixed inside the truck's cab near the gear shift lever, reading as follows:

WARNING Overloading this vehicle beyond its "as manufactured" GVW can result in loss of control or a rollover resulting in serious personal injury or death. (For additional information please refer to owner's manual). *Id.* at 361.

have been heeded, liability would follow under the strict theory—no *ex ante* judgment about appropriateness would take place.

Notwithstanding the language of the *Restatement (Second)*, courts have increasingly admitted that the test for "informational defect" is essentially negligence-based. Some courts refuse to forthrightly acknowledge this; they concede, though, that "any posited distinction between strict liability and negligence principles is illusory";[12] or that instructing the jury only on negligent failure to warn was "harmless error," even though "[w]e do not mean to suggest that a cause of action for negligent failure to warn or warn adequately is identical to one brought under strict liability."[13] Even staunch defenders of strict liability have concluded that failure to warn caselaw is hard to reconcile with their vision.[14]

The relevance of the negligence-strict liability distinction arises in several different kinds of warning cases, as illustrated here.

A. The Never–Before–Seen, Yet Conceivable Risk

In *Lewis v. Sea Ray Boats, Inc.,*[15] plaintiff's decedent had purchased a ten-year old Sea Ray® boat from a dealer. The boat was equipped with a gasoline generator to power accessories, including the air conditioning system. During a jaunt, he "side-tied" the boat to a beach and went to sleep in cabin, with the air conditioner running. He was overcome by carbon monoxide poisoning and died.

Carbon monoxide detectors did not exist when the boat was manufactured. But the generator's manufacturer had equipped the generator with this warning:

WARNING

ENGINE EXHAUST GAS (CARBON MONOXIDE) IS DEADLY!

Carbon monoxide is an odorless, colorless gas formed by incomplete combustion of hydrocarbon fuels. Carbon Monoxide is a dangerous gas that can cause unconsciousness and is potentially lethal. Some of the symptoms or signs of carbon monoxide inhalation are:

Dizziness	*Vomiting*
Intense Headache	*Muscular Twitching*

12. Olson v. Prosoco, Inc., 522 N.W.2d 284, 289 (Iowa 1994).

13. Crislip v. TCH Liquidating Co., 556 N.E.2d 1177, 1183 (Ohio 1990).

14. *See, e.g.,* Anderson v. Owens–Corning Fiberglas Corp., 810 P.2d 549, 563 (Cal. 1991) (Mosk, J., concurring in part and dissenting in part) ("We should consider the possibility of holding that failure to warn actions lie solely on a negligence theory.").

15. Lewis v. Sea Ray Boats, Inc., 65 P.3d 245 (Nev. 2003).

Weakness and Sleepiness   *Throbbing in Temples*

If you experience any of the above symptoms, get out into fresh air immediately. The best protection against carbon monoxide inhalation is a regular inspection of the complete exhaust system. If you notice a change in the sound or appearance of the exhaust system, shut the unit down immediately and have it inspected and repaired at once by a competent mechanic.

In addition, a national association of boat builders had recommended a second warning, which the defendant duly added:

WARNING: *Use care in running the engine continuously when the boat is closed up in bad weather, particularly when the boat is not in motion. Exhaust fumes and carbon monoxide may accumulate in the passenger areas, so be alert to any indication that exhaust fumes are present, and ventilate accordingly.*

All parties agreed, however, that exhaust fumes had not caused the tragedy. Rather, a process described as "migrating carbon monoxide" had occurred. This takes place when carbon monoxide, though safely exhausted from the generator into the open air, is blown back into the boat by the precise configuration of winds and anchorage entering the passenger cabin through small openings. If the boat is anchored from the bow, rather than the side, wind currents blow away from the stern. Sea Ray had not warned of this particular eventuality *because no incidents of this type had ever been reported.* The manufacturer argued that it could not be liable for failure to warn of an unprecedented event. The trial judge agreed and a defense verdict promptly followed.

The Nevada Supreme Court reversed, however, holding that it was a jury question whether Sea Ray's warning was adequate, and that "the jury should use its common sense" in making its determination.[16]

Questions

- If a negligence rule applied, do you think the plaintiff produced any evidence of a negligent failure to warn? If not, he may not reach the jury.

- Does the fact that no similar accident had ever occurred resolve this question, or should the jury be allowed to find that the boat manufacturer could have anticipated this particular risk?

- If strict liability applies, is it sufficient for liability that the plaintiff claim that the decedent would have heeded a warning had one been given?

16. *Id.* at 350.

Questions About Julian Felipe's Case

• Had Ford warned, in its owner's manual or perhaps on a sticker glued to the dashboard, that the roof of the Aerostar would only withstand a force equal to 1.5 times the weight of the van, that many rollovers involved a greater force than that, and that compression of the roof could therefore be expected in many rollovers, would this warning have been sufficient to immunize Ford from design defect liability? Note in this regard that Comment j of the *Restatement (Second)* provides in part:

> "Where warning is given, the seller may reasonably assume that it will be read and heeded; and a product bearing such a warning, *which is safe for use if it is followed,* is not in defective condition, nor is it unreasonably dangerous."[17]

The *Restatement (Third)* adds:

> "Reasonable designs and instructions or warnings both play important roles in the production and distribution of reasonably safe products. *In general, when a safer design can reasonably be implemented and risks can reasonably be designed out of a product, adoption of the safer design is required over a warning that leaves a significant residuum of such risks.* For example, instructions and warnings may be ineffective because users of the product may not be adequately reached, may be likely to be inattentive, or may be insufficiently motivated to follow the instructions or heed the warnings. However, when an alternative design to avoid risks cannot reasonably be implemented, adequate instructions and warnings will normally be sufficient to render the product reasonably safe. *Compare* Comment *e. Warnings are not, however, a substitute for the provision of a reasonably safe design.*[18]

It should be noted that sometimes the physical design of a product includes a non-verbal warning. Thus, a clear liquid used for cleaning might be defective in design unless an odor and a color were added during the manufacturing process to alert users that the liquid is not potable water and that cloths drenched in the liquid are not washcloths that may be used to clean one's face.[19]

B. The Warned–Of but Allegedly Underemphasized Risk

In *Murray v. Wilson Oak Flooring Co., Inc.,*[20], plaintiff owned a small brick residence in Chicago, and was preparing to install a

---

17. RESTATEMENT (SECOND) OF TORTS § 402A cmt. J (1977). (Emphasis added.)

18. RESTATEMENT (THIRD) OF TORTS, PRODUCTS LIABILITY § 2 cmt. l. (1998); *see also* Uniroyal Goodrich Tire Co. v. Martinez, 977 S.W.2d 328 (Tex. 1998).

19. *See, e.g.*, Hayes v. Kay Chemical Co., 482 N.E.2d 611 (Ill. App. 1985).

20. Murray v. Wilson Oak Flooring Co., Inc., 475 F.2d 129 (7th Cir. 1973) (applying Illinois law).

parquet floor on a portion of the second story of his building. The five-gallon can of adhesive for the flooring contained these two labels:

CAUTION: INFLAMMABLE MIXTURE
DO NOT USE NEAR FIRE OR FLAME

N. Y. F. D. C. of A. No. 2360
CONTAINS HEPTANE — USE IN WELL VENTILATED AREA
Do not smoke — Extinguish flame — including pilot lights
KEEP LID TIGHTLY CLOSED   KEEP AWAY FROM CHILDREN

Keep
AWAY
From Fire,

HEAT and OPEN flame LIGHTS

CAUTION

LEAKING Packages Must be Removed to a Safe Place

DO NOT DROP

Plaintiff was severely injured when the vapors from the adhesive were ignited by a pilot light, either of a water heater located four feet away behind a closed door, or (less likely) of a stove located in the adjacent kitchen, eight feet away but with no closed door. It turned out that federal and state hazardous substance laws required the use of the words "danger" rather than "caution," and "extremely flammable" rather than "inflammable."[21] Overturning

---

21. The word "inflammable" is derived from the Latin " 'inflammare," "to set fire to," where the prefix "in-" means "in" as in "inside", rather than "not" as in "invisible" and "ineligible." Nonetheless, "inflammable" is often erroneously thought to mean "nonflammable". However, given the text

the trial court's judgment *nonobstante verdicto* in favor of the defendant, the Seventh Circuit court of appeals found that the word "near" in the first warning was insufficient to alert plaintiff to pilot lights in other or adjacent rooms.[22]

Questions

- Should the adhesive manufacturer have realized that it was required to add, after the word "near" in the first warning above, the words "including in adjacent rooms?" Is this question relevant to "negligence" analysis, to "strict liability" analysis, or to both?

- Should *Murray* have reached the jury? If so, is the question about the prominence of the warning against overloading in *General Motors v. Saenz*[23] not also for the jury?

The *Restatement (Third)* treats failure to warn cases as negligence cases:

§ 2. Categories Of Product Defect

A product is defective when, at the time of sale or distribution, it contains a manufacturing defect, is defective in design, or is defective because of inadequate instructions or warnings. A product:

. . .

(c) is defective because of inadequate instructions or warnings when the foreseeable risks of harm posed by the product could have been reduced or avoided by the provision of reasonable instructions or warnings by the seller or other distributor, or a predecessor in the commercial chain of distribution, and the omission of the instructions or warnings renders the product not reasonably safe.[24]

The Restatement states that it declines to take a side in the negligence-strict liability debate,[25] but of course it does,[26] as the underlined terms above show.

immediately following, the word "inflammable" and given the plaintiff's testimony, it is evident that he did not consider the product to be fireproof.

22. *Murray*, 475 F.2d at 132.

23. See *supra* note 9.

24. RESTATEMENT (THIRD) OF TORTS, PRODUCTS LIABILITY § 2 (1998) (emphasis added).

25. *Id.* § 2, cmt. n ("The rules are stated functionally rather than in terms of traditional doctrinal categories.... As long as these requisites are met, doctrinal tort categories such as negligence or strict liability may be utilized in bringing the claim.").

26. See David G. Owen, *Defectiveness Restated: Exploding The "Strict" Products Liability Myth*, 1996 U. ILL. L. REV. 743.

Question

- When lightning strikes, we all know to head indoors. But it is unlikely that that many of us know about other risks of electrical storms. In fact, deadly shocks are possible if one performs any of the following activities during a lightning storm: 1) working on a laptop computer; 2) playing a video game; 3) talking on a corded phone; 4) riding in a car with a fiberglass or plastic body;[27] 5) taking a shower or bath.[28] Should laptop computers, corded phones, Corvettes and shower doors come with warnings about lightning? If so, how prominent should these warnings be? [Phones often have such warnings buried in an owner's manual, but studies indicate that almost no users retain that information after installation of the phone.]

C. Obvious but Infinitesimal Risks

The author of this Book uses Gillette® After Shave Skin Conditioner Gel.

---

27. It is the metal body of most cars that protects from lightning, *not* (as most believe) the rubber tires.

28. *See, e.g.*, Liam Pleven & Dionne Searcey, *If Lightning Strikes, Drop PlayStation and Pick Up a Book*, WALL St. J., October 27, 2007, at A1.

The reverse side of the container lists the ingredients: Water, SD Alcohol 408, Cyclomethicone, Fragrance, Dimethicone Copolyol, Triethanolamine, Phenoxethanol, Isodecyl Oleate, Carobmer 940, Polysorbate 80, Disodium EDTA, and artificial colors Green #3 and Yellow #5.

The entirety of the instruction on how to use the product, seen in boldface below, is "Apply after shaving or anytime."

Upon researching the issue, the author has discovered that Dimethicone Copolyol, a surfactant, is an eye irritant that can cause reddening and irritation of the eyes.[29] One 2004 report indicates that Triethanolamine causes an increased incidence of tumor growth in the liver in female B6C3F1 mice, but not in male mice or in Fischer 344 rats.[30] The "Environmental Working Group" has a page devoted to its belief about the multiple health risks of Phenoxethanol (aromatic ether alcohol), including allergies, skin irritation, and organ toxicity and neurotoxicity.[31]

29. See Ma Wen Jie, What Is Dimethicone Copolyol?, EHow, http://www.ehow.com/about_5057373_dimethicone-copolyol.html (last consulted March 23, 2010).

30. W. Stott, *et al.,* "Evaluation of the potential of triethanolamine to alter hepatic choline levels in female B6C3F1 mice". 79 TOXICOL. SCI. 242 (2004).

31. Environmental Working Group, *Phenoxyethanol*, Cosmetic Database, http://www.cosmeticsdatabase.com/ingredient.php?ingred06=704811 (last consulted March 23, 2010).

Questions

- Why does Gillette not warn against the risk of tumors, eye irritation, skin irritation, allergies, or organ/neuro toxicity on the bottle of its After Shave Skin Conditioner?

- Why does Gillette not warn against problems that will occur if the user (or the user's child) ingests the contents of the 3.25–ounce container or pours it into his eyes?

- Why is there no warning about against the dangers of applying after-shave while driving (recall, the directions suggest "apply anytime")?

Courts unanimously hold that warnings must be "adequate." When is the absence of any warning adequate? Knives come with no warnings that they may cut human flesh, and heavy hardcover books have no warning that they may injure users if the book falls (or is thrown) onto their heads. These risks are obvious to any human being who is not a candidate for a Darwin award.[32]

Over-warnings such as those cited in the introductory section of this Chapter are superfluous if the goal is to avoid liability. Moreover, they are in fact hazardous in that they "crowd out" more important warnings. As one court pointed out, "[E]xcessive warnings on product labels may be counterproductive, causing 'sensory overload' which literally drowns crucial information in a sea of mind-numbing detail."[33] Over-warning may in fact create a liability risk.

This creates a tricky balancing act for corporate counsel, because under-warning also exposes a manufacturer to liability. Warning "SLIPPERY WHEN WET" on a roofing compound that creates "the slickest roof in the world" was, decided one court, the equivalent of warning "cat on the premises" when a full-grown, hungry cheetah lurks behind the fence.[34] On the other hand, warning (via a proposed sticker beside the shift lever) the driver of a standard shift car that he should depress the clutch before starting the car in gear was held not to be required as a matter of law—the "intricacies of standard transmissions" are deemed known to drivers of stick-shift cars.[35]

What about allergies or other hypersensitivities? By definition allergies are *abnormalities*—no one speaks of an "allergy to lead" because lead is toxic for all of us. In allergy cases the "defect," in

32. Darwin Awards, http://www. darwinawards.com (last consulted March 23, 2010).

33. Aetna Cas. & Sur. Co. v. Ralph Wilson Plastics Co., 509 N.W.2d 520, 523 (Mich. App. 1993).

34. Spillane v. Georgia Pacific Corp., 1995 WL 71183 (E.D. Pa. 1995).

35. Conti v. Ford Motor Co., 743 F.2d 195, 199 (3d Cir. 1984) (applying Pennsylvania law).

other words, is in the allergic person, not in the allergenic product. An overwhelming number of products induce allergies in *someone*.[36] If enough people are allergic, however, and if their allergy is severe, then the "Learned Hand Test"[37] might require a warning that the product is allergenic. But if an allergy is exceedingly uncommon or even unknown to potential sufferers, warnings are not required.[38]

3.   The How, Who and When of Warnings

A.   How

Sometimes warnings can be placed on a product itself. Ladders have lots of space, so warnings tend to be glued on.[39] In other cases the product is too small, or has no convenient spot to place a warning, and so most warnings are in a user's manual. But no product has an infinite space on which to write warnings, and every manual could display warnings more prominently than it does. How much is enough? Can a manufacturer ever shield itself from exposure to a jury's second-guessing its warnings' placement and format?

The general view, as indicated in the previous section, is that the manufacturer must behave as would a reasonably prudent maker of this product. To succeed the plaintiff must produce evidence that the manufacturer has breached this duty. In reality the law here is little different than as regards proof of negligence in non-product cases. Here are some representative cases:

- In *Meyerhoff v. Michelin Tire Corp.*,[40] a tire from a tractor-trailer rig developed "circumferential wrinkling" from being run while severely underinflated. It turns out that the load on an underinflated tire weakens or breaks internal steel belts, causing significant weakening of the tire sidewall.

---

36. *See Medico–Legal Aspects of Allergies*, 24 Tenn. L. Rev. 840 (1957).

37. *See* United States v. Carroll Towing Co., 159 F.2d 169, 173 (2d Cir. 1947) (holding that liability depends on whether the burden of adequate precautions is less than the product of the probability that injury will occur and the seriousness of the resulting injury).

38. *See, e.g.*, Kaempfe v. Lehn & Fink Prods. Corp., 231 N.E.2d 294, 295 (N.Y. 1967), In *Kaempfe* the injury was dermatitis from aluminum sulphate in deodorant, and the court found no liability for failure to warn where manufacturer had received four complaints in 600,000 sales: "the manufacturer has no special duty to warn the unknown few potential users who might suffer some allergic reaction not common to the nor-

mal person ... plaintiff failed to prove that she was one of the substantial number or of an identifiable class of persons who were allergic to aluminum sulphate and that defendant knew or should have known of the existence of such number or class of persons ... specific words of caution would serve no purpose as to those who knew of their allergy, since they would be adequately warned by notice on the container of the presence of aluminum sulphate in the product, and notice would be meaningless to those who did not know of their allergy." *Id.*

39. Your author once counted forty warnings on a tall ladder.

40. Meyerhoff v. Michelin Tire Corp., 70 F.3d 1175 (10th Cir.1995) (applying Kansas law).

Upon reinflation, the force of the air ruptured the weakened sidewall, causing the air to escape suddenly and, in this case, with fatal consequences. The suit against Michelin first argued that a warning against reinflating a tire that had been used while severely underinflated should have been placed in yellow on the sidewall of the tire. The Tenth Circuit approved the trial court's decision not to allow an "expert" to testify that this was feasible, since that expert had no scientific or market-based foundation for his opinion.[41] That left plaintiffs with their fallback theory that Michelin should have placed a warning about this in black letters on the tire. But even the plaintiff's "expert" doubted that a black on black warning would have had any effect. Michelin had warned about "circumferential wrinkling" warnings in the literature accompanying the tire. This was deemed by the court to be adequate as a matter of law.

• In *Hubbard–Hall Chemical Co. v. Silverman*,[42] defendant sold bags of Parathion® insecticide to a farmer, who hired two Puerto Rican farm workers to spread the product. One worker could read some English while other could not. The farmer claimed he warned his employees about the risks of Parathion®, but in any event both became quite sick after work. They were transported in a semi-comatose condition to a hospital, where they died from Parathion® poisoning. Wrongful death suits against the manufacturer acknowledged that the verbal poison warning (in English) met all federal regulatory requirements, but claimed a skull and crossbones pictogram would have alerted non-English speakers, and that the manufacturer could have expected that farm workers might not be literate in English. This claim was allowed to reach the jury, given universal understanding of the skull and crossbones symbol and the ease of including it on the label.[43]

B. Who

The "who" question has two components.

1). *To Whom Should a Warning be Given?*

Quite often the purchaser of product is not the person who will be using it. As this book has shown in countless examples, the end-user is frequently an employee of the purchaser. The manufacturer

41. See Chapter 7 Section 3 *supra.*

42. Hubbard–Hall Chem. Co. v. Silverman, 340 F.2d 402 (1st Cir. 1965).

43. *See also* Stanley Industries, Inc. v. W.M. Barr & Co., 784 F.Supp. 1570, 1576 (S.D. Fla. 1992) ("It is for the jury to decide whether a warning, to be adequate, must contain language other than English or pictorial warning symbols.")

could warn the purchaser and count on the latter to transmit this warning to employees, but sometimes this doesn't happen. Employers' incentive to transmit information may be dulled by the tort immunity they enjoy as a result of Workers' Compensation legislation, discussed in Chapter 5.

Hubbard–Hall Chemical Co. v. Silverman, discussed immediately above, implies that the manufacturer must take reasonable steps to have warnings reach the final user. Again, this case is a rather routine application of negligence principles. How expensive would a direct warning have been to make, and how valuable would it have been had it been made?[44] Normally, in a complicated chain of distribution, one who supplies a poison in bulk is less able to efficiently warn "downstream" users than would be a "midstream" sophisticated party who packages, labels and distributes the finished bulk product in individual containers.[45] In other words, while manufacturing and design defect claims typically result in liability for every seller in the chain of distribution, this is not necessarily the case as regards informational defect suits.[46]

On the other hand, if bystanders are typical victims of a design characteristic (imagine, for example, a lawn mower designed to frequently project stones far away from the mower), a warning to the purchaser of the mower might not be effective—and of course a warning to bystanders is impossible. In such cases, the design characteristic itself will likely be seen to be a defect.[47]

2). *Who Should Give the Warning?*

Determining who should receive a warning also resolves the issue of who must provide one. A vivid illustration of this in the medical field occurred in a series of lawsuits against the DuPont Corporation after the tragic use of TMJ implants, discussed in Chapter 2. To recall, thousands of Americans received insufficiently

---

44. RESTATEMENT (SECOND) OF TORTS § 388(c) cmt. n (1965); RESTATEMENT (THIRD) OF TORTS, PRODUCTS LIABILITY § 2 cmt. i. (1998).

45. Higgins v. E.I. DuPont de Nemours & Co., 671 F.Supp. 1055, 1062 (D. Md. 1987).

46. RESTATEMENT (THIRD) OF TORTS, PRODUCTS LIABILITY § 5 (1998). Liability Of Commercial Seller Or Distributor Of Product Components For Harm Caused By Products Into Which Components Are Integrated.

One engaged in the business of selling or otherwise distributing product components is subject to liability for harm to persons or property caused by a product

into which the component is integrated if:

(a) the component **is defective in itself,** as defined in this Chapter, and the defect causes the harm; or

(b)(1) the seller or distributor of the component substantially participates in the integration of the component into the design of the product; and

(b)(2) the integration of the component causes the product to be defective, as defined in this Chapter; and

(b)(3) the defect in the product causes the harm.

47. *See, e.g.,* Karns v. Emerson Elec. Co., 817 F.2d 1452 (10th Cir. 1987) (applying Oklahoma law).

tested artificial jaw implants that caused severe pain and debilitating permanent damage to facial and skull bones when the Teflon® disintegrated. DuPont had feared this might happen, and had in fact warned the surgeons who experimented with this technique that its product had never been tested, and was neither warranted nor approved, for this surgical use. DuPont largely escaped liability for failure to pass this warning to surgery patients. The sole duty to warn belonged to the surgeon, courts held.[48]

C. When

Obviously, if a warning is required it is normally required before or during sale. A warning transmitted after sale is possibly too late to be of use—and of course an effective warning might preclude any sale at all, the purchaser being unwilling to confront the risk once he is made aware of it.

What if a danger is not known to anyone at the time of sale, but becomes known to a manufacturer or downstream seller subsequently? A manufacturer does not have a general duty to retrofit old products when *new designs* become available: old cars need not be refitted with airbags now that these are technologically feasible.[49] But what of *newly discovered dangers*? If the manufacturer or seller can easily warn the consumer of these dangers, must it do so to avoid liability for subsequent injuries? Similarly, what if a risky design characteristic in the product, unavoidable at the time of manufacture, is now known and avoidable? Is the seller's duty to now warn of this design characteristic? Is liability for failure to warn part of a misrepresentation doctrine that applies only once, at the moment of sale, or would a manufacturer owe a continuing duty to users to provide cheaply available information that might save life or limb?

The *Restatement (Third)* covers this eventuality in language that, again, is reminiscent of negligence:

§ 10. Liability Of Commercial Product Seller Or Distributor For Harm Caused By Post–Sale Failure To Warn

(a) One engaged in the business of selling or otherwise distributing products is subject to liability for harm to persons or property caused by the seller's failure to provide a warning after the time of sale or distribution of a product *if a reasonable person* in the seller's position would provide such a warning.

(b) A reasonable person in the seller's position would provide a warning after the time of sale if:

---

48. *See, e.g.,* In re TMJ Implants Products Liability Litig., 872 F.Supp. 1019 (D. Minn. 1995).

49. *See, e.g.,* Ostendorf v. Clark Equip. Co., 122 S.W.3d 530 (Ky. 2003).

(1) the seller knows or reasonably should know that the product poses a substantial risk of harm to persons or property; and

(2) those to whom a warning might be provided can be identified and can reasonably be assumed to be unaware of the risk of harm; and

(3) a warning can be effectively communicated to and acted on by those to whom a warning might be provided; and

(4) the risk of harm is sufficiently great to justify the burden of providing a warning.

Several cases prior to the publication of the *Restatement (Third)* resulted in liability for failure to issue a post-sale warning.[50] The publication of § 10 and the use of overt negligence principles will likely exacerbate this movement.[51]

4.   Special Case: Prescription Drugs

A.   General Principles

In some countries, prescriptions are optional for the purchase of all ethical drugs.[52] In the United States this was once the case. Today, many ethical drugs may only be acquired after consultation with a medical practitioner who counsels their use. In addition, these drugs must have been approved for use by the FDA, though they need not be approved for the condition for which the medical practitioner prescribes them.[53] As is the case for many other products, approved drugs have unwanted side effects, some but not all of which can be prevented in advance through warnings.

---

50. *See, e.g.,* LaBelle v. McCauley Indus. Corp., 649 F.2d 46 (1st Cir. 1981) (manufacturer's duty to warn of a defect or dangerous condition in an airplane propeller extended to the purchaser of its product, even if the defects were discovered after the initial sale); Patton v. TIC United Corp., 859 F.Supp. 509 (D. Kan. 1994) (punitive damages warranted for failure to issue post-sale warning about newly discovered danger in previously sold cultivator); Walton v. Avco Corp., 610 A.2d 454 (Pa. 1992) (helicopter manufacturer had independent duty to warn of defect in engine, derived from its knowledge of the defect communicated by the engine manufacturer).

51. *See, e.g.,* Brown v. Crown Equip. Corp., 501 F.3d 75 (1st Cir. 2007) (Maine courts did not adopt the rule of *Restatement (Third)* § 10 but held, regardless, that a post-sale duty to warn existed under a straightforward negligence theory); Stanger v. Smith & Nephew, Inc., 401 F. Supp. 2d 974 (E.D. Mo. 2005) (holding there is no strong indication that the Missouri Supreme Court would adopt the *Restatement (Third)*, defendant is liable for post-sale failure to warn of a new discovery that a knee implant had only a five year shelf life).

52. These countries include India, Egypt, Turkey and Mexico. *See* Joanne Christie, *No prescription, no problem*, THE GUARDIAN WEEKLY, Dec. 20, 2007.

53. *See* Michael I. Krauss, *Loosening the Food and Drug Administration's Drug Certification Monopoly: Implications for Tort Law and Consumer Welfare*, 4 GEO. MASON L. REV. 457 (1996).

The unusual regulatory régime for prescription drugs has had implications for products liability law. The *Restatement Second, Torts* § 402A, comment k, provides that ethical drugs, vaccines, and the like are exempt from design defect strict liability as "unavoidably unsafe products."[54] An unavoidably unsafe product may be shielded under Comment k, despite its danger, when it is accompanied by proper directions and warnings. But to whom should these warnings be communicated?

The basic rule for prescription drugs is that the warnings need not be communicated to the patient. The reasoning behind this rule is that the physician is a *learned intermediary* between the manufacturer and the consumer of a prescription drug. Thus, as a general matter, manufacturers must provide detailed warnings to physicians, who are liable (not as product sellers, but under negligence-based medical malpractice law) to reasonably transmit and tailor warnings to their patients. One influential judge put it this way:

> We cannot quarrel with the general proposition that where prescription drugs are concerned, the manufacturer's duty to warn is limited to an obligation to advise the prescribing physician of any potential dangers that may result from the drug's use. This special standard for prescription drugs is an understandable exception to the *Restatement's* general rule that one who markets goods must warn foreseeable ultimate users of dangers inherent in his products. See *Restatement (Second) of Torts, Section 388 (1965)*. Prescription drugs are likely to be complex medicines, esoteric in formula and varied

54. RESTATEMENT (SECOND) OF TORTS § 402A cmt. k (1965) *Unavoidably unsafe products*. There are some products which, in the present state of human knowledge, are quite incapable of being made safe for their intended and ordinary use. These are especially common in the field of drugs. An outstanding example is the vaccine for the Pasteur treatment of rabies, which not uncommonly leads to very serious and damaging consequences when it is injected. Since the disease itself invariably leads to a dreadful death, both the marketing and the use of the vaccine are fully justified, notwithstanding the unavoidable high degree of risk which they involve. Such a product, properly prepared, and accompanied by proper directions and warning, is not defective, nor is it unreasonably dangerous. The same is true of many other drugs, vaccines, and the like, many of which for this very reason cannot legally be sold except to physicians, or under the prescription of a physician. It is also true in particular of many new or experimental drugs as to which, because of lack of time and opportunity for sufficient medical experience, there can be no assurance of safety, or perhaps even of purity of ingredients, but such experience as there is justifies the marketing and use of the drug notwithstanding a medically recognizable risk. The seller of such products, again with the qualification that they are properly prepared and marketed, and proper <u>warning is given, where the situation calls for it</u>, is not to be held to strict liability for unfortunate consequences attending their use, merely because he has undertaken to supply the public with an apparently useful and desirable product, attended with a known but apparently reasonable risk." (emphasis added).

in effect. As a medical expert, the prescribing physician can take into account the propensities of the drug, as well as the susceptibilities of his patient. His is the task of weighing the benefits of any medication against its potential dangers. The choice he makes is an informed one, an individualized medical judgment bottomed on a knowledge of both patient and palliative. Pharmaceutical companies then, who must warn ultimate purchasers of dangers inherent in patent drugs sold over the counter, in selling prescription drugs are required to warn only the prescribing physician, who acts as a 'learned intermediary' between manufacturer and consumer."[55]

To successfully sue a pharmaceutical manufacturer for failure to warn, therefore, the plaintiff must produce evidence that the manufacturer communicated an insufficient warning to the patient's physician. A few examples serve as useful illustrations.

- In *McNeil v. Wyeth*,[56] a physician prescribed Reglan® to treat plaintiff's gastroesophageal reflux disease symptoms. The prescription was for six months, though the Food and Drug Administration had approved the drug only for no more than twelve weeks use. Thereafter, a second doctor continued McNeil's prescription for six months, then a third doctor for two more months. The clinical pharmacology section of Reglan's FDA-approved label explains that, like other drugs for this purpose, Reglan "may produce extrapyramidal reactions, although these are comparatively rare." One such reaction, tardive dyskinesia is characterized by grotesque involuntary movements of the mouth, tongue, lips, and extremities, involuntary chewing movements, and a general sense of agitation. The plaintiff developed tardive dyskinesia after fourteen months' use of Reglan, and sued Wyeth for failure to adequately warn of this. Wyeth moved for summary judgment, which the trial court granted, concluding that the Reglan label was "adequate as a matter of law" because it "specifically mentions the circumstances complained of...."

The Circuit Court of Appeals reversed and sent the case back for jury trial. Plaintiff had presented evidence that long-term prescription of Reglan was common, and that Wyeth was aware of this practice. Because Wyeth advertised that the risk of developing EPS is "comparatively rare," 0.2 percent for short-term use, merely noting that the risk is "higher" for long-term

---

55. Reyes v. Wyeth Labs., 498 F.2d 1264, 1276 (5th Cir. 1974) (Wisdom, J.) (applying Texas law) (footnotes omitted).

56. McNeil v. Wyeth, 462 F.3d 364 (5th Cir. 2006) (applying Texas law).

use would not put physicians on notice that certain studies have found that the risk could be one hundred times higher.

- When a name-brand drug goes "off-patent," and generic manufacturers produce the same chemical composition, are they shielded if they use the same warning as had been used by the name-brand manufacturer? If this warning is found to have been inadequate, the fact that the name-brand manufacturer had used it will not shield the generic drug-maker.[57] What if the FDA had declined to require the inclusion, in the name-brand or generic drug, of the warning the plaintiff deems to have been required by products liability law? That question is dealt with in Chapter 10 below.[58]

- For certain prescription drugs, such as contraceptive pills, regulations promulgated by the FDA require warnings to be given directly to consumers. In such cases, the content of the warning to the consumer will be examined as an exception to the learned intermediary doctrine.[59]

- Where an ethical drug's side effect injures a third party (for example, if drowsiness is a side effect, and a driver injures a third party after having consumed the drug), there is generally held to be no duty to warn the third party, who is neither a user nor a consumer of the drug, both under the "learned intermediary doctrine" and on proximate causation grounds.[60]

- Where a fatal side effect of a prescription drug is discovered only after the drug is on the market, leading to the drug's recall, the manufacturer has a duty to take all reasonable steps to notify individual patients, not merely physicians, of the danger and of the recall, since many patients fail to communicate with their physicians.[61]

- Finally, where a drug is administered in a mass immunization program, without the participation of physicians, many courts decline to apply the learned intermediary doctrine.[62] Since it is virtually impossible for manufacturers to communicate individually with each person vaccinated in a mass clinic setting (many will be illiterate and unable to read pre-printed sheets, etc.) and since public health authorities may

57. *See, e.g.,* Dorsett v. Sandoz, Inc., 699 F.Supp.2d 1142 (C.D. Cal. 2010).

58. *See* Chapter 10 *infra.*

59. *See, e.g.,* Lindsay v. Ortho Pharm. Corp., 637 F.2d 87 (2d Cir. 1980) (applying New York law).

60. *See, e.g.,* Gourdine v. Crews, 955 A.2d 769 (Md. 2008).

61. Nichols v. McNeilab, Inc., 850 F.Supp. 562 (E.D. Mich. 1993) (fatal allergic reaction to a pill prescribed for menstrual pain).

62. *See, e.g.,* Reyes v. Wyeth Labs., 498 F.2d 1264 (5th Cir. 1974) (applying Texas law); Allison v. Merck & Co., 878 P.2d 948 (Nev. 1994).

have chosen risky vaccines with full knowledge of risks,[63] liability holdings such as these arguably were a moving force behind the no-fault vaccine liability system summarized below.

B. The Impact of Mass Marketing of Prescription Drugs

No one with a television set is unaware of the fact that prescription drugs may be legally marketed to the general public. The *Restatement (Third)*, which retains the learned intermediary rule,[64] suggests that direct marketing might forfeit the manufacturer's ability to invoke the learned intermediary doctrine.[65] Manufacturers must, in other words, communicate warnings directly to consumers to whom they market the drug. Today, thirty-or sixty-second ads have carefully crafted warnings mixed in with praise for the benefits of the drug.

In *Perez v. Wyeth Laboratories, Inc.*[66] the New Jersey Supreme Court held that the learned intermediary doctrine did not shield a manufacturer that had warned physicians of the risks of the Norplant contraceptive device, while failing to reveal important side effects of Norplant in its voluminous marketing in women's magazines. Other cases have declined to follow *Perez*.[67] Even recent New Jersey caselaw indicates that only active concealment or positive misstatement of risks in a mass advertisement would result in liability.[68]

As this Book goes to press, over 1,000 lawsuits have been filed against Bayer HealthCare claiming health risks from Yasmin® and Yaz® birth control pills.[69] These "fourth-generation" contraceptives contain estrogen and another progestin, drospirenone. The drugs

---

63. Public health authorities selected Sabin (live) polio vaccine for many years because of its "vicarious immunization" effects, even though they knew that this would result in some people (mostly, but not exclusively, mothers of immunized infants) acquiring the disease. The Salk (killed) vaccine presented no risk to third parties, but only immunized those vaccinated. Who, as between health authorities and the manufacturer of the Sabin vaccine, should be liable when an innocent third party gets polio from the vaccine? The answer is clear.

64. RESTATEMENT (THIRD) OF TORTS, PRODUCTS LIABILITY § 6(d). (1998).

65. RESTATEMENT (THIRD) OF TORTS, PRODUCTS LIABILITY § 6 cmt. e (1998) (Council Draft No. 1A 1994).

66. Perez v. Wyeth Labs., Inc., 734 A.2d 1245 (N.J. 1999).

67. *See, e.g.*, In re Norplant Contraceptive, 215 F. Supp. 2d 795 (E.D. Tex. 2002). (granting summary judgment for defendant on claims of failing-to-warn consumers directly for all states, except New Jersey)*; see also* Aaron Twerski, *Liability for Direct Advertising of Drugs to Consumers: An Idea Whose Time Has Not Come*, 33 HOFSTRA L. REV. 1149 (2005).

68. McDarby v. Merck & Co., Inc., 949 A.2d 223 (N.J. App.Div. 2008).

69. Tammy Worth, *Birth control pill concerns bring lawsuits but few solid answers*, L.A. TIMES, April 19, 2010, A1, *available at* http://www.latimes.com/features/health/la-he-yaz–20100419,0,2851244.story (last consulted April 20, 2010).

were created not just to prevent pregnancy but to also reduce the side effects of other contraceptive pills, and to treat acne and acute premenstrual disorders (severe cases of depression, anxiety, headaches and other symptoms). Yaz® especially was heavily marketed to consumers and is the most widely sold oral contraceptive in the country.

The suits all claim that drospirenone causes health problems including deep vein thrombosis (blood clots in the deep veins), strokes, heart attacks and gallbladder disease, and that Bayer insufficiently warned of these risks. Bayer received a warning from the FDA in 2009 for overstating Yaz®'s effectiveness in treating pre-menstrual syndrome (PMS) and acne while minimizing the risks of the medication on its website and television commercials. In response, the company altered its advertising, declining to tout any acne benefit and specifying that only premenstrual depression disorder (more severe than PMS) justifies Yaz®. Blood clots in Yaz users will continue to generate failure to warn lawsuits in the near term, however, for Bayer will not be able to prove that an affected user viewed the second, not the first, ad for Yaz®.

C. National Childhood Vaccine Injury Act ("NCVIA")

Pressure from parents (upset when their children, and sometimes the parents themselves, acquired a disease after a compulsory or recommended childhood vaccination) and from vaccine manufacturers (held liable under exceptions to the learned intermediary doctrine despite the absence of any negligence, with resulting adverse consequences for the availability of vaccines) strained our legal system after a seminal event in the 1970's.

On January 27 1976, an outbreak of flu was identified at Fort Dix, New Jersey. On February 4, after leaving his sick bed and making a forced, five-mile night march, Private David Lewis collapsed and died. On February 12 the Center for Disease Control ("CDC")'s influenza laboratory notified the CDC Director that swine influenza virus strain H1N1 had been isolated. One death, thirteen hospitalizations and up to 500 soldiers who apparently caught but resisted the disease led to fear of a massive epidemic.

President Ford recommended a mass immunization program, but vaccine manufacturers refused to produce the vaccine absent some guarantee they would not be held liable for side effects. To resolve the liability problem, legislation was passed in August 1976 under which the federal government assumed liability for personal injuries or death resulting from the swine flu vaccine. Ultimately, the H1N1 virus never reached our shores (with the bizarre exception of Fort Dix). Nevertheless, thousands of lawsuits for side effects were filed against the federal government, and 316 claims were settled for $12.3 million.[70] Then in the 1980s further production crises affecting the availability of the Diphtheria, Pertussis and Tetanus ("DPT") combination vaccine were caused by liability fears.

These events led Congress to create an insurance system for vaccine side effects. Under the *National Childhood Vaccine Injury Act of 1986*,[71] a Vaccine Injury Compensation Trust Fund was constituted with the proceeds of an excise tax on every dose of covered vaccine. (This tax is obviously built into the price of the vaccine, and constitutes in essence an insurance premium paid by each recipient.) If a named side effect of a covered vaccine occurs, payment is made from the fund without any need to prove negligence, failure to warn, etc. Compensation (which must be demanded in an action before the United States Court of Claims) includes up to $250,000 for a vaccine associated death, all past and future unreimbursed medical expenses, custodial and nursing home care, any lost earned income and up to $250,000 for pain and suffering. Claimants may turn down awards from the Court of Claims and sue manufacturers, but then they must prove products liability under the requirements discussed in this book.

Recently the Court of Claims (which, unlike common law courts, sits without a jury) rejected controversial demands for compensation for the costs of autism allegedly caused by the preservative thimerosal in DPT vaccines.[72] The court released 600 pages of findings rejecting the claim that thimerosal causes autism. Meanwhile, during the 2009 Swine Flu scare, upwards of 200 million doses of vaccine were produced. Out of every million people who get a flu shot, one or two will have a serious neurological reaction called Guillain–Barre syndrome (GBS)—and these will be compensated through the NCVIA. Other alleged side effects, that might otherwise have resulted in jury trials replete with expensive "Daubert" challenges of new causal claims,[73] will now likely be tried before the Court of Claims.

---

70. A few other plaintiffs obtained $900,000 more after trials.

71. 42 U.S.C. §§ 300AA–10 *et seq.*

72. Hazlehurst v. Secretary of Health and Human Services, 88 Fed. Cl. 473 (2009).

73. *See* Chapter 7 Section 3 *supra.*

Chapter 9

THE PLAINTIFF'S CASE: CAUSATION[1]

1. Introduction

Consider the following scenarios.

- A trespasser dives into an above ground pool, and breaks his neck when the hands he stretches out in front of him separate on the slippery liner. What caused the broken neck?[2]

- An aged agricultural worker contracts pulmonary fibrosis. Which of the many chemicals to which he was exposed over the course of his life was "the cause" of his disease? Or was his genetic makeup "the cause?"[3]

- A drunk driver exceeds the speed limit, loses control of his car and crashes into the wall of a building. He sues the manufacturer of his car, on the ground that because of its design he suffered too severe an injury from the crash. What caused his injury?[4]

The plaintiff in a products liability suit must produce evidence of "defect," a complex term that has been described in preceding chapters. But a defect alone is not enough to result in products liability. Rather, only the harm "thereby caused,"[5] or "caused by the defect,"[6] may be recovered. When a defect in a boiler blows the boiler up, and shrapnel injures the plaintiff, it is evident that the defect is the cause of the injury. But what if the defect, directly, "causes" nothing at all? Julian Felipe's mother's Aerostar's roof is not like an exploding boiler—the roof did not collapse on Julian from its own internal forces.

---

1. Additional Reading: Aaron Gershonowitz, *What Must Cause Injury In Products Liability?*, 62 IND. L.J. 701 (1986/1987).

2. O'Brien v. Muskin Corp., 463 A.2d 298 (N.J. 1983), discussed in Chapter 7, *supra*.

3. Ferebee v. Chevron Chem. Co., 736 F.2d 1529 (D.C. Cir. 1984).

4. Tunnell v. Ford Motor Co., 330 F. Supp. 2d 748 (W.D. Va. 2004).

5. RESTATEMENT (SECOND) OF TORTS § 402A (1965).

6. RESTATEMENT (THIRD) OF TORTS, PRODUCTS LIABILITY § 1 (1998).

128

As Julian Felipe's example illustrates, products liability presents unique and interesting causal issues, which this chapter examines.

2. Cause in Fact (Necessary Condition)

This Book uses causation terms in the way in which it is usually (but not always) employed. A "cause in fact" is a "necessary condition." Was the (manufacturing, design, or informational) defect a necessary condition of the plaintiff's harm? If the universe were exactly the same save for the lack of a defect, would the injury have happened anyway? A "proximate cause" is a cause in fact that is deemed closely enough connected with the plaintiff's injury.

Sometimes evidence of cause in fact will be conflated with evidence of the defect itself. Thus, in *Stewart v. Von Solbrig Hospital*,[7] a "Rush pin" was inserted into the tibia of the plaintiff's left leg following a fracture. Sometime later the pin broke while in the plaintiff's leg. Several operations and complications concerning the plaintiff's leg transpired after this break. The plaintiff alleged that these subsequent operations and complications were caused by the break in the pin and that a defect in the pin was the cause of the break. The defendant claimed overuse of the leg during convalescence caused the pin to break. If there is no defect, there is no causation—at trials like this one the evidence of defect and of causation will be practically conflated.[8]

Conceptually the two notions remain distinct. Thus, proof that there is cause in fact, i.e., that an injury would not have occurred had the product been designed differently, is not sufficient to establish that the product has a design *defect*. Products are not defective just because they were not designed to prevent the precise injury that actually happened. Often the defense will concede cause in fact and argue that the product is not defective.[9] Understanding the concepts helps determine an effective trial strategy.

A. Whodunit?

In negligence law, if plaintiff proves merely that defendant was driving while drunk and that plaintiff was struck by a drunk driver, plaintiff's tort suit will be dismissed. For it is necessary to prove that defendant (not some other drunk driver) struck plaintiff. Proving negligence alone is insufficient. Similarly, in products liability cases, the plaintiff must produce evidence that it was

---

7. Stewart v. Von Solbrig Hosp., 321 N.E.2d 428 (Ill. App. 1974).

8. It is possible that there is a defect and no causation, in that the overuse would have caused even a non-defective "Rush pin" to break.

9. *See, e.g.,* Jones v. Hutchinson Mfg., Inc., 502 S.W.2d 66 (Ky. 1973) (grain auger "swallows" minor child, yet design is still not defective).

defendant's (defective) product that caused her injury. If the injury was caused by someone else's product, defendant is not liable even if defendant's product was defective.

Usually this is a cause-in-fact issue—the defect in the defendant's product was not a necessary condition of the plaintiff's injuries from some other source. But sometimes this is a proximate cause issue. The following examples illustrate both kinds of situations:

- In *Powell v. Standard Brands Paint Co.,*[10] plaintiff used defendant's lacquer thinner to remove a sealer from a tile floor. The next day, he finished the project with another brand, then used an electric buffer. An explosion followed. The defendant's thinner had not warned of the risk, but the second thinner did contain an adequate warning. Plaintiff, having read the first label, thought himself instructed on proper use and did not bother to read the label on the second product. The Court, deciding the matter as an issue of proximate cause, held that the explosion of the second product was not a reasonably foreseeable consequence of Standard Brands' failure to warn on its own label, and that "the manufacturer's duty is restricted to warnings based on the characteristics of the manufacturer's own products."[11] In *obiter dictum*, the Court entertained the possibility of liability if the defendant's product had been chemically identical to the product that caused injury and if *none* of the manufacturers provided a warning.[12] But if the products are generic *and the second manufacturer provided adequate warnings,* should plaintiff's suit fail on causation grounds?

- In *Foster v. American Home Products Corp.,*[13] a plaintiff died after consuming a generic drug. Suit was filed against the name-brand manufacturer on the grounds that the manufacturer's label, which plaintiff claimed contained an inadequate warning, had been copied by the generic manufacturer. Summary judgment to the name-brand manufacturer was granted and confirmed on appeal. There was no need to decide the question of the adequacy of the warning, the court held, since in any case the generic drug, not defendant's product, harmed plaintiff. But in *Conte v. Wyeth, Inc.,*[14] it was held that if the name brand prescription drug manufacturer inadequately warns a physician who subsequently pre-

---

10. Powell v. Standard Brands Paint Co., 212 Cal.Rptr. 395 (Cal. App. 1985).

11. *Id.* at 398.

12. *Id.* at 399.

13. Foster v. American Home Prods. Corp., 29 F.3d 165 (4th Cir.1994) (applying Maryland law).

14. Conte v. Wyeth, Inc., 85 Cal. Rptr.3d 299 (Cal. App. 2008).

scribes the drug to a patient for whom it is dangerous, causation is satisfied even if the patient receives a generic form of the drug. *Conte* has been criticized on causation grounds.[15] One court wrote that,

> "*Conte* is the lone outlier against the overwhelming weight of authority on this point. As of the date of the summary-judgment hearing here, thirty-four decisions had applied the laws of twenty different states to hold that name brand manufacturers are not liable for injuries caused by generic products... No case before or after *Conte* has agreed with its reasoning."[16]

- In *Brown v. Stone Mfg. Co.*,[17] plaintiff claimed that the design of defendant's nightgown was defectively flammable,[18] injuring her daughter. The nightgown was destroyed in a fire, and the store where the nightgown was purchased sold models from several different manufacturers. Who made the nightgown worn by plaintiff's daughter? The victim testified that the nightgown she wore was "sort of like" defendant's model, but the washing directions remembered by the mother differed from those on defendant's gown. The trial judge refused to let this case go to the jury, on the grounds that it would have to speculate about whether the right defendant was being held liable.

- In every state save Washington, Wisconsin, Michigan and New York, one may not sue all manufacturers of a generic product for an alleged design defect in the particular product that injured plaintiff. "Market share liability," which would allow plaintiffs to waive the obligation to prove that a products liability defendant actually produced the product that injured the plaintiff, is generally not accepted.[19]

B. Why Did It Happen?

As mentioned above, liability does not result merely because the plaintiff has proved that the defendant's product (as opposed to another product) caused her injury. Rather, it must be that the *defect* in the defendant's product caused the injury. If an automo-

15. *See, e.g.*, Mensing v. Wyeth, Inc., 588 F.3d 603, 613 (8th Cir. 2009) (applying Minnesota law).

16. Dietrich v. Wyeth, Inc., 2009 WL 4924722 (Fla. Cir. Ct., Dec. 21, 2009).

17. Brown v. Stone Mfg. Co., 660 F.Supp. 454 (S.D. Miss. 1986).

18. Or is it inflammable? See *supra*, Chapter 8.

19. *See, e.g.*, Kurczi v. Eli Lilly & Co., 113 F.3d 1426, 1434–35 (6th Cir. 1997) (holding that under Ohio law the theory of market share liability, or a plaintiff not demonstrating which defendant manufactured the DES, only that they had a substantial share of the market, was not applicable to a lawsuit based on exposure to DES). See also Chapter 14, *infra*, for a discussion of DES mass products liability suits.

bile has a defective roof, but the victim was killed by the crash before the vehicle rolled over, there is no cause in fact.

1). *Causation and Manufacturing and Design Defects*

The connection between the defect and the injury is often the focus of expert testimony and *Daubert* debates[20] at trial. Plaintiff attempts to introduce expert testimony causally linking the defect and the injury. Defendant's expert claims that the defect was foreign to the damage sustained, and typically attributes the damage to some other cause. Note that if plaintiff alleges that a product contains several defects, plaintiff's experts may disagree about which of the defects caused the injury. Despite this disagreement plaintiff will have satisfied his burden of production of evidence of causation, allowing the jury to determine which (if any) defect caused the harm.[21] Similarly, if plaintiff testifies non-speculatively[22] that defendant's defective product caused plaintiff's injury, while defendant's expert opines that the damage was caused by a competitor's product, plaintiff has satisfied his burden of production and the jury gets to decide whom to believe.[23]

It is often difficult to "reverse engineer" an accident to find a defect. If, for instance, the product has been consumed by fire or detonation, the cost of finding the defect might be prohibitive. Should *res ipsa loquitur* be available to prove causation in such instances? In negligence law, if most occurrences of an accident result from negligence, then the occurrence of the accident itself shifts the burden of proof on negligence to the defendant.[24] In products cases, can one hold that a particular kind of malfunction was, as a statistical matter, likely caused by a defect and not by some other cause (consumer misuse, tampering by a third party, etc.)?

The *Restatement (Third)* deals with this issue as one of circumstantial evidence of defect:

> **§ 3. Circumstantial Evidence Supporting Inference Of Product Defect**
>
> It may be inferred that the harm sustained by the plaintiff was caused by a product defect existing at the time of sale or

---

20. See Chapter 7 for a discussion of *Daubert*.

21. *See, e.g.*, Henderson v. Sunbeam Corp., 46 F.3d 1151 (10th Cir. 1995) (applying Oklahoma law).

22. *See* Brown v. Stone Mfg. Co., *supra* note 17.

23. *See, e.g.*, Speller v. Sears, Roebuck & Co., 790 N.E.2d 252 (N.Y. 2003).

24. Byrne v. Boadle, 159 Eng. Rep. 299 (Exch. 1863) (holding that where an accident is of the type that does not ordinarily occur in the absence of negligence, negligence may be presumed). In *Byrne* the plaintiff was walking by a flour shop when a barrel fell out of a window and injured plaintiff. *Id.* The court found the defendant negligent because the barrel was in the defendant's possession and the accident could not transpire absent negligence. *Id.*

distribution, without proof of a specific defect, when the incident that harmed the plaintiff:

(a) was of a kind that ordinarily occurs as a result of product defect; and

(b) was not, in the particular case, solely the result of causes other than product defect existing at the time of sale or distribution.

In some cases, establishing the elements of paragraph (a) will be sufficient to shift the burden of proof to defendant as regards paragraph (b). Thus, if witnesses on the ground see both wings suddenly and unexpectedly fall off a new aircraft, plaintiff will be able to invoke paragraph (a) to infer that the crash was caused by a manufacturing defect (e.g., welding on this plane only) or a design defect (e.g., weakness of wing structure for the entire model run). Presumably, the older the product the weaker this inference will be, and at some point a judge will declare that plaintiff needs to produce actual evidence of defect at the factory. Even for new products the inference is rebuttable (e.g., defendant will be allowed to produce evidence that both wings of the new plane were shot off by a surface-to-air missile).

It is often the case that evidence of defect itself makes causation plausible. In *Sanchez v. Hillerich & Bradsby Co.*,[25] a college baseball pitcher suffered serious injuries when struck by a line drive hit by a player using a new model of aluminum bat. The pitcher sued the bat manufacturer, alleging the bat's design significantly increased the risk that a pitcher would be hit by a line drive. The manufacturer obtained summary judgment based in part on the pitcher's inability to prove causation (the speed at which the ball was travelling could not be determined, obviously). The appellate court reversed, ruling that it was sufficient that the plaintiff establish that the particular model of aluminum bat was defective because it significantly increased the speed of a hit ball.[26] The jury could then determine whether that defect caused this particular injury or not.

2). *Causation and Informational Defects*

Special considerations apply when the alleged defect is neither of design nor of manufacture. When the allegation is one of *failure to warn*, plaintiff must prove that the absence or inadequacy of the warning caused plaintiff's injury. This requires proving that a warning would have been read and followed. Often such evidence consists of plaintiff's sworn testimony that he always reads warnings and would have read and complied with an adequate warning

25. Hillerich & Bradsby Co., 128 Cal.Rptr.2d 529 (Cal. App. 2002).

26. *Id.* at 533.

had one been provided. Many jurisdictions declare that there is a rebuttable "read and heed" presumption to this effect—but in practice plaintiffs will still wish to tell jurors that they always read warnings assiduously.

Such testimony is often hard to rebut. Typically courts rule that the witness's self-interest affects the credibility of her evidence, not its admissibility. In rare instances, however, plaintiff's behavior leads courts to conclude that the plaintiff lacks any "basis" for his statement that he would have read and complied with a warning had one been given. Thus, in *Van Dike v. AMF, Inc.*[27] plaintiff was seriously injured when he unsuccessfully attempted to perform a double back somersault on a trampoline owned by friends. He sued the manufacturer on the ground that the trampoline should have contained the following label:

> "WARNING–CRIPPLING INJURIES CAN OCCUR DURING SOMERSAULTS. Somersaulting should never be attempted without an overhead safety harness operated by a trained instructor. Refer to instruction manual. Almost all the benefits and enjoyment of the Trampoline can be obtained by learning the non-somersaulting, twisting skills and routines provided in the manual furnished with this Trampoline.

> "Any activity involving motion or height creates the possibility of accidental injury. This equipment is intended for use ONLY by properly trained and qualified participants under supervised conditions. Use without proper supervision could be DANGEROUS and should NOT be undertaken or permitted. Before using, KNOW YOUR OWN LIMITATIONS and the limitations of this equipment. If in doubt, always consult your instructor.

> "Always inspect for loose fittings or damage and test stability before each use."

Plaintiff testified that had this label been on the trampoline he never would have attempted a double back somersault. He admitted, however, that he had *not* read the following label that *was* on the trampoline:

> "CAUTION

> "Misuse and abuse of this trampoline is dangerous and can cause serious injuries.

> "Read instructions before using this trampoline.

> "Inspect before using and replace any worn, defective or missing parts.

> "Any activity involving motion or height creates the possibility of accidental injuries. This unit is intended for use only by

27. Van Dike v. AMF, Inc., 379 N.W.2d 412 (Mich. App. 1985).

properly trained and qualified participants under supervised conditions. Use without proper supervision could be dangerous and should not be undertaken or permitted."

Plaintiff insisted that even had he read this label he would have performed the somersault, because the label contained no specific warning about this activity. Defendant objected to this testimony as speculative. This interesting exchange then ensued between the judge and the plaintiff, outside the presence of the jury:

"THE COURT: I thought you just indicated that, prior to getting on the trampoline to do your double back somersault, you didn't see any label. Is that correct or not correct?

"THE WITNESS: [Plaintiff] That is correct.

"THE COURT: At this time, you seem to be saying that, if the label that has 'WARNING' on it was on there instead of the one that has 'CAUTION' written on it, it is your opinion you would have seen it.

"THE WITNESS: Yes.

"THE COURT: Why do you think you would have seen the one that says 'WARNING' on it and not seen the one that says 'CAUTION' on it, particularly in light of the fact that 'CAU-TION' is about twice, if not more times, bigger than the word 'WARNING'?

"THE WITNESS: Well, possibly subconsciously I may even have seen the 'CAUTION' one, but the 'WARNING' one, when you see something like that, it grabs your attention. You see it, and it registers, and you look at it. The other one, I didn't even know that one meant for a user or anything. It could have meant for shipping purposes or anything. I know I didn't see it."

The judge refused to allow plaintiff to testify that he would have read his suggested warning when he did not read the warning that was on the device. Note, however, that had plaintiff claimed that the existing warning was *too small* (as opposed to too vague), he would have been able to testify that he would have noticed and read a more prominent warning.[28]

An additional causal wrinkle in some failure to warn cases involves defects in products other than the one sold by the defendant. Thus, in *Garman v. Magic Chef, Inc.*,[29] plaintiffs purchased a

---

28. *See, e.g.,* Johnson v. Johnson Chem. Co., Inc., 588 N.Y.S.2d 607 (N.Y. App. 1992) (warning on roach spray not read, but alleged to be both too vague and insufficiently prominent).

29. Garman v. Magic Chef, Inc., 173 Cal.Rptr. 20 (Cal. App. 1981).

motor home with a propane gas system. About two weeks later while at a rest stop, appellant's wife lit the stove to make soup. Approximately five minutes later an explosion and fire occurred. A copper tube extended from the propane gas tank upwards to a point where it flared out in two directions. One branch of the tubing extended to the gas stove, which was not defective in manufacture or design, while the other extended to the gas hot water heater. The branch of tubing that extended to the hot water heater separated at its attachment to the T-joint permitting propane gas to leak out and form a pool of flammable vapor. The flame on the stove, when lit by the victim, provided a source of ignition for the leaking gas.

The stove manufacturer was sued for having failed to warn that a properly operating stove might nonetheless ignite gas leaking from some other place in the home. Noting that, even had such a warning existed and been read, the fire could just as easily have happened as a result of lighting a cigarette, the court granted summary judgment to the stove manufacturer.

C. When Did the Defect Get Introduced?

Showing that a product failed, with catastrophic results, is not the same as showing that it was defective when it left the defendant's hands. For the failure might be the result of normal wear and tear, for instance—a product that deteriorates over time, becoming less safe, is not for that reason a defective product. Nor is there any reason to warn that a product will deteriorate over time, as this is obvious and there is no need to warn of obvious dangers. As mentioned above, and as implied by the *Restatement (Third),* § 3(b), the older a product gets, *ceteris paribus*, the harder it will be to produce credible evidence that its defect was present before defendant sold it.

In such cases courts may claim that plaintiff failed to establish causation. That is sloppy language. What such rulings *mean* is that plaintiff failed to produce evidence of any defect attributable to the defendant. The plaintiff must ensure that his evidence either directly or inferentially establishes that the alleged defect existed at the relevant time.

Thus, in *Nissan Motor Co. Ltd. v. Armstrong*,[30] plaintiff's parents purchased a 1986 Nissan 300ZX in January 1986, then transferred the car to plaintiff five years later with more than 90,000 miles on the odometer. On a rainy day in October 1992, immediately after resigning from her job, plaintiff got into her car and shifted into reverse. After she allegedly "barely touched" the accelerator, the car "took off" backwards and hit a brick building,

30. Nissan Motor Co. Ltd. v. Armstrong, 145 S.W.3d 131 (Tex. 2004)

though she claimed to be pressing the brake pedal as hard as she could. When she shifted into drive and again allegedly "barely touched" the accelerator, the car "shot forward" and this time struck a telephone pole, again despite alleged application of the brakes. These collisions resulted in two broken bones in her foot and nerve damage, injuries the jury assessed at $900,000 in their verdict against Nissan. On appeal, the jury verdict was quashed, as the existence or non-existence of a defect when the vehicle left Nissan's possession had not been established. Chapter 10 discusses this further.[31]

D. "Substantial Factor" Cause-in-fact

If Smith's negligence, Jones's negligence, and Robinson's negligence all combine to cause harm (imagine that all three lose control of their cars, which ram into the victim's car at the same moment, killing the victim), it is impossible to know how much of the indivisible damage was caused by each defendant. In such cases, liability of all three defendants is "joint and several" (that is, each is liable for the entire damage caused) under common law.

Thus, in *Mavroudis v. Pittsburgh–Corning Corp.*,[32] plaintiff had contracted mesothelioma while working for the U.S. Navy, from his exposure to products (stipulated at this juncture to be defective) containing asbestos. He could not single out which manufacturer's product caused his injury, but his exposure to the asbestos-containing products of each of the several defendants alone would have been sufficient to cause the illness, according to his physicians. The court concluded that this is exactly the situation that calls for application of the substantial factor test, "in order that no supplier enjoy a causation defense solely on the ground that the plaintiff probably would have suffered the same disease from inhaling fibers originating from the products of other suppliers."[33] Because mesothelioma (unlike asbestosis[34]) can result from even short-term expo-

31. See Chapter 10 Section 3 *infra.*

32. Mavroudis v. Pittsburgh–Corning Corp., 935 P.2d 684 (Wash. App. 1997).

33. *Id.* at 689; *see also* In re Methyl Tertiary Butyl Ether (MTBE) Products Liability Litigation, 379 F. Supp. 2d 348 (S.D.N.Y. 2005).

34. Mesothelioma, unlike asbestosis, can develop from infrequent exposure to a relatively small amount of asbestos. Mesothelioma, also known as asbestos cancer, is similar to other types of cancers: tumors grow in the mesothelium, the lining that encloses the inside of the body. Asbestosis is a non-cancer illness that requires prolonged exposure to asbestos fibers. The fibers are inhaled and are able to travel deep into the lungs, embedding themselves within the alveoli, the air sacs that handle daily oxygen intake. The body recognizes them as foreign bodies and tries to expel them, activating an immune response. However, the asbestos fibers become lodged and the body cannot remove them. The body's immune response creates an inflammation that eventually results in scar tissue in the inner walls of the lungs. This condition leads to shortness of breath that comes on gradually and typically worsens during exercise.

sure to asbestos, the "substantial factor" test can result in joint liability for multiple producers and distributors of asbestos and of products containing asbestos.[35]

Similarly, when a father negligently buckles up his child in a defective child seat, and the child is incapacitated for life after a collision (evidence indicating that damages would not have been so severe had the seat not been defective), the seat manufacturer is liable to the child as a "substantial factor" of the child's its entire injury, even if the father's negligence caused the collision.[36]

Beware, though: concurrent tort is not the same as alternate tort! Plaintiff attempted in vain to invoke "substantial factor" analysis in *McLaughlin v. Acme Pallet Co.*,[37] which involved a worker injured when a pallet broke and buckets of joint compound fell on him. Plaintiff sued two pallet distributors, one of whom had supplied the pallet that injured him. Plaintiff's theory was that the injurious pallet must have contained a manufacturing flaw. The pallet had been destroyed[38] after the accident, preventing anyone from identifying its manufacturer. Plaintiff sought to use the theory of alternative liability,[39] but the court would have none of it, and granted defendant distributors' motion for summary judgment, because,

> "[n]either of the Restatement's requirements have been satisfied by plaintiffs .... Because this is a manufacturing defect case, *either* [defendant] acted tortiously, *not both*. Thus, there was no justification to join both."[40]

3. Proximate Causation

A. Introduction

Should it be sufficient for liability that a product defect was a cause in fact of plaintiff's injury? We know that in basic negligence doctrine, the combination of wrongdoing and cause in fact is not sufficient for liability. Thus:

- If Dr. X negligently misperforms a tubal ligation on Y, with the result that Y gives birth to Z ten months later, and if Z drives negligently eighteen years hence, injuring A, X is not

---

35. *See, e.g.*, Buttitta v. Allied Signal, Inc. et al., 2010 WL 1427273 (N.J. App. 2010) (among those held liable for plaintiff's mesothelioma was General Motors, where plaintiff's father worked on brake pads containing asbestos, raising the possibility that the father had brought home asbestos dust from the workplace).

36. Farr v. Evenflo Co., Inc., 705 N.W.2d 905 (Wis. App. 2005).

37. McLaughlin v. Acme Pallet Co., 658 A.2d 1314 (N.J. App. 1995).

38. See Chapter 5 *supra* for a discussion of employer's moral hazard in workers' compensation cases.

39. Summers v. Tice, 199 P.2d 1 (Cal. 1948).

40. *McLaughlin*, 658 A.2d at 1316.

liable to compensate A for her damages, notwithstanding the fact that X's negligence was a cause in fact of A's injuries.

- If X negligently injures Y, who is airlifted to another city for emergency surgery, and who is struck by a bus while exiting the hospital after the successful surgery, X is not liable for Y's bus injuries, notwithstanding the fact that X's negligence was a cause in fact.

Any injury has many causes in fact. What if one of those causes in fact is a product defect, which intervenes with other causes in fact (such as product misuse)? Should the rules of proximate causation determine *which* cause in fact results in liability, or, as some have argued,[41] should the advent of strict liability for products relax legal standards of causation?

As mentioned above, many cases that discuss "proximate cause" are in reality cases about the existence or non-existence of a defect. If an industrial meat grinder injures a child operator, the court may declare that it refuses to allow the case to the jury on "proximate cause" grounds (the child's use was "unforeseeable"; the parent's negligence was "superseding," etc.), but this is sloppy language. What it *means* is that the grinder, meant for adult use, was not "defective" merely because it was not child-proof.[42] Conversely, if a power mower propels a stone one hundred feet into a passerby's eye, the mower manufacturer's claim that the event was unforeseeable (because the manufacturer had warned against mowing with "anyone in the area") may be camouflage designed to hide the fact that the design of the mower is defective and unreasonably dangerous if it allows such propulsion to occur.[43] Finally, if a drug manufacturer warns a physician that a prescribed drug may not be used with alcohol, but the physician negligently fails to transmit this warning to the patient, with fatal results, a court may sloppily say that the doctor's malpractice is a "superseding cause"—but what it really means is that the "learned intermediary" doctrine makes the drug non-defective. In all such cases, a party's claim that injury is or is not "foreseeable" or "proximately caused" is essentially a claim that the design need not have guarded against a particular risk. Such cases are better understood substantively as debates about the existence of a defect.

On many occasions courts will leave true "proximate causation" issues to the common sense application of the jury. But sometimes judges intervene to determine whether juries should be

41. See, e.g., Peter Zablotsky, *Eliminating Proximate Cause As An Element Of The Prima Facie Case For Strict Products Liability*, 45 Cath. U. L. Rev. 31 (1995).

42. *See, e.g.,* Darsan v. Globe Slicing Machine Co., 606 N.Y.S.2d 317 (N.Y. App. 1994).

43. *See, e.g.,* Dugan v. Sears, Roebuck & Co., 454 N.E.2d 64 (Ill. App. 1983).

allowed to find that there is indeed proximate causation. Consider the following scenarios:

B. Product Danger X, Harm Y

- In *Greenfield v. Suzuki Motor Co.*,[44] a defective outboard motor stalled on Long Island Sound. The husband restarted the motor, but did so without withdrawing the anchor line he had dropped. The line became entangled dangerously in the motor. He tried to cut the line, slipped, and fell into the water, tipping the boat violently. His wife tried to approach the side of the boat to throw him a life buoy, but she was washed below deck by the water coming on board. The boat then capsized, and the wife drowned. The court held that the husband, on his wife's behalf, could reach a jury with her products liability suit against the motor manufacturer. Does the reader agree that there was evidence of proximate causation?

- In *Crankshaw v. Piedmont Driving Club, Inc.*,[45] three women were dining at defendant's restaurant when one became ill from defendant's tainted shrimp. The ill woman proceeded to the rest room, where she vomited on the floor and in the sink. Her companion rushed into the rest room a minute later to provide assistance, and slipped on the vomit covering the floor, breaking her hip. The court held that the suit for the broken hip could not go to the jury, as the fracture was not proximately caused by the serving of tainted food.[46] Does the reader agree that there was no evidence of proximate causation?

- In *Moran v. Fabergé*,[47] an adolescent, "[a]pparently ... at a loss for entertainment," poured a bottle of Tigress® Cologne over a burning candle, ostensibly to scent the candle. The cologne ignited and burned her. She argued that the product was defective because it contained no warning that cologne is highly flammable. The defendant argued that product had been misused and that the damage was unforeseeable. The court concluded that so long as there was some risk of fire, proximate causation could be found.[48] Does the reader agree that there was evidence of proximate causation?

44. Greenfield v. Suzuki Motor Co., 776 F.Supp. 698 (E.D.N.Y. 1991).

45. Crankshaw v. Piedmont Driving Club, Inc., 156 S.E.2d 208 (Ga. App. 1967).

46. For those tempted to apply (then) Judge Cardozo's famous "danger invites rescue" maxim (Wagner v. International Ry. Co., 133 N.E. 437 (N.Y. 1921)), note that in *Wagner* the risk that injured the plaintiff-rescuer (falling from a trestle) was the same risk that had endangered the rescuee.

47. Moran v. Fabergé, 332 A.2d 11 (Md. 1975).

48. *Id.* at 20.

- In *Wallace v. Owens–Illinois, Inc.*[49] plaintiff was in his kitchen opening a glass soft drink bottle when it exploded because of a defect in its manufacture. Fragments of glass and the soda fell to the floor. The explosion caused no injury to plaintiff. He left the kitchen unharmed, returning with his wife five minutes later to clean up the floor. He first picked up the larger fragments of glass by hand, then began placing paper towels on the floor to absorb the soda. In the course of cleaning up, he got liquid on the smooth leather soles of his bedroom slippers, which caused him to slip, fall, and sustain bodily injuries. It was held that he could recover for this injury. Does the reader agree that there was evidence of proximate causation?

It is hard to reconcile these decisions. Are either the defendant's case (*Crankshaw*) or one or more of the plaintiffs' cases mistaken? Would the plaintiff in *Crankshaw* have been allowed to recover had she been a stranger walking in the restaurant who slipped on just-disgorged vomit from the tainted shrimp (quite possibly—perhaps plaintiff's assumption of risk in rushing after a friend she knew would vomit "broke the causal chain" in *Crankshaw*). Would the wrongful death suit in *Greenfield* have been able to reach the jury had the victim jumped into the water, not fallen back into the boat, and had then been strangled by a giant octopus?[50] If the husband in *Wallace* had removed his sneakers to don the slick slippers, just to see if he was nimble enough to avoid slipping on soda, would assumption of risk[51] have been found? Should a *stalling* motor and an *exploding* motor have the same causal consequences, or does the fact that the first "fails passively" while the second "fails actively" have causal implications?

The *Restatement (Third)* alludes[52] to general causation principles in its discussion of proximate cause in products liability. This presumably refers to the *Restatement (Third) of Torts: Liability for Physical and Emotional Harm*, § 29:

> An actor's liability is limited to those harms that result from the risks that made the actor's conduct tortious.

Question[53]

- A container of ten pounds of nitroglycerin is defective and unreasonably dangerous, because it contains no warning of its

49. Wallace v. Owens–Illinois, Inc., 389 S.E.2d 155 (S.C. App. 1989).

50. http://digg.com/educational/ Angry_Octopus (last consulted March 26, 2010).

51. See *infra* Chapter 11.

52. RESTATEMENT (THIRD) OF TORTS, PRODUCTS LIABILITY § 15 (1998); *see also id.* § 29 cmt. l.

53. Warren A. Seavey, *Mr. Justice Cardozo and the Law of Torts*, 39 COLUM. L. REV. 20 (1939). *see also* RESTATEMENT (THIRD) OF TORTS: LIABILITY FOR PHYSICAL

contents' explosive power. A clerk receives the unlabeled container and leaves it on a table near playing children (thinking it no more dangerous than a ten pound canister of water). A child knocks over the canister, which (thank Goodness) freakishly does not explode. But the canister breaks the child's big toe. Should the product manufacturer be liable for the broken toe under *Restatement (Third) of Torts: Liability for Physical and Emotional Harm,* § 29?

C. Superseding ("Intervening") Causes

Some cases use the language of proximate causation to deal with plaintiff's "contributory negligence." Sometimes the use of proximate causation language occurs because the jurisdiction's contributory negligence doctrine has been abolished and replaced by comparative negligence, which reduces but does not preclude recovery by a negligent plaintiff. Yet a court may feel that in a particular case there should be no recovery at all. Accordingly, since it may no longer phrase the case as one of contributory negligence, it determines that both the defect and plaintiff's misdeeds were causes in fact but that only the plaintiff's misdeeds were the proximate cause of injury.[54] Since this Book deals with user misuse as an affirmative defense in Chapter 10, it does not address that question in this chapter.

Other forces than plaintiff misuse may of course intervene between the discovery of the defect and the injury. To what extent should these factors "take over" the case, causally, depriving the defect of legal significance?

1). *Third party misconduct*

In some cases, the possibility of third party misconduct is precisely what plaintiff claims the manufacturer should have guarded against. In these cases the lack of a "foolproof" protection becomes the product's defect. Especially in the employment context, when workers' compensation immunity creates a moral hazard, this can be a troubling possibility for manufacturers.

Thus, in *Anderson v. Dreis & Krump Manufacturing Corp.,*[55] a multi-purpose press was sold with a two-button control (each hand must press a button to activate the press, reducing the possibility of an arm being caught in the press) and, as an alternate activation mechanism, a foot control. There was no hand protection while

AND EMOTIONAL HARM, § 29, Comment d, illustration (3) (no liability, it is claimed).

54. *See, e.g.,* Buckley v. Bell, 703 P.2d 1089 (Wyo. 1985). *Buckley* involved negligent filling of gas tank with diesel followed by plaintiff's purging of diesel with spark. *Id.* at 1090. The court held

that plaintiff's negligence alone was the proximate cause of the injury, notwithstanding Wyoming's pure comparative negligence rule. *Id.* at 1096.

55. Anderson v. Dreis & Krump Mfg. Corp., 739 P.2d 1177 (Wash.App. 1987), *cert. denied,* 109 Wash.2d 1006 (1987).

using the foot control—presumably the foot control would be used only if the employee had to grasp an unwieldy object with his two hands. The employer however modified the press to permit one-button hand activation, and an employee using one-button activation severely injured his other hand when it was caught in the press. The alleged design defect was the foot activation mechanism, though that was not being used at the time of the accident! The trial judge dismissed the complaint because the employer's modification was an intervening cause—but this ruling was overturned by a majority of Washington's Supreme Court, which found that the absence of hand guards while using the foot treadle was a defect. The dissent's argument that the alleged foot treadle design defect does not satisfy proximate causation requirements seems hard to resist.

Clearly, if an employer alters a product and makes it more dangerous, the thrust of some states' caselaw rejects the plaintiff's design defect claim that the product was defective because it was not "impossible to alter."[56] Caselaw from other states, however, seems to require manufacturers to prevent foreseeable dangerous alterations by the employer, under pains of having sold a defective product.[57]

2). *User negligence (other than misuse)*

In *Yun v. Ford Motor Co.,*[58] Mr. Yun and his daughter, the driver of the automobile, had been advised by a mechanic nearly one month before the accident that the spare tire assembly attached to the rear of their vehicle was defective. Despite that warning, repairs were not made and the Yun family continued to use the car. One day the spare tire assembly fell off the vehicle onto the roadway. Neither the tire nor the vehicle harmed any other motorist. The sixty-five year old Mr. Yun made two attempts to retrieve the bald tire and its assembly parts by running across the Garden State Parkway. He was struck and injured during his second attempt. A majority of the New Jersey Supreme Court overturned the intermediate appellate court, which had granted summary judgment to defendant on proximate cause grounds. The majority held that it was foreseeable that someone would try to retrieve the broken assembly.[59]

---

56. *See, e.g.,* Robinson v. Reed–Prentice Div. of Package Mach. Co., 403 N.E.2d 440 (N.Y. 1980).

57. *See, e.g.,* Brown v. U.S. Stove Co., 484 A.2d 1234 (N.J. 1984); Chairez v. James Hamilton Const. Co., 215 P.3d 732 (N.M. App. 2009).

58. Yun v. Ford Motor Co., 669 A.2d 1378 (N.J. 1996).

59. If, however, instead of trying to retrieve the wheel assembly, Mr. Yun had gone home and, distraught at the danger his lost tire assembly was creating for other motorists, had had nightmares that caused him to fall out of his bed, injuring himself, even the New Jersey Supreme Court apparently might have found that this was not proximately caused by the defective wheel assem-

3). *Criminal action by a third party*

In *Hollenbeck v. Selectone Corp.*,[60] plaintiff police officer was injured while attempting to effectuate an arrest. He had tried to summon "backup" using defendant's pager, but it failed to function. Plaintiff alleged (and the procedural posture of the case required that the court presume) that defendant had represented that its product was marketed specifically for use by police agencies. The court held that the criminal action of resisting arrest did not break the chain of proximate causation, since such action was precisely one of the reasons for buying the pager.

Questions

- Given *Hollenbeck*, would the court have enforced a limitation of liability in the contract between defendant and the police force (say, limiting recovery to a refund of the purchase price)? [Hint: Is this a tort case or a contract case?]

- How would the court have decided the case had the chief of police purchased the pagers while in civilian clothing at Radio Shack? [Hint: If there would have been proximate causation in this instance, a huge adverse selection process would be set off— for it would be virtually impossible to determine a market-clearing price for pagers at Radio Shack.[61]]

Hollenbeck's proximate causation ruling makes eminent sense, given the implied warranty of fitness for a particular purpose.[62] What of goods sold to the general public? Often the issue in these cases is whether the criminal act was merely the occasion for the actualization of the product's defect or in some sense "the cause" of the injury. Thus, if a criminal hi-jacks my car, with me in it, and then loses control and crashes (but my defective airbag does not deploy, exacerbating my injuries) I will be able to recover from the auto manufacturer—the car-jacking was the occasion of, but not the legal cause of, the exacerbated injuries. This is the case even if I had decided to store my car and not drive it for awhile. In *Price v. Blaine Kern Artista*,,[63] plaintiff had purchased a very large, heavy face mask of President George H.W. Bush for use in his employment as a casino entertainer. He was pushed to the ground by someone (perhaps someone who disagreed with the former presi-

---

bly. *See* Jensen v. Schooley's Mountain Inn, Inc., 522 A.2d 1043 (N.J. App. 1987), *cert. denied*, 528 A.2d 11 (1987) (serving alcohol to a visibly intoxicated patron did not proximately cause injuries sustained when the patron subsequently drove his car eight miles, parked, climbed a tree, fell out of the tree, rolled into the river and drowned).

60. Hollenbeck v. Selectone Corp., 476 N.E.2d 746 (Ill. App. 1985).

61. See Chapter 2, *supra.*

62. See Chapter 4, *supra.*

63. Price v. Blaine Kern Artista, Inc., 893 P.2d 367 (Nev. 1995).

dent's politics) and, he claimed, the mask's defect (it was top-heavy with no retaining harness) caused injury to his neck. The case was allowed to go to the jury.

If the crime was intended to injure the plaintiff, both proximate causation and the very notion of defect are somewhat more problematic. Is fertilizer defective because it is foreseeable that a terrorist will fill a truck with it and set it off? Likely not. On the other hand, were the Boeing airplanes hi-jacked on September 11, 2001 defective because their cockpit doors did not lock? That seems to be a much closer case, likely because of the very risk that a simple lock would have minimized.[64]

Questions About Julian Felipe's Case

- Imagine that Mrs. Felipe had read, and been alarmed by, a news report about the relatively weak roof strength of the 1993 Aerostar. If she continued to drive the van, ultimately injuring Julian in the rollover, should Julian still be able to reach a jury with his design defect claim?

- Should it matter to Ford's liability to Julian how his mother was driving at the moment of the rollover? If so, why?

- Imagine that Mrs. Felipe, having read about the relative weakness of the roofs of minivans, had declined to drive the car because of the danger. One day, reluctantly, she loaned it to her neighbor, who requested it urgently to drive his pregnant wife to the hospital? Imagine that Mrs. Felipe had explicitly warned the neighbor of the dangers from roof compression if there was a rollover for any reason. Should the neighbor's wife have a suit against Ford if she is injured from roof compression in a rollover en route to the hospital?

---

64. *See* In re September 11 Litig., 280 F.Supp.2d 279 (S.D.N.Y. 2003) [failure of manufacturer to design impenetrable cockpit door was one of the proximate cause of the crashes of the planes].

Chapter 10

THE DEFENDANT'S CASE: AFFIRMATIVE DEFENSES TO DEFECTIVENESS CLAIMS[1]

1. Introduction

Suppose plaintiff has produced enough evidence to survive a summary judgment motion in a products liability case. Whether the case is styled as one of negligence, warranty or "strict liability," plaintiff has arguably produced evidence that a product was defective, that that defect rendered the product dangerous, and that that dangerously defective product injured her.

Now it is the defendant's turn. The defendant's case will either contest that the product was defective or will deny that the alleged defect was the cause of plaintiff's injury. In the former case, defendant will typically argue that the product was fine if used correctly and as instructed, or that the product became defective only after it left defendant's possession. In the latter case, defendant will claim that, even if the product was defective, the legal cause of the harm plaintiff suffered is plaintiff's own (or a third party's) misconduct or voluntary acceptance of a dangerous situation. Other affirmative defenses might involve particularities of the contract between defendant and plaintiff, or some legal immunity the defendant claims to enjoy.

In many instances defendant will be content to deny the allegations of plaintiff's complaint, and to produce witnesses who will contradict those who testified for plaintiff. Often, however, defendant will add an affirmative defense. What follows are examples of the type of evidence defendant might offer at this juncture.

2. The Injured User (or Her Employer) Chose to Use the Product in a Dangerous Way

A. The Product Was Misused

If a person experiments with Drano® by drinking it for breakfast in the hope that the product will cleanse his colon, his estate is

---

1. Additional Readings: Michael I. Krauss, *Federalism and Product Liability: One More Trip to the Choice-of-Law Well*, 2002 B.Y.U.L. REV. 759; THOMAS O. MCGARITY, THE PREEMPTION WAR (2008); David G. Owen, *Special Defenses in Products Liability Law*, 70 MO. L. REV. 1 (2005).

exceedingly unlikely to prevail in a subsequent wrongful death claim against the product's manufacturer.[2] The maker of a knife will not be liable for damages incurred when its product is used as a toothpick.[3] A speeding car must be crashworthy, but a car is not uncrashworthy merely because its frame will not withstand a (combined) 160 mph head-on collision with a tanker trailer. These three examples introduce the interesting and complicated issue of user misuse.

Consider these cases, two of which are from the same state and two of which concern children:

1. In *Halliday v. Sturm, Ruger & Co., Inc.*,[4] a three-year old boy allegedly discovered his parents' semi-automatic handgun under their mattress. The child allegedly was capable of loading the ammunition magazine into the handgun because he had seen similar weapons loaded and fired while watching television. As he played with the loaded pistol, it accidentally discharged and the young child suffered a fatal bullet wound to the head. Plaintiffs alleged that the gun was defective because a competently made gun would not be able to be fired by a three-year-old. The Appellate court affirmed the trial judge's summary judgment in favor of the gun manufacturer, on the grounds that the handgun was not defective and that the parents' misuse (by storing it under a mattress, accessible to their child) was the cause of their son's death.

Question

- Do you believe the parents' claim that they stored the gun under their mattress (for fast access) but that the gun was unloaded (making access slower)? Do you think the court believed them? Is there a systemic problem with products liability suits alleging facts that a defendant cannot directly contradict?

2. In *Venezia v. Miller Brewing Co.*,[5] an eight-year old found a discarded Miller Beer bottle and threw it against a telephone pole, where it shattered and sent shards of glass into his eye. Plaintiff claimed that the non-returnable bottle was defective because it was more "thin-walled" than returnable bottles. The appellate court upheld the trial judge's dismissal of the suit on the grounds that that there was no implied warranty (the Massachusetts version of

---

2. Tucci v. Bossert, 385 N.Y.S.2d 328 (N.Y. App. 1976).

3. General Motors Corp. v. Hopkins, 548 S.W.2d 344, 349 (Tex. 1977).

4. Halliday v. Sturm, Ruger & Co., Inc., 770 A.2d 1072 (Md. App. 2001).

5. Venezia v. Miller Brewing Co., 626 F.2d 188 (1st Cir. 1980) (applying Massachusetts law).

strict liability) that an empty glass bottle discarded by unknown persons would safely withstand being intentionally smashed against a solid, stationary object.[6]

3. In *Ellsworth v. Sherne Lingerie*,[7] plaintiff was severely burned when the flannelette nightgown she was wearing ignited in proximity to a front burner of her electric stove. Plaintiff had walked into her kitchen to make coffee early in the morning. She admitted she was wearing her nightgown inside out, and as a result the lining of the two pockets was flapping or protruding. Plaintiff claimed that the nightgown was excessively flammable (though it met federal flammability standards for adult nightgowns). Overturning the directed verdict for defendant given at trial, Maryland's high court ruled that the federal regulations did not shield the manufacturer,[8] and that plaintiff's wearing of the nightgown inside out, though possibly careless, was reasonably foreseeable and not misuse of the product.[9]

Questions

- What distinguishes *Ellsworth* from the two other cases?

- Is it "reasonably foreseeable" that a young boy will toss a beer bottle against a tree, or that a three-year-old will want to play with a gun he finds under his parents' mattress?

- On the other hand, is it not the case that the plaintiff in *Ellsworth* was "using" the nightgown in a way related to its marketed purpose, while in the other two cases the "use" was outside the scope of the products' marketing? If so, is misrepresentation, yet again, the theme that explains the "product misuse" defense?[10]

Several conclusions may be drawn from these examples. First, a successful "user misuse" defense sometimes means nothing other than that the court has decided a product is not defective as a matter of law. If one drives a car without one or more tires, and a wheel rim eventually drops off, causing injury, don't bother suing on the grounds that the rim should have been stronger.

---

6. *Id.* at 190.

7. Ellsworth v. Sherne Lingerie, 495 A.2d 348 (Md. 1985).

8. See in Section 5 of this Chapter, *infra*.

9. *Id.* at 355.

10. *See, e.g.,* U.C.C. § 2–314(2)(c) (1977) (indicating that a product is unmerchantable if it is not fit for "ordinary" purposes).

On other occasions, more controversially, a defendant invoking product misuse is claiming that even if there is a defect, the misuse precludes proximate causation.[11] One example is the dissent in *Moran v. Fabergé*.[12] It hypothetically accepted that defendant's perfume might be defective for lacking a warning that its flash point is a mere 73°F, and it admitted that this might result in liability to a user who accidentally spilled perfume over an open flame. But the dissent denied that this liability would extend to a consumer who was using the perfume to scent candles and not people.[13] Is using perfume to scent candles more like wearing a nightgown inside out, or more like throwing an empty beer bottle against a tree?

When seen from the perspective of misrepresentation, these cases are arguably clarified. Imagine that an automobile's brakes are designed so poorly that they fail if the car is ever driven for any distance with the parking brake engaged.[14] Few would imagine such a failure would occur—a car with brakes designed that way would therefore be defectively designed, i.e., the plaintiff's omission to release the parking break would not constitute "misuse." Similarly, if a new car with a 425 horsepower engine is driven at 100 mph (in a 55 mph zone) and its tires (original equipment from the manufacturer but only suitable for a maximum 85 mph) explode, the car as marketed is defective and unreasonably dangerous even if the speeding was in a residential zone.[15] On the other hand, if a vacuum cleaner is used for erotic stimulation,[16] resulting in the partial amputation of a "body part," few would argue that any implied misrepresentation has resulted. In this case either lack of defect or lack of proximate causation (through misuse) should preclude recovery.

"Normal" use includes uses other than the typical use of a product. Chairs are used to stand on, even if they are "meant for sitting," so they should bear a grown man's weight.[17] Nightgowns are, worn by sleepy people, who may wear them inside out. Tougher

11. *See, e.g.,* Daniell v. Ford Motor Co., 581 F.Supp. 728 (D.N.M. 1984) (holding no recovery on theory of defective design of lock mechanism for failure to have an internal release or opening mechanism, or for failure to warn of such condition where buyer had crawled into trunk and closed lid behind her in attempt to commit suicide, before changing her mind and remaining locked in the vehicle's trunk for nine days).

12. Moran v. Fabergé, 332 A.2d 11 (Md. 1975). See discussion *supra* in Chapter 9.

13. *Id.* at 24. (O'Donnell, J., dissenting).

14. This example is inspired by Knapp v. Hertz Corp., 375 N.E.2d 1349 (Ill. App. 1978).

15. LeBouef v. Goodyear Tire & Rubber Co., 451 F.Supp. 253 (D. La. 1978).

16. Apparently this practice is not uncommon. *See* R. C. Benson Jr., "Vacuum cleaner injury to penis: A common urologic problem?" 25(1) UROLOGY 41 (1985).

17. RESTATEMENT (SECOND) OF TORTS § 395 cmt. k (1965).

cases abound, however. Consider window screens. Are they defective if they cannot withstand the weight of a 20–lb child who leans his full body weight on one? Assuming a proper warning was given, such a use is arguably not "normal" and need not be anticipated when designing the attachment system for the screen.[18]

More generally, if a manufacturer warns against a particular kind of use, does non-compliance with the warning constitute misuse precluding products liability? The answer, alas, is, "it depends." On the one hand, many cases contain a sentence similar to this one: "Where warning is given, the seller may reasonably assume that it will be read and heeded."[19] Ironically, such courts sometimes write that misuse is "unforeseeable" (precluding liability) precisely when it is foreseen and warned against by the manufacturer.

If a product is specifically NOT designed for a particular use, and the warning makes this clear (and is not contradicted in the marketing of the product), then non-compliance with the warning is especially likely to constitute "unforeseeable" misuse.[20] On the other hand, a manufacturer cannot avoid liability by warning against "normal" use of the product. Non-compliance with a hypothetical warning on an SUV, "Do not take off-road, as the high center of gravity might lead to a rollover" would be insufficient to preclude a design defect claim.[21] As discussed in Chapter 8, a warning has its greatest impact when design alternatives are expensive. If an alternate design is appropriate for a particular use, the warning itself may be to no avail.

B. The Product Was Obviously Dangerous

In Chapter 6 it was noted that moral hazard is minimized if liability is confined to cases where a *hidden* defect is the cause of plaintiff's injury. If a danger is obvious, allowing recovery may discourage due care by users, which may in turn require that the price of the product incorporate an exhorbitant "insurance premium." In extreme cases, as we have seen, this could price the product out of existence because of "unraveling" of the market.[22] For example, chain saws would likely be priced out of existence if courts allowed recovery every time a saw cuts through a user's arm.

---

18. *See, e.g.,* Brower v. Metal Indus., Inc., 719 A.2d 941 (Del. 1998).

19. *See, e.g.,* Uptain v. Huntington Lab., Inc., 723 P.2d 1322 (Colo. 1986); Restatement (Second) of Torts § 402A cmt. j (1965) ("'(a) product bearing such a warning, which is safe for use if it is followed, is not in defective condition, nor is it unreasonably dangerous.'").

20. *See, e.g.,* Lightolier, A Div. of Genlyte Thomas Group, LLC v. Hoon, 876 A.2d 100 (Md. 2005) (light fixture specifically designed *not* for in-ceiling use, and so warned—no liability if fire ensues due to heat buildup after in-ceiling use).

21. *See, e.g.,* Lewis v. American Cyanamid Co., 715 A.2d 967 (N.J. 1998).

22. See Chapter 3 Section 3 *supra.*

As noted above in Chapter 7, the "consumer expectations" test is closely associated with the view that obvious dangers are not defects. Thus, in a case involving a collision between a car and a motorcycle, resulting in injuries to the biker's legs, his claim that the failure to provide crash bars (available as a dealer-installed option) as standard equipment failed as a matter of law in Colorado's intermediate appellate court. The absence of crash bars was obvious, the court held, and the manufacturer has no obligation to offer every feasible safety device as standard equipment.[23] This decision was overturned by the Colorado Supreme Court, which held that under the rival "risk-utility," test, the question whether the motorcycle should have come equipped with crash bars as standard equipment was for the jury.[24] As the "consumer expectations" test is replaced by "risk-utility," therefore, the obviousness of the danger ceases to be a legal trump card for manufacturers in design defect cases. Rather, it is one of many facts in defendant's "assumption of risk" causal defense for the jury (see Chapter 11).

To the extent plaintiff's case in chief is based on *informational* defect (failure to warn), "obvious danger" can still be a total defense. Thus, it was recently held that the manufacturer of a siren does not need to warn firefighters that repeated exposure can damage their hearing.[25] Similarly, a manufacturer does not need to warn of the dangers of riding unrestrained in the open cargo bed of a moving pickup truck.[26] Therefore, the more obvious the danger, the more likely it is that plaintiff will sue under design defect, not failure to warn.

C. The Product Was Inherently Dangerous

What is the difference between an "inherent danger" and an "obvious danger?" The former is a subset of the latter. Some products are precisely designed to do dangerous things. A firearm is designed to project small lead objects at very high speed. Knives and chainsaws are designed to cut. Alcoholic beverages are designed to inebriate.[27] Trampolines are bouncy (though some users claim they are more bouncy than they appear to be, giving rise to a duty to warn).[28] Pools contain water that can drown swimmers. Ham-

23. Camacho v. Honda Motor Co., 701 P.2d 628 (Colo. App. 1985).

24. Camacho v. Honda Motor Co., 741 P.2d 1240 (Colo. 1987).

25. Fitzgerald v. Federal Signal Corp., 883 N.Y.S.2d 67 (N.Y. App. 2009).

26. Maneely v. General Motors Corp., 108 F.3d 1176 (9th Cir. 1997) (applying California law).

27. *See, e.g.*, Bruner v. Anheuser–Busch, Inc., 153 F. Supp. 2d 1358 (S.D.

Fla. 2001) ($2 billion dollar suit against defendant for manufacturing a known "psychoactive substance" that caused plaintiffs "not to achieve their maximum potential and station in life" dismissed).

28. Parish v. Jumpking, 719 N.W.2d 540 (Iowa 2006). See discussion in Chapter 7 *supra*.

burgers and French fries are fatty and (for that reason) tasty, though they do not contribute to a balanced diet.[29] These products are not defective in design just because they do what they are designed to do![30] Similarly, there is no duty to warn of an inherent risk. Suits claiming the contrary are often seen as part of the "torts crisis."

Which risks are "inherent" to a product, and which are part of a design choice that might have been made differently? Plaintiffs obviously have an interest in characterizing the feature to which they object as *not* being inherent to the product that injured them. Thus, famously, in *Liebeck v. McDonald's Restaurants, P.T.S. Inc.*,[31] it was alleged that though coffee is inherently hot, the defendant's coffee was *too hot*—twenty to forty degrees hotter than coffee sold by other fast-food restaurants, and hot enough to cause third-degree burns if spilled onto human skin (a foreseeable event given defendant's "drive-through" sales to customers wearing shorts and skirts). In a different case, an appellate court noted that plaintiffs had failed to produce evidence that 179°F is unusually hot for coffee—and a summary judgment against them was affirmed.[32] The two cases are not incompatible. Rather, they highlight the need for plaintiffs to respond with detailed evidence to defendants' claims that the dangers that caused injury were inherent to the products purchased.

The issue of tobacco presents a special case in this regard. The *Restatement (Second)* opined that tobacco was inherently dangerous,[33] and tobacco packaging has warned of this danger since 1969. A few jurisdictions have held the inherent dangers of tobacco products are fact issues for the jury.[34] Others have held that tobacco companies' one-time denials of health risks of their products preclude them from claiming that these risks are inherent to the product.[35]

---

29. *See, e.g.,* Michael I. Krauss, *Suits Against "Big Fat" Tread On Basic Tort Liability Principles,*18(6) LEGAL BACKGROUNDER, WASHINGTON LEGAL FOUNDATION (2003), *available at* http://www.wlf.org/upload/03–14–03krauss.pdf (last consulted April 1, 2010).

30. "Good whiskey is not unreasonably dangerous merely because it will make some people drunk, and is especially dangerous to alcoholics." RESTATEMENT (SECOND) OF TORTS § 402A cmt. i (1965).

31. Liebeck v. McDonald's Restaurants, P.T.S. Inc., 1995 WL 360309 (D.N.M. 1994).

32. McMahon v. Bunn–O–Matic Corp., 150 F.3d 651 (7th Cir. 1998) (applying Indiana law).

33. RESTATEMENT (SECOND) OF TORTS § 402A cmt. i (1965).

34. *See, e.g.,* Hearn v. R.J. Reynolds Tobacco Co., 279 F. Supp. 2d 1096 (D. Ariz. 2003).

35. *See* Michael I. Krauss, Liggett Group v. Engle: *Florida High Court's Imperfect Response to Class Action Abuse*, (Wash. Legal Found. Critical Legal Issues, Working Paper Series No. 145, March 2007), *available at* http://www.wlf.org/upload/KraussWPfinal.pdf (last consulted April 1, 2010).

The issue of inherent danger relates to design defect claims with difficulty, especially if courts are sensitive to the issue of judicial restraint and reluctant to become public regulators. The inherent danger of driving is arguably different if one's car is equipped with an airbag than if it is not. Does this mean that a car legally manufactured and sold with fewer than the maximum feasible number of airbags is defective in design? The answer depends, it seems, on one's position vis-à-vis the *Camacho* case.[36] The fact that the inherent danger of motorcycling can be lessened with the use of an airbag (currently available as an option on the Honda Gold Wing) does not signify that a jury should be allowed to decide that a motorcycle *sans* airbag is defective and unreasonably dangerous.

In *Jordon v. K–Mart Corp.*,[37] a ten-year-old plaintiff was injured when he lost control of his sled and hit a tree. The sled was alleged to have two design defects; (1) molded runners that rendered the sled unsteerable and (2) no independent steering or braking mechanism. The sled in this case was an inexpensive model, while more sophisticated ones featured additional control possibilities. The appellate court affirmed the trial judge's summary judgment, holding "that the dangers inherent in sledding with a toboggan-like sled with limited steering capacity is one which an ordinary ten-year-old child would recognize and appreciate as part of the risk of sledding."[38] What if plaintiff had been visiting from Florida?

Less inclined to accept the inherent danger doctrine was the New Jersey Supreme Court in *O'Brien v. Muskin.*[39] That court allowed a jury to decide whether above-ground swimming pools as a whole were "too dangerous" as compared with more expensive in-ground models. In contrast to this ruling, the *Restatement (Third)* rejects *almost* entirely the idea that entire categories of products may be defective for their inherent characteristics. Only a very tiny subset of products would qualify for such liability according to the comment: "manifestly unreasonable designs" for which "the extremely high degree of danger posed by its use or consumption so substantially outweighs its negligible social utility that no rational, reasonable person, fully aware of the relevant facts, would choose to use" it.[40] The example provided is a prank cigar that blows up in the face of its surprised victim. The minimization of "product line" liability is a good thing. Public ordering institutions (consumer

---

36. *See* Camacho v. Honda Motor Co., 741 P.2d 1240 (Colo. 1987).

37. Jordon v. K–Mart Corp., 611 A.2d 1328 (Pa. Super. 1992).

38. *Id.* at 1331–32.

39. O'Brien v. Muskin Corp., 463 A.2d 298 (N.J. 1983); see *supra* Chapter 7.

40. RESTATEMENT (THIRD) OF TORTS, PRODUCTS LIABILITY § 2 cmt. e (1998).

protection agencies, regulators, legislatures capable of banning products, etc.) are fully motivated to act where they deem it appropriate.

D. The Product Was Altered

A defendant is liable for injuries legally caused by a product that was defective and unreasonably dangerous when the defendant sold it.[41] As has been seen, if a product is packaged in a sealed container (e.g., a bottle of Coca–Cola®) it may be difficult for defendant to prove that tampering has occurred further along in the stream of production.[42]

In practice, a high percentage of all changes to products by mid-stream buyers is made by employers, against whom workers' compensation is the injured worker's exclusive remedy. Should the absence of a tort remedy against the employer, and the moral hazard to which this immunity gives rise, justify a cause of action against a manufacturer or distributor who furnished the product to the employer? A representative case is *Liriano v. Hobart Corp.*,[43] with these facts:

> "Luis Liriano, a seventeen-year-old employee in the meat department at Super Associated grocery store ('Super'), was injured on the job in September 1993 when he was feeding meat into a commercial meat grinder whose safety guard had been removed. His hand was caught in the 'worm' that grinds the meat; as a result, his right hand and lower forearm were amputated.

> "The meat grinder was manufactured and sold in 1961 by Hobart Corporation ('Hobart'). At the time of the sale, it had an affixed safety guard that prevented the user's hands from coming into contact with the feeding tube and the grinding 'worm.' No warnings were placed on the machine or otherwise given to indicate that it was dangerous to operate the machine without the safety guard in place. Subsequently, Hobart became aware that a significant number of purchasers of its meat grinders had removed the safety guards. And in 1962, Hobart began issuing warnings on its meat grinders concerning removal of the safety guard.

> "There is no dispute that, when Super acquired the grinder, the safety guard was intact. It is also not contested that, at the

---

41. RESTATEMENT (SECOND) OF TORTS, § 402A(1)(b) requires, for liability, that the product "is expected to and does reach the user or consumer without substantial change in the condition in which it is sold."

42. *See* Pulley v. Pacific Coca–Cola Bottling Co., 415 P.2d 636 (Wash. 1966) in Chapter 2 *supra*.

43. Liriano v. Hobart Corp., 700 N.E.2d 303 (N.Y. 1998).

time of Liriano's accident, the safety guard had been removed. There is likewise no doubt that Hobart actually knew, before the accident, that removals of this sort were occurring and that use of the machine without the safety guard was highly dangerous. And Super does not question that the removal of the guard took place while the guard was in its possession."[44]

New York's high court held that a manufacturer could still be liable in cases where a substantial alteration had made the product unsafe, in two circumstances: 1) if plaintiff establishes that it designed the product purposefully to permit its use without the safety feature, thereby making the manufacturer an accomplice of the downstream user who modifies the product;[45] or 2) if the alteration is foreseeable and presents non-obvious risks, generating a duty for the manufacturer to at least warn, if feasible, the end user about such risks.[46]

E. The Product Was "Made to Order"

Imagine that a product is normally manufactured within certain design parameters, but that the purchaser of this particular item (often the victim's employer) orders one with different design parameters. Should the manufacturer be subject to the claim that the specified design was defective and unreasonably dangerous?

Consider *Bloemer v. Art Welding Co., Inc.*[47] with these facts:

"In 1983, Lever Brothers, a detergent manufacturer, undertook a project to upgrade its existing facilities in the north tower of its St. Louis plant. The project involved, among other construction services, the fabrication and installation of six new "cyclones" in the north tower. A cyclone is a three-story tall cylindrical tank which is designed to remove detergent particles from the air. The cyclone contains a fan, a separator pot and access doors.

Lever Brothers' engineering department designed the entire north tower upgrade and the cyclones were built and installed according to Lever Brothers' specifications. Lever Brothers retained Montgomery as the general contractor for the project and, pursuant to its contract, Montgomery subcontracted with Art who then subcontracted a portion of the fabrication of various components to Metro. After installation, Lever Brothers' engineering department redesigned the access doors with a quick-release latch. Originally, the access doors were designed

---

44. *Id.* at 305.

45. *See also* Lopez v. Precision Papers, Inc., 492 N.E.2d 1214 (N.Y. 1986).

46. *See also* Welch Sand & Gravel, Inc. v. O & K Trojan, Inc., 668 N.E.2d 529 (Ohio App. 1995).

47. Bloemer v. Art Welding Co., Inc., 884 S.W.2d 55 (Mo. App. 1994).

with lug nuts to restrict the speed and angle at which the doors could be opened. Montgomery installed the quick-release handles in accordance with Lever Brothers' specifications. The completed cyclones were accepted by Lever Brothers in 1983.

After a period of operation, detergent would periodically coat the cyclone's interior, necessitating cleaning. On December 18, 1987, Plaintiffs were injured while they were attempting to clean cyclone #1 in the north tower. Cleaning was accomplished by flushing heated water along the walls of the cyclone. The heated water was inserted at the top of the cyclone and steam was inserted on the sixth floor to heat up the water and assist in the cleaning process. The water was then discharged through a port at the bottom of the cyclone. Plaintiffs noted that no water was flowing from the port at the bottom of cyclone #1 and suspected a blockage. Plaintiffs turned the water and steam off, opened the access door on the fifth level, and attempted to dislodge the blockage with an iron rod. When this procedure proved unsuccessful, Plaintiffs went to the sixth level, hoping to dislodge the clog from there. Plaintiffs saw water seeping out around the edges of the access door on the sixth level. Plaintiff Bloemer used a metal pole to manipulate the quick-release handle of the access door. When the door opened, hot water gushed out and burned Plaintiffs."[48]

The appeals court affirmed the trial court's summary judgment. Its reiteration of the "specifications rule" is typical. A manufacturer "is not subject to liability if the specified design or material turns out to be insufficient to make the chattel safe for use, unless it is so obviously bad that a competent contractor would realize that there was a grave chance that his product would be dangerously unsafe."[49]

The "obvious danger" exception applied quite clearly in the New Jersey case, *Michalko v. Cooke Color and Chemical Corp.*[50] In *Michalko*, a worker's hand was amputated when, pursuant to her employer's order and in a poster-child illustration of the moral hazard created by Workers' Compensation laws, she used a press shorn of all safety devices. The press's manufacturer, Cubby,

> "was aware of the types of safety devices that could be used on the transfer presses. However, it had a policy of not questioning the absence of safety guards when it was not building a complete machine. Cubby knew that assembly drawings usually showed the machine as a finished product ready to operate and that, in this case, the drawings furnished to it by Elastimold

48. *Id.* at 57.

49. *Id.* at 59.

50. Michalko v. Cooke Color and Chem. Corp., 451 A.2d 179 (N.J. 1982).

did not indicate any safety devices. Even though Cubby's personnel had visited Elastimold and seen the presses operating without safety devices, Cubby assumed that Elastimold would install safety devices itself. It is undisputed that Cubby knew the transfer presses were dangerous without safety devices."[51]

Liability in *Michalko,* where a simple device was knowingly supplied in a form grossly unsafe for use, is compatible with lack of liability in *Bloemer,* where the employer specified a complicated, unique device in painstaking detail.[52]

Questions About Julian Felipe's Case

• Should Julian Felipe's case against Ford be dismissed if:

-Ms. Felipe was driving with underinflated tires?

-Ms. Felipe had driven the tires until their treads were separating?

-Ms. Felipe was driving at 100 mph at the time of the rollover?

-Ms. Felipe had repeatedly carried extremely heavy loads on her Aerostar's roof, weakening it over time?

3. Too Much Time Has Passed to Hold Defendant Liable

No human lives forever, and the same goes for his artifacts. Determining when the passage of time relieves the defendant from products liability is an interesting exercise in legal theory.

A. The Product's Useful Life Had Expired

1). *Deterioration*

Drive a car long enough ("long enough" varies by brand of car and tire) and its tires will become dangerously used. Should this expose the tire manufacturer to products liability? Should the answer to this question depend on how long it takes for the tires to go bald? If so, where do juries get the knowledge and authority to determine optimum tire durability?

Plaintiff will often attempt to rely on a *res ipsa loquitur* instruction (the failure of the product is itself evidence of defect). The defendant will respond that "normal" deterioration, not defect, explains the failure. Sometimes even an expert opinion that the

---

51. *Id.* at 181–82.

52. *See also* RESTATEMENT (SECOND) OF TORTS § 404 cmt. a (1965) ("[T]he contractor is not required to sit in judgment on the plans and specifications or the materials provided by his employer. The contractor is not subject to liability if the specified design or material turns out to be insufficient to make the chattel safe for use, unless it is so obviously bad that a competent contractor would realize that there was a grave chance that his product would be dangerously unsafe.").

failure of the product was due to a manufacturing or design defect will not overcome, in law, evidence of deterioration.

Mullen v. General Motors Corp.[53] illustrates this. On February 9, 1969, Mr. and Mrs. Mullen were injured when Mrs. Mullen lost control of their 1967 Chevrolet station wagon, causing it to leave the highway and overturn. The cause of the accident was a blowout of the left rear tire. The Mullens sued General Motors Corporation and Uniroyal, Inc. Evidence revealed that from the time of purchase until the time of the accident, the auto had been driven 23,600 miles. The Mullens used it mainly for traveling to and from a suburban railroad station, for shopping and for pleasure. They had driven it on two extended vacation trips, from Illinois to Mexico in 1967 and to Minnesota in 1968. When the tire blew, they were traveling at 65–70 mph on a highway. The vehicle had not previously been involved in an accident, nor, according to plaintiffs' testimony, had it ever been driven over rough terrain or over curbs, logs, or unusual bumps. It had not been used to trailer anything. Mrs. Mullen was aware that tires wear out, but testified that she paid little attention to the maintenance of the tires, since it was family practice to trade in their car for a new model before it became necessary to replace tires. She did not know whether the tires had ever been rotated. At intervals, she would ask gas station attendants to "check the tires," but she specified no particular air pressure for them. The day before the Mullens departed for their fateful trip, they left the car at a service station, asking that the oil be changed and the car "checked for a trip."

Plaintiffs' expert opined that the tire had a vague "incipient defect" causing the blowout, but defendants' experts noted that 90 percent of the tread on the blown tire had been consumed and that the tire had been used for a considerable period while grossly underinflated. Reversing the trial jury's verdict for plaintiffs, the Illinois Court of Appeals ruled that they had not produced evidence capable of convincing an unbiased jury that the tire had a defect when it left defendants' possession.

Mullen is an important case. On the one hand, the consumer's "misuse" of the car (her failure to maintain the tires) is "foreseeable"—many inattentive drivers fail to monitor the safety of their tires. Indeed, Consumers Union's senior vice president for technical policy has admitted that for "too long, people have viewed tires simply as things that, if they weren't flat, they were probably O.K."[54] Failing to manufacture maintenance-free tires, however, is not the equivalent of manufacturing defective tires.

53. Mullen v. General Motors Corp., 336 N.E.2d 338 (Ill. App. 1975).

54. R. David Pittle, *Tire Safety: Start With The Consumer*, 18th Annual Tire Industry Conference, Feb. 27, 2003,

Had the tire failed after 5,000 miles, would the court have reached the same conclusion as a matter of law? This seems unlikely—and yet the difference between 5,000 miles and 24,000 miles might appear to be one of fact (for the jury), not of law. Some tires deteriorate much more rapidly than others—should different tire wear ratings[55] result in different summary judgment results? If *premature* deterioration was something that a manufacturer should have considered when designing the product, it may be liable for a design defect.[56]

Other representative cases where plaintiffs' products liability claims were rejected as a matter of law because of deterioration include:

- Glass v. Allis–Chalmers.[57] A combine was equipped with four strips of painted non-skid surface (called "Safety Walk") on the deck between the engine and the fuel tank. These strips had obviously[58] worn away by the time plaintiff purchased the combine from its previous owner. The court held that the combine was not defective at manufacture merely because non-skid paint could wear away;

- In *Bourgeois v. Garrard Chevrolet*.[59] The court ruled that the failure of a police car's antilock braking system is no evidence that this high-use car was defective when originally sold, and refused to issue a *res ipsa loquitur* instruction.

2). *Disposal and Destruction*

Imagine that a manufacturer of ductwork loosely connected two pieces. Fortunately, throughout the life of the ductwork this loose connection causes no mishap. However, after the useful life of

http://www.consumersunion.org/products/tire2-consumer.htm (last consulted April 5, 2010).

55. The National Highway Traffic Safety Administration ("NHTSA") requires tire manufacturers to grade tires. This grading system, known as the Uniform Tire Quality Grading System, provides guidelines for making relative comparisons when purchasing new tires. NHTSA specifies that, "[t]readwear grades are an indication of a tire's relative wear rate. The higher the treadwear number is, the longer it should take for the tread to wear down. For example, a tire grade of 400 should wear twice as long as a tire grade of 200." NHTSA adds that, "[a]lthough this rating system is very helpful when buying new tires, it is not a safety rating or guarantee of how well a tire will perform or how long it will last. Other factors such as personal driving style, type of car,

quality of the roads, and tire maintenance habits have a significant influence on your tire's performance and longevity." *Tire Safety,* U.S. DEP'T OF TRANS., NAT'L HIGHWAY TRAFFIC SAFETY ADMIN., http://www.nhtsa.dot.gov/cars/rules/Tire Safety/ridesonit/brochure.html (last consulted April 5, 2010).

56. *See, e.g.,* Mickle v. Blackmon, 166 S.E.2d 173 (S.C. 1969) (use of substandard material in car part leading to premature deterioration exposes manufacturer to liability).

57. Glass v. Allis–Chalmers, 789 F.2d 612 (8th Cir. 1986) (applying Missouri law).

58. Had the danger been non-obvious, a failure to warn claim might have been available.

59. Bourgeois v. Garrard Chevrolet, 811 So.2d 962 (La. 2002).

the heating system has expired the ductwork is dismantled. During disassembly the two loosely connected pieces unexpectedly separate, with one piece falling on a hapless worker. Should the manufacturer of the ductwork be liable for this injury?

In *Wingett v. Teledyne Industries*[60] it was held that strict liability under § 402A required that injury take place during "normal" or "reasonably foreseeable" "use" of the product. Destruction and disposal are not "uses." There is other caselaw to this effect, though the question remains controversial. Comment 1 to Section 402A states that "users" of products include

> "those who are passively enjoying the benefit of the product, as in the case of passengers in automobiles or airplanes, as well as those who are utilizing it for the purpose of doing work upon it, as in the case of an employee of the ultimate buyer who is making repairs upon the automobile which he has purchased."

Comment 1 also defines "consumers" as including "not only those who in fact consume the product, but also those who prepare it for consumption." Thus in 2000, Indiana's Supreme Court narrowed *Wingett* by finding that a maintenance worker, as an employee of the final purchaser of the transmission system was a "user" of the product.[61] But it is hard to see why maintenance of a product is "use," while disposal is not.[62] Indeed, in many cases where it is held that destruction and disposal are not "use" (precluding strict liability), the facts lead one to believe that the *manner* of the disposal was so bizarre as to constitute misuse.

For example, in *Boscarino v. Convenience Marine Products, Inc.*[63] plaintiff found a used fire extinguisher among certain used marine parts and other rubbish. The extinguisher had been removed from the engine room of a vessel owned by a third party. The extinguisher had a broken electrical system, and plaintiff decided it was useless and should be discarded. However, he and his friend believed that disposal of the charged extinguisher might create a hazard, so they decided to manually discharge the extinguisher before throwing it away. To do so, they mounted the extinguisher to an interior wall. Then, using a pair of needle-nosed pliers, they attempted to manually discharge the extinguisher by removing two springs from the sprinkler head portion on the top of the cylinder. Nothing happened. A few minutes later, the friend placed the extinguisher in a trashcan. Almost immediately after it

---

60. Wingett v. Teledyne Indus., 479 N.E.2d 51 (Ind. 1985).

61. Butler v. City of Peru, 733 N.E.2d 912, 919 (Ind. 2000).

62. *See* Charles Cantu, *The Recycling, Dismantling, and Destruction of Goods as a Foreseeable Use Under Section 402A of the Restatement (Second) of Torts*, 46 ALA L. REV. 81 (1994).

63. Boscarino v. Convenience Marine Prods., Inc., 817 F.Supp. 116 (S.D. Fla. 1993).

was placed in the trash, the extinguisher flew out of the can, over Mr. Ferris's shoulder, and struck Mr. Boscarino in the head. It then bounced off of two walls and flew out the door, eventually landing underneath a truck. The court granted summary judgment to defendant on the ground that the disposal of the extinguisher was not "use." But this case could just as easily have been decided on grounds of proximate causation, or lack of defect, or unforeseeable misuse.

Significantly, the plaintiff in *Boscarino* did not sue for failure to warn, perhaps the most effective legal argument for disposal injuries. For instance, "NiCa" rechargeable batteries contain cadmium, a metal that causes blood and reproductive damage among other problems. These batteries are commonly used in portable telephones, power tools, radios and video tape recorders. Several states now prohibit consumers from dumping these batteries into the normal trash, as they are hazardous in landfills. If a battery contains an inadequate warning against improper disposal and cause in fact is presumed or proven, it is likely that the injured disposal worker would be deemed to be a product "user."

B. The Harm Was Intergenerational (Not Caused to the User)

Often the product purchaser is not the person injured. Mrs. Felipe purchased the car, but Julian was injured. A young baby injured by the crash of a defective and unreasonably dangerous car is not deprived of a cause of action merely because she was not alive when the car was produced.[64]

Julian Felipe and the baby passenger were "using" the car when their injuries occurred. Diethylstilbestrol (DES), however, when used to prevent miscarriage, causes ovarian cancer in some female children of the user, approximately fourteen years after their birth. (All male and some female offspring are unaffected.[65]) These female children never "use" the product. In *Grover v. Eli Lilly & Co.*, the Ohio Supreme Court was silent about "DES daughters'" right to sue, but refused to extend liability to DES grandchildren:

64. *See, e.g.,* Lough by Lough v. Rolla Women's Clinic, Inc., 866 S.W.2d 851, 854 (Mo. 1993) ("Assume a balcony is negligently constructed. Two years later, a mother and her one-year-old child step onto the balcony and it gives way, causing serious injuries to both the mother and the child. It would be ludicrous to suggest that only the mother would have a cause of action against the builder but, because the infant was not conceived at the time of the negligent conduct, no duty of care existed toward the child.").

65. One small study in the Netherlands suggested that the sons of DES daughters had a fairly high risk of a birth defect called hypospadias (wherein the urethra opens along the shaft of the penis rather than at its tip). A later study suggested that the risk of hypospadias was much smaller than was first thought.

When a pharmaceutical company prescribes drugs to a woman, the company, under ordinary circumstances, does not have a duty to her daughter's infant who will be conceived twenty-eight years later. Because of remoteness in time and causation, we hold that [the grandchild] does not have an independent cause of action. . . A pharmaceutical company's liability for the distribution or manufacturer of a defective prescription drug does not extend to persons who were never exposed to the drug, either directly or in utero.[66]

Two different kinds of causal considerations are at play here. The longer the causal chain, temporally, the more uncertainty there is about whether intervening causes ultimately determined the plaintiff's fate.[67] Alternatively, if the harm is too distanced from the product's alleged defect, a "duty" question may arise.[68] If a product "causes" a withered right arm in the user and in all the user's descendants, *ad infinitum,* should each generation have a cause of action against the manufacturer?

Suppose for example that the defect in a male pharmaceutical product is that it fails to warn users not to give blood or let women touch the drug, which can have teratogenic effects on her offspring.[69] It is hard to see why the injured offspring could not sue for the damages suffered as a result of this informational defect. The child may not be the "user," but she is the very reason why the product is defective.

C. The Legislature Has Said It's Too Late to Sue

As has been seen, the common law's treatment of the defect requirement itself provides a ready-made limit to many products liability lawsuits in cases of deterioration. In addition to the time constraint provided by deterioration, statutes of limitation and statutes of repose affect a defendant's liability for a product by the passage of time.

1). *Statutes of Limitation*[70]

Most state tort statutes of limitation[71] bar civil claims from one to six years after they "accrue."[72] The rub is in the word "accrue."

---

66. Grover v. Eli Lilly & Co., 591 N.E.2d 696, 700 (Ohio 1992).

67. This alludes to Judge Andrews' dissent in Palsgraf v. Long Island R. Co., 162 N.E. 99 (N.Y. 1928).

68. This alludes to Chief Judge Cardozo's opinion in Palsgraf v. Long Island R. Co., 162 N.E. 99 (N.Y. 1928).

69. Avodart®, the brand name for dutasteride (an effective treatment for benign prostate hyperplasia), can be carried in the blood and could cause birth defects if a pregnant women receives, many months later, a transfusion with blood that contains the drug.

70. Statutes of limitation are the typical ways that legislatures address the inevitable issues of staleness and unreliability of evidence that occur as time passes.

71. Note that if a suit is brought against a seller in contractual privity, for breach of warranty, whether implied or express, the Uniform Commercial

If a product explodes, courts traditionally hold that the right of action accrues on the date of the explosion, not the date of manufacture or sale. If a child is injured, the statute may be tolled until the age of majority. If a defective and unreasonably dangerous product causes harm right away, but the harm is reasonably undiscovered for a time (as where a drug causes a latent condition that gradually manifests itself), most jurisdictions toll the statute of limitations until the date of reasonable discovery.

2). *Statutes of Repose*

These tolling issues have led tort reformers to propose, and in some cases adopt, statutes of repose. Essentially, a statute of repose is a firm (non-tollable save rare exceptions[73], and accrued immediately upon manufacture or sale) statute of limitations, typically ten years in length.[74] Several states have adopted statutes of repose, which are typically deemed "substantive" (i.e., they apply whenever the substantive tort law of the state applies, even if the case is heard in another state). The federal government arguably rescued the light aircraft industry from the brink of economic oblivion by enacting an 18–year statute of repose for "general aviation aircraft and the components, systems, subassemblies and other parts" of the aircraft.[75]

The federal aviation statute of repose has been effective. But a frequent political argument against state statutes of repose has been that they protect (often) out-of-state defendants to the detriment of (usually) in-state plaintiffs. At the margin this problem has likely dissuaded states from adopting statutes of repose. It also sometimes leads forum courts to decline to enforce another state's statute of repose, on the grounds that the forum court does not want to hurt its own residents.[76]

Code's 4–year statute of limitations (which runs from the date of retail sale, not the date of the accident) will apply. *See, e.g.,* Britt v. Schindler Elevator Corp., 637 F.Supp. 734 (D.D.C. 1986) (tort actions stale through statute of repose; contract warranty actions stale because of U.C.C.). Where "breach of implied warranty" is the term used for strict products liability of a seller not in privity, the tort statute of limitations applies. *See, e.g.,* Salvador v. Atlantic Steel Boiler Co., 389 A.2d 1148 (Pa. Super. Ct. 1978).

72. *See generally* 1 Prod. Liab. Rep. (CCH) P 3420 (Charts of State Statutes of Limitation). This book will not deal with issues such as the choice of which statute of limitation applies in federal courts, class actions, or choice of law issues that can affect the decision about where to file a products liability suit.

73. Some statutes of repose have incorporated exceptions for certain long latency disease personal injury claims.

74. See generally Frank E. Kulbaski, *Statutes of Repose and the Post–Sale Duty to Warn: Time for a New Interpretation,* 32 Conn. L. Rev. 1027 (2000).

75. General Aviation Revitalization Act of 1994, 49 U.S.C. § 40101.

76. See Gantes v. Kason Corp., 679 A.2d 106 (N.J. 1996), for an extraordinary case where the New Jersey Supreme Court's desire to hold manufacturers liable led it to ignore a Georgia statute of repose *in a suit by a Georgia*

4. "State of the Art" Defense (The Product Was as Safe as It Could Be)

A. General Comments

Many characteristics of products are safety-related, and over time the profit motive results in greater knowledge and constant improvements. This affects both hidden and overt safety features. Consider just two of the astounding array of safety features made available over time on automobiles:

- Airbags provide tremendous protection in case of crashes. Allen Breed received a patent[77] to a "sensor and safety system" in 1968, the world's first electromechanical automotive airbag system. The 1973 Oldsmobile Toronado was the first American car with a passenger airbag intended for sale to the public. General Motors later offered the option of driver side airbags in full-sized Oldsmobiles and Buicks in 1975 and 1976 respectively. Cadillacs were available with driver and passenger airbags options during those same years, as were Mercedes. By the mid–1980s other manufacturers started to offer them, and in 1988 Chrysler became the first to make driver's airbags standard equipment. The 1987 Porsche Turbo was the first car to equip both front seats with standard airbags. Volvo introduced optional side airbags in 1995, and the 1996 Kia Sportage had the first knee airbag. The first rear curtain airbag (where a bag inflates over a window) was introduced in the 2008 Toyota iQ. In 2006, Honda introduced the first motorcycle airbag on the Gold Wing. Airbag suits are also available for motorcycle Grand Prix riders.[78]

  Question: Assuming they are not required by government regulations, might cars, or motorcycles, without airbags become defective at some point? If so, should there be a duty to retrofit earlier models?

- Xenon high-intensity-discharge headlights produce a slightly bluish light up to three times brighter than halogen head-

---

worker against a New Jersey manufacturer.

77. U.S. #5,071,161. U.S. #5,071,-161. This 1991 invention for "an airbag that vents air as it defaults... was designed to 'reduce the risk of secondary injuries by reducing the inflated bag's rigidity." Lisa Wade McCormick, *A*

Short History of the Airbag, CONSUMER-AFFAIRS.COM, http://www.consumer affairs.com/news04/2006/airbags/airbags_invented.html.

78. *See* McCormick, *Id.*; *see also* Hazel Morgan, "The History of Airbags", *E–How*, http://www.ehow.com/about_5393997_history-airbags.html (last consulted April 5, 2010).

lights. Xenon headlights tend to last two to three times longer, reducing the dangers caused by sudden burnout. They also provide much more uniform intensity. Studies have demonstrated that drivers react faster and more accurately to roadway obstacles with good HID headlamps rather than halogen ones.[79] Xenons were first introduced in 1991 by BMW on one model. Now they are offered on several but not all car models.

> **Question:** if an accident happens in reduced visibility on a car equipped with halogen headlights, should the lack of xenon lights make the car defective?

- Thanks to OnStar® and similar systems, cars can now alert central reporting stations in case of a collision, enabling instant calls to emergency services and even gradual immobilization of a vehicle that has been stolen (with, for example, a baby on board).[80]

> **Question:** If a car is not equipped with OnStar® and crashes in a rural location, with fatal consequences for the driver, is the car defective as un-crashworthy[81] because it is not equipped with this modern convenience? Suppose older GM cars can be retrofitted with OnStar® for $400. Would it then be incumbent on GM to recall its older vehicles for this purpose? If so, who should pay for the retrofit? Finally, must OnStar® be standard equipment, or should consumers have the right to opt out of this important safety device by not paying the monthly maintenance fee?

Those improvements were apparent. *Hidden* safety improvements are perhaps even more impressive. Today the roofs of vans can be made much more sturdily than in the past, at little cost in additional weight, because of improvements in metallurgical and steel molding technology. Tires can withstand increasingly higher speeds and are much more resistant to blowouts.[82] Many cars stop

---

79. John van Derlofske et al., Evaluation of High Intensity Discharge Automotive Forward Lighting, Rensselaer Polytechnic Institute, 2001, *available at* http://www.lrc.rpi.edu/programs/transportation/pdf/PAL/PAL2001-vanderlofske.pdf (last consulted April 5, 2010).

80. OnStar,® General Motors' Technology (Lexus has its own, different, system) is an in-vehicle safety and security system intended to protect drivers and their families on the road. The hands-free calling system provides 24–hour access to Advisors and an automat-ic connection to emergency roadside assistance whenever airbags are deployed. *See OnStar Explained,* ONSTAR, http://www.onstar.com/web/portal/onstarexplained.

81. *See* Chapter 7 *supra* for a discussion of design defects.

82. A 2000 report details how Goodyear invented a blowout-resistant tire for passenger cars. Z. Bareket D., F. Blower C, & MacAdam, *Blowout Resistant Tire Study for Commercial Highway Vehicles,* UNIV. OF MICH. TRANSP. RESEARCH INST., Aug. 31, 2000, *available at* www.retread.org/PDF/umtris.pdf.

more quickly[83] and adjust to slippery surfaces more rapidly and automatically.[84]

The point of these illustrations is that today's cars become more or less obsolete tomorrow. And so it goes with other products. Visit any "Home Show" and you will see gadgets that are safer than previous models. The relentless march of technology poses two important questions for products liability. The first has been explored in Chapter 7, when the notion of strict liability for design defect was examined: is it defective to make and market a product that is not "as safe as it can be?" Should consumers be allowed to purchase (at lower cost) products that are less safe, both for them (fewer airbags) and for third parties (less powerful brakes)?

The second set of questions has not yet been explored. When a product IS made "as safe as it can be", does that product become defective after time passes and the old item becomes "unreasonably dangerous?" Should it matter how extensive or widespread the new knowledge of safety technology is? Should it even matter that the new invention is actually "known" for the product to be "unreasonably dangerous," or might it suffice that the improvement was "knowable" when the product was manufactured? After all, anything that *has become* known *could have been* learned one week sooner! Should there be liability for failure to warn of a danger, if the danger was not known to anyone when the product was made? What if the danger becomes known after the product is sold, but before the accident occurs? Finally, are jurors capable of judging products made in the past (perhaps before their birth), or should determinations about their fitness be made as a matter of law by judges?

If products liability is truly "strict," it is presumably not a defense that the allegedly defective and unreasonably dangerous product could not have been made safer. After all, the manufacturer could have chosen not to make the product at all. Yet in many

---

83. See James R. Healey, *Smarter cars require smarter drivers to avoid dumb mistakes*, USA TODAY, May 19, 2010 available at http://content. usatoday.com/communities/driveon/post/ 2010/05/smarter-cars-require-smarter-drivers-to-avoid-dumb-crashes—/ 1?csp=34 (remarking that "anti-lock brakes have become the norm in new cars"). Anti-lock brakes are now mandated on all new cars, and pressure is building to mandate them on new motorcycles, where ABS systems are arguably even more valuable: *See* Christopher Jensen, *Agency Urged to Require Antilock Brakes for Motorcycles,* N.Y. TIMES, Mar. 6, 2010, available at:http:// wheels.blogs.nytimes.com/2010/05/06/ agency-urged-to-require-antilock-brakes-on-motorcycles/ (last consulted on May 31, 2010).

84. Electronic stability control, which seeks to automatically reduce speed and brake to avoid car skidding, emerged in the 1990s and has become available on many car models since. *See* Ann Job, *Mandatory Stability Control,* MSN, *available at http://editorial.autos. msn.com/article.aspx?cp-documentid= 435633.* In 2007, the National Highway Traffic Safety Administration announced it is requiring that all future vehicles have standard stability control by 2012. *Id; see also* 49 C.F.R. Parts 571 & 585 (2007).

states, statutes or caselaw or both protect sellers from design and informational defect claims if "the product [including its warning] conformed to the state of the art in existence at the time...."[85] Accepting the state of the art defense is an indirect admission both that design defect law is negligence-based, not strict (for manufacturer and sellers cannot be faulted for marketing the safest product possible). Interestingly, the defense does *not* shield sellers from liability for marketing a product that contains a manufacturing defect.[86] This comports with the representational theory of liability sketched in Chapter 4—the "lemon" has been misrepresented, even if it was made with as much quality control as was available.

"State of the art" issues therefore affect informational and design defect cases.

B.   "State of the Art" and Informational Defects

Manufacturers typically have the most knowledge of the risks of their products. In some situations, however, risks only become known after the product has been used for some time. If a user succumbs to such risks, and claims he would not have used the product had he been warned of them, the question is whether the manufacturer should be liable for not having issued this warning.

In *Rogers v. Miles Laboratories, Inc.*[87] Jeremy Rogers was born in 1980 with severe hemophilia, requiring numerous transfusions of donated blood. Since April 1985, blood banks have employed a test to detect the presence of the human immunodeficiency virus ("HIV"). However, prior to April 1985, no test was available to test plasma for this purpose. In November 1985, Jeremy tested positive for the presence of HIV antibodies. In February 1988, he was diagnosed as suffering from acquired immune deficiency syndrome ("AIDS"). Washington's Supreme Court held, following Comment k of the *Restatement (Second)*,[88] that the trial court had correctly dismissed plaintiff's strict liability suit against the blood bank. According to the court, the blood bank would be liable only if it negligently failed to warn of the risk of hepatitis, and if that risk caused injury to Jeremy. Since Jeremy needed transfusions to survive in any case, and since no blood bank was screening for HIV, no warning would have made any difference. Comment k, of course,

---

85. *See, e.g.,* Iowa Code § 668.12(1), (2). The Iowa statute, and many others, do however require that a warning be communicated as soon as the significant danger does become known.

86. *See, e.g.,* McGuire v. Davidson Mfg. Corp., 258 F. Supp. 2d 945 (N.D. Iowa 2003), *aff'd*, 398 F.3d 1005 (8th Cir. 2005) (holding that even though Iowa statute offers "state of the art" defense in both manufacturing and design defect suits, the former will result in liability for negligence if a "lemon" is produced)

87. Rogers v. Miles Laboratories, Inc., 802 P.2d 1346 (Wash. 1991).

88. RESTATEMENT (SECOND) OF TORTS § 402A cmt. k (1965). See Chapter 8, *supra.*

explicitly abandons the pretense of strict liability in favor of a frank negligence rule for "unavoidably unsafe products." So long as known risks are warned of, and so long as the state of the art allows for no better design of the product, there is no liability for prescription drugs, blood, vaccines and medical devices.

Comment k is often restricted to the medical field. Is there any theoretical reason for this restriction? The very existence of "failure to warn" suits implies that there are some risks that cannot feasibly be "designed out" of a product and that must be warned of if possible.[89] Consider the following cases.

- In *Anderson v. Owens–Corning Fiberglas Corp.*,[90] plaintiff filed suit in 1984, alleging that he contracted asbestosis and other lung ailments through exposure to asbestos while working as an electrician at the Long Beach Naval Shipyard from 1941 to 1976. Plaintiff encountered asbestos while working in the vicinity of others who were removing and installing insulation products aboard ships. Plaintiff referred to catalogs and other literature depicting workers without respirators or protective devices. In addition, he offered proof that, until the mid–1960s, defendants had given no warnings of the dangers associated with asbestos, that various warnings given by some of the defendants after 1965 were inadequate and that defendants removed the products from the market entirely in the early 1970s. Defendants responded that the state of the art during the period 1943–1974 was their defense to any cause of action for failure to warn. Defendants' claimed that even those at the vanguard of scientific knowledge at the time the products were sold could not have known that asbestos was dangerous to users in the tiny concentrations associated with plaintiff's injuries. California's Supreme Court ruled that this was a viable defense, as one cannot be held liable for failing to warn of an unknown and not reasonably knowable risk.

- In *Sternhagen v. Dow Co.*[91] Charles Sternhagen was employed by a crop-spraying business in Montana during the summer months of 1948, 1949 and 1950. His survivors claimed that during that time, Sternhagen was exposed to defendants' herbicide 2,4–D. In 1981, Sternhagen, by then a radiologist, was diagnosed as having a form of cancer that his survivors claimed was caused by his exposure to 2,4–D thirty years earlier. Defendants disputed the claim that there was any causal link between the herbicide and the type of

89. *See, e.g.,* Purvis v. PPG Indus., 502 So.2d 714 (Ala. 1987) (dry cleaning chemicals not defective if known risks warned of to direct buyer).

90. Anderson v. Owens–Corning Fiberglas Corp., 810 P.2d 549 (Cal. 1991).

91. Sternhagen v. Dow Co., 935 P.2d 1139 (Mont. 1997).

cancer from which Sternhagen died. Alternatively they asserted, under Comment j of § 402A, that such causal links were utterly unknown at the time and that they therefore had no duty to warn of it.[92] The Montana Supreme Court, answering a certified question, decided to "reject the state-of-the-art defense, as this defense is contrary to the doctrine of strict products liability as that body of law has developed in Montana."[93] The court did recognize that the caselaw of most states admitted "state of the art" evidence, but insisted that the social functions of strict liability would be served only if state of the art evidence was inadmissible.[94] The court declined to indicate how a manufacturer or seller should price an item if unknowable risks might affect expected liability in unpredictable ways, or how a liability insurer should fix premiums for unknowable risks.[95]

The *Restatement (Third)*, as stated above, holds that a product is defective only if manufactures fail to warn about "foreseeable" product dangers.[96] Clearly, "state of the art" evidence is admissible in failure to warn cases under this rule.

C. "State of the Art" and Design Defect

- *Boatland of Houston, Inc. v. Bailey*[97] arose after Samuel Bailey was killed in a boating accident in May 1973. Bailey's boat, sold by defendant, had struck a partially submerged tree stump, throwing Bailey into the water. With the boat's motor still running, the boat turned sharply and circled back toward the stump. Bailey was killed by its propeller. Plaintiff claimed the boat as designed was defective and unreasonably dangerous, because it was not equipped with a "kill switch" cord attached to the body of the boater that would switch off the motor if the boater were ejected. As it turns out, four months earlier, one George Horton had obtained a patent for just such a kill switch, which he branded "Quick Kill." According to Horton, his invention required no breakthroughs in manufacturing or production. The Texas Supreme Court upheld the jury's defense verdict, ruling that "in response to the Baileys' evidence of kill switch use in 1978, the time of trial, Boatland was properly allowed to show that they were not used when the boat was sold in

92. Comment j notes that that "the seller is required to give warning ... if he has knowledge, or by the application of reasonably, developed human skill and foresight should have knowledge, of the presence of the ... danger." RESTATEMENT (SECOND) OF TORTS § 402A cmt. J (1965).

93. *Sternhagen*, 935 P.2d at 1142.

94. *Id.* at 1147.

95. *See* Chapter 2 *supra*.

96. RESTATEMENT (THIRD) OF TORTS, PRODUCTS LIABILITY § 2(c) (1998).

97. Boatland of Houston, Inc. v. Bailey, 609 S.W.2d 743 (Tex. 1980).

1973. To rebut proof that safety switches were possible and feasible when Bailey's boat was sold because the underlying concept was known and the "Quick Kill," a simple, inexpensive device had been invented, Boatland was properly allowed to show that neither the "Quick Kill" nor any other kill switch was available at that time."[98]

Questions: Is *Boatland* a "state of the art" case or a "custom" case?[99] Even today, "quick kill" switches are optional, and boat buyers, the overwhelming majority of whom do not wish to be tied to their boat by a lanyard, rarely select this option. Are boats sold without "Quick Kill" defective and unreasonably dangerous?

Properly understood, "state of the art" is not rigorously a defense in a design defect case. Rather, it is a claim that plaintiff has not made out his case in chief that defendant's product is defective. On occasion, though, the availability of an alternative design at the time of manufacture and first sale is assumed from the fact that alternate designs are available at the time of trial. Thus, state of the art evidence will usually have to be presented by the defense.[100]

- In *Allen v. Minnstar, Inc.,*[101] Allen went for a midnight boat ride with some friends on Lake Powell in 1985. The boat was a 1978 Wellcraft Marine, powered by an OMC 140 hp inboard/outboard engine. Allen was sitting in the front of the boat when, in order to avoid an obstacle in the water, the driver made a sharp turn, causing Allen to fall overboard. The boat ran over Allen who was struck and severely injured by the boat's unguarded propeller. The propeller lacerated his left leg to the bone, necessitating amputation. Allen brought suit against OMC and others, alleging that the boat was defectively designed because it was not equipped with a propeller guard. OMC moved for summary judgment, arguing that Allen had failed to produce evidence that a safer commercially feasible engine design was available when the boat was manufactured in 1977. Plaintiff's proposed expert,

---

98. *Id.* at 749.

99. *Id.* at 752 (dissent).

100. *See, e.g.,* Champion v. Great Dane Ltd. Partnership, 286 S.W.3d 533 (Tex. App. 2009) (holding that injured truck driver failed to prove that refrigerated truck trailer with floor gutter to collect water was defective, by evidence of alternative design with a grating to cover gutter which might have reduced or eliminated risk of pallet-jack wheels falling into gutter and causing him injury; there was evidence that a grate was neither technologically nor economically feasible because the metal would pose problems of corrosion, added weight, and would need to be very thick to sustain heavy loads, driver did not show such grates were technologically feasible when trailer left manufacturer's control, and there was expert testimony that this design was safer.)

101. Allen v. Minnstar, Inc., 8 F.3d 1470 (10th Cir. 1993) (applying Utah law).

testifying in 1989, reported that he had just developed two prototypes, which he claimed could be applied to a 70–hp, 140–hp or 200–hp engine. The expert conceded that he had not actually built the prototype for a 140–hp engine, but that "all the numbers and all the shapes and designs will transfer very easily and simply to the 140–horsepower engine that's involved in this case." The following discussion then ensued:

> Q. Do you have an opinion as to whether this particular boat and engine should have been equipped with a propeller guard when it left the hands of Outboard Marine Corporation back in the early Seventies, and in the late Seventies?
>
> A. I really don't. My opinion would be that I think boats should have guards on them; and that if it could have been, it should have been. My opinion is that if it could have had a guard on it, it should have.
>
> . . . .
>
> Q. What I'm trying to get at, Bryan, is whether you have an opinion as to whether this boat and engine specifically, the 140–horsepower stern drive unit, should have been equipped with some sort of people protecting propeller guard when it left the hands of Outboard Marine Corporation in the late Seventies.
>
> A. My opinion is that if it could have had a guard, it should have had a guard on it. And if the boat was going to be used as a waterskiing boat, around people, that it should have a guard on it. Is that- That's the best I can answer that.
>
> Q. Do you have an opinion as to whether there was a guard in existence at the time this 140–horsepower stern drive left the hands of Outboard Marine Corporation that could have been equipped on that particular stern drive unit?
>
> A. I didn't have one for that horsepower at this time, no. So all I could say is that at that time I couldn't put one on it.
>
> Q. Were you aware of any guards in existence back in the late Seventies when this guard left the hands of Outboard Marine Corporation; this lower unit left the hands of Outboard Marine Corporation?
>
> A. For that particular lower unit, as far as I was aware of, there were no guards for that at that time.

Summary judgment for the defense was affirmed.

- In *Caterpillar Inc. v. Shears,*[102] plaintiff Shears was seriously injured in a collision of two front-end loaders. The removable rollover protective structure ("ROPS") for the loader operated by Shears was not installed. Shears alleged that Caterpillar, the manufacturer of the loader, and B.D. Holt, which sold the loader to Shears' employer, were strictly liable because the ROPS was removable. The trial court affirmed a jury verdict for Shears for actual and punitive damages. But the Texas Supreme Court reversed, stating that the availability of other models with non-removable ROPS was irrelevant, because some uses of loaders require low clearance on level ground, making removal of the rollover protective structure mandatory. The court noted, "We evaluate whether a product has a design defect in light of the economic and scientific feasibility of safer alternatives.... The degree of feasibility is one factor courts weigh in balancing the utility of a product versus its risks.... However, if there are no safer alternatives, a product is not unreasonably dangerous as a matter of law."[103]

What if the jurisdiction where a design defect suit is heard is among the small minority that still uses "consumer expectations" instead of the "risk utility" test? Presumably plaintiff need not even prove the existence of an alternate design in such cases—she need merely prove that the design used was expected to perform flawlessly or at least without the mishap that occurred. However, the distinction may be a semantic one. If defendant claims its product is "unavoidably unsafe" under Comments j and k (see above), plaintiff must then, even in some "consumer expectations" jurisdictions, show that an alternate design was feasible.[104]

The *Restatement (Third),* discussed above, requires plaintiff to prove that a "reasonable alternative design" would have avoided or reduced the risk, *and* that the absence of this design makes the product unreasonably safe. This entrenches the relevance of "state of the art" in design defect cases, and also allows safety devices to be optional equipment. It is required, however, that as in *Caterpillar* the "less safe" model is still "reasonably safe."[105]

D. "State of the Art" and Post–Sale Duties

Chapters 7 and 8 demonstrated that liability for design and informational defects, allegedly "strict" under the *Restatement*

---

102. Caterpillar Inc. v. Shears, 911 S.W.2d 379 (Tex. 1995).

103. *Id.* at 384.

104. *See, e.g.,* Jenkins v. Amchem Prods., 886 P.2d 869 (Kan. 1994) (Plaintiff need not specifically prove safer, cost-effective alternative unless defendant claims that its product is unavoidably unsafe.)

105. *See also* RESTATEMENT (THIRD) OF TORTS, PRODUCTS LIABILITY § 2 cmt. d (1998).

(Second), is in fact inevitably premised on some kind of wrongdoing. We have seen that the *Restatement (Third)* recognizes this.

When the "state of the art" changes, after the sale of the impugned product, some cases have found that the product becomes defective unless the seller either recalls it where feasible (to retrofit the new device) or at least warns of any now-known hidden danger (where retrofitting is not feasible). This can happen in several different kinds of cases.

- It may be that a hidden danger of the product is not reasonably discoverable when the product is first sold. Later, experience reveals this hidden danger makes the product irreparably defective and unreasonably dangerous.[106]

- A design risk might not have been reasonably discoverable pre-sale, but once discovered post-sale it might give rise to a duty to recall and repair the product.[107]

- On the other hand, if a new safety device is developed, but the old device was not defective/unreasonably dangerous when sold, there is generally held to be no obligation to recall and retrofit the new device.[108] Even if the manufacturer (perhaps to enhance goodwill) voluntarily upgrades some units to reflect new technology, that does not prove the non-upgraded products are defective.[109]

Of course, an *involuntary* recall pursuant to a government mandate[110] might be powerful evidence of the existence of a design defect, though plaintiff will still bear the burden of proving that that particular defect caused her injury. But agencies such as NHTSA have no authority to order free upgrades, e.g., to force carmakers to recall legally produced old cars and make them "state of the art."[111] Most jurisdictions admit recall letters (whether volun-

---

106. *See, e.g.,* Kociemba v. G.D. Searle & Co., 707 F.Supp. 1517 (D. Minn. 1989) (post-sale duty to warn of newly discovered contra-indication for IUD).

107. *See, e.g.,* Cover v. Cohen, 461 N.E.2d 864 (N.Y. 1984) (duty under common law to recall car after newly discovered throttle spring problem causing unintended acceleration).

108. *See, e.g.,* Anderson v. Nissan Motor Co., Ltd., 139 F.3d 599 (8th Cir. 1998) (no obligation under Nebraska law to warn of or recall forklift simply because newer models are less likely to tip over). Ford Motor Co. v. Reese, 684 S.E.2d 279 (Ga. App. 2009) (no obligation to recall automobile to install safer design of seat).

109. *See, e.g.,* Zychowski v. A.J. Marshall Co., Inc., 590 N.W.2d 301 (Mich. App. 1998) (meat slicer).

110. *E.g.,* National Highway Traffic & Motor Vehicle Safety Act, 49 U.S.C. § 30101 *et seq.,* especially § 30117–21.

111. Typically, after several people complain to NHTSA about the same mechanical or safety-related problem, NHTSA will investigate the issue to determine whether the consumer or the manufacturer is at fault. If the manufacturer is found to be responsible for a serious defect that compromises the *safety* of the vehicle, a recall is ordered. In other instances, an auto manufacturer may find a defect that occurred during the design or manufacturing process of a vehicle and issue a recall voluntarily

tary or mandated) as evidence of the existence of the defect.[112] Obviously, if the letter concerns a manufacturing defect that affects only a small subset of recipients, receipt of the letter does not prove that the recipient's vehicle had the defect.

Under the *Restatement (Third),* one engaged in the business of selling or otherwise distributing products is not subject to liability for harm to persons or property caused by the seller's failure to recall a product after the time of sale or distribution, unless a government body had ordered the recall or unless the failure to recall was negligent.[113] This essentially codifies existing law. Negligence will be established the usual ways. If there are few current users, and if they are easy to contact, post-sale warnings will be cheaper, *ceteris paribus.* If the hidden danger is quite acute, post-sale warning will be more valuable, *ceteris paribus.*

Finally, a comment about a pure evidentiary question is in order. Chapter 7 revealed that if, post-injury, the manufacturer alters the design of the impugned product to make it safer, a federal evidentiary rule prohibits use of that modification to prove that the original version of the product was defective.[114] In any case any modification *via* recall or "technical service bulletin"[115] may be admissible in partial fulfillment of the plaintiff's burden to show a feasible alternate design existed.[116] As for subsequent product warnings, they are covered by § 407. In any case, post-injury warnings are obviously not evidence that knowledge of a substantial risk existed *ex ante* the injury.

Questions About Julian Felipe's Case

- If in subsequent model years the Aerostar is marketed with stronger roofs, would evidence of this design modification help or hurt Julian Felipe's case?

(the NHTSA still receives notification, though). Whatever the circumstances, a recall requires the manufacturer to send an official notice, in a particular form, to registered owners of vehicles found to be defective.

112. *See, e.g.,* Farner v. Paccar, Inc., 562 F.2d 518 (8th Cir. 1977) (applying South Dakota law).

113. RESTATEMENT (THIRD) OF TORTS, PRODUCTS LIABILITY § 11 (1998).

114. Fed. R. Evid. § 407. See Chapter 7, *supra.*

115. Manufacturers issue TSB's for less serious problems that affect normal operation of a vehicle. Sometimes called "secret warranties," TSB's cover known problems and provide repair instructions for service technicians whenever a customer brings a vehicle in for this or (sometimes) any other reason. The NHTSA maintains a database of TSB's.

116. *See, e.g.,* Bramlette v. Hyundai Motor Co., 1992 WL 350683 (N.D. Ill. 1992) (denying defendants' motion in limine to exclude evidence of a recall). *But see* Rutledge v. Harley–Davidson Motor Co., 364 Fed.Appx. 103 (5th Cir. 2010) (upholding the exclusion of plaintiff's recall notice evidence to establish, in part, the feasibility of an alternative design based on Fed. R. Evid. 407).

- Would the filing of suits such as the Felipes' serve to encourage or discourage Ford, at the margin, from improving the roofs of its vans?

5. Regulatory Preemption Defense (The Product Was as Safe as the Government Said It Had to Be)

A. The Problem

Products liability law is part of private ordering.[117] However, public ordering increasingly determines product safety. Interstate commerce in products has resulted in federal authorship of most (though not all) such regulation. From ATF[118] to CPSC[119] to CSB[120] to EPA[121] to FDA[122] to NHTSA to OSHA,[123] the alphabet soup of product regulators is large and growing. Violation of regulations duly enacted[124] can result in hefty fines and a finding that the offending product was defective in design or by lack of warning. For though there is no (state) private right of action automatically accruing from the violation of a federal regulation,[125] a violation of a state or federal design or warning rule can be either per se[126] or persuasive[127] evidence of defectiveness.

The focus of this section is the opposite state of affairs. Suppose that a product *complies* with validly enacted regulations governing design or warnings. May plaintiff, allegedly injured because the product didn't contain more warnings than required, or was not designed more safely than required, nonetheless successfully sue in products liability?

---

117. Michael I. Krauss, *Tort Law and Private Ordering,* 35 St. Louis U. L.J. 623 (1992).

118. Bureau of Alcohol, Tobacco, and Firearms, 28 U.S.C. § 599A *et seq.* (2006).

119. Consumer Product Safety Commission, 15 U.S.C. § 2053 *et seq.* (2006).

120. U.S. Chemical Safety and Hazard Investigation Board, 42 U.S.C § 412 *et seq.* (2006).

121. The Environmental Protection Agency was formed under President Nixon's Executive Order titled Reorganization Plan Number 3. Congressional Record, Vol. 116, H 6523 (91st Congress, 2nd Session). Unlike other agencies, it has no single enabling statute.

122. Food and Drug Administration, 21 U.S.C. § 301 *et seq.* (2006).

123. Occupational Safety and Health Administration—29 U.S.C. § 651 *et seq.* (2006).

124. Challenging adverse or undesirable regulations is a preemptive element of products liability defense work. If the enabling statute does not authorize a regulation, for example, it can be challenged and voided. *See, e.g.,* Southland Mower Co. v. CPSC, 619 F.2d 499 (5th Cir. 1980) (law preferred performance requirements for mowers, while enacted rule was a design requirement; quashed).

125. Merrell Dow Pharms., Inc. v. Thompson, 478 U.S. 804, 811 (1986).

126. *See, e.g.,* Palmer v. A.H. Robins Co., Inc., 684 P.2d 187 (Colo. 1984).

127. *See, e.g.,* Deyoe v. Clark Equip. Co., Inc., 655 P.2d 1333 (Ariz. App. 1982) (holding OSHA standards admissible in strict liability action against manufacturer of earth compactor for injury sustained by worker when compactor rolled over).

Inevitably, where *federal* regulation is involved, constitutional concerns rear their heads.[128] In some cases, federal regulations preempt state laws unless they impose requirements identical to federal requirements. When there is *express preemption,* the Supremacy Clause of the Constitution[129] resolves any conflict (unless of course the federal statute is for some reason unconstitutional).

Most federal statutes have some kind of preemption provision. For example, The *National Traffic and Motor Vehicle Safety Act* ("NTMVSA") contains this preemption clause:

"(b) Preemption.

(1) When a motor vehicle safety standard is in effect under this chapter, a State or a political subdivision of a State may prescribe or continue in effect a standard applicable to the same aspect of performance of a motor vehicle or motor vehicle equipment only if the standard is identical to the standard prescribed in this chapter."[130]

But in most statutes, preemption clauses have uncertain effects. This is in part because such statutes also typically contain *savings clauses* which preserve state rules that are not incompatible with the federal rule. Without clear express preemption, in other words, courts must decide whether there is *implied preemption,* that is, whether there is sufficient *conflict*[131] between the federal and state rules that they cannot function together, or whether the federal government has totally occupied a field such that any intervention by a state would defeat the federal scheme.[132] The NTMVSA savings clause reads as follows:

"Common law liability.—Compliance with a motor vehicle safety standard prescribed under this chapter does not exempt a person from liability at common law."[133]

Several different conjugations of these clauses are possible.

- What if a federal statute compels a manufacturer to do "at least X?" Is that requirement incompatible with a state common law holding that "only 3X or more" avoids liability?

- Likewise, if a federal statute gives a manufacturer a choice between doing X, Y or Z, is the statute incompatible with a state common law ruling that it is liable if it does X or Y, but not liable if it does Z?

---

128. When state regulations are involved, some states' laws explicitly provide that compliance establishes a *rebuttable* presumption of non-defectiveness.

129. U.S. Const. art. VI, cl. 2.

130. 49 U.S.C.A. § 30103(b)(1).

131. This type of implied preemption is often called "conflict preemption."

132. This type of implied preemption is often called "field preemption."

133. 49 U.S.C.A. § 30103(e).

In neither of these cases is it impossible to comply with both federal and state obligations, but in both cases the federal objective may be more or less stymied by state liability decisions.

Representative of the judicial treatment of implied preemption are these two cases:

- *Cellucci v. General Motors Corp.*[134] Daniel Cellucci suffered serious brain injuries when the 1986 Chevrolet Cavalier in which he was a passenger went off the road and collided with a tree. The Cavalier was equipped with three-point lap and shoulder harness safety belts and a dashboard warning light and buzzer designed to promote occupant use of the belts. This setup was one of the three safety options for occupant crash protection allowed by FMVSS 208. Cellucci sued General Motors, claiming that he was wearing his seat belt at the time of the accident but that the Cavalier was defectively designed because airbags were not installed. The court refused to allow this claim to reach the jury, ruling that "since Congress gave manufacturers three passive restraint options to choose from and indicated that such options must be uniform throughout the country, any state liability claim that deviates from allowing a manufacturer to use any of the three options that Congress allowed conflicts with the Safety Act and the regulations promulgated under it."[135]

- *Doyle v. Volkswagenwerk.*[136] While Victoria Doyle was driving her new Volkswagen Jetta in August, 1989, she was struck in the rear by another vehicle, causing severe injuries to her right breast. Ms. Doyle's expert opined that her injuries were caused by the Jetta's restraint system, which included a shoulder belt but lacked a lap belt to absorb a portion of the impact force, a majority of which was focused on Ms. Doyle's right breast. Instead of a lap belt, the Jetta utilized the following combination: (a) a torso shoulder belt with automatic locking retractor; (b) an energy absorbing knee bolster; (3) a specially designed anti-submarining seat; and (4) outboard seat belt anchorage. This setup was another of the three options allowed by FMVSS 208. Plaintiff maintained that a Georgia jury should be allowed to decide whether the option chosen by Volkswagen was defective and unreasonably dangerous. Defendant argued that because the Jetta seat belt system complied with FMVSS 208, defendant was entitled to judgment as a matter of law because they either had no duty under Georgia common law to exceed federal

---

134. Cellucci v. General Motors Corp., 706 A.2d 806 (Pa. 1998).

135. *Id.* at 810.

136. Doyle v. Volkswagenwerk Aktiengesellschaft, 481 S.E.2d 518 (Ga. 1997).

standards, or, if Georgia common law required more than FMVSS 208, the latter preempted the former. The Eleventh Circuit Court of Appeals certified this question to Georgia's Supreme Court, which ruled for plaintiff. Since federal safety standards were "minimum" standards, the court decided that a state's common law may require more. Citing what eventually became § 4(b) of the *Restatement (Third)*,[137] the Georgia court held that a jury has discretion to consider minimum federal regulations along with other elements in determining whether the restraint system passes a "risk-utility" test.[138]

Questions About Julian Felipe's Case

- Imagine that NHTSA had enacted regulations governing the strength of the roof of 1993 Aerostars. Imagine that the regulations forbade the sale of any van whose roof could not withstand a force equal to the weight of the vehicle. Imagine also that the Julian's van (barely) met this standard. Should Julian be able to argue that the regulation establishes a floor, and that state products liability law should be able to find this floor inadequate, a van meeting this minimum therefore being defective and unreasonably dangerous?

- If Julian can win with this argument, could someone injured in a car without a side-curtain airbag argue that such an airbag, available in some vehicles since 1998, is required by common law, even if it is not required by regulation?

- If one accepts that vehicles may always (at a cost) be made safer than they currently are, should there ever be a case where compliance with regulations provides a shield for product sellers?

B. The Supreme Court's "Solution"

Until 1992, federal "savings clauses" were usually sufficient to preserve state common law, which might therefore require more than federal regulations in terms of safety equipment and design. But in *Cipollone v. Liggett Group*,[139] the Supreme Court held that the *Public Health Cigarette Smoking Act of 1969*,[140] which required warnings on cigarette packages, preempted claims based on failure

---

137. "(b) a product's compliance with an applicable product safety statute or administrative regulation is properly considered in determining whether the product is defective with respect to the risks sought to be reduced by the statute or regulation, but such compliance does not preclude as a matter of law a finding of product defect." RESTATEMENT (THIRD) OF TORTS, PRODUCTS LIABILITY § 4(b) (1998).

138. *Doyle*, 481 S.E.2d at 520–21.

139. Cipollone v. Liggett Group, 505 U.S. 504 (1992).

140. Public Health Cigarette Smoking Act of 1969, Pub.L. 91–222, 84 Stat. 87, as amended, 15 U.S.C. §§ 1331–1340 (2006).

to warn, though it did not preempt fraud or misrepresentation claims.

Post–*Cippolone*, preemption has become a significant issue in numerous products liability cases. In the view of your author the Supreme Court has still not developed a coherent vision of preemption. A chronological synopsis of post-*Cippolone* Supreme Court products liability preemption decisions follows:

- *Freightliner Corp. v. Myrick.*[141] State common-law design defect claims were brought against manufacturers of trucks and trailers that were not equipped with antilock braking systems (ABS). The federal trial judge granted summary judgment to the manufacturers on grounds of preemption (ABS was not required by regulation). The Fifth Circuit Court of Appeals reversed, and a virtually unanimous Supreme Court upheld the Circuit court on the grounds that no federal regulations had ever been adopted in the area, thus defeating any preemption claim.

- *Medtronic, Inc. v. Lohr.*[142] Lohr and her husband filed suit alleging design defect liability in the failure of her Medtronic pacemaker. The federal trial court dismissed the complaint as preempted by the *Food and Drug Act,*[143] which added the usual savings clause to this preemption clause:

  > "No State or political subdivision of a State may establish or continue in effect with respect to a device intended for human use any requirement (1) which is different from, or in addition to, any requirement applicable under [the Act] to the device, and (2) which relates to the safety or effectiveness of the device or to any other matter included in a requirement applicable to the device under [the Act]."

  A bare majority of the Supreme Court held that no claims were preempted. A plurality (no precedential status) decided that this was because common law liability did not create any "requirement."

- *Geier v. Am. Honda Motor Co.*[144] An injured motorist brought a design defect suit against Honda, contending that his 1987 Civic was defective because it was not equipped with a driver's side airbag. The trial judge entered summary judgment in favor of the manufacturer, and the Circuit Court of Appeals affirmed. The Supreme Court affirmed by a 5–4

141. Freightliner Corp. v. Myrick, 514 U.S. 280 (1995).

142. Medtronic, Inc. v. Lohr, 518 U.S. 470 (1996).

143. 21 U.S.C. § 360k(a) (2006).

144. Geier v. American Honda Motor Co., 529 U.S. 861 (2000).

majority, holding that the motorist's suit was *impliedly* preempted by FMVSS 208, despite the usual savings clause, because liability would conflict with the federal scheme that required that manufacturers place airbags in *some but not all* 1987 vehicles.

- *Sprietsma v. Mercury Marine, a Div. of Brunswick Corp.*[145] Plaintiff's wife was killed when, after falling from a boat into the water, she was struck by the propeller of an outboard motor. Plaintiff claimed that the motor was unreasonably dangerous because a propeller guard did not shield it. The Coast Guard, the regulator under the Federal Boat Safety Act of 1971,[146] had considered this exact issue and had declined to require propeller guards on motorboats. The state trial court dismissed the complaint and the intermediate court affirmed, finding that the federal statute expressly preempted the state design defect claim. The Illinois Supreme Court affirmed, but on implied preemption grounds. The Supreme Court then unanimously reversed. It reiterated its reluctance, on federalism grounds, to infer express preemption when there is a refusal to regulate. It held that the Coast Guard's decision not to require propeller guards does not logically conflict with state law liability for failing to use one.

- *Riegel v. Medtronic, Inc.*[147] Riegel and his wife sued Medtronic after its catheter ruptured in Riegel's coronary artery during heart surgery. The catheter was a Class III device that received FDA premarket approval. The Riegels alleged that the device was designed, labeled, and manufactured in a manner that violated New York common law. The Medical Device Amendments of 1976 ("MDA") calls for federal oversight of medical devices that varies with the type of device at issue. The most extensive oversight is for Class III devices that undergo premarket approval. These devices may enter the market only if the FDA reviews their design, labeling, and manufacturing specifications and determines that the specifications provide a reasonable assurance of safety and effectiveness. Manufacturers may not make changes to such devices that would affect safety or effectiveness unless they first seek and obtain permission from the FDA. The statute provides that a State shall not

---

145. Sprietsma v. Mercury Marine, a Div. of Brunswick Corp., 537 U.S. 51 (2002).

146. 46 U.S.C. §§ 4301–4311 (2006).

147. Riegel v. Medtronic, Inc., 552 U.S. 312 (2008).

"establish or continue in effect with respect to a device intended for human use any requirement-... (1) which is different from, or in addition to, any requirement applicable under [federal law] to the device, and ... (2) which relates to the safety or effectiveness of the device or to any other matter included in a requirement applicable to the device under [relevant federal law]..."

An 8–1 Supreme Court majority held that this constituted express preemption of the plaintiff's products liability claims. The majority noted that the FDA has, since 2002, favored preemption, and that had the preemption provision been ambiguous the Administration's preference would have been relevant. But since the preemption provision was unambiguous the current administration's preference was superfluous.

- *Altria Group, Inc. v. Good.*[148] Plaintiffs, who smoked "light" cigarettes for over 15 years, claimed that defendants violated the *Maine Unfair Trade Practices Act.*[149] Specifically, they alleged that defendants' advertising fraudulently conveyed the message that "light" cigarettes deliver less tar and nicotine to consumers than regular brands, despite petitioners' knowledge that the message was untrue. [Smokers of "light" cigarettes tend to puff harder and to extract more of a cigarette's tar and nicotine.] The trial court entered summary judgment in favor of defendants, accepting their argument that the *Federal Cigarette Labeling and Advertising Act*[150] preempted plaintiffs' state claim. The preemption section of that statute provides that

  > "[n]o requirement or prohibition based on smoking and health shall be imposed under State law with respect to the advertising or promotion of any cigarettes the packages of which are labeled in conformity with the provisions of this chapter."

  In a 5–4 decision, the Supreme Court held that the Maine consumer statute was neither a "requirement" nor a "prohibition," and was therefore not preempted. The dissent felt that the majority was eviscerating the Court's holding in *Cippolone*.

- *Wyeth v. Levine.*[151] On April 7, 2000, as on previous visits to her clinic, Levine received an intramuscular injection of

---

148. Altria Group, Inc. v. Good, 129 S.Ct. 538 (2008).

149. Me. Rev. Stat. Ann., Tit. 5, § 207 (Supp. 2008).

150. 15 U.S.C.A. § 1331 (2006).

151. Wyeth v. Levine, 129 S.Ct. 1187 (2009).

Demerol® for her migraine headache and Phenergan® for her nausea. Because the combination did not provide relief that day, she returned later and received a second injection of both drugs. This time, the physician's assistant administered the drugs by the "IV-push method." Phenergan® entered Levine's artery, either because the needle was negligently inserted or because (in a phenomenon called "perivascular extravasation") the drug escaped from the vein into surrounding tissue, where it came in contact with arterial blood. Levine developed gangrene, and doctors amputated first her right hand and then her entire forearm. Levine settled her claim against her health care provider, then sued Wyeth for failure to warn, claiming that the drug should have been accompanied by a sterner warning against intravenous insertion. She obtained a $7.8 million judgment at trial. Wyeth appealed on the grounds that Levine's failure to warn claim was preempted. Wyeth's FDA-approved warning about "Inadvertent Intra-arterial Injection" was in these terms:

"Due to the close proximity of arteries and veins in the areas most commonly used for intravenous injection, extreme care should be exercised to avoid perivascular extravasation or inadvertent intra-arterial injection. Reports compatible with inadvertent intra-arterial injection of Phenergan Injection, usually in conjunction with other drugs intended for intravenous use, suggest that pain, severe chemical irritation, severe spasm of distal vessels, and resultant gangrene requiring amputation are likely under such circumstances. Intravenous injection was intended in all the cases reported but perivascular extravasation or arterial placement of the needle is now suspect. There is no proven successful management of this condition after it occurs.... Aspiration of dark blood does not preclude intra-arterial needle placement, because blood is discolored upon contact with Phenergan Injection. Use of syringes with rigid plungers or of small bore needles might obscure typical arterial backflow if this is relied upon alone. When used intravenously, Phenergan Injection should be given in a concentration no greater than 25 mg per mL and at a rate not to exceed 25 mg per minute. When administering any irritant drug intravenously, it is usually preferable to inject it through the tubing of an intravenous infusion set that is known to be functioning satisfactorily. In the event that a patient complains of pain during intended intravenous injection of Phenergan Injection, the injection should be stopped immediately to provide for evaluation of possible arterial placement or perivascular extravasation."

Justice Stevens, writing for five Justices (Justice Thomas concurred in the judgment only, not in the reasoning), found that "State tort suits uncover unknown drug hazards and provide incentives for drug manufacturers to disclose safety risks promptly. They also serve a distinct compensatory function that may motivate injured persons to come forward with information." When those lawsuits are based on claims (as in the Wyeth case) of manufacturers' failure to warn about risks, Stevens added, they "lend force to the promise [of federal law] that manufacturers, not the FDA, bear primary responsibility for their drug labeling at all times."[152] Though the FDA had to approve any change in the warning, Wyeth could have (the jury found it should have) requested such a change.

In dissent, Chief Justice Roberts and Justices Alito and Scalia observed that the FDA had obviously decided that IV insertion of this drug was NOT to be banned. "This case illustrates that tragic facts make bad law," they concluded. "The Court holds that a state tort jury, rather than the Food and Drug Administration, is ultimately responsible for regulating warning labels for prescription drugs. That result cannot be reconciled with *Geier v. American Honda Motor Co.*, or general principles of conflict preemption."[153]

This flurry of activity on the part of the Supreme Court has, it is fair to say, *not* clarified the law in the eyes of practitioners. Typical of the controversial decisions rendered by lower courts after *Wyeth* is *Dorsett v. Sandoz, Inc.*[154] 26–year–old Noe Carrasco shot himself to death after having taken fluoxetine, a selective seratonin reuptake inhibitors (SSRI) and the generic version of Prozac®, for 36 days. Sandoz manufactured fluoxetine, and its warning to doctors about suicide was identical to the warning accompanying Eli Lilly's Prozac® and all other SSRI's:

Suicide: The possibility of a suicide attempt is inherent in major depressive disorder and may persist until significant remission occurs. Close supervision of high-risk patients should accompany initial drug therapy. Prescriptions for _____ should be written for the smallest quantity of tablets consistent

152. *Id.* at 1202.
153. *Id.* at 1217.

154. Dorsett v. Sandoz, Inc., 699 F.Supp.2d 1142 (C.D. Cal. 2010).

with good patient management, in order to reduce the risk of overdose.

Four months after Carrasco's suicide, Sandoz changed its warning to make it identical with Lilly's newly "enhanced warning," which now read as follows in pertinent part:

Clinical worsening and suicide risk-Patients with major depressive disorder, both adult and pediatric, may experience worsening of their depression and/or the emergence of suicidal ideation and behavior (suicidality), whether or not they are taking antidepressant medications, and this risk may persist until significant remission occurs. Although there has been a longstanding concern that antidepressants may have a role in inducing worsening of depression and the emergence of suicidality in certain patients, a causal role for antidepressants in inducing such behaviors has not been established. **Nevertheless, patients being treated with antidepressants should be observed closely for clinical worsening and suicidality, especially at the beginning of a course of drug therapy, or at the time of dose changes, either increases or decreases.** [emphasis in original]

According to plaintiff, who sued both Sandoz and Lilly, the original warning presumably read by Carrasco's physician was not strong enough, because it did not allude to the possibility that antidepressants may have a role in inducing worsening of depression and the emergence of suicidality. Both defendants moved for summary judgment on the grounds that the *Food, Drug and Cosmetic Act* and FDA regulations pursuant thereto preempted plaintiff's failure to warn suit. As it happens, the FDA had considered and rejected citizen petitions to revise the labeling of SSRI's to warn of increased risk of suicide, on the grounds that there was insufficient scientific evidence to find such a link. In fact, the FDA had consistently held that "no credible scientific evidence has caused the agency to depart from its conclusion that the current Prozac® labeling appropriately reflects the level of concern about Prozac® and suicidality."[155]

The trial judge nonetheless rejected defendants' preemption claim, finding that though the FDA had refused to require a more dire warning, it had not in fact forbidden one. Moreover, two weeks after Carrasco's suicide the FDA wrote all generic Prozac® manufacturers to instruct them to henceforth include the "enhanced warning" reproduced above, which mentions but does not endorse the view that fluoxetine enhances suicidality. The court noted that the FDA had accepted that such an association existed for pediatric patients and "was in the process of determining whether such an

155. *Id.* at 5.

association existed for adult patients a well."[156] An FDA 2007 notice that "short-term studies did not show an increase in the risk of suicidality with antidepressants compared to placebo in adults beyond age 24"[157] was, said the court, not "clear evidence" that the FDA would have disapproved a more stringent warning.

What is clear from all this is that current caselaw is Supremely fractured on the issue of preemption—the tide is presently turned against preemption, but could change in a short time. The recent and impending arrival of Justice Sotomayor (whose views on this are unknown) and Elena Kagan (the replacement for Justice Stevens, who has been an active contributor to the preemption debate) exacerbates the uncertainty. If Congress inserted clear express preemption clauses, or omitted preemption clauses in favor of clear savings clauses, these cases would not recur. Until then, the preemption saga will create uncertainty in products liability law, increasing litigation costs to the benefit of no one save attorneys.

6. The Standards Defense (Our Product Was as Safe as Our Competitors' Product)

What if a products liability defendant believes its product is not as good as possible, but as good as all others out there? Perhaps the industry to which defendant belongs has adopted a voluntary safety code, which defendant's impugned product meets. Perhaps industry standards have been fully complied with? Is this compliance relevant to a design defect or failure to warn suit?

Though not legally dispositive, compliance with industry standards and widely respected safety codes can be a powerful defense tool. On the one hand, if standards (for example, of the American National Standards Institute[158]) are detailed and complied with, and adopted by the entire industry, it will be much harder to establish that the design is defective and unreasonably dangerous,[159] or that the alternative design proposed by plaintiff's expert is really feasible.[160] If the risk-utility test for design defect is followed, it will be extremely difficult for plaintiff to assert that a design followed by

---

156. *Id.* at 14.

157. *Id.* at 14, n.14.

158. The American National Standards Institute is a private non-profit organization that oversees the development of voluntary consensus standards for products, services, processes, systems, and personnel. The organization also coordinates U.S. standards with international standards so that American products can be used worldwide. ANSI accredits standards developed by repre-

sentatives of standards developing organizations, government agencies, consumer groups, companies, and others. *See* www.ansi.org (last consulted April 10, 2010).

159. *See, e.g.,* Alderman v. Wysong & Miles Co., 486 So.2d 673 (Fla. App. 1986).

160. *See, e.g.,* Hubbard v. McDonough Power Equip., Inc., 404 N.E.2d 311 (Ill. App. 1980).

all is worse than the alternative design he alone proposes.[161] If no one warns of a particular risk, that is perhaps a persuasive indication that the risk is obvious or inherent, or so rare as not to merit warning.

Question About Julian Felipe's Case

- Should it be relevant to Julian's case if the 1993 Aerostar roof's strength was the same as that of other 1993 vans?

161. *See, e.g.,* Bragg v. Hi–Ranger, Inc., 462 S.E.2d 321 (S.C. App. 1995).

Chapter 11

THE DEFENDANT'S CASE: CAUSATION AND OTHER PEOPLES' BEHAVIOR[1]

1. Introduction

"Many authorities blame human error for almost all accidents, attributing 80 percent to 90 percent of accidents to human error."[2]

"[O]ver 2/3 of all injuries related to consumer products have nothing to do with the design or the performance of the product. They relate to the misuse or abuse of the product."[3]

The recipients of Vitek® jaw implants did nothing wrong. Dr. Holmsby's complaints about premature chewing shouldn't be taken seriously—clearly the defective implants were the cause of their harm.[4] But who is truly responsible for Julian Felipe's injuries? Assuming for the purposes of discussion that the Felipes' Aerostar's roof was defectively weak, are there other candidate donkeys on which to pin the "proximate causation" tail? What if Mrs. Felipe was driving too fast, or poorly maintained her tires, or was inattentive in some way that caused the rollover? Perhaps another driver cut the Felipes off, causing the rollover? Why should Ford buyers, shareholders and workers subsidize that driver's negligence? What if the tire manufacturer or installer was to blame for the blowout? Assume Ford has no liability for defective tires. Should that affect Ford's liability for the defective roof?

In this chapter the affirmative defenses examined boil down to the claim that "the product didn't do it." Readers know that in tort law mere proof of wrongdoing is insufficient to hold defendants liable—sometimes the victim herself, or a third party, or even a natural event concur to relieve the defendant of responsibility for the victim's fate.

---

1. Additional Reading: Gary T. Schwartz, *Contributory And Comparative Negligence: A Reappraisal*, 87 YALE L. J. 697 (1978).

2. Marc Green, *Human Error Vs. Design Error*, 53 TRIAL June 1, 2006, *available at* http://www.visualexpert.

com/Resources/humanvsdesignerror. html (last consulted April 11, 2010).

3. Mary Fisk, *An Interview with John Byington, Chairman, Consumer Product Safety Commission*, 14 TRIAL 25 (1978).

4. Chapter 2, *supra*.

2. Contributory Negligence

The study of contributory negligence as it relates to products liability is endlessly fascinating.

On the one hand, the doctrine of "foreseeable misuse" is universally accepted. This doctrine excuses some consumer misbehavior precisely because the likelihood of this misbehavior was part of the risk that made the seller's design or warning defective. Chapter 10 related the case of a woman who wore her too-flammable nightgown inside out and was allowed to recover for fire damages from its manufacturer, even though her "misuse" caused the linings of the pocket to come into close contact with the burners on a stove[5] and even though the jurisdiction in question recognizes contributory negligence.[6] Similarly, in many workers' injury cases the worker's carelessness, irrelevant to her workers' compensation claim, will also be found irrelevant to her products liability claim.

On the other hand, in all jurisdictions, even those that purport to have abandoned the contributory negligence doctrine, some types of consumer use obviate all seller liability. When an 8–year old child was injured while smashing an empty "non-returnable" beer bottle he had found against a tree, his Massachusetts design defect suit against the manufacturer was rejected, notwithstanding the fact that Massachusetts does not recognize contributory negligence.[7]

Buckley v. Bell[8] is an insightful case in this regard. Buckley ordered a delivery of regular gasoline from the Bells. When the driver arrived in Bells' fuel truck he handed Buckley a hose that, as it turned out, was connected to the *diesel* compartment of the fuel truck. Buckley filled a portable tank in his truck with diesel fuel. Buckley then drove to a field and filled his gasoline-engine hay baler with the diesel from the portable tank. When he attempted to operate the baler Buckley discovered that he had filled it with diesel fuel. Buckley returned to Bells' place of business to inform the Bells that they had delivered the wrong fuel. The Bells recognized the error and said they would replace the diesel fuel with regular gasoline. They drained the portable tank on Buckley's truck and refilled it with regular gasoline. After the portable tank had been filled Buckley went back to his hay baler in the field. He drained the diesel fuel from the baler onto the ground and filled the

---

5. Ellsworth v. Sherne Lingerie, 495 A.2d 348 (Md. 1985), see discussion in Chapter 10 *supra*.

6. As mentioned above, Alabama, Maryland, North Carolina, Virginia and the District of Columbia continue to recognize contributory negligence in tort law. As is seen immediately *infra*, the reach of contributory negligence in prac-

tice goes far beyond the borders of these five jurisdictions.

7. Venezia v. Miller Brewing, 626 F.2d 188 (1st Cir. 1980), see discussion in Chapter 10 *supra*. At any rate the plaintiff was likely too young to be found negligent.

8. Buckley v. Bell, 703 P.2d 1089 (Wyo. 1985).

baler with the regular gasoline. To purge the fuel line of the last bit of diesel, Buckley disconnected it at the carburetor and turned the engine by jumping the solenoid to pump the diesel out of the line. Buckley had his hand over the carburetor to choke the engine and at about the time the gasoline began to flow from the fuel line he removed his hand from the carburetor. The engine backfired and the gasoline ignited. The fire spread to the ground and, fueled by dry grass and the diesel fuel that Buckley had dumped there, it destroyed the hay baler.

Buckley sued Bell both in negligence and in products liability, as the diesel gasoline was unfit for the specific purpose to which Buckley had alerted Bell and was therefore allegedly "defective and unreasonably dangerous." The trial judge dismissed the suit and the Wyoming Supreme Court affirmed, despite the fact that Wyoming had recently jettisoned contributory negligence in favor of pure comparative negligence. Buckley's argument that this modification required that he recover at least some of his damages was dismissed on the ground that his negligence, not the product defect, was the sole proximate cause of the damage he suffered.

The doctrine of contributory negligence in products liability is, in sum, difficult to parse. Often, as in *Buckley*, the term "contributory negligence" is never mentioned. The talented practitioner should not conclude from this that plaintiff's conduct is irrelevant. It is in fact semantically, but not substantively, irrelevant. Rather, the practitioner should conclude that in this particular jurisdiction plaintiff's conduct will be examined to help determine defendant's "scope of duty," or whether there is "proximate causation" of plaintiff's injury by the defect.

In virtually all cases where the *concept* of contributory negligence is involved (even if the *language* of contributory negligence is not invoked) one of the following scenarios exist:

- A negligent plaintiff *does not* recover from the product seller, because the product is found to be non-defective (i.e., the only "defective" aspect of the accident was plaintiff's own behavior).[9]

- The product may be defective, but the negligent plaintiff subsequently misused the product after discovering the defect, "causing the entire injury."[10]

9. *See, e.g.,* Simpson v. Standard Container, 527 A.2d 1337 (Md. App. 1987) (gas can not defective merely because it was not designed to be child-proof—held, no duty to prevent children of users from drinking the gasoline).

10. *See, e.g., Buckley,* 703 P.2d 1089; *see also* RESTATEMENT (SECOND) OF TORTS § 402A cmt. n (1965) ("If the user or consumer discovers the defect and is aware of the danger, and nevertheless proceeds unreasonably to make use of the product and is injured by it, he is barred from recovery.").

- The product is defective, but the negligent plaintiff's misuse was such that he would have been injured even had there been no defect.[11]

- A careless plaintiff *does* recover all his damages (even in "contributory negligence" jurisdictions) because his misbehavior is mild, and failure to protect against this mild misbehavior was precisely the defect complained of.[12]

- Children are injured, the manufacturer should have known that the product would be used near and with children, and it was reasonably possible to safeguard against the danger in question. The negligence of the parent in allowing the child to misuse the product will not be imputed to the child.[13]

3. Comparative Negligence

A. General Remarks

§ 17(a) of the *Restatement (Third)* provides that "A plaintiff's recovery of damages for harm caused by a product defect may be reduced if the conduct of the plaintiff combines with the product defect to cause the harm and the plaintiff's conduct fails to conform to generally applicable rules establishing appropriate standards of care."[14] Obviously, this section is inapplicable in states that follow the contributory negligence rule. "Comparative negligence" states are roughly divided between "pure" states (where plaintiff, no

---

11. *See, e.g.*, Madonna v. Harley–Davidson, 708 A.2d 507 (Pa. 1998) (motorcycle driver claimed an accident occurred because of a defective bolt in the caliper of his brakes; but defendant produced evidence that the accident occurred because plaintiff was riding while intoxicated, and would not have occurred had he been sober); *see also* Campbell v. Cutler Hammer, Inc., 646 So.2d 573 (Ala. 1994).

12. This is the case for virtually all "crashworthiness" cases involving automobiles—see Chapter 10. However, automotive defects other than crashworthiness can implicate this reasoning. *See, e.g.*, Ford Motor Co. v. Bartholomew, 297 S.E.2d 675 (Va. 1982) (driver who had been assured by the dealership that her vehicle was operating well even though the transmission arrow never hit "P" failed to put gearshift lever firmly into "Park," parked car, and left it momentarily with motor running; lever slipped into reverse with resulting damage; held, no contributory negligence).

13. *See, e.g.*, Porter v. United Steel & Wire Co., 436 F.Supp. 1376 (N.D.

Iowa 1977) (young child attempts to climb into grocery cart, which topples; suit for defective design; held that the parents negligence in failing to supervise the child cannot be imputed to the child).

14. In automobile crashworthiness cases, where the manufacturer is liable only for exacerbated injuries caused by a defective design (see Chapter 7 above), the question arises whether this liability should be reduced by some percentage corresponding to plaintiff's negligence that in fact causes the collision. Though caselaw is divided on this point, the logically more sound view is that which holds that the concept of "enhanced injury" already effectively apportions damages on a comparative basis, since defendant is liable only for the increased injury caused by its own conduct, not for the injury resulting from the crash itself. Thus no further reduction should be made because of plaintiff's negligence. *See, e.g.*, Jimenez v. Chrysler Corp., 74 F. Supp. 2d 548, 566 (D.S.C. 1999), *rev'd in part and vacated in part by* Jimenez v. DaimlerChrysler Corp., 269 F.3d 439 (4th Cir. 2001).

matter how negligent recovers some percentage of his damages from the culpable defendant) and "modified" states (where, roughly, plaintiffs recover no damage at all when they are more negligent than are defendants).

Here again the reader is warned of severe semantic confusion in the caselaw. If it is difficult to compare plaintiff's and defendant's negligence in a typical tort case, it is even more difficult to do so when defendant is allegedly liable "irrespective of fault." How does "degree of fault" of plaintiff compare with "liability despite no fault" of defendant?

Of course an easy way out is to decide that the comparison of plaintiff's and defendant's behavior is "for the fact-finder"—but it is still necessary to instruct the jury. In one noteworthy case the Hawaii Supreme Court decided that, though by statute the state had adopted modified comparative negligence in tort cases based on negligence, in strict liability products cases the rule would be pure comparative negligence (though, again, what the plaintiff's negligence is "compared with" is left to the tender and unsupervised mercies of the jury.)[15] For its part, a Comment to the *Uniform Comparative Fault Act* concedes that strict products liability bears a strong similarity to negligence, and that "the trier of fact should have no real difficulty in setting percentages of fault. Putting out a product that is dangerous to the user or the public involves a measure of fault that can be weighed and compared, even though it is not characterized as negligence."

It would be dishonest to claim that theoretical coherence has emerged from the caselaw, but several clarifying examples may be usefully summarized here.

1. *Daly v. General Motors Corp.*[16] Decedent, a 36–year–old attorney, was driving his Opel while intoxicated in Los Angeles. At a speed of 50–70 miles per hour, he collided with 50 feet of guard rail. He was forcibly ejected from the car and sustained fatal head injuries. A wrongful death suit alleged a design defect, namely, an improperly designed door latch allegedly activated by the impact. Plaintiffs' expert testified that the Opel's door was caused to open when the latch button on the exterior handle of the driver's door was forcibly depressed by a protruding portion of the guard rail. It was his opinion that the exposed push button on the door constituted a design "defect" which caused injuries greatly in excess of those that would otherwise have been sustained. Defendants introduced evidence indicating that the Opel was equipped with a seat belt-

15. Armstrong v. Cione, 738 P.2d 79 (Hawaii 1987).

16. Daly v. General Motors Corp., 575 P.2d 1162 (Cal. 1978).

shoulder harness system and a door lock, either of which, if used, would have prevented Daly's ejection from the vehicle after the door opened.

The jury verdict was for the defense, and plaintiffs appealed on the grounds that the victim's fault should not have been considered. The California Supreme Court held that the failure to use the seat belt could reduce, but not preclude, recovery under the state's comparative negligence rule. The intoxication would not reduce recovery at all, however, as this case was about the "secondary collision" or "crashworthiness." The majority recognized that it is semantically difficult to reconcile "comparative fault" to strict liability, but apparently had confidence that juries would somehow perform this feat. For his part, Justice Mosk, dissenting, was of the view that none of the victim's misconduct should reduce recovery in any way. He lamented that "This will be remembered as the dark day when this court, which heroically took the lead in originating the doctrine of products liability and steadfastly resisted efforts to inject concepts of negligence into the newly designed tort inexplicably turned 180 degrees and beat a hasty retreat almost back to square one."[17]

2. *Larue v. National Union Electric Corp.*.[18] Plaintiff, 11 years old, was playing with his parents' canister-type vacuum cleaner. He and his sister were home alone; his father was at work and his mother at school. The previous evening his mother had taken out the two filters that rested above the fan housing and motor of the vacuum cleaner in order to clean them. She left the vacuum cleaner in a hallway, plugged in, with the filters not yet replaced and the hood that covered its top half left open. According to plaintiff's testimony, he was sitting on the yellow plastic filter support, which in turn rested on the metal casing that covered the fan and engine, riding the vacuum cleaner as if it were a toy car. He was dressed in pajamas. His older sister was in another room watching television. At some point in his play he turned on the motor. He continued to ride the vacuum cleaner until his penis slipped through openings in the filter support and casing into the fan. He immediately suffered an amputation of part of his penis. He rushed outside to seek help, was taken to the hospital, and underwent the first of a number of complicated operations to

---

17. *Id.* at 1881; *see also* Greenman v. Yuba Power Prods., 377 P.2d 897 (Cal. 1963), discussed in Chapter 2 *supra* and Cronin v. J.B.E. Olson Corp., 501 P.2d 1153 (Cal. 1972), discussed in Chapter 6 *supra*.

18. Larue v. National Union Elec. Corp., 571 F.2d 51 (1st Cir. 1978).

repair the damage. The products liability suit claimed that the vacuum was defective in design in two ways: it did not have a shield over the opening in the engine and fan casing to prevent insertion of stray parts of the human body, and it was not equipped with an "interlock" switch that would prevent the motor from turning on while the hood was up. The Massachusetts Supreme Judicial Court found that the issue of comparative negligence of the plaintiff had been properly submitted to the jury, which had found the plaintiff 25 percent comparatively negligent.

3. *Shipler v. General Motors Corp.*[19] Plaintiff, the passenger in a Chevrolet SUV, was rendered quadriplegic after the vehicle rolled over. She sued, as Julian Felipe did, claiming that the SUV was defective in design because its roof compressed during the rollover. At trial, GM sought to present evidence of plaintiff's alleged contributory negligence: she and the driver had been drinking before the accident. The trial court excluded evidence regarding alcohol consumption, on the ground that such evidence was not relevant in a crashworthiness case. In addition, when the accident occurred plaintiff's infant son was sitting in her lap, and the seatbelt was fastened over both of them. The infant was ejected in the rollover, and GM tried to prove that the infant's presence under the seatbelt created slack and enhanced plaintiff's injury. The trial court excluded evidence of plaintiff's misuse of the seatbelt (though it reduced her damages by 5 percent under Nebraska's seatbelt law). The jury returned a $19 million verdict for the plaintiff.

The Nebraska Supreme Court affirmed the correctness of excluding all evidence of plaintiff's negligence, as this was a products liability case. It concluded, "We believe it is inconsistent to hold that the user's negligence is material when the seller's is not."[20]

Needless to say, this book's (and the *Restatement (Third's)*) contention that liability for design and informational defects is ultimately based on negligence is relevant to the evaluation of *Shipler*. Even in Nebraska, of course, defendants are free to attempt to prove that plaintiff assumed the risk (see below) or that their product is not defective, as discussed in Chapter 10. But when product defect is conceded or difficult to rebut, the issue dividing *Shipler* from *Daly* will arise, and arguments for one or the other

19. Shipler v. General Motors Corp., 710 N.W.2d 807 (Neb. 2006). *See* Chapter 7, *supra*.

20. *Id.* at 829.

will require a subtle understanding of the various grounds for products liability.

B. Complicating Factor: Multiple Defendants

Often both the manufacturer and subsequent resellers of a product are sued. In these cases, a reseller called on to compensate a plaintiff may almost always avail herself of an indemnity suit against the manufacturer (unless the reseller altered the product or was negligent in some way). But in other instances (as in *Shipler*) the plaintiff has a cause of action against multiple tortfeasors, some liable in negligence, others "strictly liable." Typically all defendants will be found jointly liable to plaintiff, and in comparative negligence jurisdictions this joint liability will be for the percentage of the total harm that is not attributable to the fact-finder's evaluation of the plaintiff's negligence. However, numerous complications arise when these principles are applied to specific fact scenarios. Consider these cases:

1. *Jahn v. Hyundai Motor Co.*[21] A vehicle driven by Burke blew through a stop sign and struck an automobile non-negligently operated by Jahn. After impact, the driver-side airbag in Jahn's Hyundai failed to deploy. As a result of the accident, Jahn sustained multiple serious injuries including a fractured skull. Jahn sued Hyundai and Burke, and reached a settlement with the latter. Jahn claimed that since it could not be determined what damages would have occurred had the airbag deployed, Hyundai should be liable for the entirety of his damages, minus the dollar amount of the settlement with Burke (joint and several liability minus "claim reduction"). Hyundai argued that its "fault" had to be compared with Jahn's, and that the total damage apportioned between them comparatively (joint and several liability minus "share reduction"). The federal court hearing this diversity case certified the dispute to the Iowa Supreme Court. That court was confronted with an earlier precedent that *plaintiff's* comparative fault should never reduce recovery in a crashworthiness case unless it is shown to be a proximate cause of the enhanced injury.[22] Reversing this decision, it held that plaintiff's negligence was a proximate cause of the entire injury (including the enhancement).[23] It then extended this holding to a *third*

21. Jahn v. Hyundai Motor Co., 773 N.W.2d 550 (Iowa 2009).

22. Reed v. Chrysler Corp., 494 N.W.2d 224, 229–230 (Iowa 1992).

23. *Id.* at 559–60. This view is contrary to that of cases such as Jimenez v. Chrysler Corp., 74 F. Supp. 2d 548, 566, *rev'd in part and vacated in part by* Jimenez v. DaimlerChrysler Corp., 269 F.3d 439 (4th Cir. 2001), where the court held that when a manufacturer's defective design "enhances" or exacerbates plaintiff's injuries the manufactur-

party's negligence, thereby agreeing with Hyundai's position.

2. *Schneider Nat., Inc. v. Holland Hitch Co.*[24] This case's facts are colorfully summarized by a dissenting state Supreme Court Justice:

> "A tractor-trailer being operated by a driver for ... (Schneider) separated, the trailer crossing into the oncoming lane, ... killing three persons. Suit was filed against Schneider to recover wrongful death damages. Schneider, a perceptive, knowledgeable defendant, did not just fall off a turnip truck. It recognized the lawsuit as one likely to result in a large verdict and began to look for help in paying the loss. And so, as commonly occurs, it asserted the third party claims against the road contractor ... and the trailer hitch manufacturer ... neither of whom had anything to do with hooking up the trailer. These third party defendants, incensed at being sued at all, refused to contribute to a settlement. So Schneider, after five days of trial and unable to frighten the third party defendants into contributing, weakened, decided discretion was the better part of valor, and settled, paying the total amount necessary to cause [the plaintiff] to dismiss the case against Schneider with prejudice."[25]

The federal trial court certified to the Wyoming Supreme Court the question whether that state's pure comparative negligence applied when one of the liable parties is a "strictly liable" manufacturer. The court held that comparative negligence required negligence by both sides, and thus could not apply when one defendant is strictly liable. In such a circumstance, the negligent party who has settled (in this case, Schneider) may recover 100 percent of what it paid from a strictly liable product manufacturer, provided that the negligent party was only "passively" negligent in failing to discover the defect. If the negligent settling party was "actively negligent," recovery against the defective product manufacturer would be "equitable," i.e., in a proportion to be decided by the fact-finder.

3. If plaintiff is at fault, the modified comparative negligence rule (roughly, allowing recovery only for persons less than "51 percent negligent") in effect in a plurality of states can

er is only liable for the such increased injury, but no further reduction is taken to this liability based on plaintiff's negligence.

24. Schneider Nat., Inc. v. Holland Hitch Co., 843 P.2d 561 (Wyo. 1992).

25. *Id.* at 588.

produce a jumble, since the plaintiff's fault may be less than that of some defendants and greater than that of others. Similarly, if any defendants having to pay subsequently seek contribution from those not held liable to the plaintiff, the outcome is uncertain and when counterclaims arise no logical solution seems available. Regardless of whether a jurisdiction utilizes the 49 percent modified rule (a plaintiff must be less negligent than the defendant to recover) or the 50 percent modified rule (a plaintiff must not be more negligent than the defendant to recover), it still must determine <u>the manner in which a plaintiff's negligence should be compared to that of multiple defendants</u>. In a pure comparative negligence state, all negligent defendants are liable to the plaintiff even though some may have been less negligent than he; the extent of that liability is a function of the state's joint and several liability rules. In a modified comparative negligence jurisdiction, however, there are two competing approaches. Under the so-called "unit rule," also termed the "aggregate rule," plaintiff is entitled to recover so long as his fault is less than (or at most equal to, in a fifty percent state) the fault of *all defendants combined.*[26] This is the position of the great majority of "modified comparative" states. Under the "Wisconsin rule," also called the "individual rule," however, the plaintiff can recover from any individual defendant only when his negligence was less than (or at most equal to, in a fifty percent jurisdiction) *the fault of the particular defendant.*[27]

[handwritten margin notes: pure comparative negligence → joint and several liability rules.]

[handwritten margin notes: modified comparative negligence → EITHER unit/aggregate rule OR Wisconsin/individual rule]

4. Some states have eliminated joint and several liability, holding each tortfeasor liable only for its "share of negligence." In some instances reforms like these have been held to apply both to negligent defendants and to "strictly liable" products defendants, preventing the original injured party from recovering from the manufacturer damages attributable to another tortfeasor.[28] Juries must somehow determine how much harm each defendant "caused"—easy enough conceptually in "crashworthiness" cases but not in every products case.

In any case, whether they purport to adhere to contributory or comparative negligence for products liability, or whether (as is the

26. *See, e.g.,* Walton v. Tull, 356 S.W.2d 20, 26 (Ark. 1962).

27. *See* Walker v. Kroger Grocery & Baking Co., 252 N.W. 721, 727–28 (Wis. 1934).

28. *See, e.g.,* O'Quinn v. Wedco Tech., Inc. 746 F.Supp. 38 (D. Colo. 1990).

case in Nebraska following *Shipler*) they reject both doctrines, all jurisdictions retain some form of assumption of risk defense.

4. Assumption of Risk

Comment n to the *Restatement (Second)* § 402A notes that a *plaintiff's negligence* is not a defense to strict liability action if it consists merely of the failure to discover defects or to guard against the possibility of the product being defective. The Comment adds, however, that *assumption of risk* (which it defines as "voluntarily *and unreasonably* proceeding to encounter a known danger") still constitutes a complete defense. The comment adds that three elements are required for assumption of risk to avail: subjective knowledge of a risk, voluntary "encounter" of the risk, and negligence ("unreasonable" proceeding). Presumably, then, assumption of risk should reduce, not eliminate, the liability of the seller of the defective product in jurisdictions that have adopted the comparative negligence rule—assumption of risk seems to be an instantiation of comparative negligence.[29]

On the other hand, cases such as *Buckley v. Bell*[30] show that if plaintiff's assumption of risk is seen as the *only proximate cause* of plaintiff's injury, liability of the seller will be precluded even in comparative negligence jurisdictions.[31] And to repeat, there is no need to invoke "assumption of risk" when one really means "there was no evidence of defect"—cutting oneself while playing with knives results in no liability for the knife manufacturer for the latter reason alone.

The reader might be excused for wondering whether the court's choice among all these doctrines is merely conclusory—that is, whether it uses one set of terms when it wishes for some reason to deny recovery, and another set of terms when it wishes for some reason to allow it. It is hard to respond in absolute terms, but assumption of risk does seem to have an independent conceptual content. The following cases illustrate how detailed plaintiff's knowledge and confrontation of a risk must be to constitute assumption of risk:

- If the victim's "best choice" is to face the risk, or if he is required to do so under the terms of his job description, his

29. *See, e.g.,* Kennedy v. City of Sawyer, 618 P.2d 788, 796–97 (Kan. 1980).

30. Buckley v. Bell, 703 p.2d 1089 (Wyo. 1985).

31. *See also* Correia v. Firestone Tire & Rubber Co., 446 N.E.2d 1033

(Mass. 1983) (plaintiff "may not recover if it is found that, after discovering the product's defect and being made aware of its danger, he nevertheless proceeded unreasonably to make use of the product and was injured by it," despite pure comparative negligence rule).

encounter will likely not be deemed "voluntary" under Comment n;[32]

- If the defect creates a peril, which plaintiff must address, and if she addresses the peril clumsily but without premeditation about the risk at hand, assumption of risk will generally not prevail;[33]

- On the other hand, where there is no obligation to act, and there is gross negligence by the victim, assumption of risk is more likely to be found. Thus, if plaintiff knows that liquid propane gas is dangerous, is specifically aware that lighting a cigarette in a room filled with such gas would cause an explosion, recognizes the smell of gas in the basement and nevertheless lights the cigarette, this is a good assumption of risk case.[34]

- Where the victim *should have been aware of* the precise risk, but evidence shows that this particular victim was not, there is no assumption of risk (though there might be comparative negligence).[35]

Subjective standard

Question About Julian Felipe's Case

- Imagine that Mrs. Felipe had, in the company of her son, attempted to trade her 1993 Aerostar in on a newer vehicle one week before her crash. The salesperson offered her a very low trade-in value. When Mrs. Felipe expressed incredulity at the low offer, the salesman responded that the Felipe's Aerostar was known to be quite dangerous, that its roof could not support more than the van's weight in a rollover, and that "the market" knew this, greatly lowering demand for the vehicle. If the Felipes verify the salesman's claim, confirm it, and continue to use the Aerostar, should they be vulnerable to an assumption of risk defense after Julian's injury?

5. "Last Clear Chance"

"Last Clear Chance" is the mirror image of contributory negligence. In the typical contributory negligence case a plaintiff observes defendant's negligence, then carelessly reacts. In these cases contributory negligence often overlaps with assumption of risk. But in "last clear chance" cases, it is the defendant who observes plaintiff's negligence, then carelessly reacts. Since manufacturing

---

32. *See, e.g.,* Brown v. Quick Mix Co., 454 P.2d 205, 208 (Wash. 1969) ("It could never be said as a matter of law that a workman whose job requires him to expose himself to a danger, voluntarily and unreasonably encounters the same.")

33. *See* Wallace v. Owens–Illinois, 389 S.E.2d 155 (S.C. App. 1989) (clean-

ing up exploded soda while wearing slick slippers is not assumption of risk).

34. Andren v. White–Rodgers Co., Div. of Emerson Electric Co., 465 N.W.2d 102 (Minn. App. 1991).

35. *See, e.g.,* Howard v. General Cable Corp., 674 F.2d 351 (5th Cir. 1982) (applying Texas law).

and selling normally occurs well before negligent use of a product, last clear chance has virtually no application in products cases.

One could imagine a situation where a retailer sells a vehicle without functioning brakes to a driver whom he knows to be hopelessly drunk. This would constitute a long-lost "last clear chance" products liability case—but a careful search has failed to reveal any such situation in published cases!

The closest "last clear chance" has come to products liability seems to be a case where a tire manufacturer (who normally must indemnify tire retailers when the latter are held liable for tire defects in a new car) was held to have a contribution suit against a retailer who had installed defective tires even though the retailer should have known they were unsuitable for the automobile in question.[36]

36. Barth v. B. F. Goodrich Tire Co., 92 Cal.Rptr. 809 (Cal. App. 1971).

Chapter 12

THE DEFENDANT'S CASE: OTHER AFFIRMATIVE DEFENSES[1]

1. "I Made It, But *Someone Else* Designed It."

We have seen that manufacturers are potentially liable for manufacturing defects, for design defects and for informational defects. But the extent of this liability depends to a certain extent on the contractual relationships the manufacturer has developed. For example, if a manufacturer produces a good for an expert user, the product may not require the kind of warning needed if it had been marketed to the general public.

A parallel problem occurs when a manufacturer uses design specifications from a co-contracting party. The manufacturer clearly remains liable for manufacturing defects, but is it liable for design defects when it had no hand in the product's design?

Examples:

- Suppose a supplier wins a General Motors bid to manufacture wheels for a particular GM SUV. The bid includes detailed design specifications provided by GM. If the supplier competently manufactures these wheels, which turn out to be too weak for the gross vehicle weight of the SUV for which they were made, should the supplier be strictly liable to the injured consumer?

- An SUV manufacturer wins an Army contract to produce off-road vehicles according to a design provided or approved by federal procurement officials. Suppose a roll bar designed according to the contract specifications gives way in a roll-over accident, injuring the soldier who was at the wheel. The soldier cannot sue the United States.[2] Should he be permitted to sue the manufacturer that produced the SUV following the government's design under a design defect theory?

1. Additional Reading: Ronald A. Cass & Clayton P. Gillette, *The Government Contractor Defense: Contractual Allocation Of Public Risk*, 77 VA. L. REV. 257 (1991).

2. Feres v. United States, 340 U.S. 135 (1950).

Question Concerning Julian Felipe's Case

- Imagine that the 1993 Ford Aerostar was in fact manufactured under license granted by Ford to Magna International.[3] Ford specified, *inter alia*, the Aerostar's roof materials and strength, and Magna produced the Felipes' vehicle according to those specifications. Should Magna have any defense to a design defect claim against it?

A. Contracts Specification Defense

Both examples above concern the manufacturing of a product (or a component) according to the specifications of a third party. Should the manufacturer be liable in such cases?

One approach to this problem was presented by the Nebraska Supreme Court in *Moon v. Winger Boss Co., Inc.*[4] In *Moon*, the victim worked on an assembly line at a meat processing plant. While on the job he fell and his arm became entangled at a "pinch point," where a chain and a sprocket merged in a conveyor system. After the accident, screen guards were placed over these pinch points, but prior to the accident no such safety devices had been installed. The worker filed suit against the manufacturer of the conveyor system, alleging design defect. Defendant had built the conveyor system in strict compliance with the specifications of the employer, after being invited to bid on the project. Defendant did not assist in designing the product in any way. The employer's plans and specifications did not include a safety device over the pinch points. Furthermore, the employer had refused to give the defendant a full layout of the section of the plant where the system was to be used.

Agreeing with a Comment to § 404 of the *Restatement (Second)*,[5] which holds subcontractors liable for design defect only in cases of blatant danger, the Nebraska Supreme Court ruled that the defendant could not be "strictly liable." Only "when the plans are so obviously, patently, or glaringly dangerous that a manufacturer exercising ordinary care under the circumstances then existing would not follow them"[6] would there be liability. *Moon* acknowledges the basis in negligence of design defect liability, and holds harmless a non-negligent manufacturer who had no reason not to trust the design proposed by the co-contracting party. The

---

3. This Canadian–Austrian auto parts maker has built several models under contract, including most recently BMW's X3 crossover vehicle, built at a Magna factory in Graz, Austria.

4. Michalko v. Cooke Color and Chem. Corp., 451 A.2d 179 (N.J. 1982).

5. RESTATEMENT (SECOND) OF TORTS § 404 cmt. a (1965) ("[T]he contractor is not required to sit in judgment on the plans and specifications ... provided by his employer. The contractor is not subject to liability if the specified design ... turns out to be insufficient to make the chattel safe for use, unless it is so obviously bad that a competent contractor would realize that there was a grave chance that [the] product would be dangerously unsafe.").

6. *Moon*, 287 N.W.2d at 434.

latter, who was the victim's employer, was of course immune to products liability because of the workers' compensation bar.

A different approach to this question was offered by the New Jersey Supreme Court in *Michalko v. Cooke Color and Chemical Corp.*[7] In *Michalko*, plaintiff operated a thirty-five ton vertical press that soldered wires to cable transformers inside a cavity. Rubber strips from the press would occasionally fall out during the soldering process. Plaintiff had been instructed by her employer to hold these strips in the cavity with her left hand while she used her right hand to operate the press control. The plaintiff followed these instructions, and her left hand was amputated when it got stuck between the mold and the cavity. The press was not equipped with safety devices that could have prevented the plaintiff's injury. The employer's parent company had manufactured the press many years earlier, but Cubby Manufacturing had been contracted to "rebuild" it. Cubby's contract with the victim's employer required that Cubby follow the employer's drawings and specifications. Cubby knew that safety devices could be installed, but it adhered to the design supplied by the employer, which did not provide for any type of safety device. The New Jersey Supreme Court held that Cubby could be held liable, even though it was not negligent, since its liability for defective design is "strict."[8] Under the New Jersey holding, it was irrelevant that Cubby had no role in the product's design, that it did not create the defect or even that it did not know of the defect. Rather, it was sufficient that Cubby built a product that was defective.

Moon has been widely emulated[9], while *Michalko* has had a relatively small following. Indeed, a subsequent New Jersey statute limits the case's holding to situations where the designer is insolvent or otherwise unreachable.[10] The sub-contractor becomes in effect a surety bond for the designer, and will be liable in settings where the designer is an employer shielded from liability by workers' compensation. In such cases, the "rebuilder" would do well to obtain a contractual indemnity clause from the employer for whom it provides the "rebuilt" machine.

---

7. Michalko v. Cooke Color and Chem. Corp., 451 A.2d 179 (N.J. 1982).

8. *Id.*, at 183.

9. *See, e.g.*, Austin v. Clark Equip. Co., 48 F.3d 833, 837 (4th Cir. 1995) (Virginia law); Garrison v. Rohm & Haas Co., 492 F.2d 346, 351 (6th Cir. 1974) (Kentucky law); Housand v. Bra-Con Indus., Inc., 751 F.Supp. 541, 544–45 (D. Md. 1990) Lesnefsky v. Fischer & Porter Co., 527 F.Supp. 951, 953–55 (E.D. Pa. 1981); Castaldo v. Pittsburgh–Des Moines Steel Co., 376 A.2d 88, 90 (Del. 1977); Luna v. Shockey Sheet Met-

al & Welding Co., 743 P.2d 61, 62 (Idaho 1987); Vaughn v. Daniels Co., Inc., 841 N.E.2d 1133 (Ind. 2006); McCabe Powers Body Co. v. Sharp, 594 S.W.2d 592, 595 (Ky. 1980); Huff v. Ford Motor Co., 338 N.W.2d 387, 390 (Mich. App. 1983); Fisher v. State Highway Comm'n of Mo., 948 S.W.2d 607, 612 (Mo. 1997); Houlihan v. Morrison Knudsen Corp., 768 N.Y.S.2d 495 (App. 2003).

10. N.J. Stat. Ann. §§ 2A:58C–8 & 2A:58C–9(b).

B. Government Contractor Defense

Outside of employer workers' compensation immunity, one of the few status-based immunities that remains is sovereign immunity. If government defectively designs a helicopter, it will not be liable to the Marines and soldiers killed when the copter crashes.[11] Should the private firms who contract with government to build that copter benefit from the same immunity?

In *Boyle v. United Technologies, Corp.*,[12] the copilot of a Marine Corps helicopter was killed during a training exercise when his craft crashed in the ocean due to pilot error. The Marine survived the crash, but as the helicopter sank in the water he was unable to exit the copter and drowned. A wrongful death suit was filed against the helicopter's manufacturer, claiming that the escape hatch was defectively designed because it opened out rather than in; this precluded opening the hatch in a submerged craft because of water pressure. As a matter of federal common law, a 5–4 majority of the United States Supreme Court endorsed a "government contractor defense." This defense immunizes contractors from liability to third parties for design defects if: 1) the federal government had approved reasonably precise product specifications; 2) the product conformed to those specifications; and, crucially, 3) the contractor had warned the federal government about any product-related dangers of which the contractor and not the government had knowledge. Writing for the majority, Justice Scalia opined, "It makes little sense to insulate the Government against financial liability for the judgment that a particular feature of military equipment is necessary when the Government produces the equipment itself, but not when it contracts for the production."[13]

If the government essentially rubber-stamps the design of a product, as when it selects from several competing designs, *Boyle* does not apply.[14] Conversely, if the government appreciates the design risks and warns its service members, the manufacturer can avoid "failure to warn" liability even if it was the designer of the product.[15] Note that government contractor immunity under *Boyle* may be invoked in either state or federal court.

---

11. Richard Ausness, *Surrogate Immunity: The Government Contract Defense and Products Liability*, 47 Ohio St. L.J. 985, 987 (1986) (explaining how the discretionary function exception to the Federal Tort Claims Act "prevents litigants from bringing tort suits against the government to challenge the correctness of policy decisions by members of the executive branch).

12. Boyle v. United Techs. Corp., 487 U.S. 500 (1988).

13. *Id.* at 512.

14. *See, e.g.*, Trevino v. General Dynamics Corp., 865 F.2d 1474 (5th Cir. 1989) (Navy set only general performance standards of diving hangar and left contractor with complete design discretion).

15. Snell v. Bell Helicopter Textron, Inc., 107 F.3d 744 (9th Cir. 1997).

Whether contractors who manufacture and sell products for state and local government use receive similar protection from design and warnings defect claims is a matter for local products liability law. Several states, however, have enacted products liability reform statutes that mimic *Boyle* and protect state government contractors. Note that without *Boyle* immunity, contractors will factor heightened insurance costs into their bid prices, depriving governments of the economic benefits of the immunity granted by statute.

2. "It Wouldn't Have Made a Difference if I Had Warned You."

In informational defect cases, plaintiff's case in chief will produce (typically expert-provided) evidence that a hazard of defendant's product was significant and non-obvious, and should have been warned of (or, as the case may be, should have been warned of more prominently than it was). Plaintiff will then vow that, had the appropriate warning been provided, she would have both noticed the warning and complied with it, thereby by avoiding the hazard that ultimately injured her.

More often than not, plaintiffs declare that they did read the (inadequate) warnings that were provided by the manufacturer, and so would certainly have read an adequate one had it been furnished. In some instances the claim is that a third party read the inadequate warning to the plaintiff,[16] or that though plaintiff did not read the existing warnings *someone else* at plaintiff's workplace read them and would have read an adequate warning and transmitted it to plaintiff.[17] However suspect such claims might appear (the seller is never present to witness the alleged reading of the inadequate warning and so cannot rebut this claim), they constitute evidence of causation, and frequently allow the failure to warn cause of action to go to the jury.

In wrongful death cases, however the decedent is not available to claim that existing warnings were read. In such cases plaintiffs (the named survivors in the state's wrongful death statute) must rely on a legal presumption often called "read and heed:" that an adequate warning would have been heeded had it been given.[18] The burden will typically be on defendant to rebut this presumption.

---

16. *See, e.g.,* Gainey By and Through Gainey v. Perkins, 500 So.2d 272 (Fla. App. 1986).

17. *See, e.g.,* Ferebee v. Chevron Chem. Co., 736 F.2d 1529 (D.C. Cir. 1984) (applying Maryland law).

18. Comment j, § 402A of the *Restatement (Second)* provides, "Where warning is given, the seller may reasonably assume that it will be read and heeded...." RESTATEMENT (SECOND) OF TORTS § 395 cmt. j (1965); *see, e.g.,* Ross Labs., Div. of Abbott Labs. v. Thies, 725 P.2d 1076 (Alaska 1986). Almost all states incorporate "read and heed" in tort cases. Connecticut, Mississippi,

How might defendant offer contrary evidence that would allow a jury to possibly decide that the lack of an adequate warning was not "causal?" As one court pithily stated, if "the user was blind, illiterate, intoxicated at the time of use, irresponsible or lax in judgment," defendant can reach the jury with a persuasive claim that any failure to warn on defendant's part had no causal effect.[19] In one case where the victim, a service station employee, had no impairment and insisted he would have read a warning on a tire rim against mismatching with a tire of a different dimension, defendant produced expert psychiatric testimony that the victim had an antisocial personality disorder that made it exceedingly unlikely that he would have read anything on the tire rim. The psychiatric testimony was held sufficient to allow the jury to find that the lack of warning had no causal effect.[20]

Rarely can defendants hope for more than the chance to persuade the jury that causation is lacking. Still, there are a few failure to warn cases where courts have ruled that defendants are entitled to a judgment as a matter of law on causation grounds, even though plaintiff has made out a *prima facie* case that a better warning should have been provided. Here is a representative sample of these cases.

A. Plaintiff Did Not Read the (Allegedly Inadequate) Warning That Was Given, and Therefore Would Not Have Read the Warning She Claims Should Have Been Given

In *Johnson v. Niagara Mach. & Tool Works,*[21] defendant manufactured and sold to plaintiff's employer a general-purpose punch press. The press was equipped with two palm buttons that had to be simultaneously pressed in order to activate its mechanism. This safety feature prevents the operator from placing a hand between the die and the ram while using the press. The press was also manufactured with a receptacle for a foot switch. [The foot switch method is necessary in strip-feeding applications where the operator must use both hands to position and hold materials in the press. This makes the two-palm technique impossible—only the foot remains available to activate the mechanism.] The employer converted the press from the two-palm method of operation to the foot

Montana and Nevada do require plaintiff to produce evidence that he would have read an adequate warning in cases other than wrongful death. The difference here is superficial—invariably in non-death cases plaintiff will testify that she would have read an adequate warning, as testimony tends to be a more powerful influence on a jury than is a legal instruction.

19. Technical Chem. Co. v. Jacobs, 480 S.W.2d 602, 606 (Tex. 1972).

20. Crowston v. Goodyear Tire & Rubber Co., 521 N.W.2d 401 (N.D. 1994).

21. Johnson v. Niagara Mach. & Tool Works, 666 F.2d 1223 (8th Cir. 1981) (applying Minnesota law).

switch. Plaintiff was strip-feeding the press at the time of the accident. Defendant did not equip its press with any barrier-type guards that would physically prevent an operator from placing any part of the body in the press. Defendant did, however, attach the following warning plate on the front of the press at eye level:

WARNING

TO PREVENT SERIOUS BODILY INJURY

NEVER Place any part of your body under the slide (ram) or within the die area unless power is off, flywheel is stopped and the slide (ram) is blocked up.

NEVER Operate, install dies, or maintain this machine without proper instruction and without first reading and understanding the operator's or machine manual.

It is the employer's responsibility to implement the above and also to provide proper dies, guards, devices or means that may be necessary or required for any particular use, operation, set-up or service.

Do not remove this sign from this machine.

In addition, the press's operation manual provided this bold-faced warning:

CAUTION: For utmost safety, press operators should never be allowed to place their hands into the die area. To this end, Niagara strongly urges the use of point-of-operation guards for all modes of operation. It is specifically pointed out that when foot switches are used, most state codes make the use of point-of-operation guards mandatory. Point-of-operation guards are the user's responsibility, as their design must conform to the type of die used, which is beyond the knowledge and control of the press manufacturer.

Plaintiff had never used this press before. He was instructed how to operate it by his foreman. Plaintiff began to work and had produced about forty parts when a piece of material became stuck in the press. Plaintiff then reached into the press to knock the material out. When that failed, he reached up with his right hand to press the STOP button in order to interrupt the electric current and extract the material. In so doing, he inadvertently placed his left hand in the press and then, while reaching up with his right hand, pressed the foot switch activating the press. Plaintiff's left hand was partially crushed in the press. He lost his left index and middle fingers and 75 percent of the use of his left thumb. He sued

the manufacturer for, *inter alia,* failing to adequately warn operators of the dangers involved in operating the press with a foot
switch.

Plaintiff's claim, in essence, was that the warning contained in
the operator's manual should have been on the faceplate. However,
at trial he testified that he had never read the warning that *was* on
the faceplate, even though he knew a warning of some kind was
there as he had glanced at it. This testimony, according to the
Circuit Court of Appeals, justified the trial judge's directed verdict
dismissing the failure to warn claim.[22]

In such cases, the plaintiff's strategy could be to argue that the
warning that *was* present was inadequate both because it was
substantively lacking *and* because it was insufficiently conspicuous
to attract his attention Had he been drawn to this inadequate
warning he would have read it, inferring that had he been drawn to
a conspicuous and substantively adequate warning he would have
read that one, too. For example, if a poison warning is in written
text, a plaintiff who did not or cannot read the text might claim
that a "skull and crossbones" symbol would have attracted his
attention.[23]

Similarly, if a warning (whether substantively adequate or not)
is not read but is insufficiently prominent in color or size, given the
danger at hand, a failure to warn case can get to the jury if properly
grounded in expert testimony. Typically, this testimony will be by
psychologists who testify as to feasible methods of communicating
the warning, and its psychological impact.[24] Without expert testimony, the naked claim that an impugned warning was not prominent
enough will often be held to be insufficient to allow jury consideration.[25]

An interesting combination of several of these factors existed in
the important Texas decision, *General Motors v. Saenz.*[26] In *Saenz,*

---

22. Why, the reader might ask, did
plaintiff make this admission at trial?
One plausible answer is that his informational defect claim was a multifaceted
one. Likely he wanted to conserve the
option of arguing that the faceplate was
too small, or insufficiently visible or
poorly placed.

23. *See, e.g.,* Hubbard–Hall Chem.
Co. v. Silverman, 340 F.2d 402 (1st Cir.
1965) (affirming judgment against manufacturer of crop-dusting chemicals in
failure to warn action for death of two
Puerto Ricans where English language
label on chemical container did not display skull and crossbones symbol in addition to written warning).

24. *See, e.g.,* Spruill v. Boyle–Mid-
way, Inc., 308 F.2d 79, 87 (4th Cir. 1962)
(affirming judgment against manufacturer of furniture polish in failure to
warn action for death of a 14–month–old
child whose mother did not read a warning on the bottle, where the warning
was "not calculated to attract the user's
attention, due to its position, size, and
. . . coloring").

25. *See, e.g.,* Town of Bridport v.
Sterling Clark Lurton Corp., 693 A.2d
701 (Vt. 1997).

26. General Motors v. Saenz, 873
S.W.2d 353 (Tex. 1993).

two employees were travelling in their employer's water tanker truck when a rear tire blew out, causing the driver to lose control of the vehicle. The truck overturned, killing both employees. The tanker, it turns out, was built in two stages. General Motors manufactured the base truck—without the water tank—in 1972. The base was designed so that it could be modified for a wide variety of uses. The original owner installed a winch on the vehicle and used it as a tow truck. Fifteen years later the base truck (the winch had been removed) was resold to a paving and utility contractor. That contractor added a 2,000-gallon water tank to the truck, so that it could be used to haul water around construction sites. But that contractor's plans must have changed, for a few weeks later he sold the truck, water tank intact, to the construction company that employed the decedents. When the water tank was full, the truck greatly exceeded its gross vehicle weight rating (GVWR)—the maximum safe weight for the entire vehicle, loaded. The GVWR was imprinted on a metal plate that GM had attached to the doorjamb on the driver's side at eye level, in conformity with federal regulations. In addition, an **"IMPORTANT INFORMA-TION ON VEHICLE LOADING"** appeared on page two of the owner's manual in boldfaced block letters. The text then stated, in part:

> **"OVERLOADING SAFETY CAUTION:** . . . Overloading can create serious potential safety hazards and can also shorten the service life of your vehicle."

The doorplate and owner's manual were in place when the employer purchased the truck. One of the construction company's owners noticed that when the truck was driven with a full tank on a bumpy road, it was so heavy that the fenders hit the tires. To try to correct this problem, an employee welded spacers to the truck's frame. However, no one attempted to determine whether the load on the truck was too heavy when the tank was full. On the day of the accident the victims, Saenz and Ramirez, were directed to drive the truck to a job site over 100 miles away. Saenz drove, though he had no valid driver's license, while Ramirez rode in the passenger seat. The accident occurred while the truck was traveling at high-way speeds.

The victims' families sued GM and five other defendants for wrongful death. They claimed that GM did not sufficiently promi-nently warn of the dangers occasioned by weights that would result from foreseeable uses of the truck, including as a water tanker. Against GM, they argued that a sticker with the following language should have been affixed inside the truck's cab near the gearshift lever:

WARNING Overloading this vehicle beyond its "as man-ufactured" GVW can result in loss of control or a roll-over resulting in serious personal injury or death. (For additional information please refer to owner's manual.)

Plaintiffs settled with four of the six defendants before trial and with a fifth during trial, receiving $1,600,000. GM was the only remaining defendant. The jury found that the accident was caused by GM's inadequate warnings and instructions for the safe use of the truck, and by the paving contractor's defective design and construction of the completed water tanker. The jury apportioned responsibility for the accident, 70 percent to GM and 30 percent to the paving contractor, and found plaintiffs' damages to be $3,115,000. The jury also found GM liable for punitive damages of $2,500,000. The trial court rendered judgment on the verdict against GM for 70 percent of actual damages and all punitive damages, court costs and interest, for a grand total of $4.8 million.

GM appealed, alleging that its warning about overloading was sufficient as a matter of law, and arguing in the alternative that plaintiff failed to prove causation, since all parties admitted the victims had not read the warnings that were given. The Texas Supreme Court felt there was sufficient evidence that the warning was inadequate, but that the "read and heed" presumption of causation did not apply. Thus, plaintiff could not reach the jury on causation. In the words of the court,

"Every warning can always be made bigger, brighter and more obvious. GM could have placed the warning where it could not possibly have been overlooked, perhaps engraved upon the dashboard, or backlit on the instrument panel. But it clearly would not be possible for GM to place every important warning in such a position of maximum prominence. It can always be argued that a single instruction should have been given more prominence and if it had, an accident might have been prevent-ed. This argument, however, must be considered in the context of the product involved. When, as here, it is important to give a number of instructions concerning the operation of a vehicle, not all of them can be printed on the dashboard. Indeed, the more instructions and warnings that are printed in one place-on the dashboard, on a doorplate, or in the owner's manual-the less likely that any one instruction or warning will be noticed.

The issue is not whether GM could have placed its warning against overloading in a more prominent position, such as a sticker near the gear shift lever as plaintiffs argue; rather, the issue is whether the warning where it was actually placed was sufficient to give reasonable notice against overloading. GM's warning was posted where gross vehicle weights are customarily placed in compliance with federal regulations. . . . It was at eye level on the driver's doorjamb. The owner's manual was in the glovebox. There is nothing in the record, and nothing in plaintiffs' arguments, to suggest why the warning GM gave was not sufficient to give reasonable notice against overloading. To the contrary, the evidence establishes that the warning did give reasonable notice. In these circumstances, plaintiffs' contention that the warning could have been more prominent does not entitle them to the presumption that it would then have been followed.''[27]

1). *Note: "warning pollution" and failure to warn causation*

Courts are increasingly aware that "warning pollution" can desensitize product users to dangers. This is especially the case for products whose large surface area potentially lends itself to a proliferation of warning decals, such as automobiles (as in *Saenz* above) and ladders.

Typical of "warning pollution" cases involving ladders is *Kane v. R.D. Werner Co., Inc.*[28] In *Kane* a school custodian fell and injured himself while climbing an extension ladder in the school gymnasium. He claimed that the warning labels attached to the ladder were inadequate because: (a) they did not warn users that the rubber feet would wear out over time; (b) they did not inform users how to replace the rubber feet; (c) they recommended that the ladder be set up in a manner that resulted in its leaning at an angle four degrees (!) less than the ideal angle for minimizing the chance of slippage; and (d) they were not in conformance with the 1956 American Standards Association standard pertaining to the proper angle (four degrees less steep) for erection of extension ladders. Defendant moved for and obtained summary judgment, based on plaintiff's deposition concession that he never read warning labels attached to ladders.

B. A Third Party Warned the Victim, So the Lack of Warning on the Product Was of No Consequence

Typical here is *Menard v. Newhall.*[29] In *Menard*, a child playing with a BB gun shot and injured a friend. The plaintiffs argued that the manufacturer should have warned of this danger. The child's father, however, testified that he had instructed his son in the use of the weapon, including what kinds of things he may and may not shoot. (Presumably the father testified to this effect to avoid a suit for contribution by the manufacturer if it were held liable.) The

---

27. *Id.* at 360–61.
28. Kane v. R.D. Werner Co., Inc., 657 N.E.2d 37 (Ill. App. 1995).

29. Menard v. Newhall, 373 A.2d 505 (Vt. 1977).

child ignored those instructions when he shot at his playmate. The court found as a matter of law that there was no reason to believe a child who ignored his father would comply with a label on a gun.

C. A Learned Intermediary Knew of the Risk, Despite the Lack of Warning, and the Intermediary Failed to Warn the Victim; *or* the Intermediary Ignored the Inadequate Warning and Would Have Ignored an Adequate One

Most pharmaceutical warnings are directed to physicians, as discussed in Chapter 8. "Read and heed" applies to the physician, so plaintiff need not prove that the physician would have read an adequate warning had it been made.[30] On the other hand, if the pharmaceutical manufacturer proves that a patient's physician did not read the inadequate warning, the adequate warning in its place would have made no difference.[31] Similarly, if the physician is not aware of a particular condition in a patient that would make the argued-for warning affect his prescription choice to prescribe the drug, the lack of such warning by the manufacturer might have no causal effect. In either case the patient's failure to warn suit may fail as a matter of law.[32] Finally, if the physician already knew of the danger of which the pharmaceutical manufacturer failed to warn, the plaintiff's suit against the manufacturer again fails on causation grounds, whether or not the physician made the patient aware of this danger.[33]

D. The Circumstances of the Injury Make It Virtually Impossible That a Warning, Had It Been Given, Would Have Been Heeded

In *Greiner v. Volkswagenwerk Aktiengesellschaft*,[34] plaintiff was riding as a passenger in a Beetle that was being driven on the wrong side of the road when a car approached at high speed. The driver veered sharply to the right, headed for a guardrail, then veered sharply left, at which point the Volkswagen Beetle overturned—its rear-wheel-drive, rear-engine dynamics requiring different steering techniques in a "spin" than do most other cars.[35]

---

30. Wooderson v. Ortho Pharm. Corp., 681 P.2d 1038 (Kan. 1984).

31. *See, e.g.*, Strumph v. Schering Corp., 626 A.2d 1090 (N.J. 1993).

32. *See, e.g.*, Chambers v. G. D. Searle & Co., 441 F.Supp. 377, *aff'd* 567 F.2d 269 (4th Cir. 1977) (applying Maryland law).

33. The physician's failure affects her own liability for malpractice for failure to obtain informed consent, not the manufacturer's liability. *See, e.g.*, Garside v. Osco Drug, Inc., 976 F.2d 77 (1st Cir. 1992) (applying Massachusetts law).

34. Greiner v. Volkswagenwerk Aktiengesellschaft, 429 F.Supp. 495 (Pa. 1977).

35. The author of this Book was, as a law student, a passenger in a Volkswagen Beetle whose driver lost control on an icy road in exactly these circumstances, with exactly these results. That Beetle was one week old, and the driver

Plaintiff alleged that this design was defective, but the jury disagreed. Plaintiff also alleged that Volkswagen should have warned drivers of these steering characteristics and how to counter them. The court refused to submit the failure to warn claim to the jury, finding that the driver's reaction was instinctive and would not have been different even if the warning she advocated had been given: "[u]nder the circumstances of this case, a warning, even if read, could not have been heeded."[36]

Questions: What if the driver had testified that a warning would have convinced her not to buy a Beetle? In fact, the passenger-plaintiff did attempt to argue this claim, but the court was unimpressed. The plaintiff had produced no evidence providing a basis for this argument, and so the jury was not allowed to hear it. What, though, if the driver had testified that she test-drove several vehicles, and never would have purchased a Beetle had she known of its characteristics in a spin? Would this testimony have solidified a failure to warn case, or would it have been relevant only to plaintiff's (failed) design defect argument?

3. "We Agreed I Wouldn't Be Liable for This."

Fundamental to the "products liability revolution" has been the unanimous judicial refusal (from *Henningsen*[37] onwards) to enforce limitations on the "implied warranty of merchantability," at least when these limitations are incompatible with an express warranty or with the implied representation that a new product is not defective. However, there are occasions, especially when used products are sold, when both parties find it advantageous for the consumer to assume the risk of defect in the contract of sale or rental by waiving the right to sue. Comment m to § 402A of the *Restatement (Second)* contemplates that the strict liability of manufacturers and sellers "is not affected by limitations on the scope and content of warranties." On the other hand, Comment n provides that "the form of contributory negligence which consists in voluntarily *and unreasonably* proceeding to encounter a known danger, and commonly passes under the name of assumption of risk, is a defense under [§ 402A] as in other cases of strict liability."[38]

But why must the user's use be both voluntary *and negligent* in cases involving used products? What if the contract alerts the user to the existence of a possible defect, which the user non-

---

had never before driven a rear-engine, rear-wheel-drive vehicle.

36. *Greiner*, 429 F.Supp. at 498.

37. Henningsen v. Bloomfield Motors, 161 A.2d 69 (N.J. 1960), see *supra* Chapter 4 Section 4.B,

38. RESTATEMENT (SECOND) OF TORTS § 402A (1965) (emphasis added).

negligently decides to risk? Echoing *Henningsen*, Comment a to § 18[39] of the *Restatement (Third)* provides that:

"A commercial seller or other distributor of a new product is not permitted to avoid liability for harm to persons through limiting terms in a contract governing the sale of a product. It is presumed that the ordinary product user or consumer lacks sufficient information and bargaining power to execute a fair contractual limitation of rights to recover. . . . *The rule in this Section applies only to 'sellers or other distributors of new products.'*"[40]

Therefore, an automobile manufacturer would not be protected by a hypothetical clause in a *new* car sales contract by which a purchaser accepts that one car in 10,000 will be a dangerous "lemon." Nor will the mere mention in a sales contract that the buyer takes a *used* product "as is" shield a professional seller from liability for a latent defect that renders the product unreasonably dangerous.

For both new and used products, though, Comment d to § 18 adds,

"This Section does not address whether consumers, especially when represented by informed and economically powerful consumer groups or intermediaries, with full information and sufficient bargaining power, may contract with product sellers to accept curtailment of liability in exchange for concomitant benefits. . ."[41]

What rule does and should apply to used products that are sold with warnings about specific defects? If the last used hang-glider available at the rental shop has a small tear in it, the seller points out this tear, and the consumer decides to rent the hang-glider anyway, will a clause waiving any liability suit for defects in the glider help the renter[42] when he is sued by the purchaser? If not, there is likely no price at which a solvent businessman will be willing to rent this hang-glider. If the seat belts don't work well on the last car available at the rental lot, and the driver, informed of the problem, insists that he urgently needs the car to drive his pregnant wife to the hospital, should they be able to sue the car

---

39. RESTATEMENT (THIRD) OF TORTS, PRODUCTS LIABILITY § 18 (1998) ("Disclaimers and limitations of remedies by product sellers or other distributors, waivers by product purchasers and other similar contractual exculpations, oral or written, do not bar or reduce otherwise valid products liability claims against sellers or other distributors of new products for harm to persons.").

40. *Id.* § 18 cmt. a. (emphasis added).

41. *Id.* § 18 cmt. d. Presumably the "concomitant benefits" do not include "lower purchase price"—otherwise the very nature of § 18 would be contradicted.

42. See Chapter 5, *supra*, for a discussion of lessors' strict liability.

rental agency if a crash causes injuries more grievous than those they would have sustained had the seat belts worked properly, assuming they both had waived such a right as a condition of obtaining the vehicle?

Many jurisdictions refuse to allow potential defendants to waive liability for future negligence. In addition, virtually all jurisdictions decline to enforce express waivers when the subsequent tort is intentional (e.g., fraud). The following statement is typical of courts' response to this issue: "[S]trict liability in tort for personal injuries resulting from defectively designed product cannot be disclaimed by one who places a product on market, knowing that it is to be used without inspection for defects, that proves to have a defect that causes injury to a human being."[43]

On the other hand, as illustrated in Chapter 11, voluntary acceptance of a known defect in a product can result in denial of recovery *via* the defense of assumption of risk.[44] Indeed, in many states a product is not "defective and unreasonably dangerous" unless it creates a risk of physical harm "to an extent beyond that contemplated by the ordinary consumer who purchases it with the ordinary knowledge about the product's characteristics common to the community of consumers."[45]

Presumably this knowledge is altered when a seller informs the buyer of additional latent risks. Why should it matter if the defect becomes "known" through its revelation in a contract as opposed to through sensory perception? What if the seller or distributor wishes to avoid liability for a particular manufacturing defect, or for some poor design feature, *that he specifically points out*? In theory the barrier to recovery for open and obvious defects should both: 1) apply in cases where the defect is made obvious through contract; and 2) benefit all previous sellers of the product through express assumption of risk.

There are few cases on point, however, and they are nuanced. In *Westlye v. Look Sports, Inc.*,[46] for example, plaintiff, an insurance broker by profession, was injured when the allegedly defective bindings on his ski equipment failed to release during a fall. In the rental agreement, plaintiff:

43. Ruzzo v. LaRose Enters., 748 A.2d 261, 267 (R.I. 2000) (citing Greenman v. Yuba).

44. *See, e.g.,* Colson v. Allied Products Corp., 640 F.2d 5 (5th Cir. 1981) (fact that plaintiff knew that the mowers did not have guarding and would throw rocks precluded him from recovering under Georgia law); Delvaux v. Ford Motor Co., 764 F.2d 469 (7th Cir. 1985) (plaintiff may not recover for injuries sustained after rollover of Ford Mustang convertible under Wisconsin law on grounds that it was not equipped with a roll bar, since this feature was obvious)

45. McGraw–Edison Co. v. Northeastern Rural Elec. Membership Corp., 678 N.E.2d 1120 (Ind. 1997) (citing IND. CODE § 33–1–1.5–2 (1993 & Supp.1995)).

46. Westlye v. Look Sports, Inc., 22 Cal.Rptr.2d 781 (App. 1993).

(1) accepted the equipment for use "as is";

(2) agreed that he understood that bindings "will not release under ALL circumstances and are no guarantee for the user's safety";

(3) acknowledged there is "an inherent risk of injury in the sport of skiing, and the use of any ski equipment, and expressly assume[d] the risks for any damages to any persons or property resulting from the use of this equipment"; and

(4) agreed to hold the rental agency harmless and release it from any and all responsibility or liability for damage and injury "whether resulting from the negligence (active or passive/past, present or future) or whether resulting from the selection, inspection or adjustment of this equipment (active or passive/past, present or future) by [the rental agency] and/or its employees or whether resulting from the use of this equipment by the user."

The trial judge granted summary judgment to the lessor and to the distributor of the bindings on the following grounds:

"That agreement releases Klein from all liability. The agreement also contains express language by which the plaintiff acknowledged the inherent risk of skiing and assumed the risk of injury. Finally, the agreement acknowledges that plaintiff accepted the equipment 'as is' and understood that the bindings would not release in all circumstances."

The appellate court was unimpressed with the waiver. First, it held that a waiver signed at the bequest of the rental agency could not benefit the distributor of the bindings. The distributor's claim that an express assumption of risk by plaintiff was absolute and good "against the world" was rebuffed:

"Although in the academic literature 'express assumption of risk' often has been designated as a separate, contract-based species of assumption of risk, ... cases involving express assumption of risk are concerned with instances in which, as the result of an express agreement, the defendant owes no duty to protect the plaintiff from an injury-causing risk."[47]

Second, as regards the rental agency, the court concluded that a "product supplier's attempt to contract away strict liability in tort is void as against the public interest."[48]

In *Bauer v. Aspen Highlands Skiing Corp.*,[49] the facts were virtually identical to those of *Westlye,* except that plaintiff was a

47. *Id.* at 787 (citing Knight v. Jewett, 834 P.2d 696, 703, n.4 (Cal. 1992)).

48. *Id.* at 796–97.

49. Bauer v. Aspen Highlands Skiing Corp., 788 F.Supp. 472 (D. Colo. 1992).

travel agent, not an insurance broker. Only the rental agency was sued. The suit was dismissed based on the waiver, which was held to be fully enforceable.

Questions

- Is it relevant that *Bauer* was decided under Colorado law, and that Colorado is more of a "ski state" than California?

- Following these cases, in which state would one expect ski rental prices to be higher, *ceteris paribus*?

- Is there any way for patrons of California slopes to avoid the liability premium for undetectable binding "defects," other than by purchasing their own equipment (accidents may not happen for months, and in that case the purchasers will be unlikely to be able to prove that the bindings were defective when sold— and this fact will greatly reduce the liability premium)?

Questions Regarding Julian Felipe's Case

- Suppose a used car dealer wishes to sell the 1993 Aerostar to Mrs. Felipe. He has heard about problems regarding the Aerostar's roof's collapsing in rollovers, however, and he fears that the risk of future products liability more than offsets any profits he might derive from the sale. So he informs Mrs. Felipe of this risk, and tells her that he will not sell her the Aerostar unless she signs a waiver of any right to sue him for design defect if ever the roof collapses following a rollover.

  - Should this waiver be enforceable against Mrs. Felipe?

  - Should the waiver be enforceable against Julian Felipe? If not, is there any way the dealer can protect himself from a suit by the passenger?

  - Should the waiver benefit Ford in any way?

4. "You're Paid to Face These Dangers."

A large number (perhaps the majority) of cases cited in this Book involve injuries to workers whose only suit lies against the manufacturer and the resellers of products implicated in their injury. It is clear that the fact that these workers are paid to do their jobs does not preclude them from launching products liability suits.

Some workers, however, are paid precisely to confront situations that result from product defects (and other dangers). The "firefighter's rule" generally holds that such workers (police officers, firefighters, emergency medical technicians, etc.), if injured, may not sue the person who tortiously created the dangerous situation they were paid to confront. Thus, where a defective product causes a fire, the extinguishment of which results in injury to a firefighter, it is traditionally held that no suit lies against the defective product's manufacturer.

The doctrine is possibly in decline as regards products liability. In *Mahoney v. Carus Chemical Co.*,[50] a firefighter sued the manufacturer of potassium permanganate, which it had shipped in fiber-paper drums that caused a fire in its customer's chemical plant. While combating this fire, a structural wall collapsed on a firefighter, trapping him inside the building and injuring him. The New Jersey Supreme Court held that since the firefighter's rule is an exception to liability for negligence, and since manufacturing a defective product is the functional equivalent of negligence, there is no justification for denying manufacturers the immunity afforded by the firefighter's rule. Seven years after *Mahoney*, however, the New Jersey legislature abrogated the firefighter's rule, both for products manufacturers and for negligent tortfeasors.[51] Even in states where the doctrine is still viable, if a defective product injures a firefighter called to the scene of a fire *started by other causes*, caselaw tends to permit recovery much more readily. Thus, in *Furch v. General Electric Co.*,[52] defendant was not protected by the firefighter's rule where it installed materials that, during a fire set by other causes, released toxic gases that injured responding firemen.[53]

50. Mahoney v. Carus Chem. Co., 510 A.2d 4 (N.J. 1986).

51. *See* N.J.S.A. 2A:62A–21 ("In addition to any other right of action or recovery otherwise available under law, whenever any law enforcement officer, firefighter, or volunteer member of a duly incorporated first aid, emergency, ambulance or rescue squad association suffers any injury, disease or death while in the lawful discharge of his official duties and that injury, disease or death is *directly or indirectly the result of the neglect, willful omission, or willful or culpable conduct of any person or entity,* other than that law enforcement officer, firefighter, or first aid, emergency, ambulance or rescue squad member's employer or co-employee, the law enforcement officer, firefighter, or first aid, emergency, ambulance or rescue squad member suffering that injury or disease, or, in the case of death, a representative of that law enforcement officer, firefighter or first aid, emergency, ambulance or rescue squad member's estate, may seek recovery and damages from the person or entity whose *neglect, willful omission, or willful or culpable conduct* resulted in that injury, disease or death.").

52. Furch v. General Elec. Co., 535 N.Y.S.2d 182 (App. 1988).

53. In another case, when a firefighter suffered second- and third-degree burns in a residential fire, allegedly because his firefighting clothing was defective, the firefighter's rule was quite properly held not to apply to preclude recover from the clothing manufacturer. Price v. Tempo, Inc., 603 F.Supp. 1359 (E.D. Pa. 1985). *Price* is surely a case of warranty of fitness for a particular purpose. See *supra* Chapter 4.

Chapter 13

DAMAGES[1]

1. Introduction: Additional Facts About Julian Felipe's Case

Please read paragraphs 15 and 44–55 of Julian Felipe's complaint against Ford Motor Co. (Non-lawyers, please note that "talk is cheap"; in other words, the insertion of an allegation in a complaint does not constitute proof of that allegation.)

15. As a direct and proximate result of the subject incident described above, Plaintiff Julian Felipe suffered severe and permanent physical injuries, including but not limited to C5 spinal fracture with C4 to C6 spinal cord injuries, pain and suffering, disability, disfigurement, mental anguish, loss of capacity for the enjoyment of life, aggravation of a previously existing disease or injury, expense of hospitalization, medical, rehabilitation and nursing care and treatment, transportation expenses and loss of earnings and ability to earn money.

44. Defendant Ford has known since the 1960s that a statistical relationship exists between roof strength, roof intrusion, and neck injuries in belted occupants during rollover accidents. At that time, Ford was aware of how to protect passengers by ensuring that roofs retained their integrity during a foreseeable rollover, and also had the technology available to ensure the necessary roof strength without altering basic roof design.

45. Nonetheless, instead of protecting the occupants of its vehicles, Ford followed an internal policy of evaluating whether it would implement safety measures based on a monetary comparison of the cost of the safety measure per car versus the overall cost of the likely litigation and settlement costs of paying injured victims and decedents' families if the safety measures were not implemented. This policy was memorialized by Ford in writing in the 1960s, and was communicated to Ford engineers during the 1970s and 1980s as well.

46. Specifically, Ford management advised Larry Bihlmeyer, an engineer in its light truck division, that it would not

---

1. **Additional Readings:** Michael I. Krauss, *'Retributive Damages' and the Death of Private Ordering*, 158 U. Pa. L. Rev. Pennumbra 167 (2010), *available at* http://www.pennumbra.com/responses/response.php?rid=86; W. Kip Viscusi, *Corporate Risk Analysis: A Reckless Act?*, 52 Stan. L. Rev. 547 (2000).

authorize $600 in safety testing to identify rollover issues in one of its light truck models, because "it was okay to kill people rather than spend money on safety testing." When Mr. Bihlmeyer went to higher management seeking clarification as to what he had been told, higher management confirmed that this was indeed Ford's policy.

47. During his career with Ford, Mr. Bihlmeyer was involved in higher level management meetings, including ones involving the Aerostar and other light trucks, in which Ford openly discussed safety hazards with these vehicles, withholding information from the federal government, and falsifying documents to NHTSA.

48. Ford followed its policy of cutting safety expenditures to save money, and chose not to implement the safety recommendations regarding roof strength of its own safety engineers, instead placing vehicles on the road with weak, inadequate roofs that would crush and injure occupants during rollovers.

49. To ensure that Defendant Ford did not have to absorb even the "litigation expenses" of this policy, it took the further step of pre-charging upfront a percentage of the wholesale price of the vehicles that would be placed into a litigation account and paid out as claims arose—attempting to buffer itself from the financial consequences of a willful policy of permitting occupants to be injured and to die in its vehicles.

50. Julian Felipe was one such occupant, and he was catastrophically injured in a foreseeable rollover incident when the roof, inadequately designed and constructed, foreseeably crushed in on him.

51. Defendant's conduct was willful, wanton, reckless, or so grossly negligent as to amount to an intentional tort tantamount to at least a third degree misdemeanor.

52. Defendant's acts and omissions are so outrageous that they are not tolerable in a civilized society or community.

53. Defendant's wrongful conduct subjects Defendant to an assessment against it of substantial punitive damages, to punish Ford for its bad acts, and to deter others from acting in a similar way in the future.

54. Moreover, the negligence and the acts and omissions of the Defendant as defined in this complaint in connection with the intentional acts of certain of its employees serves as a further basis for the imposition of punitive damages against Defendant.

55. The evidence in this case establishes that Defendant engaged in conduct which showed such an entire lack of care that

the Defendant must have been consciously indifferent to the consequences; that Defendant engaged in conduct that showed wanton or reckless disregard for the welfare of the public, and that they engaged in conduct which showed a reckless indifference to the rights of others. As a result, Plaintiff is entitled to punitive damages against Defendant.[2]

Questions About Julian Felipe's Case

- If you were Julian's attorney, how would you go about attaching dollar figures to the compensatory damages claims of paragraph 15? How would you attach a figure to the punitives claim of paragraph 55?

- If you were Ford's attorneys, would you contend that any of Julian Felipe's compensatory claims are weak?

- Do any of the paragraphs (44–49) written to justify Julian Felipe's punitive damages claim seem objectionable to you?

2. Compensatory Damages for Personal Injury and Death

Many issues relating to damages are common to tort suits in general. However, product malfunction often leads to lifelong disabilities and death. It is therefore worthwhile to briefly revisit these areas.

A. Wage Loss[3]

It is difficult to generalize, given the variety of state (and even individual courtroom) rules here, but it is safe to say that juries have considerable leeway in fixing damages for lost wages. Typical, if striking, is *Shipler v. General Motors,*[4] a rollover case discussed in Chapter 7. In *Shipler* plaintiff produced an "expert" with a Ph.D. in Business Administration who presented evidence of plaintiffs' most recent two years' (1996–1997) pre-accident earnings as a bartender. She had been earning $6.50 per hour plus unspecified tips. The expert testified that average earnings for a 35–39 year old female with a high school education were $25,811 in 2001 (when the trial took place), and that plaintiff would have had a work life expectancy of 19.5 years from the date of her testimony. The expert explained variables, including the future growth rate of plaintiff's compensation and the various options that could be used to discount future income to present value.[5] The "expert" refused to

2. Second Amended Complaint § 15, 44–55, Felipe v. Ford Motor Corp., 2006 WL 4702029 (Fla. Cir. Ct. 2006).

3. *See generally,* for a detailed treatment of wages issues in tort adjudication, Michael I. Krauss & Robert A. Levy, *Calculating Tort Damages For Lost Future Earnings: The Puzzles Of Tax, Inflation And Risk*, 31 Gonz. L. Rev. 325 (1995–96).

4. Shipler v. General Motors Corp., 710 N.W.2d 807 (Neb. 2006).

5. *Id.* at 838.

provide a figure for lost earning capacity. Defendant presented no evidence to rebut anything this "expert" said.[6]

The jury returned a verdict of $19,562,000.00 without indicating specific amounts allocated for lost wages, medical expenses, and pain and suffering. Incredulous, General Motors moved for a new trial on the grounds that the award was excessive and evidence of jury bias. The Nebraska Supreme Court affirmed the trial court's rejection of this motion thusly:

> "The fact that Shipler would incur damages in the future was reasonably certain. The question for the jury was the amount of her damages. The jury was given sufficient evidence from which it could determine a range of damages for Shipler's future loss of wages. The amount of damages to be awarded is a determination solely for the fact finder, and the fact finder's decision will not be disturbed on appeal if it is supported by the evidence and bears a reasonable relationship to the elements of the damages proved."[7]

B. Pain and Suffering

As one court famously noted years ago,

> "Earning power and dollars are interchangeable; suffering and dollars are not. Two persons apparently suffering the same pain from the same kind of injury might in fact be suffering respectively pains differing much in acuteness, depending on the nervous sensibility of the sufferer. Two persons suffering exactly the same pain would doubtless differ as to what reasonable compensation for that pain would be. This being true, it follows that jurors would probably differ widely as to what is reasonable compensation for another's pain and suffering, no matter how specific the court's instructions might be. ..."[8]

Every jurisdiction allows the recovery of (to use the generic term) pain and suffering[9] damages, which are damages not measured by any loss of a tangible thing. In many products cases, physical contact with the product itself is enough to allow for

---

6. Often, if defendant vigorously claims not to be liable, excessive defense attention paid to damages issues might be seen by jurors as tacit admission of liability. Also, when plaintiff is in a pitiful physical state as in *Shipler*, excessive defense rebuttal of damage claims might be seen as cruel and sadistic.

7. *Shipler*, 710 N.W.2d at 839.

8. Herb v. Hallowell, 154 A. 582, 584 (Pa. 1931).

9. Other terms for non-economic damages, which this Book refers to as "pain and suffering," include: emotional distress, mental anguish, disfigurement, physical impairment, loss of consortium, awareness of loss of life expectancy, loss of companionship, loss of parental guidance, loss of enjoyment of life, humiliation, embarrassment, inconvenience, and loss of society. Not all of these will be allowed in any given products case (for example, loss of consortium is severely restricted). The general rules in this regard are available in any Torts hornbook.

recovery for pain and suffering, even if no physical ailment ensues. Thus the "worm in the cola bottle" case will result in (usually small) awards for pain and suffering because of the revulsion experienced upon seeing the worm. Often some threshold of seriousness will be applied, likely in order to avoid the moral hazard of concocted damages,[10] though this threshold falls short of any requirement that there be physical injury.

There is no explicit market for the kinds of "goods" (general contentedness, professional satisfaction, lack of pain, fulfillment, sexual gratification, etc.) lost by the plaintiff who claims pain and suffering damages. Thus, testimony on these matters is much more subjective than is evidence of lost wages, medical expenses or property damage. Plaintiffs' counsel will often create "day in the life" videos for juries to consider in their evaluation of pain and suffering. The visual images of daily indignities allegedly caused by a defective product are often more effective in illustrating "suffering" than thousands of words. "Pain" is sometimes also demonstrated this way, as in *Lanclos v. Rockwell Intern. Corp.*,[11] where the jury viewed images of the plaintiff, a carpenter who lost several fingers in defendant's wood shaper, feeling pain in his hand from the cold or whenever it was touched.

Jury awards for pain and suffering, not surprisingly, vary tremendously. Was Mr. Lanclos' aversion to bumps, to the cold and perhaps to unwelcome stares worth $150,000 (as was adjudged), or perhaps $15,000, or perhaps $1 million? The range of jury awards for pain and suffering greatly affects insurability, as the small chance of a gigantic award may raise premiums considerably. Some states[12] have reacted legislatively to this problem by setting caps that "cut off the tail" of the distribution of pain and suffering damages. Juries are normally not informed of the existence of these

---

10. *See, e.g.*, Ford v. Aldi, Inc., 832 S.W.2d 1 (Mo. App. 1992) (psychological distress must be "medically diagnosable" for recovery—when a woman allegedly "became ill" after seeing a ¾ inch long insect on her fork, but never consulted a doctor afterwards, she was not allowed to reach the jury with her pain and suffering claim).

11. Lanclos v. Rockwell Intern. Corp., 470 So.2d 924 (La. 1985).

12. Alaska, ALASKA STAT. ANN. § 9.17.010 (West 2010) (limiting non-economic damages to the greater of $400,000 or the injured persons life expectancy multiplied by $8,000), Colorado, COLO. REV. STAT. ANN. § 13–21–102.5 (West 2010) (limiting non-economic damages to $250,000), Hawaii, HAW. REV.

STAT. § 663–8.7 (West 2010) (limiting damages for pain and suffering to $375,000 for most tort actions), Idaho, IDAHO CODE. ANN. § 6–1603 (West 2010) (limiting non-economic damages to $250,00), Kansas, KAN. STAT. ANN. § 60–1903 (West 2010) (limiting non-pecuniary damages to $250,000), Maryland, MD. CODE ANN. § 11–108 (West 2010) (limiting non-economic damages to $680,000 as of Dec. 1, 2010, to rise by $15,000 each January 1st), and Ohio, OHIO REV. CODE ANN. § 2315.18 (West 2010) (limiting non-economic damages to $250,000 per plaintiff, or three times the economic loss, up to $300,500 per plaintiff and not to exceed $500,000), have general caps on non-economic damages that are applicable to products liability cases.

caps on damages.[13] Obviously, in states with caps on pain and suffering, general jury verdicts (which fail to itemize which damages are for lost income, which for medical expenses, and which for pain and suffering) are not permitted.[14] But if there are no caps on pain and suffering damages, juries can easily substitute high pain and suffering awards to neutralize legislative or constitutional limitations on punitive damages (discussed below).

Courts do occasionally (though quite rarely) strike down jury damage awards as excessive even in the absence of a cap. Thus, in *In re Vioxx Products Liability Litigation*,[15] a 58–year–old former FBI agent sued Merck for failure to warn his physician that Vioxx®, prescribed to him to relieve chronic neck and back pain, increased the chance of a heart attack, which plaintiff suffered. A jury found Merck liable and awarded plaintiff $50 million in compensatory damages. The court struck down this award and ordered a new trial solely to re-determine damages. Clearly the court felt the jury was biased in its determination of the pain-and-suffering component of the damage award, though it was unable to allude to any objective formula to calculate these damages:

> "The Court finds that the $50 million compensatory damages award is excessive under any conceivable substantive standard of excessiveness. The evidence suggests that the Plaintiff *may* have lost nine or ten years of life expectancy as a result of his use of Vioxx. He also has past medical bills for which he may be compensated, and perhaps future medical bills as well. Furthermore, the Plaintiff is entitled to compensation for his pain and suffering and other intangible losses. However, the Plaintiff is retired, and therefore he cannot recover for lost wages or lost earning capacity. While the Plaintiff may be experiencing a decrease in energy, it appears that he has been able to return to many of his daily activities. Therefore, no reasonable jury could have found that the Plaintiff's losses totaled $50 million."[16]

---

13. Many states have pain and suffering damage caps that apply, not to products cases, but only to medical malpractice cases. These caps create a suspicious distinction—medical malpractice defendants who benefit from them are more likely to be located in-state, while products manufacturers are more likely from out of state. This kind of distinction between local and out-of-state defendants has led some caps to be quashed by state Supreme Courts on "equal protection" grounds. *See e.g.,* Brannigan v. Usitalo, 587 A.2d 1232 (N.H. 1991) (finding $875,000 cap on non-economic loss in personal injury action in violation of New Hampshire's equal protection clause); Ferdon v. Wisconsin Patients Compensation Fund, 701 N.W.2d 440 (Wis. 2005) (striking down Wisconsin's $350,000 cap on non-economic medical-malpractice damages as a violation of Wisconsin's equal protection clause).

14. *See* note 4, *supra,* and corresponding text.

15. In re Vioxx Products Liability Litigation, 448 F.Supp.2d 737 (E.D. La. 2006).

16. *Id.* at 740–41.

Question About Julian Felipe's Case

- Julian Felipe recovered $6 million in damages. The six-person Florida jury awarded him roughly $3 million for past and future medical expenses, about $1 million for lost earnings, and roughly $2 million for past and future pain and suffering.[17] How did the jury reach the pain and suffering figure? Are they "wild guesses?" Is it easier to calculate lost earnings and medical expenses? What confidence should one have in these figures?

- If jury calculations are arbitrary, should a fixed schedule of pain and suffering damages be available as a matter of law, depending, for example, on the age and extent of injury of the victim? Would this be preferable to hearing numerous and expensive expert witnesses opine about pain and suffering?

C. Fear of Future Injury and Medical Monitoring

When exposed to an allegedly defective product, victims sometimes suffer no physical injuries. But they may fear a *future* physical ill effect. In such situations, two possibilities arise. First, the victim might sue for the pain and suffering (a.k.a. "emotional distress") caused by this fear. This type of claim is problematic, as many jurisdictions refuse recovery for "fear of disease" damages unless there is some current manifestation of the disease.[18] In lieu of or in addition to "fear of disease" damages, however, victims have recently sued for economic damages representing the cost of the present and future medical monitoring they claim is needed as a result of their exposure to the defective product.

This recent development in products liability law seems promising. It was held *In Re Paoli R. Yard PCB Litigation,*[19] for instance, that the cost of medical monitoring to detect latent diseases brought about by exposure to polychlorinated biphenyls (PCBs) that can damage the immune system was recoverable in Pennsylvania. Other jurisdictions have not yet recognized claims for medical monitoring unless some present injury is diagnosed.[20]

A suit for medical monitoring costs is conceptually different from a suit for "enhanced risk of" or "fear of" (cancer, etc.). The latter claim seeks damages for the anticipation of future harm and is a dubious subset of pain and suffering. Medical monitoring

---

17. In Florida non-economic damages are called both pain and suffering damages and damages for lost enjoyment of life.

18. *See, e.g.,* Bondy v. Texas Eastern Transmission Corp., 701 F.Supp. 112 (M.D. La. 1988), *affirmed,* 872 F.2d 422 (5th Cir. 1989), holding that state law requires a physical or present injury as a predicate for recovery for mental anguish.

19. In re Paoli R. Yard PCB Litig., 916 F.2d 829 (3d Cir. 1990).

20. *See, e.g.,* Cole v. ASARCO, Inc., 256 F.R.D. 690 (N.D. Okla. 2009); Hinton v. Monsanto Co., 813 So.2d 827, 831 (Ala. 2001); Lowe v. Phillip Morris USA, Inc., 183 P.3d 181 (Or. 2008); Paz v. Brush Engineered Materials, Inc., 949 So.2d 1 (Miss. 2007).

recovery, however, is gaining momentum as a traditional cause of action for future medical costs caused by the defective product.[21] In mass class actions by smokers against cigarette manufacturers, for example, the cost of lung cancer medical monitoring for every member of the class can be enormous. Defendants might be better advised to contesting any legal liability as per Chapters 11, 12 and 14 than to challenge the admissibility of the medical monitoring claim.[22]

Many jurisdictions have not yet addressed this issue, but awards of medical monitoring costs do appear to be consistent with traditional torts claims, so long as the increased risk giving rise to the medically recognized need for testing is significant.[23]

One interesting gloss on this issue was provided in *Khan v. Shiley, Inc.*[24] In *Khan* plaintiff had had an artificial heart valve implanted. Her life improved thereafter, until she discovered that the valve had been recalled due to a 1 percent risk of fracture. This risk of failure was so minute that it was determined that she should not have the removal-replacement surgery, since in her particular case the surgery itself would be riskier than leaving the suspect valve inside her body. Plaintiff sued in products liability, claiming that she experienced anxiety attacks about the valve failing at any moment, like a ticking time bomb. For this anxiety she sought compensation. But was the product inside her body even defective (triggering strict liability)? The California Court of Appeals held that she could not sue for products liability unless her valve in fact did malfunction. On the other hand, had the removal-replacement surgery taken place and the plaintiff suffered side effects, the court has held that recovery would have been allowed.[25] Is this logical?

21. *See, e.g.,* Ball v. Joy Techs., Inc., 958 F.2d 36 (4th Cir. 1991) (applying West Virginia law); Cook v. Rockwell Int'l Corp., 755 F.Supp. 1468 (D. Colo. 1991); Miranda v. Shell Oil Co., 15 Cal. Rptr.2d 569 (App. 1993).

22. Donovan v. Philip Morris USA, Inc., 914 N.E.2d 891 (Mass. 2009).

23. *See* Abuan v. General Elec. Co., 3 F.3d 329 (9th Cir. 1993) (increased risk not significant, therefore monitoring not medically needed under Guam law). Despite a number of states' recognition of claims for medical monitoring, plaintiffs who bring medical monitoring suits as class actions have had trouble achieving certification in these states. (See also Chapter 14, *infra*.) *See, e.g.,* Gates v. Rohm & Haas Co., 265 F.R.D. 208 (E.D. Pa. 2010) (denying plaintiffs' motion for class certification given the presence of significant legal issues); In re Fosamax Prods. Litig., 248 F.R.D. 389 (S.D.N.Y. 2008) (holding class certification improper given the existence of too many individual questions of fact under Federal Rules of Civil Procedures 23(a) and 23(b)).

24. Khan v. Shiley, Inc., 266 Cal. Rptr. 106 (App. 1990). The court did, however, indicate that a suit for fraud would survive summary judgment. Plaintiff of course would have to produce evidence of fraud.

25. *See also* Larsen v. Pacesetter Systems, Inc., 837 P.2d 1273 (Hawaii 1992).

D. Wrongful death

As is well known to those who have studied tort law, a somewhat contentious interpretation of extant common law by a Nineteenth Century English court terminated all tort suits if and when the victim died, even if the death was proximately caused by the tort. America imported this common law tradition, which was overcome (as in England *via* Lord Campbell's Act[26]) by legislation in all fifty states. This legislation allowed persons named in each statute to launch "wrongful death" or "survivor" suits (or both) if their relative was tortiously killed. A wrongful death suit compensates the persons named in the state statute for *their own* losses, not for the decedent's pre-death damages (the latter are recovered through survivor suits). Most state statutes provide that both such causes of action must be merged into one judicial proceeding.

Since, apparently, no "wrongdoing" need be committed for strict products liability to ensue, one might wonder whether "wrongful" death suits are even possible in products liability cases.[27] Rest assured: they are.[28] As is the case with all compensatory damage awards, calculating compensation for persons other than the direct victim in products liability suits is problematic for a variety of reasons.[29]

Very high wrongful death awards can easily be the functional equivalent of punitive damages (see below). Note also that depending on the precise wording of each state's wrongful death statute, statewide legislative caps on pain and suffering damages may not be held to apply to wrongful death suits. This is because the state caps may specifically apply to "personal injury" situations. As statutes are often interpreted restrictively, at least one court has held that *deaths* are not included in the statutory limits on damages in *injury* cases.[30]

---

26. The Fatal Accidents Act 1846 (9 & 10 Vict. c.93).

27. Exceptionally, the remedy under Alabama's *Wrongful Death Act* is apparently entirely punitive; the jury's monetary award should not reflect ordinary compensable items such as loss of support, funeral expenses, or perhaps loss of society, but is solely meant to punish the tortfeasor for causing the decedent's demise. *See, e.g.,* Roe v. Michelin North America, Inc., 637 F. Supp. 2d 995 (M.D. Ala. 2009).

28. *See, e.g.,* Stiltjes v. Ridco Exterminating Co., Inc., 347 S.E.2d 568 (Ga. 1986).

29. *See, e.g.,* Mikolajczyk v. Ford Motor Co., 870 N.E.2d 885 (Ill. App. 2007) (holding part of a products liability wrongful death award of $25 million

for loss of society was so large as to "shock the judicial conscience"; plaintiff's decedent had been killed in an automobile accident that occurred when a driver rear-ended decedent's vehicle, and his defective seat ramped back, causing him to be fatally strike his head on the back seat of the car).

30. *See, e.g.,* United States v. Streidel, 620 A.2d 905 (Md. 1993) (holding that the state noneconomic damages cap for "personal injuries" does not apply to wrongful "death" actions. The case was superseded by statute (1994 Md. Laws 2292 (codified as amended at MD. CODE ANN., CTS. & JUD. PROC. §§ 11–108, 11–109 (1995))) but the alert to readers remains: these are *statutory* provisions, not interpreted the same way *common law* provisions are.

3. Other Compensatory Damages

A. Economic Damage to Tangible Property (Other Than to the Product Itself)

In addition to recovery for personal injuries, products liability plaintiffs may recoup the value of destroyed property. If a defective herbicide destroyed a crop, its value may be recovered;[31] if dairy cows must be euthanized because a defective product has ruined their milk, the value of the cows as milk cows as well as other net economic damage (see immediately below) caused may be recouped.[32] These are economic damages for loss of tangible property, and they are universally treated identically to personal injury.

For intangible economic losses (loss of wealth without loss of tangible property) there are two complications, however.

B. "Pure" Economic Loss

What if a plaintiff suffers no tangible property loss, but "only" loss of income (whether profits or clientele)? In this situation, distinctions must be made. Did the accident injure anyone or not? Did the action damage someone else's tangible property or not? Was the only economic damage to the product itself?

1). A Third Party Suffers Physical Injury

If physical injury occurs to the *plaintiff*, that plaintiff's lost earnings and other lost moneys are recoverable economic losses as a matter of course. If *someone other than the plaintiff* is injured, then the plaintiff's lost of wealth may still be recoverable. (Plus, of course, the injured party may sue.) For example, a father has a legal duty to care for his son, so the father's lost income while tending to his injured son at the hospital is deemed proximately caused and foreseeable.

A Comment to the *Restatement (Third)* illustrates another type of possible occurrence.

> "A machine that is used to anesthetize dental patients was delivered to Dr. Smith with the labels for nitrous oxide and oxygen reversed. Dr. Smith, believing she was administering oxygen to a patient, mistakenly administered nitrous oxide, which caused the patient to die. Due to the adverse publicity arising from accurate media reporting of the case, Dr. Smith suffered a sharp drop in her practice and substantial economic loss. Dr. Smith's interest in her professional reputation is an interest protected by tort law against economic loss arising

---

31. Lowe v. E. I. Du Pont de Nemours & Co., 802 F.2d 310 (8th Cir. 1986).

32. Snyder v. Bio–Lab, Inc., 405 N.Y.S.2d 596 (1978).

from harm to a patient in her care. Thus, Dr. Smith's damages for economic loss are recoverable . . . ."[33]

On the other hand, if under general state common law tort rules an individual may not recover pure economic damages caused by physical injury to a third party, the fact that the injury occurred because of a defective product will not change matters. Again, the *Restatement (Third)* illustrates:

Robert, a skilled electrical engineer, was employed by ABC Contractors, Inc. Robert was killed in an automobile accident caused by a defect in an automobile manufactured by XYZ. ABC suffered substantial economic loss as a result of Robert's death because ABC was unable to complete a building contract in a timely fashion. ABC cannot recover its economic loss from XYZ *because an employer does not have a tort cause of action against a third party for deprivation of the services of an employee arising from personal injury to the employee.*[34]

2). *No One Is Physically Injured, But Property Damage Occurs*

What if no one suffers any physical injury, and the only tangible property damage is *suffered by a third party*? Imagine, for example, that a defective product causes a fire in a commercial establishment whose employees had the habit of patronizing a particular restaurant. The commercial establishment closes, and the ex-employees disperse. This results in an economic loss to that restaurant. The restaurant may not recover against the manufacturer of the defective product.[35]

However, where there *is* damage to *plaintiff's* tangible property (other than the product itself), plaintiff can more easily claim that her economic harm was proximately caused. Imagine, for instance, that a defective car smashes into a storefront, not damaging the car but causing the closing of the store during repairs. The store owner may recover lost profit (not merely the cost of the replacement glass) from the manufacturer of the defective car.[36]

---

33. RESTATEMENT (THIRD) OF TORTS, PRODUCTS LIABILITY § 21, Illustration 1 (1998). What about Dr. Smith's pain and suffering (for the horror she felt at "killing" her patient)? Caselaw varies considerably, but many jurisdictions do not allow recovery for pain and suffering unless the plaintiff was either injured or could have been injured (was in the "zone of danger").

34. *Id.* § 21, Illustration 2 (1998) (emphasis added).

35. *See* William Bishop, *Economic Loss In Tort*, 2 OXFORD J. L. STUDIES 1 (1982).

36. *See, e.g.,* Clay v. Missouri Highway and Transp. Comm'n, 951 S.W.2d 617, 629 (Mo. App. 1997) (explaining that plaintiffs could have recovered for lost profits if they were "made reasonably certain by proof of actual facts which present data for a rational estimate of such products").

When the United States suffers economic loss due to cleanup of a defective oil well, whether onshore or offshore, it can recover these costs through statute, under the *Water Pollution Control Act*,[37] unless the operator can prove that that the discharge was caused solely by an act of God, an act of war, negligence on the part of the United States Government, or an act or omission of a third party. Proof of negligence by the operator is not required to recoup federal economic losses. However there is no remedy under *Water Pollution Control Act* for state government or private citizens' losses, for example in their tourist or fisherman revenue.

The damage horrifically caused by the massive oil slick in 2010 when a British Petroleum ("BP") offshore rig exploded in the Gulf of Mexico will certainly cause tens of billions in tangible and intangible economic loss, in addition to the eleven workers' lives lost in the explosion. The United States Supreme Court noted in *Askew v. American Waterways Operators, Inc.*[38] that states remain free to impose liability in damages for losses suffered both by the states and by private interests. In *In re Exxon Valdez*,[39] which was not a products liability case, it was held that the general maritime law rule prohibiting recovery for purely economic harm (such as loss of livelihood or trade) was inapplicable if strict liability applied, as it would to the manufacturer and seller of defective equipment, if it is determined that such defect caused the BP spill.

3). *Damage Occurs To the Product Itself*

§ 21 of the *Restatement (Third)* provides as follows:

Definition Of "Harm To Persons Or Property": Recovery For Economic Loss

For purposes of this Restatement, harm to persons or property includes economic loss if caused by harm to:

(a) the plaintiff's person; or

(b) the person of another when harm to the other interferes with an interest of the plaintiff protected by tort law; or

(c) **the plaintiff's property other than the defective product itself.**[40]

When a defective product breaks and becomes worthless, perhaps causing other economic losses to its owner or even to others, contract law, not tort law, is generally seen to apply. Privity of

---

37. Federal Water Pollution Control Act, 33 U.S.C.A. § 1321(f, g), Section 311(f, g).

38. Askew v. American Waterways Operators, Inc., 411 U.S. 325 (1973).

39. In re Exxon Valdez, 767 F.Supp. 1509 (D. Alaska 1991).

40. RESTATEMENT (THIRD) OF TORTS, PRODUCTS LIABILITY § 21 (1998) (emphasis added).

contract and consensual limitations on recovery may all become relevant to the success of the plaintiff's recourse, depending on the law of the state.[41] The *Restatement (Third)* provides the following example:

> "ABC Rubber Company sells a conveyor belt to XYZ Automobile Company. XYZ installs the belt in its engine assembly line. A defect in the conveyor belt causes it to break, stopping the assembly line. Until the assembly belt is repaired, no engines can be assembled. Because no engines are available, the production lines for automobiles shut down as well. XYZ loses many days of production at a critical time when its best-selling new model has just appeared in the showroom. Expert witnesses testify and the trier of fact finds that as a consequence of this shutdown, XYZ not only lost the sales of the automobiles that would have been produced but for the shutdown, but also lost the crucial race to be the first in the market with its new model, thereby losing additional millions of dollars of sales to its arch rival MNO Motor Cars, which introduced its new model a week ahead of XYZ instead of a week behind it. Under Subsection (c), XYZ's losses were caused by harm to the defective product itself. XYZ may not recover those losses from ABC under the rules in this Restatement [but must rely on the terms of its contract and on provisions of the UCC]."[42]

It is, however, sometimes difficult to know if the product has merely "injured itself," or if it has caused other damage. When a defective and unreasonably dangerous tire blows up and destroys a car, a products liability suit for the car's value should lie against the tire manufacturer.[43] On the other hand, if a home loses value because one of its component parts (say, the concrete) is defective, the homeowner's rights are traditionally determined by contract law, not products liability.[44] One glaring exception concerns asbestos, where removal costs have been allowed on products liability (as opposed to contract) theories even if there is no injury or damage to

---

41. *See, e.g.,* Alloway v. General Marine Indus., L.P., 695 A.2d 264 (N.J. 1997) (holding that buyer of luxury boat that sank while docked but did not cause personal injury or damage to other property may not bring strict liability action to recover for economic losses against manufacturer's successor, but must rely on contractual remedies).

42. RESTATEMENT (THIRD) OF TORTS, PRODUCTS LIABILITY § 21, Illustration 3 (1998); *see also* East River Steamship Corp. v. Transamerica Delaval, Inc., 476 U.S. 858 (1986) (plaintiff discovered that the supertanker it just purchased had defective turbines, and brought a product liability suit (in admiralty) against the manufacturer of the turbines for the cost of repair and for profits lost while the tankers were out of service. Affirming summary judgment for the defendant, the Court held that the plaintiff could not recover in tort).

43. *See, e.g.,* Saratoga Fishing Co. v. J.M. Martinac & Co., 520 U.S. 875 (1997) (fishing vessel is "other property" when its hydraulic system fails with catastrophic results).

44. *See, e.g.,* Casa Clara Condominium Ass'n. Inc. v. Charley Toppino & Sons, Inc., 620 So.2d 1244 (Fla. 1993).

any other property, indeed (and intriguingly) even if the asbestos itself presents no substantial danger to health until and unless it is being removed.[45]

Finally, if the product damages only itself *but also causes personal injury,* the *East River* rule is inapplicable. Thus, a substantial amount of Chinese drywall imported to America in the 2000s was apparently manufactured in gypsum mines that used fly ash, a waste material that is a byproduct from power plants using coal. This drywall apparently creates a noxious odor and allegedly causes "headaches, nosebleeds, difficulty breathing and other physical afflictions," as well as corroding copper and other metal surfaces. The drywall has led to contract actions against builders as well as a successful products liability suit.[46]

C. Additional Compensatory Damages in Case of Alleged Fraud

If a manufacturer is held liable for a massively marketed defective product (either for a design defect or for failure to warn), its share price (almost all products defendant are public corporations) can be seriously affected. If, in addition, fraud is alleged (in other words, if it is claimed that the company knew of the design or warning defect and fraudulently continued to market the defective product to unsuspecting consumers), punitive damages (see below) are available as well as statutory remedies *via* state consumer fraud statutes and federal securities laws.

As an example of the latter, when Merck & Co. withdrew Vioxx® in 2004 after reports that the pain reliever doubled the risks of heart attack and stroke, after having defended the drug through three years of FDA investigations, shareholders lost tens of billions in wealth overnight. A class action suit by investors claiming securities fraud[47] (alleging that Merck and individual officers and directors had made misrepresentations and omissions to lenders and shareholders regarding Vioxx®'s safety and commercial viability) was deemed timely by the Supreme Court if filed within two years of the withdrawal of the drug.[48] This suit, if successful, could recoup from Merck the losses investors incurred from buying shares in purported reliance on the success of Vioxx®.[49]

45. *See* Richard C. Ausness, *Tort Liability for Asbestos Removal Costs,* 73 OR. L. REV. 505 (1994).

46. In re Chinese Manufactured Drywall Products Liability Litig., 680 F.Supp.2d 780 (E.D. La. 2010) (applying Virginia law).

47. § 10(b), *Securities Exchange Act of 1934,* 15 U.S.C. § 78j(b), has been seen to authorize these suits.

48. Merck & Co., Inc. v. Reynolds, 130 S.Ct. 1784 (2010).

49. Of course, any sums paid by Merck must come either from insurers or from its own capital; in the latter case investors are paying themselves...

In addition, insurance plans (state Medicaid plans as well as private insurers) have sued Merck for the cost of their reimbursement of prescription costs, allegedly a result of the insurers being fraudulently induced to add Vioxx® to their formularies. Even uninsured individual consumers who did not suffer heart attacks or strokes have sued Merck, claiming that they would not have paid as much for the pain-killer at the pharmacy had they known of its dangers.[50] Fraud obviates the need to show other than financial damages.

4. Punitive Damages[51]

Four states have abolished punitive damages by caselaw,[52] while a fifth has done so legislatively.[53] Several other states have capped punitive damages by statute. For all other states, the following story highlights the tensions surrounding the doctrine of punitive damages in products cases.

Mayola Williams sued Philip Morris, manufacturer of Marlboros, for the wrongful death (from lung cancer) of her husband Jesse, a lifelong Marlboro smoker.[54] Jesse Williams had smoked, despite warnings from the federal government, family, and many others, because he had allegedly believed Philip Morris's early claims that smoking had not been proven dangerous.[55] An Oregon jury awarded Ms. Williams $821,000 in compensatory damages (reduced to $521,000 because of a state law cap on pain and suffering) and *$79.5 million* in punitive damages (of which legislation[56] provided that sixty percent would be diverted to the Oregon government.)[57] The punitive award was upheld by Oregon's appel-

---

50. *See, e.g.,* Julie Kay, *More Vioxx Pain: Despite $4.85 Billion Settlement, Merck Faces Slew Of U.S., Foreign Suits,* BROWARD DAILY BUS. REV., December 10, 2007, p. 8, available at 2007 WLNR 28027003.

51. Much of this section is inspired by Krauss, *supra* note 1.

52. *See* International Harvester Credit Corp. v. Seale, 518 So.2d 1039, 1041 (La. 1988) ('Under Louisiana law, punitive or other 'penalty' damages are not allowable unless expressly authorized by statute."); Distinctive Printing & Packaging Co. v. Cox, 443 N.W.2d 566, 574 (Neb. 1989) ("[P]unitive, vindictive, or exemplary damages contravene Neb. Const. art. VII, § 5...."); Dailey v. North Coast Life Ins. Co., 919 P.2d 589, 590 (Wash. 1996) (noting the "court's long-standing rule prohibiting punitive damages without express legislative authorization"); Flesner v. Tech-

nical Commc'ns Corp., 575 N.E.2d 1107, 1112 (Mass. 1991) ("Punitive damages are not allowed in this Commonwealth unless expressly authorized by statute.").

53. *See* N.H. REV. STAT. ANN. § 507:16 (2009) ("No punitive damages shall be awarded in any action, unless otherwise provided by statute.").

54. Williams v. Philip Morris Inc., 48 P.3d 824, 828 (Or. Ct. App. 2002), vacated sub nom. Philip Morris USA Inc. v. Williams, 540 U.S. 801 (2003).

55. *Id.* at 829.

56. *See* OR. REV. STAT. § 31.735 (2007) (directing sixty percent of all punitive damage awards into the "Criminal Injuries Compensation Account").

57. *Williams,* 48 P.3d at 828. In fact Philip Morris has contested this sum, and has not paid it yet, because of

late and Supreme Courts and was reaffirmed on remand after the United States Supreme Court ordered it reconsidered in light of its ruling in *State Farm Mutual Automobile Insurance Co. v. Campbell.*[58] The Oregon Supreme Court upheld the award under *Campbell* because Philip Morris's behavior was "extraordinarily reprehensible."[59] Philip Morris again appealed to the United States Supreme Court.

A sharply divided Court again reversed, finding that the punitive-damages award against Philip Morris violated the latter's constitutional right to due process of law.[60] These rights were violated, held the majority, when the jury was instructed that it should calculate punitives based on the number of people killed by tobacco products. Justice Breyer's majority opinion ruled for the first time that a factfinder must be instructed that it may not increase punitives because of harm caused to nonparties to a lawsuit.[61] Such harm, Breyer conceded, is relevant to the question whether *any* punitive damages may be awarded, but may play no role in determining the amount of the punitive award.[62] The majority declined to consider a separate question—whether the 100–1 ratio of punitive to compensatory awards in *Williams* flouted the constitutional standards of *BMW of North America v. Gore*—presumably because the Court expected the punitive damages award to be reduced on remand.[63]

In any case, after *Williams*, judges must tell jurors to think about harm to nonparties injured by a defective product in deciding *whether* the defendant's conduct merits a punitive award. To calculate *the amount* of punitive damages, however, jurors must somehow consider only the harm to the plaintiff. How jurors are to conceptually separate these two steps is unclear—what seems clear, though, is that this issue is destined to come back before the Court.

One view on this issue is that awards of punitive damages in products cases almost always violate a key characteristic of tort law (of which products liability is a subset) by breaching the private ordering/ public ordering divide.[64] *Private ordering* is between citi-

language contained in the Master Agreement settling the fifty Attorneys' General 1998 suit against cigarette manufacturers.

58. State Farm Mut. Auto. Ins. Co. v. Campbell, 538 U.S. 408 (2003). *Campbell* declined to establish a "bright line rule" to limit the amount of punitive damages, but declared that few awards exceeding a single-digit multiplier of compensatory damages would likely satisfy due process requirements. It did allow for higher ratios where the harm inflicted was minimal and the misbehavior "particularly egregious."

59. Williams v. Philip Morris Inc., 127 P.3d 1165, 1177, 1181–82 (Or. 2006), *vacated sub nom.* Philip Morris USA v. Williams, 549 U.S. 346 (2007).

60. *Id.* at 353–55.

61. *Id.* at 355.

62. *Id.*

63. *Id.* at 352 (citing BMW of N. Am., Inc. v. Gore, 517 U.S. 559 (1996)).

64. *See generally* Michael I. Krauss, *Tort Law and Private Ordering*, 35 St. Louis U. L.J. 623 (1991).

zens. Property law, contract law, tort law, and family law exist to regulate this ordering. *Public ordering* is between citizens and the State. Criminal law, administrative law, tax law, and welfare law are components of public ordering.[65]

Seeing products liability as part of private ordering has several implications. One is that when a defective product damages someone, compensation must be full. Compensation is a function of damages wrongfully incurred rather than that of the extent of wrongdoing. A manufacturer whose defective product negligently burns down a $50,000 house is liable in tort to pay $50,000 to make the homeowner whole. If that house were worth $1 million, the manufacturer would likewise be required to pay $1 million to its owner. Tort law equally respects the poor and the rich. Each tort victim has the right to be returned to her former state by the tortfeasor who harmed her—that far but no farther. Similarly, rich tortfeasors owe full compensation to their victims, as do poor tortfeasors.[66]

By contrast, if products liability incorporated penalties it would resemble public ordering. The use of state agencies to recover penalties is properly seen as subject to constitutional protections, including Fifth Amendment protection against self-incrimination and double jeopardy, Eighth Amendment protection against excessive fines, Due Process requirements that the law alleged to have been broken was duly adopted and clearly published, and the Article I prohibition of *ex post facto* laws subjecting individuals to federal prosecution for crimes not previously clearly defined. Most products liability trials today offer none of those protections. Thus, compulsory discovery compels self-incrimination, while one defective design may lead to many successful punitive damage awards.

Clearly, this view of punitive damages in products cases has not prevailed, despite the explicit statutory conversion of such damages into state revenues (which greatly resemble "fines") as was demonstrated in the *Williams* case. But the explosion of punitive awards has been recent, and has followed the strict liabili-

---

65. Public ordering is the *only* kind of legal order in totalitarian societies. In such a society there is no such thing as property as Americans experience it. Nor is there freedom of contract between consenting adults—private contracts would allow self-determination without state supervision and would thus be impermissible, to the extent it is totalitarian, a state can have no tort law: there's no such thing as a private wrong because every wrong is a wrong against the state. On the other hand, tort law is an essential com-

ponent of private ordering. It is contract law's necessary counterpart—regulating non-contractual interaction among humans. This rectification of private imbalances takes place without the intervention of prisons and police, quintessential components of public ordering.

66. Of course, if the tortfeasor is so poor that he has insufficient assets to compensate the victim (and insufficient insurance to make him solvent), then he cannot be adequately reached in tort.

ty "revolution." Until 1976, there were a total of three reported appellate court decisions upholding punitive damages awards in product liability cases, and in each case the punitive award was quite modest.[67] Today multi-million dollar punitive awards are common, and punitive damages are awarded in approximately 3 percent of products liability judgments.

Questions About Julian Felipe's Case

- As indicated in his complaint (relevant paragraphs are reproduced at the beginning of this Chapter), Julian's attorney asked for punitive damages (presumably totalling millions of dollars). Though many states limit punitive damages to cases where "oppression, fraud or malice" has been established,[68] the United States Supreme Court has never declared this to be a constitutional requirement. Julian Felipe's attorney cited *Owens–Corning v. Ballard*,[69] where the Florida Supreme Court determined that if a manufacturer "knew of dangers of its product, yet consciously made a purely economic decision not to warn of danger, or not to change the product with a readily available safe alternative," punitive damages would be available. Indeed, the court opined that in such cases punitive damages could exceed the state's normal statutory limit of three times compensatory damages.[70] Ford knew of course that it could design a stronger roof than it did design. Does that make Ford eligible for punitive damages?

- If so, would manufacturers be exposed to punitive damages for every conscientious design tradeoff?

- Presumably, manufacturers aware of design limitations, who decide not to correct them, engage in some kind of cost-benefit analysis in order to determine the proper course of action. Some courts have found that the very act of weighing the increased production costs of a contemplated design improvement against the savings in possible accidents is obnoxious and makes the company eligible to be liable for punitive damages. Thus, the Wisconsin Supreme Court in *Wangen v. Ford Motor Co.* held that "punitive damages may be particularly appropriate in a product liability case because . . . [s]ome may think it cheaper to pay damages or a forfeiture than to change a business prac-

67. *See* Gillham v. Admiral Corp., 523 F.2d 102 (6th Cir. 1975) ($125,000 compensatory damages, $50,000 attorneys' fees, $100,000 punitive damages); Toole v. Richardson–Merrell, Inc., 60 Cal.Rptr. 398 (App. 1967) ($175,000 compensatory, $250,000 punitive damages); Moore v. Jewel Tea Co., 253 N.E.2d 636 (Ill. App. 1969) ($920,000 compensatory damages, $10,000 punitive damages).

68. *See, e.g.,* Calif. Civ. Code, § 3294(a).

69. Owens–Corning v. Ballard, 749 So.2d 483 (Fla. 1999).

70. Felipe v. Ford Motor Co., 2006 WL 4808629 (Plaintiff's Reply to Defendant Ford's Memorandum in Opposition to Plaintiff's Motion for Leave to Amend Complaint to Add Punitive Damages).

tice.''[71] Similarly, in *Grimshaw v. Ford Motor Co.*, the California Court of Appeals permitted a $3.5 million punitive damage award because the defendant had "decided to defer correction of the [Ford Pinto's] shortcomings by engaging in a cost-benefit analysis balancing human lives and limbs against corporate profit.''[72] This, however, is puzzling. The risk/utility test that governs design defect adjudication in most jurisdictions is based on the notion that manufacturers should make design decisions by trying to determine whether the expected societal benefits of a contemplated design or warning outweigh the expected societal costs of that design or warning. How can this be done without a cost-benefit analysis?[73] If a cost-benefit analysis alone is insufficient to ground a claim for punitive damages, what facts would be sufficient?

• In 1968, Ford safety engineer J. R. Weaver wrote a memo in which he argued for strengthening the roofs on Ford vans and SUV's. Weaver stated, "It is obvious that occupants that [sic] are restrained in upright positions are more susceptible to injury from a collapsing roof than unrestrained occupants who are free to tumble about the interior of the vehicle. It seems unjust to penalize people wearing effective restraint systems by exposing them to more severe rollover injuries than they might expect with no restraints.''[74] Should this memo make punitive damages available to Julian Felipe?

• In late 1992, Value Rent-a-Car ("Value"), a Florida company owned at the time by Ford competitor Mitsubishi Motors, apparently suffered a series of rollover accidents involving Aerostars that had been rented to groups of tourists. The vans apparently rolled over more often if loaded with people and cargo. Value sent the following memo to Ford:

> "This letter is to inform you that Value had experienced a number of accidents involving rollover incidents in the Ford Aerostar vans. We are interested in knowing if you have any information regarding any problems or increased incidents of rollovers for the Ford Aerostar vans. We would appreciate your providing us with any relevant information regarding these concerns, including the vehicles [sic] compliance with safety standards. [The Aerostar met all federal standards.] In addition, please provide us with any information you have which may be helpful to

---

71. Wangen v. Ford Motor Co, 294 N.W.2d 437, 451 (Wis. 1980).

72. Grimshaw v. Ford Motor Co., 174 Cal.Rptr. 348 (App. 1981).

73. See, for a cogent defense of cost-benefit analysis in product design and warning development, W. Kip Viscu-

si, *Corporate Risk Analysis: A Reckless Act?*, 52 Stan. L. Rev. 547 (2000).

74. J.R. Weaver, Ford Intracompany Memo to H.G. Brilmyer, Roof Strength Study, July 8, 1968 (produced as Exhibit C in *Felipe v. Ford Motor Co.*).

our renters in handling this vehicle other than the information provided in the owners [sic] manual . . . ."

Ford allegedly responded to Value's letter by suggesting that Value "not put things like this in writing." It allegedly declined Value's subsequent demand that the Aerostar be "recalled and fixed" by asserting that the van was "safe" if "used properly," and by insisting that "it would be cheaper to pay the claims involving the Aerostar" than to recall it or redesign it.[75] Does Ford's insistence that its vehicles are "safe," its preference not to create a paper trail of alleged design defects, and its reluctance to redesign the Aerostar after learning from a company controlled by a direct competitor that some have apparently rolled over, make Ford eligible for punitive damages? Should it be relevant to your answer to this question that Julian's van was not fully loaded with baggage nor occupied by more than two people?

- Should this photo, of a billboard in the Detroit, Michigan area created by a rollover "activist" group, be admissible in evidence as part of Julian Felipe's claim for punitive damages?

- In a 2007 research paper written for NHTSA by a George Washington University "National Crash Analysis Center" member, it was determined that on average a 2002–2004 passenger minivan statistically caused $1700 in economic costs from rollovers, which could be prevented by an expenditure of $225 by manufacturers.[76] Would this figure, if it were applicable to 1993 models, establish gross negligence on the part of Ford (and of virtually every other van and SUV manufacturer)? Would it make Ford eligible for punitive damages to Julian Felipe?

75. *Stopping Rollovers: The Dual–Wheel Solution for 15–Passenger Vans,* PUBLIC CITIZEN, November 2002 at p. 11 (footnotes omitted).

76. Carl E. Nash, *What NASS Rollover Cases Tell Us*, NHTSA research paper #07–0141, at 3, 10, 2007, *available at* http://www-nrd.nhtsa.dot.gov/pdf/esv/esv20/print14.pdf (last consulted April 28, 2010).

- In *Gryc v. Dayton–Hudson Corp.*[77] the Minnesota Supreme Court allowed a jury to consider a punitive damages award in a case involving allegedly ultra-flammable children's pajamas, even though the manufacturer had met (but not exceeded) the federal regulatory standard for flammability in clothing. The regulatory test was generally regarded as a poor one, and one of the defendant's officials had written in a memorandum entitled "Flammability–Liability," that, "we are always sitting on somewhat of a powder keg as regards our flannelette being so inflammable." Does this case argue for punitive damages for Julian Felipe, despite Ford's having met applicable NHTSA standards?

- The most significant punitive damages have been awarded in cases where a defect made the product very dangerous, where that defect was not readily discoverable by users, where the product diverged from customary (presumably cost-effective) design, and where the manufacturer was aware both of this divergence and of the unreasonable danger its product created. A famous (infamous?) example is the "McDonald's Coffee" case, where the fast food maker allegedly prepared its beverage at a much higher temperature than did competitors, then sold it to mobile customers at drive-through lanes.[78] After reduction by the trial judge, punitive damages were adjudged at $480,000, or three times compensatory damages. For a more appalling example, consider *Tetuan v. A.H. Robins Co.*,[79] where millions in punitive damages were allowed against the maker of the IUD known as the Dalkon Shield®:

  > "In the present case, the jury made a specific finding of fraud. A review of the record indicates that there was substantial evidence tending to show Robins knew the Dalkon Shield was not safe or effective; that Robins knew of the wicking nature of the tail string; that Robins knew of a high rate of PID and septic abortion associated with the Dalkon Shield; that Robins misled doctors through claims of safety and efficacy while it knew there was no basis for a claim of safety, and all responsible tests for the Dalkon Shield's effectiveness showed a much higher pregnancy rate than Dr. Davis' "1.1 percent" figure; that Robins similarly misled consumers through a misleading lay promotional campaign; that Robins never publicly retracted its claims of "effectiveness" even though it had privately acknowledged the 1.1 percent rate as invalid; and that Robins knew there were serious problems with

---

77. Gryc v. Dayton–Hudson Corp., 297 N.W.2d 727 (Minn. 1980).

78. Liebeck v. McDonald's Restaurants, P.T.S., Inc., 1995 WL 360309 (N.M. Dist. Ct., August 18, 1994).

79. Tetuan v. A.H. Robins Co., 738 P.2d 1210 (Kan. 1987).

its open-ended nylon multifilament string in maintaining its integrity within the body. But not only was there substantial evidence to conclude that Robins fully comprehended, by 1974 at the latest, the enormity of the dangers it had created, but that it deliberately and intentionally concealed those dangers; that it put money into "favorable" studies; that it tried to neutralize any critics of the Dalkon Shield; that Robins was motivated by a desire to avoid litigation judgments rather than a concern for the safety of the users of the Dalkon Shield; that it consistently denied the dangers of the Dalkon Shield for nearly fifteen years after its original marketing of the Dalkon Shield; that it commissioned studies on the Dalkon Shield which it dropped or concealed when the results were unfavorable; and, ultimately, that it consigned hundreds of documents to the furnace rather than inform women that the Dalkon Shield carried inside their bodies was a bacterial time bomb which could cause septic abortions, PID, and even death."[80]

The Kansas Supreme Court went on to justify the punitive award for fraud.

"The $6.2 million punitive damage award against Robins in *Palmer*[81] was rendered by the jury on July 30, 1979. Loretta Tetuan first experienced symptoms of PID in late September of that year. It is entirely possible that plaintiff's injuries could have been avoided if the company had reacted to the verdict by immediately moving to recall the product or to at least warn of its dangers. Instead, Robins responded with the same position it had taken for the last decade-that the Dalkon Shield was "safe and effective." Robins issued a statement on July 31, 1979, that the verdict was "an aberration" and that it was confident "this unwarranted verdict will not survive" on appeal.

The first Dalkon Shield case to proceed to trial on the merits occurred in Kansas in *Deemer v. A.H. Robins Co.*, Case No. C–26420. On March 1, 1975, the jury awarded punitive damages against Robins in the amount of $75,000. Robins did not recall the product; it did not warn users of the Dalkon Shield's dangers; it did not warn physicians. It certainly did not warn Loretta Tetuan or the physicians who treated her. Instead, it reacted to the modest punitive damages award in *Deemer* by promptly attempting to destroy all evidence of its knowledge of the Dalkon Shield's dangers, consigning hundreds of documents to the draft furnace. To punish Robins for its

---

80. *Id.* at 1240.   **81.** Palmer v. A.H. Robins Co., Inc., 684 P.2d 187 (Colo. 1984).

conduct and to discourage others from committing like wrongs in the future, the punitive damages award is justified."[82]

Does *Tetuan* argue for or against punitive damages to Julian Felipe?

- In *Ammerman v. Ford Motor Corp.*,[83] the Indiana Court of Appeals confirmed a compensatory award of $4.4 million and a punitive award of $13.8 million to two plaintiffs in a case where a Ford Bronco II rolled over and injured them severely. The issue in this case was the propensity to roll over, not the strength of the roof once the vehicle had in fact rolled. Appeals to the Indiana Supreme Court and to the United States Supreme Court were dismissed.[84] Why do you think the jury awarded punitive damages (in fact they awarded $58 million; the amount was reduced by the trial judge to correspond to constitutional requirements) in *Ammerman*, but not in Julian Felipe's case? Do discrepancies in the award of punitive damages weaken the Rule of Law? One court put the problem this way:

  "[These cases] have the attributes of a national lottery. For essentially the same conduct, defendants are punished in some cases, as here, with millions of dollars in punitive damages; in other cases the awards are in the hundreds of thousands of dollars; and in still others no punitive damages at all are returned. In all of the cases, we must posit that the plaintiffs have been fully compensated by the compensatory awards. Yet the survivors in some cases are made instant millionaires; in others they merely receive amounts sufficient to pay their attorneys and trial expenses or nothing at all. Potential legislative solutions abound, including pending legislation in the Congress and State Legislature that would establish caps on punitive damages awards, yet the lottery wheel still turns."[85]

---

82. *Tetuan*, 738 P.2d at 1246 (footnote added).

83. Ford Motor Corp. v. Ammerman, 705 N.E.2d 539 (Ind. App. 1999).

84. Ford Motor Corp. v. Ammerman, 726 N.E.2d 310 (Ind. 1999); Ford Motor Corp. v. Ammerman, 529 U.S. 1021 (2000).

85. Ripa v. Owens–Corning Fiberglas Corp., 660 A.2d 521, 533–34 (N.J. App. 1995).

Part Three

SPECIAL SITUATIONS AND PRO-
POSED ALTERNATIVES TO
PRODUCTS LIABILITY LAW

Chapter 14

SPECIAL TYPES OF PRODUCT LITIGATION: TOXIC SUBSTANCES AND CLASS ACTIONS[1]

1. Introduction

The reader of this Book should by now have a good appreciation for the "what, when, why and how" of American products liability law. In this penultimate chapter, the focus shifts away from general principles and onto two special types of products suits.

In 2003, John Grisham's *King of Torts* starred a public defender who amassed millions in a collusive settlement of a dubious class action products suit. Grisham's novel came on the heels of law suits involving, among other products, items as varied as the herbicide Agent Orange,[2] asbestos, certain IUD's,[3] silicone breast implants and a gasoline additive called MTBE.[4] Much of the "torts explosion" of the 1980s, 1990s and early 2000s was in fact a toxic products liability explosion. Much of that litigation was related to asbestos, as it became known that exposure to asbestos fibers could cause lung cancer (especially if the exposed party was also a smoker), mesothelioma and asbestosis, and that the latency period for the latter two diseases was from twenty to forty years.[5]

Toxic and other "mass" products liability litigation has waxed and waned over the years, and the widespread publicity surrounding U.S. District Court Judge Janis Jack's dismissal[6] of fraudulent claims involving silica (then touted as "the next asbestos") has triggered investigations by a congressional committee, federal pros-

---

1. Additional Reading: Deborah R. Hensler, *Has the Fat Lady Sung? The Future of Mass Toxic Torts*, 26 Rev. Litig. 883 (2007); Stephen J. Carroll et al., *Asbestos Litigation*, Rand Corp., 2005, *available at* http://www.rand.org/pubs/monographs/MG162/.

2. *See, e.g.,* Peter H. Schuck, Agent Orange on Trial (1988).

3. *See, e.g.,* Ronald J. Bacigal, The Limits Of Litigation: The Dalkon Shield Controversy (1990).

4. *See, e.g.,* Michael I. Krauss, *Judge Scheindlin v. The Constitution:*

The MTBE Multi–District Litigation, 7(2) Engage 155 (2007).

5. Stephen J. Carroll et al., *Asbestos Litigation*, Rand Corp., 2005, *available at* http://www.rand.org/pubs/monographs/MG162/ (last consulted May 2, 2010).

6. Judge Jack revealed that the same physicians who had diagnosed asbestosis among asbestosis claimants had also diagnosed silicosis among those same people. In re Silica Prods. Liab. Litig., 398 F. Supp. 2d 563, 572–3 (S.D. Tex. 2005).

ecutors in New York and Texas's Attorney General. The silica debacle has raised important questions about the future of toxic and mass products liability litigation.[7]

There are two different types of mass products liability actions: single accident cases, where many people are injured by a catastrophic product failure occurring at one time and place; and toxic products cases where injuries result from a series of events occurring over considerable time. Due to the complexity of the individual issues presented by toxic products cases, class certification is typically easier to obtain in single accident cases than in toxic products cases.[8] Most of this chapter will focus on particular problems inherent in the toxic products case.

In most toxic products cases, it is claimed that a manufacturer has produced a defective and unreasonably dangerous product that has poisoned many people in obscure ways, creating damage that will not become fully apparent for a long time. Toxic products cases present acute problems for plaintiffs and for defendants. Here are eight issues confronting these cases.

1. The time lag between exposure to the product and development of a pathology makes it likely that evidence will become stale and/or that defendant manufacturers may disappear or be insolvent by the time individual injuries become manifest. This time lag also reduces the likelihood that non-tort compensation of victims will ever occur. Estimates are that only a small percentage of those who suffer from workplace toxicity ever receive workers' compensation awards, in large part because of these latency issues.[9]

2. The latent nature of the alleged harm also makes it difficult for individual plaintiffs to prove cause in fact. Did exposure to the product cause the harm, or did other intervening events do so?

3. The various ways in which people react to an allegedly toxic product make class actions (claimed to be the most efficient way to manage mass tort cases) problematic. Rule 23 of the Federal Rules of Civil Procedure (emulated in most but not all states) has authorized class actions since 1966.[10] However, the Advisory Committee that published Rule 23 felt it ill suited to most "mass accidents" that

---

7. *See, e.g.,* Lester Brickman, *On the Applicability of the Silica MDL Proceeding to Asbestos Litigation,* 12 CONN. INS. L.J. 35 (2006).

8. Teris, LLC v. Chandler, 289 S.W.3d 63, 69–70 (Ark. 2008).

9. W. Kip Viscusi, *Compensating Workplace Toxic Torts,* 37(1) PROC. ACAD. OF POL. SCI. 126 (1988).

10. Rule 23. Class Actions

(a) **Prerequisites.** One or more members of a class may sue or be sued as representative parties on behalf of all members only if:

(1) the class is so numerous that joinder of all members is impracticable;

injured many people, because of the individual issues of damages, causation and defenses to liability that might be involved.[11]

4. The (sometimes) *ex ante* unknowable nature of the injuries raises "state of the art" issues discussed in Chapter 10.[12]

5. On the other hand, the repetitive nature of litigation often results in accumulated knowledge through discovery, which may eventually expose defendants to significant punitive damages.[13]

6. Since the factual and legal issues of toxic products litigation are similar across all claims, the marginal cost to a law

(2) there are questions of law or fact common to the class;

(3) the claims or defenses of the representative parties are typical of the claims or defenses of the class; and

(4) the representative parties will fairly and adequately protect the interests of the class.

(b) **Types of Class Actions.** A class action may be maintained if Rule 23(a) is satisfied and if:

(1) prosecuting separate actions by or against individual class members would create a risk of:

(A) inconsistent or varying adjudications with respect to individual class members that would establish incompatible standards of conduct for the party opposing the class; or

(B) adjudications with respect to individual class members that, as a practical matter, would be dispositive of the interests of the other members not parties to the individual adjudications or would substantially impair or impede their ability to protect their interests;

(2) the party opposing the class has acted or refused to act on grounds that apply generally to the class, so that final injunctive relief or corresponding declaratory relief is appropriate respecting the class as a whole; or

(3) the court finds that the questions of law or fact common to class members predominate over any questions affecting only individual members, and that a class action is superior to other available methods for fairly and efficiently adjudicating the controver-

sy. The matters pertinent to these findings include:

(A) the class members' interests in individually controlling the prosecution or defense of separate actions;

(B) the extent and nature of any litigation concerning the controversy already begun by or against class members;

(C) the desirability or undesirability of concentrating the litigation of the claims in the particular forum; and

(D) the likely difficulties in managing a class action.

11. Advisory Committee Notes to Proposed Rules of Civil Procedure, 39 F.R.D. 69, 103 (1966).

12. Asbestos claims became viable only after an influential case held that asbestos manufacturers were liable for exposed workers' injuries even if the manufacturers did not know of the likelihood of such injuries, and that asbestos manufacturers as a group could be found to contribute to these injuries regardless of who produced any individual stock of asbestos. Borel v. Fibreboard Paper Products Corp., 493 F.2d 1076, 1095–6 (5th Cir. 1973) (applying Texas law).

13. The infamous "Sumner Simpson Papers," purporting to reveal that American asbestos manufacturers were aware of but hid data revealing the lethal toxicity of their product, were obtained in an asbestosis suit's discovery process. These papers arguably led to the downfall of the asbestos industry. See Jackson v. Johns–Manville Sales Corp., 750 F.2d 1314, 1317–8 (5th Cir. 1985) (applying Mississippi law).

firm of representing an additional plaintiff is small. But if each plaintiff is represented on a contingent basis, the marginal benefits of taking on that additional plaintiff can be substantial.[14] Huge groups are thereby assembled, and this transforms many toxic products suits into "bet the company" gambles, which lead many corporate boards to settle, even if the suits are in fact unfounded and filed by unscrupulous attorneys precisely because of their *in terrorem* effect. Conversely, the settlements might be unfavorable to plaintiffs, if class lawyers are "paid off" in return for a pittance for legally deserving victims. Class actions for toxic or mass torts typically settle after certification for these reasons. Indeed, most are filed with the sole intention of settling.

7. The "loading cost" of treating toxic products cases in tort, as opposed to insurance, is high. A 2005 RAND Corporation report on asbestos litigation found that only 42 percent of the $70 billion paid out by asbestos manufacturers through 2002 went to compensate plaintiffs.[15] This is typical of other areas of tort law,[16] and compares with a 90 percent payout rate for first party insurance premiums.[17] At least 73 asbestos manufacturers went bankrupt through 2004 (many more have since gone under), possibly because of these excess costs. The social expense of these bankruptcies (harms to shareholders, to employees, and to other "stakeholders") may be even more wasteful, since a significant portion of expenditures has gone to non-injured people.[18] State legislatures and Congress[19] arguably moved workers' accidents from tort law to compulsory insurance (*via* Workers' Compensation statutes) for this reason. But the pressures of toxic products litigation are such that even Workers' Compensation statutes have not shielded employers in all cases, especially as "common pool problems" (discussed below) deplete the resources of the manufacturers and sellers of the toxic products. Some courts have allowed plaintiffs to prove that employers intentionally exposed their employees to the product (thereby waiving employers' immunity to tort suits).[20] Other courts have

---

14. *See, e.g.,* Francis McGovern, *An Analysis of Mass Torts for Judges,* 73 TEX. L. REV. 1821, 1827–36 (1995).

15. Carroll et al., *supra* note 1, at 88.

16. See Chapter 3, *supra.*

17. George L., Priest, *The Current Insurance Crisis and Modern Tort Law,* 96 YALE L.J. 1521 (1987).

18. Carroll et al., *supra* note 1, at xxvi.

19. *See, e.g.,* Federal Coal Mine Health and Safety Act, 30 U.S.C.A. §§ 801–862 (1982).

20. *See, e.g.,* Wilson v. Asten–Hill Mfg. Co., 791 F.2d 30 (3d Cir. 1986) (applying Pennsylvania law); Duncan v. Northwest Airlines, Inc., 203 F.R.D. 601

allowed lawsuits against the employer for "fraudulent concealment" of the toxicity of the product.[21]

8. The recent decline of toxic products litigation (the asbestos well is almost dry) may have led firms with a specialization in this area to compete for *non*-toxic class action products. This may be the best explanation of the legal upshot of Toyota's 2010 "sudden acceleration" liability crisis, for instance.[22] In this way toxic products issues spread to other areas of products liability.

2. Judicial Administration of Toxic Products Cases

The Judicial Panel for Multi–District Litigation ("MDL"), which consists of seven federal judges appointed by the Chief Justice of the Supreme Court, may transfer individually filed cases to a particular federal district judge for collective treatment.[23] This judge then holds discovery and pre-trial rulings, sometimes dismissing the suit entirely for substantive reasons[24] or because (following the Supreme Court's landmark *Amchem Prods. Inc. v. Windsor* ruling)[25] it is not well suited to a class action under Rule 23. If the MDL results in class certification, an ensuing settlement is almost inevitable, as the case will have become a "bet the company" gamble.

Sometimes cases are initially filed as multistate class actions, without any MDL transfer. Efforts to create a gigantic national class consisting of "all smokers and nicotine dependent persons and their families," suing major cigarette manufacturers for fraud, failed because state laws and individual facts varied too much to allow for class certification.[26] This led to state class actions, which

(W.D. Wash. 2001) (State worker's compensation law did not preclude flight attendant's suit against airline alleging personal injury from exposure to second-hand smoke on international flights, since flight attendant alleged that airline "had actual knowledge that injury was certain to occur, and actual knowledge that injury did in fact occur.")

21. *See, e.g.*, Millison v. E.I. du Pont de Nemours & Co., 501 A.2d 505 (N.J. 1985) (alleged fraudulent concealment of dangers of asbestos).

22. *See, e.g.*, Walter Olson, *Exorcising Toyota's Demons*, NATIONAL REVIEW ONLINE, Mar. 15, 2010, http://www.nationalreview.com/articles/229316/exorcising-toyotas-demons/walter-olson (last consulted May 3, 2010) (statistics indicate that it is likely that acceleration problems usually result from poor drivers, often elderly people, stomping on the gas when they think they are hitting the brakes).

23. 28 U.S.C. § 1407.

24. *See, e.g.*, Meridia Prods. Liab. Litig. v. Abbott Labs., 447 F.3d 861 (6th Cir. 2006); In re TMJ Implants Prods. Liab. Litig., 880 F.Supp. 1311 (D. Minn. 1995).

25. *See, e.g.*, Amchem Prods. Inc. v. Windsor, 521 U.S. 591 (1997) (massive asbestos MDL suit found ill-suited for class action because the class was not cohesive enough (under Rule 23(b)(3)'s requirement that "questions of law or fact common to class members predominate over any questions affecting only individual members") to warrant the class action); *see also* Ortiz v. Fibreboard Corp., 527 U.S. 815 (1999).

26. Castano v. American Tobacco Co., 84 F.3d 734 (5th Cir. 1996).

were also often dismissed because individual fact variations remain. Famously, in Florida's *Engle* case,[27] the appellate court's rejection of the trial judge's class certification was accompanied by a declaration that the *Engle* jury's findings of fact would be binding on subsequent individual cases. This "issue preclusion" has been devastating for the defendants. They may no longer contest that cigarettes are capable of causing certain diseases, that cigarettes are defectively designed,[28] or that defendants misrepresented the risks of smoking. The individual suits that followed the *Engle* class's decertification have resulted in many multi-million dollar verdicts against "Big Tobacco." The wisdom of decertifying the class, it turns out, may be questioned.[29]

The end of asbestos litigation, the massive fraud of the silica class action, and the Supreme Court's restrictive attitude toward certification (announced in *Anchem*) have not eliminated toxic products cases. Many suits are filed individually instead of as national class actions, and (as just mentioned regarding tobacco) it is not clear that individual lawsuits are in manufacturers' best interests.[30] Defendants themselves often prefer to settle legitimate class actions economically.[31] As of this writing, multi-district class actions are ongoing regarding, among other products: Avandia,[32] Chinese Drywall,[33] Levaquin[34] and Yaz.[35] In 2007 one expert identi-

27. Liggett Group Inc. v. Engle, 853 So.2d 434 (Fla. Dist. Ct. App. 2003), *aff'd in part, rev'd in part* 945 So.2d 1246 (Fla. 2006).

28. Comment i of the *Restatement (Second)*, § 402A implements classic "inherent danger" doctrine (see Chapter 10, *supra*) by stating that, "Good tobacco is not defective merely because it causes harmful effects." The Comment cites several products, including whiskey and butter, that may be dangerous, but where products liability will not be imposed absent an additional ingredient which the ordinary consumer would not expect to be present. The *Engle* class action, and other suits, successfully weakened Comment i as it pertains to cigarettes, by listing the various chemicals added to modern cigarettes.

29. *See, e.g.,* Michael I. Krauss, *Florida Smoker's $300 Million Award to Be Reduced,* POINT OF LAW, Feb. 9, 2010, http://www.pointoflaw.com/archives/2010/02/florida-smokers.php (last consulted May 3, 2010).

30. *See, e.g.,* Michael I. Krauss, *Philadelphia Freedom: Another Round in the Prempro® Wars,* POINT OF LAW, Feb. 25, 2010, http://www.pointoflaw.com/archives/2010/02/philadelphia-fr.php

(last consulted May 3, 2010) (discussing individual lawsuits, mostly in the Philadelphia Court of Common Pleas, involving a hormone replacement therapy drug that allegedly causes breast cancer). Note that the *Class Action Fairness Act,* 28 U.S.C. § 1332(d), 1453, 1711–1715, allows defendants to remove multistate class actions to federal court even if there is less than complete diversity. However, plaintiff's attorneys can defeat removal if they limit the class definition primarily to residents of a single state.

31. Hensler, *supra* note 1, at 921.

32. In re Avandia Marketing, Sales, Practices and Prods. Liab. Litig., 2007 WL 3323362 (E.D. Pa.2007). Plaintiffs claim that this diabetes drug manufactured by GlaxoSmithKline cause an increased risk of heart attack, and that the defendant failed to provide adequate warnings.

33. In re Chinese Manufactured Drywall Prods. Liab. Litig., MDL No. 09–2047, 2010 WL 1445684 E.D. La. Drywall manufactured in China was brought into the United States and used in the construction and renovation of homes in coastal areas of the country,

fied indicators that mass products liability cases (via class or individual actions) are being contemplated or launched in the following areas:[36]

- Arsenic[b]
- Blood products[c]
- Contact lens products[a,c]
- Contraceptives[a]
- Diet products[a,b,c]
- "Heart drugs"[b]
  - Statins
  - Anti-platelets
  - ACE inhibitors
  - Anti-arrythmia
- Heart devices[a,b]
  - Catheters
  - Defibrillators[c]
  - Pacemakers[c]
  - Stents
  - Valves
- Other medical devices: e.g. orthopedic implants[a]
- Lead[a,b]
- Mold[a,b]
- NSAIDS[b]

from 2004–2006. Homeowners complain of emissions of smelly gasses, the corrosion and blackening of metal wiring, surfaces, and objects, and the breaking down of appliances and electrical devices in their homes, as well as various physical afflictions believed to be caused by the Chinese drywall.

34. In re Levaquin Prods. Liab. Litig., MDL No. 08–1943, 2010 WL 2975415 D. Minn. Plaintiffs allege that Levaquin, an antibiotic used to treat bacterial infections, causes tendon ruptures, and that defendants' (Johnson & Johnson, Ortho–McNeil Pharmaceutical, Inc., and Johnson & Johnson Pharmaceutical Research & Development, LLC) warnings regarding tendon ruptures were inadequate.

35. In re Yasmin and Yaz Marketing, Sales Practices and Prods Liab. Litig., MDL No. 09–2100, 2010 WL

3119499 (S.D. Ill.) Plaintiffs claim that this contraceptive was "over-marketed" to treat mild conditions, and that its heightened risks for Stroke, Heart Attack, Pulmonary Thrombosis and Deep Vein Thrombosis were insufficiently warned of.

36. Hensler, *supra* note 1, at 922–23.

The embedded notes are:

a Product groups for which American Attorneys for Justice (formerly, American Trial Lawyers' Association) has established litigation groups.

b Products and product groups for which Mealey's publishes litigation reports.

c Product litigation that has already been consolidated as a class action and transferred under the MDL statute.

- Cox–2 Inhibitors[a,c]

- Treatments[a] for schizophrenia[c], bi-polar disorder, dementia, depression[c] and Alzheimer's disease

- Treatments for acne[c], asthma, cancer[c], diabetes[a,b], heartburn[a], heart surgery [a], impotence[c], insomnia, Lyme disease, menopause symptoms[a], osteoporosis[a,c], ulcers

- Non-pharmaceutical consumer products: e.g. automobile components, electric blankets & heating pads, grout filler[c], iPod screens[c], digital cameras[c], Teflon, transfats, sunscreen

- Workplace products: Benzene[a], welding rods[a,b,c]

3. Causation Problems in Toxic Products Cases

The causation issue in toxic products cases typically involves the following questions: (1) whether a substance in the product *has the capacity to* cause the type of harm claimed by the plaintiff (*"the theory question"*); (2) whether the particular plaintiff's exposure to the substance *in fact was sufficient to* produce the toxic effect complained of (*the practice question*—a very fact-dependant issue that this book cannot address); and (3) whether the product in question was manufactured by the defendant and not by someone else (the whodunit question, dealt with in Chapter 5). In rare cases the plaintiff's condition is a "signature disease" (such as asbestosis and mesothelioma, which are caused only by asbestos), so there is no need to establish (1) or (2). More often, however, each of these issues is hotly contested and scientifically uncertain.

Thus, in *Earl v. Cryovac*,[37] a worker claimed that he had contracted chronic obstructive pulmonary disease on the job when he was exposed to vapors emitted from a plastic film manufactured by defendant. He settled his worker's compensation claim, then sued defendant. The trial court entered summary judgment against plaintiff, holding that he had failed to establish a causal connection between his injury and defendant's product. On appeal, the court summarized the testimony of plaintiff's expert, Dr. Reed, this way:

"The plaintiff worked in the meatpacking industry for approximately twenty-five years, of which twenty years had been spent in "slaughter" rooms and the most recent five years had been spent in a "packing" room. Until moving to the packing room, the plaintiff had not suffered any severe breathing disorders. At one time, he had been a smoker of cigarettes, but he had discontinued this habit ten years before seeing Dr. Reed. Approximately seven years before he saw Dr. Reed, the plaintiff was hospitalized briefly for shortness of breath; however, no diagnosis was made, and he suffered no severe symptoms until

37. Earl v. Cryovac, 772 P.2d 725 (Idaho App. 1989).

he began work in the packing room. In Dr. Reed's opinion, this prior history was unremarkable.

The plaintiff consulted Dr. Reed, upon reference from another physician, when he experienced a worsening problem of chest tightness and shortness of breath. He noticed that his symptoms would temporarily subside during weekends and vacations, but would resume when he returned to work in the packing room. Dr. Reed learned that the packing room contained a machine that wrapped meat in plastic bags and then heated the plastic in water at or near the boiling temperature. The hot water caused the plastic to shrink tightly around the meat; accordingly, the machine was known as a "shrink tunnel." Because the packing room was kept at a low temperature, the boiling water in the shrink tunnel produced a heavy fog. Some employees, who later submitted affidavits in this case, reported that they could smell plastic, and occasionally burning plastic, in the air.

Dr. Reed also learned that the plastic material used in the packing room was a shrinkable thermoplastic "barrier bag" manufactured by Cryovac. Dr. Reed found medical literature documenting the existence of "meatwrapper's asthma" or "meatwrapper's syndrome," a chronic lung disease observed in employees of meatpacking plants and butcher shops where plastic bags were cut by a thermal process known as a "hot wire." The disease, which produces symptoms similar to those experienced by the plaintiff in this case, has been attributed in the literature to the release of vapors during the heating of the plastic material. As noted by Dr. Reed, the researchers are satisfied that a causal connection exists between the heated plastic and the disease, although the precise chemical (or group of chemicals) responsible for the etiology of the disease has not been identified."[38]

Dr. Reed's opinion was challenged by defense counsel, both because it did not specify the particular component(s) of the plastic vapors which caused the plaintiff's disease and because the temperature in the shrink tunnel process was less than half the usual temperature of the "hot wire" implicated in "meatwrapper's asthma" cases. But the Court of Appeals reversed the summary judgment, ruling that plaintiff had produced evidence of causation for the jury. Notably, the court added that epidemiological studies are not needed to answer the theory question in every case.[39]

Often, of course, such studies will have been conducted, and attorneys attempt to introduce them as evidence. Epidemiological

38. *Id.* at 729. **39.** *Id.* at 733.

studies examine existing populations to observe associations between a disease or condition and the factor suspected of causing it. However, no epidemiological study can establish the practice question, i.e., that *the plaintiff* contracted the disease or condition complained of from the impugned product.

A "strong" version of the preponderance of evidence rule requires plaintiff to offer both epidemiological evidence that probability of causation exceeds fifty percent in the exposed population and some "particularistic" proof that the substance actually harmed the plaintiff. Such a requirement would demand more than a doubling of epidemiological risk to satisfy the civil burden of proof.[40]

Assume, for example, that a physical condition naturally occurs in six out of 1,000 people. If studies of people exposed to the impugned product show that 9 out of 1,000 contract the physical condition, it is still more likely than not (the civil standard of proof) that any given occurrence of the condition is not caused by the product. Six of nine incidences would be statistically attributable to causes other than the product, and therefore, it is not more likely than not that the product caused any single incidence of the condition, even if a particular plaintiff establishes that he was exposed to the product. However, if more than 12 out of 1,000 people exposed to the product contract the condition, then it may be more likely than not that an exposed individual's disease was caused by drug.

A relative risk of more than 2.0 is not sufficient for liability, however, for the plaintiff may fail the practice test. Her exposure may have been minimal, or she may have other strong indicators (causes) for the condition, or the timing of the manifestation of her condition may not be consistent with her exposure to the product as manifested by the study. On the other hand, even a relative risk of less than 2.0, if accompanied by practice facts making the plaintiff's non-product condition causality unlikely, could allow plaintiff to reach the jury.[41]

Whether a relative risk of 2 merits confidence is disputed. For instance, the executive editor of the *New England Journal of Medicine* has stated that "[a]s a general rule of thumb, we are looking for a relative risk of three or more [before accepting a paper for publication], particularly if it is biologically implausible or if it's a brand-new finding."[42] Thus, in *Merrell Dow Pharmaceuticals, Inc.*

40. *See, e.g.*, In re "Agent Orange" Prods. Liab. Litig., 611 F.Supp. 1223, 1261 (E.D.N.Y. 1985).

41. *See, e.g.*, Steve Gold, *Causation in Toxic Torts: Burdens of Proof, Standards of Persuasion, and Statistical Evidence*, 96 YALE L.J. 376, 395–401 (1986).

42. Gary Taubes, *Epidemiology Faces Its Limits*, SCIENCE, July 14, 1995, 168 (cited in Merrell Dow Pharms, Inc. v. Havner, 953 S.W.2d 706, 719 (Tex. 1997)).

v. Havner,[43] plaintiff claimed that her limb reduction birth defect was caused by her mother's ingestion of the anti-nausea drug Bendectin®. Post–*Daubert*,[44] plaintiff had the challenge of accrediting her experts so that their testimony on causation could be produced. She proffered testimony that relied on private epidemiological studies, including studies that considered limb reduction birth defects from Bendectin® with a relative risk greater than 2. One plaintiff's expert described studies on rabbits exposed to Bendectin® in which he saw "a lot of malformed kits." That expert opined that the probability that the malformations in this study occurred by chance were six in 10,000. With respect to another study of rabbits, he stated that the probability that Bendectin® was harmless was less than one per 1,000,000. He listed studies on monkeys, rats, and mice showing "highly significant deleterious harmful effects as far as birth defects are concerned." Based on all these animal studies, this expert was of the opinion that Bendectin was teratogenic in humans. However, he conceded that the dosage levels at which Bendectin® became associated with birth defects in rabbits was 100 milligrams per kilogram per day, the equivalent of a daily dosage of 1200 tablets for a woman weighing 132 pounds.[45] As already discussed, plaintiff's expert's studies were not published, studied, or replicated by the relevant scientific community. Yet over thirty published, peer-reviewed epidemiological studies on the relationship between Bendectin® and birth defect had failed to find the correlation seen in plaintiff's expert's studies.[46] Texas's Supreme Court quashed plaintiff's jury verdict, ruling that "there are a number of reasons why reliance on a relative risk of 2.0 as a bright-line boundary would not be in accordance with sound scientific methodology in some cases."[47]

Even if the plaintiff satisfactorily answers the "theory question" and the "practice question" (sometimes called "general causation" and "specific causation," respectively), he still must produce evidence that it was to *defendant*'s product, not to someone else's product, that he was exposed. As indicated in Chapter 9 with respect to DES claims (synthetic estrogen, produced by hundreds of companies and effective in preventing miscarriage, but carcinogenic in some female offspring), four states' courts have allowed "market share" causation to be established, while forty-six states have declined to relax common law causation requirements.

43. *Id.* at 719.

44. See *supra* Chapter 7 for a discussion of *Daubert*.

45. *Merrell Dow*, 953 S.W.2d at 728.

46. *Id.* at 726.

47. *Id.* at 719.

One of these four states, Wisconsin, has extended market share liability to cover lead paint poisoning,[48] even though paint was marketed by various companies with widely differing concentrations of lead, different types of lead, and at different periods of time. No other state has taken this route.[49] Similarly, only one appellate court has recognized market share liability for hemophiliacs harmed by tainted clotting agent "Factor VIII," obtained from one of a number of suppliers to the hospitals where they received their transfusions.[50] Even for asbestos, the "papa" of toxic substances, market share liability is not applied, as asbestos products have a very wide divergence of toxicity.[51] However, if asbestos from two or more companies is present on a worksite where a given plaintiff was exposed and injured, joint and several liability of the companies will typically result.

A. Plaintiff's Behavior as a Contributing Cause to Toxic Products Liability

In asbestos cases, one of the three diseases that may result from exposure to the product is lung cancer. Smoking multiplies the risk of lung cancer in a non-asbestos-exposed person by a factor of 10. Asbestos exposure multiplies the risk of lung cancer in a *non*-smoker by a factor of 5. The "multiplicative" effect of these two causes is that a smoker exposed to asbestos has fifty times the risk of lung cancer than does a non-smoker.[52] Should a lung cancer plaintiff's recovery against the seller of an asbestos-laden product be reduced because of her decision to smoke?

In *Dafler v. Raymark Indus.*,[53] defendant demonstrated that plaintiff's chance of contracting lung cancer from asbestos exposure was increased fifty fold by his smoking. The jury then found that

48. Thomas v. Mallett, 701 N.W.2d 523 (Wis. 2005).

49. Thus, in a case brought by the parents of a young child poisoned by the lead paint on the walls of their Philadelphia home, the Pennsylvania Supreme Court rejected market share liability theory because the lead based paint products were not fungible and some defendants had not manufactured lead paint for 100 years. Skipworth v. Lead Indus. Ass'n., 690 A.2d 169 (Pa. 1997).

50. Smith v. Cutter Biological, Inc., 823 P.2d 717 (Haw. 1991); *contra* Doe v. Cutter Biological, 852 F.Supp. 909 (D. Idaho 1994) where the court noted that, "Unlike DES, Factor VIII is not a generic, fungible drug. Each processor prepares its Factor VIII concentrate by its own proprietary processes using plasma

collected from its own sources. Each firm's Factor VIII concentrate is clearly distinguishable by brand name, package color, lot number, and number of units of Factor VIII per vial; each firm's Factor VIII concentrate is separately licensed by the Food and Drug Administration. There is no evidence that all Factor VIII products caused or were equally capable of causing HIV infection. Thus, the risk posed by the different brands of Factor VIII is not identical." *Id.* at 913.

51. *See, e.g.*, Case v. Fibreboard Corp., 743 P.2d 1062 (Okla. 1987).

52. D. Alan Rudlin, *Toxic Tort Litigation*, American Bar Association, 2007, at 348.

53. Dafler v. Raymark Indus., 611 A.2d 136 (N.J. App. 1992), *aff'd* 622 A.2d 1305 (N.J. 1993).

the plaintiff contributed 70 percent to his lung cancer by cigarette smoking and that the defendant contributed 30 percent. The New Jersey Supreme Court agreed that there was reasonable factual support for this apportionment under the state's comparative negligence principles.[54] It is not clear that this decision respects the civil burden of preponderance of evidence, at least if one interprets the jury verdict to mean that smoking, not asbestos, probably caused the plaintiff's lung cancer. Similarly, if plaintiff was warned of lung problems and told to stop smoking, but declined, a Fifth Circuit case applying Texas law confirmed that a jury may consider the continued smoking to be a failure to mitigate, precluding causation of the exacerbated damages.[55]

4. Damages Issues in Toxic Products Claims

When a large number of people have been exposed to a defective and unreasonably dangerous toxic product over time, their damages will vary greatly. If and when their individual claims are heard, the following issues will typically arise:

A. Potential but Unrealized Disease

Some victims of the toxic product may have contracted a disease or a disorder, which is compensable under normal tort principles. What of an individual exposed to the product who has no known disorder? As was seen in Chapter 13, in some cases medical monitoring has been seen as a remedy uniquely appropriate to class members. This seems perfectly compatible with basic tort theory.[56] On the other hand, "fear of cancer" pain and suffering damages are much less likely to be awarded, at least if plaintiff does not already suffer from a pre-cancerous physical condition and is not more than 50 percent likely to develop the disease.[57]

B. Property Damage and Loss of Profits

Suits claiming damages for the cost of removing asbestos products from buildings are common. A federal statute[58] requires that all schools be tested for the presence of asbestos, but does not specify liability for removal of asbestos, which in many cases might be stable and non-dangerous if it is not displaced. State law has varied, but has tended to allow suits for the cost of removal, in part

---

54. *Id.* at 146.

55. Gideon v. Johns–Manville Sales Corp., 761 F.2d 1129 (5th Cir. 1985).

56. Donovan v. Philip Morris USA, Inc., 914 N.E.2d 891 (Mass. 2009).

57. Norfolk & Western Rwy v. Ayers, 538 U.S. 135 (2003) (F.E.L.A. asbestos case; "fear of cancer" allowed be-

cause of existing asbestosis); Potter v. Firestone Tire & Rubber Co., 863 P.2d 795 (Cal. 1993) ("fear of cancer" allowed because chance of developing disease is >50 percent).

58. Asbestos School Hazard Detection and Control Act, 20 U.S.C.A. §§ 3601–3611 (1982).

because of the federal statute. Thus, in *Beavercreek Local Schools v. Basic, Inc.*[59] the defendant manufactured and sold Kilnoise®, an asbestos-containing acoustical plaster, to Beavercreek Schools between approximately 1955 and 1962. Beavercreek became aware of the health risks associated with asbestos, and in 1980 covered the ceilings containing Kilnoise® with a coat of paint. It then sued defendant for the cost of removing the product. The jury found Kilnoise® defective and unreasonably dangerous, but awarded Beavercreek only $250,000, an amount based on the cost of maintaining the plaster in the schools for twenty more years (the expected life of the schools) instead of the requested $1.8 million for removal. Defendant had produced evidence that removing the asbestos product was in fact more dangerous than leaving it encapsulated by paint. On appeal, however, it was ruled that since federal law required safe removal of the asbestos when demolishing the building (in twenty years, approximately), the cost of removal must now be paid by the defendant. What if the federal statute is modified in the interim?

What if a toxic product damages one person or her property, and that damage in turn causes pure economic harm (lost profits, for example) for others? The law here is uncertain, and nonproducts jurisprudence is instructive.

- In *Robins Dry Dock & Repair Co. v. Flint,*[60] the Supreme Court held that a ship's charterer was not entitled to recover expected profits lost as a result of delays required to repair the ship's propeller that employees of a dry dock had damaged. The court reasoned that, absent a proprietary interest in the vessel, the charterer had no basis for recovery. The loss arose only because of the lost benefit of the contract with the owners, not because of a property right, Justice Holmes ruled. He wrote this oft-quoted statement:

  > "[A] tort to the person or property of one man does not make the tortfeasor liable to another merely because the injured person was under a contract with that other, unknown to the doer of the wrong ... The law does not spread its protection so far."[61]

- But in *Petitions of Kinsman Transit Co.,*[62] the Second Circuit Court of Appeals ruled that a party could recover damages for economic losses so long as property damage was caused by an unintentional maritime tort. The plaintiffs need not

59. Beavercreek Local Sch. v. Basic, Inc., 595 N.E.2d 360 (Ohio App. 1991).

60. Robins Dry Dock & Repair Co. v. Flint, 275 U.S. 303 (1927).

61. *Id.* at 309.

62. Petitions of Kinsman Transit Co., 388 F.2d 821 (2d Cir. 1968).

~~have a proprietary interest in the property damaged, so long as their losses were neither remote nor unforeseeable.~~

- In *Pruitt v. Allied Chemical Corp.*,[63] commercial fishermen, seafood wholesalers, retailers, seafood distributors and processors, restaurateurs, marina, boat, tackle and bait shop owners, and employees of all these sued a chemical company for polluting the James River and the Chesapeake Bay with the insecticide kepone. The court accepted that the general rule in admiralty and common law is that a plaintiff may not recover for indirect economic harm.[64] Nonetheless, the defendant was held liable both to commercial fishermen[65] and to boat, tackle, marina and bait shop owners who suffered reduced sales of goods and services to sports fishermen. The court rejected any liability to businesses that would have purchased the fishermen's harvest and resold it at a profit, however.

C. Punitive Damages

When a toxic product gives rise to punitive damages, "common pool" problems abound.[66] As damages accrue and companies become insolvent following multiple punitive damage awards, there is often no money left to compensate those whose harm has manifested itself more slowly. Much as they who drink from a common source have little incentive to leave water for others, a feeding frenzy of punitive damages in mass products liability cases can both destroy defendant companies and neutralize the rights of future claimants.

This has been seen as justification to reduce or eliminate punitive damages in toxic products cases.[67] On the other hand, the United States Supreme Court has not (yet?) ruled that the Due Process Clause places a limit on repetitive awards of punitive damages in toxic products litigation. Several courts have concluded that so long as they are allowed to do so, they will let their own mass tort plaintiffs drink from the common pool, while defendant's

63. Pruitt v. Allied Chem. Corp., 523 F.Supp. 975 (E.D. Va. 1981).

64. *Id.* at 977.

65. Commercial fishermen who lose their harvest (which, of course, they do not own until they until it is captured) have been allowed to sue in tort in a wide array of cases. *See, e.g.,* Louisiana ex rel. Guste v. M/V Testbank, 752 F.2d 1019 (5th Cir. 1985), *cert. denied,* 477 U.S. 903 (1986) (defendants responsible for a maritime collision resulting in pollution of a river are liable to commercial fishermen); Union Oil Co. v. Oppen, 501 F.2d 558 (9th Cir. 1974) (commercial fishermen may recover after pollution results from defendant's oil spill); Burgess v. M/V Tamano, 370 F.Supp. 247 (D. Me. 1973) (commercial fishermen and clam diggers may recover lost profits due to tortious oil spill).

66. *See generally* Alan Schwartz, *A Contract Theory Approach to Business Bankruptcy,* 107 YALE L.J. 1807 (1998).

67. Liggett Group, Inc. v. Engle, 853 So.2d 434, 458 (Fla. App. 2003) ($143 billion punitives award quashed).

resources remain sufficient.[68] In such circumstances bankruptcy law remains the only legal way to lessen the common pool problem.

Questions About Julian Felipe's Case

- Is Julian's case best suited to an individual lawsuit against Ford, or should Julian's attorney seek to join or create a class action? If the latter, should the class be composed of all Aerostar owners? All Ford van owners? All van and SUV owners?

- Very few vans roll over. If a class action is formed, should those whose vans have never rolled over be able to recover for the "fear of rolling over?" Should they be able to recover for the reduced trade-in value of their vehicles, because of publicity ironically produced by the lawsuit itself? How should the Toyota acceleration scandal bear on this question?

Additional Question

- As this book goes to press, a federal judge has given approval for the settlement of a class-action suit that claims the rear brakes on 750,000 Honda Accord and Acura TSX cars "are wearing out much faster than they should." The suit claims the brakes wear out in 15,000 to 20,000 miles because their design causes "excessive force to be applied to the vehicles' rear wheels."[69] Is this a suitable products liability suit, or should this be dealt with *via* contract, with the ensuing warranty limitations? Are the brakes "defective and unreasonably dangerous" if they give notice of their impending failure (via squealing, warning lights, etc.)? Note that the proposed settlement will provide owners who had brake pads replaced and rotors resurfaced a maximum of $125, while class counsel will be paid $2 million.

---

68. *See, e.g.*, Spaur v. Owens–Corning Fiberglas Corp., 510 N.W.2d 854, 865–66 (Iowa 1994).

69. Christopher Jensen, *Judge Approves Preliminary Settlement of Honda Brake Suit*, N.Y. TIMES, May 3, 2010, http://tinyurl.com/33aeex4 (last visited May 5, 2010).

Chapter 15

ALTERNATIVE APPROACHES TO ENSURING PRODUCT SAFETY[1]

1. Introduction

This Book has examined the American legal response to accidents that result from the manufacturing and selling of goods in a market society. In a relatively scant forty years, our fifty-plus jurisdictions have developed a complex set of rules (not all of them coherent or settled) to determine when the cost of such accidents will be shifted to manufacturers and sellers, and when it will remain with injured parties or their first-party insurers. Current rules sometimes operate similarly to common law negligence—but on other occasions the results come closer to bundling a compulsory insurance policy with the product. An interesting analysis by two Canadian scholars in 1992 led them to conclude that American products liability law has had bizarre deterrent effects, a tenuous corrective justice impact, and a very poor distributive justice record.[2]

In this chapter, several foreign and scholarly approaches to products liability are explored. The idea here is not to exhaustively detail every proposed alternative, but rather to give readers an idea of their broad outline.

2. Replacing Products Liability With Contract

A. Libertarian Abolition of Products Liability

Before proceeding further, readers are strongly invited to read the Appendix. As the two exercises there hopefully demonstrate, products would not necessarily become unsafe if products liability law were eliminated. As long as consumers value safety and have access to information about the safety characteristics of products, manufacturers have an incentive (if they wish to maximize profits)

---

1. Additional Reading: Michael I. Krauss, *Federalism and Product Liability: One More Trip to the Choice-of-Law Well*, 2002 B.Y.U.L. Rev. 759; Geoffrey Palmer, *The New Zealand Experience*, 15 U. Haw. L. Rev. 604 (1993).

2. Don Dewees & Michael Trebilcock, *The Efficacy of the Tort System and Its Alternatives: A Review of Empirical Evidence*, 30 Osgoode Hall L.J. 57 (1992).

to produce precisely the safe products that consumers desire. Even if consumers lack information about these safety characteristics, firms may find it profitable to produce such information.

But consumers may be incapable of getting safety information, or may have a psychological inability to process information about highly unlikely risks. In those instances price signals will not provide the appropriate incentives to produce sufficiently safe products. In an imperfect world some kind of products liability law may be required to provide appropriate incentives to manufacturers and to their downstream sellers. In any case wrongful behavior by a manufacturer or a seller requires compensation of causally injured persons as a matter of corrective justice.[3] For these reasons, only a few advocate the wholesale abolition of products liability law and its replacement with pure freedom of contract.[4]

B. Free Choice of State Law

Retaining some form of products liability law does not require retaining its current iteration. As this author has pointed out elsewhere,[5] the current structure of state-based products liability rules creates what is known in Game Theory as a "Prisoners' Dilemma." In lay terms, current law may lead many or all states to adopt rules that make all of us worse off.

Understanding the game theoretical dilemma is not difficult. Assume for a moment that a product accident victim files suit in her home state, against an out-of-state manufacturer. Assume that the home state's court agrees it has jurisdiction over the suit, and that its own product liability law applies. In sum, the suit will pit an injured (usually poor) in-state physical person against a (usually wealthy) out-of-state corporation, in the plaintiff's court and subject to the plaintiff's state's laws. At the margin, will local judges (who are typically elected or appointed by governors who are elected) be tempted to transfer wealth into the state by crafting and interpreting rules with the plaintiff's welfare in mind?

To illustrate, imagine that the state law incorporates a consumer misuse defense, discussed in Chapter 10. Under the consumer misuse defense, plaintiffs injured by defective products they have misused may not recover, or their recovery may be reduced. This defense is desirable to minimize moral hazard by imparting appropriate incentives to consumers. After all, care in both the manufacture *and* the use of a product is needed to minimize the social costs of accidents.

---

3. *See* Michael I. Krauss, *Tort Law and Private Ordering*, 35 St. Louis U. L.J. 623 (1992).

4. For a recent manifestation, *see* A. Mitchell Polinsky & Steven Shavell, *The Uneasy Case For Product Liability*, 123 Harv. L. Rev. 1437 (2010).

5. Krauss, *supra* note 1, at 780–82.

But what standard will be used to measure consumer misuse? Should a plaintiff's misuse be fatal to her case even if it was foreseeable by the manufacturer? Should it matter whether the misuse was drunk driving, or driving at 100 mph, or not fastening one's seat belt? What if the cost of a consumer's misuse can be shifted to shareholders, workers, and consumers *across the nation*, while the immediate benefit of a state judge's ruling accrues to a plaintiff *inside the state*? A local plaintiff will be highly motivated to argue that the "consumer misuse" defense should be quite lenient to her. Might the local judge and the local jury be tempted to agree with the plaintiff? Chief Justice Richard Neely of West Virginia's Supreme Court disclosed in a 1988 book that he was tempted to tweak products liability rules in precisely this way whenever such an adjustment would transfer money into West Virginia.[6]

Justice Neely did not merely raise this issue theoretically—he applied his theory three years later in *Blankenship v. General Motors Corp.*[7] *Blankenship* was a "crashworthiness," or "secondary collision" case in which the West Virginia Supreme Court adopted a pro-plaintiff rule even though it stated that it found the defendant's argument more sensible. A plaintiff who had negligently caused his vehicle to crash alleged that its poor design aggravated the injuries he suffered in the collision. In "crashworthiness" cases, as seen in Chapter 7, the typical plaintiff's difficulty is establishing "cause in fact"—i.e., demonstrating the extent to which the allegedly defective design worsened an injury. Since no crash can be replicated exactly, it is hard for plaintiff to establish how a "non-defective" car would have fared. Sometimes plaintiff imagines a "perfect car" that could withstand most any crash. What should the court do if no manufacturer currently makes this perfect car? Two general approaches to this problem had emerged in pre-*Blankenship* case-law across the country:

> • One "school," following *Huddell v. Levin*,[8] places the burden on plaintiff to "offer proof of an alternative, safer design, practicable under the circumstances ... [and] of what injuries, if any, would have resulted had the alternative, safer design been used."[9] If a better, safer design is feasible, some competitor is likely producing it. If not, plaintiff is required to create and test prototypes equipped as plaintiff advocates. Failing such expensive proof, *Huddell* held that plaintiff may not reach the jury with her crashworthiness claim.

---

6. Richard Neely, The Product Liability Mess: How Business Can Be Rescued From the Politics of State Courts (1988).

7. Blankenship v. General Motors Corp., 406 S.E.2d 781 (W. Va. 1991).

8. Huddell v. Levin, 537 F.2d 726 (3d Cir. 1976) (applying New Jersey law).

9. *Id.* at 737.

● The second approach, following *Mitchell v. Volkswagen-werk*,[10] shifts to the defendant the burden of proving that the plaintiff's imagined design is not feasible or would not have reduced injuries. Any such proof would be rebuttable by the plaintiff's expert, who would therefore be assured to be able to reach the local, in-state jury on this issue.

In *Blankenship*, the West Virginia Supreme Court acknowledged that *Huddell* was the more logical rule, because it minimized the chance that the juries would engage in uninformed second-guessing of highly technical design standards. Nonetheless, the court opted for *Mitchell*. The court justified its position on the ground that West Virginia consumers were already paying markups every time a new car was purchased in West Virginia, to reflect liability payouts to plaintiffs in Minnesota and in other states that had adopted *Mitchell*. Justice Neely reasoned that West Virginians might as well derive benefit from the inefficient rule, since consumers in other states would be paying most of the rule's cost. Aware of the implications of his ruling, Justice Neely announced that henceforth, "in any crashworthiness case where there is a split of authority on any issue, ... we [will always] adopt the rule that is most liberal to the plaintiff."[11]

As indicated in greater detail elsewhere,[12] modifying and implementing a national "choice of law" rule would eliminate this dilemma while preserving state sovereignty over products liability. The idea is to allow consumers to choose among different states' legal rules when they decide where to purchase their product. This would incorporate the soundness or ridiculousness of a state's products liability rules into the prices of products sold. For Justice Neely's free-riding strategy can succeed only if price increases in other states subsidize the cost of inefficient rulings in West Virginia. Currently manufacturers cannot durably price products differently from state to state, as consumers would purchase their products in a low-liability state only to have the high-liability rules apply after an accident. Local judges and juries would not necessarily impose the costs of excessive products liability rules if they knew they and their neighbors would pay the full cost of those rules.

---

10. Mitchell v. Volkswagenwerk, 669 F.2d 1199 (8th Cir. 1982) (applying Minnesota law).

11. *Blankenship*, 406 S.E.2d at 785–86.

12. Krauss, *supra* note 1, at 802–828.

3. Replacing State Products Liability Law With a National Law

A. Federal Legislation

In Chapter 10 the tension between state products liability law and national regulation was discussed. This tension, as was seen, shows little sign of abating or of being resolved by the Supreme Court.

But direct federal legislation, if constitutional, prevails over contrary state laws under the Supremacy Clause of the Constitution. For over two decades, proposals have been floated to adopt a federal products liability law that would supersede the state rules. If decision making takes place at the national level, where (by definition) most costs are "internalized," free-riding strategies such as Justice Neely's would be unavailable. Numerous observers[13] have advocated nationalization of product liability law for this reason.

There is no strong constitutional obstacle to federal action. Because a national market exists for products, federal legislation would likely be upheld as an exercise of Congress's authority to regulate "interstate commerce." Both houses of Congress did attempt to "federalize" products liability law in 1995.[14] This effort did not survive a veto by President Clinton, who justified his action with the argument that the federal bill entailed "an unwarranted intrusion on state authority."[15]

Even if it were constitutional, however, federal dislocation of states' product liability jurisdiction may be inopportune. Federal preemption of substantive product liability laws spawns at least two major "knowledge problems."[16]

1. First, *uncertainty* about the content of "perfect" products liability legislation argues strongly against preemption by Congress. Endless and intricate calculations of utility functions, risk preferences, and philosophical outlooks of individuals would be needed to determine the correct allocation of the risks of products among manufacturers and consumers. There is no particular reason to believe in a "one-size-fits-all" solution across the nation. Moral views about liability and risk preferences may vary across individuals and regions. Diversity lessens the chance that there is one "correct" products liability rule.

---

13. *See, e.g.,* O. Lee Reed & John L. Watkins, *Product Liability Tort Reform: The Case for Federal Action,* 63 NEB. L. REV. 389 (1984); Victor E. Schwartz & Liberty Mahshigian, *A Permanent Solution for Product Liability Crises: Uniform Federal Tort Law Standards,* 64 DENV. U. L. REV. 685 (1988).

14. See H.R. 956 as passed by the House, the "Common Sense Product Liability and Legal Reform Act;" as passed by the Senate, the "Product Liability Fairness Act", 104th Cong., (1995).

15. Neil A. Lewis, *President Vetoes Limits on Liability,* N.Y. TIMES, May 3, 1996, at A1, A8.

16. Krauss, *supra* note 1, at 798–802.

2. *Lack of competition* is a second knowledge problem afflicting federal products liability legislation. State legislation, if properly arranged so that costs and benefits are apparent inside the state (as discussed above), is conducive to the competitive production of information. If a state's products liability rules are too generous to plaintiffs, or to manufacturers, and if the costs of these rules are essentially reflected within that state, their impact will eventually lead to a demand for change. The cost of a product might rise tremendously, for example, if prices in one jurisdiction had to incorporate a high premium to cover accidents that would be easily avoidable if the consumer used reasonable care. Consumers in that state might, if given a choice, prefer products liability rules in competing jurisdictions that call for a degree of user care they find more acceptable. By contrast, substantive federal legislation imposes one size on all, all at once. A federal private law rule forced on the country had better be "the right" one (and there had better be one "right" solution for our diverse population), for it is much more expensive to opt out of a country's laws than it is to use "voice" and "exit" when dissatisfied with one's state. As one commentator noted, "The choice between state authority and federal authority is the choice between competition and monopoly."[17] Indeed, shortly after President Clinton vetoed federal products liability reform legislation one observer noted, "[t]he status quo of state-law products liability may be unsatisfactory, but the alternative of federal-law products liability is keenly disadvantageous as well."[18]

B. Uniform State Laws of Product Liability

Karl Llewellyn began working on the Uniform Commercial Code after failing to interest Congress in a federal sales law.[19] Should there be a Uniform Products Liability Act?[20]

Restatements typically become law if and when state *courts* accept them. Uniform Laws, on the other hand, come into effect only if adopted by state *legislatures*. Therein lies a fundamental choice—and the ALI's adoption of the *Restatement (Third)* instead

---

17. Harvey S. Perlman, *Products Liability Reform in Congress: An Issue of Federalism*, 48 Ohio St. L.J. 503, 507 (1987).

18. Gary T. Schwartz, *Considering The Proper Federal Role In American Tort Law*, 38 Ariz. L. Rev. 917, 946 (1996).

19. *See* Zipporah B. Wiseman, *The Limits of Vision: Karl Llewellyn and the Merchant Rules*, 100 Harv. L. Rev. 465, 477–92 (1987).

20. Anita Bernstein, *Restatement Redux*, 48 Vand. L. Rev. 1663, 1682 (1995).

of a Uniform Products Liability Act expresses a distinct preference for common law evolution over legislative fiat.

The choice is an understandable one. The *Restatement (Second)* itself was arguably both excessive and misleading as regards its imposition of strict liability for design and informational defects. Judicial grappling with these excesses over the years has highlighted them and made subsequent change more likely. If concepts such as those enshrined in the *Restatement (Second)* had been frozen in legislation (via a Uniform Law) a gradual judicial retreat would have been more difficult. Legislatures can of course modify their own legislation, but political scientists have for some time shown how the "tyranny of the status quo" makes it hard to change bad laws.[21] A gradual judicial retreat from poor precedents is arguably easier to accomplish.

[handwritten margin note: whereas Rest 3d retreated to negligence some.]

C. Federal Common Law

Erie Railroad v. Tompkins,[22] which declares that federal courts are to apply state common law when applicable, was supposed to have been the *coup de grâce* for federal common law. But as has been noted by contemporary observers, *Erie* never accomplished this.[23] Federal judges still use federal presumptions or inferences (even if state presumptions or inferences point in the opposite direction) when deciding "federal cases." Of course most federal cases deal with federal statutes.[24] Thus, in more overtly "federal" areas of products liability (such as federal suits[25] against manufacturers of pharmaceuticals regulated by the *Food and Drug Act*[26]), federal judges could easily develop doctrines (for example, interpreting FDA approval of a drug as establishing a "safe harbor" against subsequent design defect claims).[27]

Congress could pass a statute declaring that products liability is a federal concern; the statute might be very simple, like the *Sherman Antitrust Act.*[28] Then a federal common law of products liability would rapidly develop, to be refined by the occasional Supreme Court decision. This is the solution promoted by former

---

21. Milton & Rose Friedman, The Tyranny of the Status Quo (1984).

22. Erie Railroad v. Tompkins, 304 U.S. 64, 82–83 (1938).

23. Henry J. Friendly, *In Praise of Erie—And of the New Federal Common Law*, 39 N.Y.U. L. Rev. 383 (1964).

24. For examples, see David R. Geiger & Mark D. Rosen, *Rationalizing Product Liability For Prescription Drugs: Implied Preemption, Federal Common Law, And Other Paths To Uniform Pharmaceutical Safety Standards*, 45 DePaul L. Rev. 395, 422–23 (1996).

25. *See* 21 U.S.C. § 334(a)(1) (1994) (providing that the manufacturer of "[a]ny ... drug ... that is ... misbranded ... or which may not ... be introduced into interstate commerce, shall be liable to be proceeded against ... in any district court of the United States").

26. 21 U.S.C. § 301 *et seq.* (2006).

27. Geiger & Rosen, *supra* note 24, at 426–27.

28. 15 U.S.C. § 1 (2006).

West Virginia Chief Justice Neely,[29] whose opinion of current products liability law was discussed earlier in this chapter. Neely's proposal has not been seriously advanced in Congress, perhaps because the proliferation of organized lobbies makes it likely that any such law passed today would contain mandates frustrating the common law process.

Professor Gary Schwartz eloquently enumerated the problems that would arise in the event Congress one day takes the "federal common law" route. These problems stem from two important facts. First, products liability is a subset of tort law, which would remain state-based—how would the two systems co-exist? Second, the Supreme Court docket is severely limited.

Schwartz derives from these facts three negative implications for any federal common law of products liability:

"[A] federal common law of products liability would maximize the problem of betting the store on whatever a particular United States Supreme Court ends up thinking. That problem can be further considered here. A state Supreme Court that decides a products liability case does so against the backdrop of all the other tort issues that belong to that court's ongoing agenda. Yet were there a federal common law of products liability and that alone, the Supreme Court would be required ultimately to decide products liability issues in isolation from any larger understanding of tort law; therefore there would be an increased prospect of unjustified disharmonies or discontinuities between products liability doctrine and tort doctrine more generally. As far as products liability itself is concerned, the situation of the Supreme Court can be contrasted with that of federal courts of appeal. Those latter courts, on account of their diversity jurisdiction, have been considering large numbers of products liability cases ever since the mid–1960s, and hence by now are generally familiar with products liability problems. Yet the Supreme Court routinely denies certiorari in mere diversity cases; until now, it has dealt with products liability only in a tiny number of cases with federal-law significance. Accordingly, the Supreme Court is currently unfamiliar not only with the larger body of tort law in general but also with the narrower body of products liability law in particular. A third problem with Supreme Court products liability decision making would be its rigidity. A state high court's docket is much less crowded than that of the United States Supreme Court itself. Given, for example, the prominence of tort cases on the California Supreme Court's docket, that court has been able to consider design defect doctrines in a series of opinions

29. Richard Neely, *The Products Liability Mess*, 1988, at 145–50, 170–75.

in 1970, 1972, 1978, 1982, and 1994; that Court has hence been able to do a reasonably good job in refining doctrine and learning from criticisms of its prior rulings. This learning process would be much less likely to occur were products liability assigned to the United States Supreme Court. Once that Court decides some particular products liability issue, as a practical matter that decision would probably remain unreviewable for perhaps a generation."[30]

4. International Approaches to Products Liability Law

As consumerism advances across the world, the influence of American products liability law has spread.

Europe

In the European Community, Product Liability Directive 85/374 governs.[31] The *Directive* was clearly inspired by § 402(A) of the *Restatement (Second)*, and imposes strict liability on manufacturers and importers (though, significantly, not on downstream sellers)[32] of defective products. There is an exception for "development risks," i.e., cases where the manufacturer can show that the defect was undiscoverable given the state of scientific and technical knowledge at the time the product was put into circulation.[33] The *Directive* departs significantly from § 402A in containing a ten-year statute of repose.

"Defects," defined by reference to objective consumer expectations, (i.e., the expectations a reasonable consumer or producer should have)[34], impliedly include manufacturing defects, informational defects and design defects.[35] A product must be used in a reasonable way for recovery to be allowed. The age of a product is an explicit factor in determining whether it is defective, and the

---

30. Schwartz, *supra* note 87, at 946–47.

31. Council Directive No. 85/374, O.J. L 210/29 (1985).

32. Downstream sellers are not liable as long as they can identify a producer. *Directive*, art. 3, § 3.

33. This is similar to Comment k of the *Restatement (Second)* and to most understandings of the "state of the art" defense. See Chapter 10 *supra*.

34. Article 6(1) of the *Directive* reads as follows:

A product is defective when it does not provide the safety which a person is

entitled to expect, taking all circumstances into account, including:

(a) the presentation of the product;

(b) the use to which it could reasonably be expected that the product would be put; and

(c) the time when the product was put into circulation.

35. The *Directive* does not differentiate between manufacturing and design defects, but the committee drafting the *Directive* indicated that Article 6(1)(a) did encompass failure to warn defects. *See* Ferdinando Albanese & Louis F. Del Duca, *Developments in European Product Liability*, 5 DICK. J. INT'L L. 193, 209 (1987).

Directive further specifies that a product is not defective merely because a better product is subsequently put into circulation.

An international law firm was asked to evaluate the impact of the directive, and produced a report in 2003.[36] Not surprisingly, the report found that products liability litigation had increased since the adoption of the *Directive*. Roughly half of all respondents surveyed thought that suits were not merely more numerous, but also that plaintiffs more frequently prevailed.[37]

Japan

Japan's 1994 products liability law, modeled on the European *Directive,* greatly expanded individual rights of action. Japan still allows fewer legal remedies than does American law—for example, only manufacturers (not downstream sellers) are strictly liable for damages caused by defective products. The Japanese law also provides more government support for alternative dispute resolution.[38]

Canada

Canada, the United States's most important trading partner, has judicially derived products liability rules in each province. In substance these rules resemble ours, from strict liability of sellers for manufacturing defects[39] to risk-utility analysis in determining design defects.[40] But practice differs greatly in that judges, not juries, decide products liability issues. These judges are federally appointed, with life tenure. These differences impact incentives, as discussed earlier in this Chapter. Notably, the lack of juries impacts discovery rules, which tend to be much more restrictive when judges participate actively in trials than when judges are relatively passive spectators.[41] Moreover, Canada's products liability litigation

36. Product Liability in the European Union: A Report for the European Commission, MARKT/2001/11/D, Feb. 2003 (Lovells law firm).

37. Of those who thought there had been no change in plaintiffs' success rates, most were from countries such as Germany, France and Belgium, where earlier national systems of product liability law generally had been equally favorable to consumers. Art. 13 of the *Directive* allows national systems of liability (e.g., Germany's *Drug Act*) that existed at the time the *Directive* was adopted to co-exist alongside the *Directive.* Germany subsequently adopted the *Products Liability Act*, which is quite similar to the *Directive* and to the *Restatement (Second). See Germany: Law*

Concerning Liability for Defective Products, 32 I.L.M. 1369 (Sandra N. Hurd & Frances E. Zollers, trans., 1993).

38. *See, e.g.,* Nancy Young, *Japan's New Products Liability Law: Increased Protection for Consumers*, 18 Loy. L.A. Int'l & Comp. L.J. 893 (1996).

39. *See, e.g.,* Katz v. Reitz, [1973] C.A. 230 (Qué. C.A.).

40. *See, e.g.,* Rentway Canada Ltd. v. Laidlaw Transport Ltd., [1989] O.J. 786 (Ont. H.C.J.), *aff'd,* [1994] O.J. 50 (Ont. C.A.). The trial judge in *Rentway* affirmatively cited Voss v. Black & Decker Manufacturing Co., 450 N.E.2d 204 (N.Y. 1983).

41. Rebekah Rollo, *Products Liability: Why The European Union Doesn't*

is not characterized by the prevalence of pure contingent fees with no "loser-pays" rule.[42] Finally, socialized "free" medical care and a national cap on "pain and suffering" damages have undoubtedly led many victims of defective products to choose not to sue. As a result of these and other structural differences, Canada did not experience the explosion of products liability claims and of damage awards that has occurred in the United States.

5.   Replacing Products Liability With Social Insurance

New Zealand's courts never adopted strict liability for product accidents.[43] However, in 1974 Parliament published a report (the "Woodhouse Report") that heavily criticized the tort system's unpredictable awards and high transaction costs.[44] New Zealand's government proceeded to create an accident compensation system that bars lawsuits for most claims involving accidental physical injury.[45] This covers most conventional accidents and some employment related diseases. A government agency reimburses medical costs, 80 percent of lost wages, a lump sum amount representing permanent loss, and wrongful death awards to spouses and children.

Perhaps unsurprisingly, in fiscal year 2007, the government agency responsible for administering this new entitlement had *1.6 million claims pending for a national population of 4.3 million*—the equivalent of over 100 million claims in the United States, fully 150 times our litigation rate.[46] The New Zealand system covers "accidents" but not diseases. Thus, a child disabled by obstetric malpractice would receive extensive benefits, while a baby genetically born with the same disability would have to rely on private insur-

Need The Restatement (Third), 69 Brook. L. Rev. 1073, 1117–8 (2004) (citing Peter Borer, "Bringt uns die EG–Richtlinie zur Produktehaftung 'amerikanische Verhaltnisse'?", in *US and EEC Product Liability: Issues and Trends*, 105, at 133–136 (Roger Zach ed., 1989)).

42. The Attorney Accountability Act of 1995, H.R. 988, 104th Cong., 1st Session (1995), adopted as a reform distinct from substantive federal products liability legislation, did provide for a modified "loser pays" system as part of the "Contract with America." This Bill was adopted by the House of Representatives, but was never considered by the Senate.

43. To judicially adopt strict liability would have been seen as "most improper," according to a leading New

Zealand jurist. *See* Palmer, *supra* note 1, at 610.

44. Joan M. Matheson, *Compensation for Personal Injury in New Zealand: The Woodhouse Report*, 18 Int'l & Comp. L.Q. 191 (1969).

45. Suits are, in brief, allowed only for intentional tort, for torts damaging property (a negligence rule is applied) and for punitive damages. *See* Peter H. Schuck, *Tort Reform, Kiwi–Style*, 27 Yale L. & Pol'y Rev. 187, 191 (2008).

46. By comparison, since the asbestos tide stemmed, roughly 660,000 tort suits are filed in state (600,000) and federal (60,000) courts each year. *See* National Center for State Courts, *Tort Caseloads in State Trial Courts of General Jurisdiction, 1998–2007*, http://www.ncsconline.org/D_Research/

ance or the very limited public system.[47] Some find it philosophically untenable that one rendered disabled by "accident" is entitled to government compensation, but that one disabled "naturally" gets no such entitlement. Several socialist backers of the New Zealand plan have advocated its extension to all illness or disadvantages.[48] It's hard to see how this would differ from a total equalization of all wealth, since arguably our conditions spring largely from the advantages or disadvantages from which we benefit or suffer.

As the costs of government outlays increased and belts were tightened, pressures grew to limit New Zealand's program. Thus, punitive damage claims (punitive damage suits for intentional torts had never been banned) were expanded, and suits are now allowed in cases of "recklessness," a concept suspiciously close to negligence.[49] Budgetary pressures have led New Zealanders to launch product liability suits in other countries if they can secure jurisdiction there.[50]

New Zealand's system has been closely examined by neighboring Australia, which held similar Parliamentary hearings but declined to adopt a socialized tort system.[51] The New Zealand government itself calculated in 2008 that the system's social costs exceed those of a tort system. The government still claims that the "social value added" more than justifies this cost.[52] A small number of critics advocate the adoption of a similar socialized risk sharing system in the United States.[53]

Questions About Julian Felipe's Case

- In the United States, pursuant to federal regulation, vehicles must be produced at some point during their nominal model year.[54] In other words, 2010 vehicles must be manufactured on

.2007_files/Table%204_07.xls (last consulted May 5, 2010).

47. Schuck, *supra* note 45, at 193.

48. *See, e.g.,* P.S. Atiyah, The Damages Lottery (1998) at 185.

49. *See, e.g.,* A v. Bottrill, [2002] UKPC 44, [2003] 2 NZLR 721 (Privy Council, from New Zealand).

50. *Australian asbestos case 'has implications for NZers'*, NEW ZEALAND HERALD, Sept. 22, 2004, http://www.nzherald.co.nz/nz/news/article.cfm?c_id=1 & objectid=3593726 (last consulted May 5, 2010).

51. Australian law professor Patrick Atiyah's book, Accidents, Compensation and the Law (1970) advocated socialization of accident risks, but that country's *National Committee of Inquiry: Compensation and Rehabilitation in*

Australia report (1974) was never acted upon.

52. PriceWaterhouseCooper, Accident Compensation Corporation New Zealand: Scheme Review, v–x (2008).

53. *See, e.g.,* Stephen D. Sugarman, Doing Away With Personal Injury Law: New Compensation Mechanisms for Victims, Consumers and Business (1989).

54. 26 C.F.R. § 48.4064–1(b)(4) (2009).

The term "model year" means the manufacturer's annual production period (as determined by the Administrator of the Environmental Protection Agency) which includes January 1 of any particular calendar year. If the manufacturer has no annual production year, the model year is the calendar year.

Jan. 1, 2010, but may be introduced earlier. Thus, for example, a 1993 model year vehicle is typically manufactured as of early 1992 and marketed from mid–1992 on.[55] Assume the Felipes' 1993 Aerostar was sold in May 1992. Their tragic accident occurred in August 2002. Thus, the Felipes' suit would have been precluded by the ten year statute of repose had their accident taken place in Europe. Is that statute of repose a good idea? Should it be implemented federally for automobiles here, as is done for small airplanes?[56] Isn't the 2010 automobile industry in just as dire financial straits as was the 1994 general aviation industry, which Congress decided to assist by adopting the statute of repose? More generally, should an industry's economic health dictate products liability laws? Does such a policy reward inefficiency with tort immunity? Should a general ten–year statute of repose be adopted for all products?

- If the Felipes had imported their vehicle from Mexico, where (hypothetically) it was first put into the stream of commerce, should Mexican products liability laws apply to their case?

---

55. Frequently the introduction of a model year is much earlier. For instance, on Jan. 28, 2010 Kia introduced some 2011 models; manufacturing had evidently begun in late 2009. *See* Colum Wood, *Geneva Preview: 2011 Kia Sportage Unveiled Ahead of Official Debut*, http://www.autoguide.com/auto-news/2010/02/geneva-preview–2011–kia-sportage-unveiled-ahead-of-official- debut.html All that is required is that these Kia models still be manufactured on Jan. 1, 2011.

56. The General Aviation Revitalization Act of 1994, Pub. L. No. 103–298, 108 Stat. 1552 (18-year statute of repose.

Appendix

THE SIMPLE ECONOMICS OF PRODUCTS LIABILITY LAW

1. Design Defects: Design Choice By Manufacturer[1]

Imagine that a company can produce a soft drink in bottles or in cans. Bottles are cheaper to produce, but accident costs are higher. This is the case both because it is easier to shatter a bottle by accidentally or intentionally striking it against a hard object, and because if a bottle shatters, glass shards are more harmful than dented or even cut aluminum.

Assume the following (arbitrarily chosen) production and accident cost numbers describe the situation:

Table I

DESIGN CHOICE (1)	UNIT PRODUCTION COST (2)	ACCIDENT RATE (3)	AVERAGE ACCIDENT COST (4)	UNIT ACCIDENT COST (5)[2]	UNIT SOCIAL COST (6)[3]
Bottle	.25	1/1,000,000	$100,000	.10	.35
Can	.28	0.5/1,000,000	$20,000	.01	.29

Though bottles are cheaper to produce than are cans, they actually cost more socially, given the accident rate. If consumers have no background preference for bottles over cans, and if there are no social costs other than production and accident costs,[4] then the "efficient" solution is to produce the drink in cans, since the total cost of a can is cheaper than the true cost of a bottle.[5]

In this exercise, the design incentives of manufacturers will be examined in the light of different legal rules and different states of knowledge.

---

1. This example is borrowed, with adaptation, from A. MITCHELL POLINSKY, AN INTRODUCTION TO LAW AND ECONOMICS 98 (2d ed. 1989).

2. Column (5) is the product of columns (3) and (4). Assume one million units are produced.

3. Column (6) is the sum of columns (2) and (5). Assume that production costs and accident costs are the sum total of costs here.

4. Thus, there are no pollution or recycling costs in this simplified example.

5. If consumers prefer bottles to cans, they will be willing to pay more for the soft drink in bottles than they would for the same soft drink in cans. If that preference is strong enough, they will be willing to pay enough of a difference in price to justify the production of bottles even when accident costs are taken into account.

A. Manufacturers and Consumers Understand Product Risks

If both manufacturers and consumers have full knowledge of the risk of drinking from cans and bottles, then regardless of the legal rule in effect, consumers will have the incentive to purchase only cans, never bottles.

To see this, imagine three legal rules, each of which is assumed to be applied perfectly and costlessly. Suppose also that consumers cannot cause "accidents" through their own negligence. In other words, only the choice of design (bottles or cans) can affect the rate of accidents:

1). Strict liability

If manufacturers are <u>liable every time there is an accident</u> (a shattered container), they will pay for all accident costs. The manufacturer's total production cost will be .35 per bottle and .29 per can. Since consumers do not prefer bottles or cans, *ceteris paribus*, <u>cans will be the design choice.</u>

2). Negligence

[margin note: but bulletproof vest?]

The <u>design choice of bottles over cans would be negligent.</u> To see this, note that the difference in accident losses for each bottle over each can (.09) is greater than the difference in cost to produce

[margin note: MUST do most cost effective thing.]

the drinks in cans (.03). In other words, for .03 in care, the manufacturer can avoid .09 in accidents.[6] <u>If the manufacturer produces soft drinks in bottles instead of cans, it will be liable for negligence and</u> its true per unit cost will be .35. If it produces soft drinks in cans it will not be liable (for it will not have been negligent) and its per unit cost will be .28. Here again, cans will be the design choice.

3). No Liability

Finally, imagine that there is no products liability law; manufacturers are never liable for design choices. All accident costs fall on consumers (who of course are free to purchase first-party insurance policies to help them bear these costs). From the manufacturer's point of view, it might appear that the design choice will be bottles, which cost less to produce than do cans. However, <u>risk-neutral consumers with information about risks will refuse to purchase bottles unless they are priced so cheaply that the savings more than overcomes the .09 accident cost disadvantage per can.</u> Manufacturers cannot price bottles more than .09 cheaper than cans, and so they <u>will produce cans</u>, which consumers will purchase.

---

6. *See* United States v. Carroll Towing Co., 159 F.2d 169, 173 (2d Cir. 1947) (holding that liability depends on whether the burden of adequate precautions is less than the product of the probability that injury will occur and the seriousness of the resulting injury).

Obviously, this example abstracts from litigation costs. Litiga- *litigation costs.* tion costs will be zero under no liability, positive under a negligence rule (plaintiffs will tend not to sue if the manufacturer is not negligent) and high under strict liability (plaintiffs will sue every time there is an accident).

B. Manufacturers Understand Product Risks, Consumers Underestimate Them

Now assume that consumers are ignorant of the possibility of a container shattering. Ignorance of this kind is perhaps implausible, given the publicity of such cases in the press. On the other hand (and as many game theorists contend), the extreme improbability of an accident may lead consumers to irrationally discount its probability to zero.[7]

The following incentives will be produced by the three possible legal rules in this scenario:

1). *Strict liability*

If manufacturers are liable for all shattering accidents, they will again internalize the costs of consumer injuries and prefer to produce cans (which will cost them .29 each) than bottles (which will cost them .35 each).

2). *Negligence*

If manufacturers are liable only if negligent, they will again not be liable if they produce cans, but they will be liable if they produce bottles, for reasons explained above. Thus, the cost of cans will be .28, while the cost of bottles will be .35. Again, they will produce cans.

3). *No Liability*

If manufacturers are never liable for shattered containers, ignorant consumers will prefer to purchase bottles (which *apparently* cost them .25 each) over cans (which will apparently cost .28), as they will "not see" the accident costs of each type of container. Since bottles are what consumers will prefer, bottles are what non-liable manufacturers will tend to produce. Of course, a competitor may try to maximize profits by producing cans and educating consumers about their superior safety, but if consumers are invincibly irrational, this competitor will not succeed.

"Inefficient" design choices are therefore likely in a no-liability world as long as consumers underestimate the risks of products.

---

7. Daniel Kahneman, & Amos Tversky, *Choices, Values, and Frames*, 39(4) AM. PSYCHOLOGIST, 341 (1984). Applied to Julian Felipe's case, this psychological theory implies that, given the choice, consumers will refuse to purchase more costly vans with sturdier roofs even if they were informed of the statistical net benefits of such roofs, since the chance of a rollover is so slim that it is irrationally discounted to zero.

This is a powerful consequential rationale for products liability law, whether negligence-based or grounded in strict liability. The choice between these two rules would then depend on how realistic the assumptions of the model are presumed to be.[8]

C. Consumers are Rational and Can Affect the Accident Rate

Subsections A and B assumed that the accident rate was "exogenous" to consumers—that is, that the rate of shattering depended solely on the design choice (bottles or cans) selected by manufacturers. Suppose now that consumers can affect the likelihood of shattering by the way they handle the soft drinks they purchase.

1). Strict liability

If manufacturers are liable every time a container shatters, all costs are borne by the manufacturer. Perfectly rational consumers in such a system will not have the incentive to use containers carefully, since care is always costly and only serves to benefit the manufacturer by reducing his liability costs. This is a "moral hazard" that will lead to "too many" accidents.[9] Thus, to work efficiently, strict liability would have to be accompanied by a "contributory negligence" defense (which might also be called a "consumer misuse" defense). Only if this defense were available and perfectly applied (which would require that the manufacturer have access to reliable information about how the injured consumer used the product) would this "modified strict liability" rule be able to operate efficiently.

2). Negligence

As has been seen, if the manufacturer makes the correct design choice it is not negligent, and the costs all remaining accidents are borne by the consumer. (Under a "no liability rule" this will occur for all accidents no matter what the design choice.) In other words, the cost of "residual" accidents is shifted to the manufacturer only under a strict liability rule. Non-shifted accident costs provide an incentive for the consumer not to misuse the product, even if there is no "consumer misuse" defense. Thus, a negligence rule provides

---

8. For instance, if many accidents resulted from consumer negligence that was difficult to prove, strict liability would create a serious "moral hazard" wherein careful consumers "subsidize" careless ones, perhaps leading the careful consumers to decline to pay the subsidy premium and creating a market failure.

9. Of course, in an important sense even one accident is "too many." But no one suggests spending stupendous amounts of money to avoid one additional accident. As this exercise points out, accidents are deplorable, but in an imperfect world some accidents will occur. The idea is to structure the law so as to provide incentives to avoid those accidents that can be avoided at reasonable cost.

incentives to both parties to take appropriate care, *if* consumers are aware of (and rationally able to process) the dangers of misusing the product.

D. What if a Third Party is Injured?

The discussion thus far has assumed that the person injured by the soft drink container is the person who purchased the product. Though this is likely to be the case for soft drinks, other products (automobiles, for instance) may injure non-purchasers. Assume then, counterfactually, that containers often injure third parties.

1). *Strict liability*

If a manufacturer is liable for all injuries caused by shattering containers, it will internalize the accident costs to third parties in making its design choice. Thus, given the data in Table 1, it will have the incentive to produce cans, not bottles. The purchase price of bottles (which would include the cost of liability) would be so high that purchasers would buy cans, thereby protecting third parties.

2). *Negligence*

Under a negligence rule, it would be negligent to produce bottles, as seen above. The purchase price of bottles would have to include liability costs, making these bottles expensive for buyers. Cans would be priced without any liability premium, since manufacturers would be non-negligent if they sold cans and therefore not liable to anyone injured by shattering. Consumers would purchase cans, indeed they would purchase a few more cans (because the price would be lower, .28 instead of .29 per can) than they would under a strict liability régime. Thus, if *only* third parties were injured by shattering containers, one would expect there to be "too many" soft drink purchases and an inefficiently high number of shattering accidents with a negligence rule. Of course, in practice, if the majority of containers exploded in consumers' (not third parties') faces, the excessive output problem would be meaningless.

Finally, and as stated earlier, if for some reason consumers are invincibly ignorant of the risks of shattering, they will over-purchase bottles under a negligence rule. One remedy for such invincible ignorance, if it exists, might be government mandates (regulations) determining design parameters. This assumes that government has the incentive to act in the public interest and not to cater to the (bottle or can or plaintiffs' lawyers') lobby.

[handwritten margin note: like drunk driving law, crashworthiness]

2. Manufacturing Defects: Quality Control[10]

Imagine that a firm produces one million glass bottles of cola per year.[11] Of the million bottles produced each year, on average thirty

---

10. This example is inspired by, though in a very different format from, that used in JAMES A. HENDERSON & AARON D. TWERSKI, PRODUCTS LIABILITY: PROB-

"lemons" (weak bottles that shatter upon hard impact with another object) will make it through the manufacturing process if no quality control is implemented. A "lemon" (shattering bottle) produces an average of $100,000 in accident costs (some folks merely suffer surprise and a cola-stained shirt; others cut an artery and either die or require very expensive surgery). The more quality control ("Q.C.") the firm purchases, the fewer lemons make it through to the consumer.[12] Initial investments in quality control are relatively inexpensive. For instance, cameras on the factory floor would detect poor handling of bottles by employees. However, as one adds more and more types of quality control, eventually one gets "less bang for the prevention buck." Eventually much more expensive measures are required to decrease the "lemon" rate further.

Table II reflects this reality. Imagine that these are the costs and benefits of up to twelve "units" of quality control designed to prevent a manufacturing defect in the glass bottles produced.

Table II

(1)	(2)	(3)	(4)	(5)	(6)	(7)
UNITS OF Q.C.	COST OF THIS UNIT OF Q.C.	TOTAL COST OF Q.C.	NUMBER OF "LEMONS"	TOTAL ACCIDENT COSTS	INJURY COST (Q.C. + ACCIDENTS)	INJURY COST PER BOTTLE
0	$0	$0	30	$3,000,000	$3,000,000	$3.00
1	$20,000	$20,000	22	$2,200,000	$2,220,000	$2.22
2	$35,000	$55,000	16	$1,600,000	$1,655,000	$1.66
3	$60,000	$115,000	12	$1,200,000	$1,315,000	$1.32
4	$90,000	$205,000	9	$900,000	$1,105,000	$1.11
5	$150,000	$355,000	7	$700,000	$1,055,000	$1.06
6	$300,000	$655,000	6	$600,000	$1,255,000	$1.26
7	$500,000	$1,155,000	5	$500,000	$1,655,000	$1.66
8	$750,000	$1,905,000	4	$400,000	$2,305,000	$2.31
9	$1,000,000	$2,905,000	3	$300,000	$3,205,000	$3.21
10	$1,300,000	$4,205,000	2	$200,000	$4,405,000	$4.41
11	$1,700,000	$5,905,000	1	$100,000	$6,005,000	$6.01
12	$2,200,000	$8,105,000	0	$0	$8,105,000	$8.11

Questions:

1. How much quality control should a profit-seeking manufacturer purchase? Given that quality control costs must be reflected in the purchase price, how much quality control do consumers want the manufacturer to purchase?

2. Under a strict liability rule, a manufacturer would be liable for all injuries from shattering bottles. How much quality

LEMS AND PROCESS Problem 2 (6th ed. 2008).

11. Assume that glass bottles are a non-defective design.

12. Assume, counterfactually, that consumers cannot affect the rate of shattering by taking more care with the bottles.

control will the manufacturer have the incentive to purchase under a strict liability rule, correctly applied?

3. Under a negligence rule, a manufacturer would be negligent (and liable) only if the cost of the "next" unit of quality control (that the manufacturer declined to purchase) is less than the expected savings (reduction in accident costs) from that "next" unit.[13] How many units of quality control would the manufacturer have the incentive to purchase under a negligence rule?

4. Many people think that strict liability for manufacturing defects leads to safer products (more quality control) than would a negligence rule. Does this example accredit that viewpoint?

5. If you have considered questions 2 and 3 closely, you will see that they produce the same answer (the manufacturer will have the incentive to purchase five units of quality control under each rule, and seven "lemons" will be sold per million bottles produced, occasioning $700,000 in injury costs). Of course that does not mean that the two legal rules are identical—for there are distributive differences. Under a strict liability rule, the injury costs from the seven "residual" lemons will be shifted to the manufacturer, as a result of products liability suits. These suits have a "loading cost" of about 55 percent[14]—so it will cost the manufacturer about $1,500,000 to get full compensation ($700,000) to injured consumers or third parties. Under a negligence rule, the residual accident costs will be borne by the injured parties themselves, since the manufacturer that purchases five units of quality control will be non-negligent and therefore not liable to them. Of course, injured parties can shift injury costs to insurance companies *via* first party (health, disability, etc.) policies. Such policies have a loading cost of about 10 percent[15]—that is, it would cost the consumers and third parties about $770,000 to obtain full compensation for their losses. In other words, consumers and third parties can have their "insurance" nominally paid for by the manufacturer at a cost of $1.5 million (factored into the sale price) or by themselves at about half that price, but paid for personally. Which rule would consumers favor? Which rule *should* they favor?

13. *See* United States v. Carroll Towing, Co., 159 F.2d 169, 173–74 (2d Cir. 1947); *see also* note 6 *supra*.

14. See Chapter 14, *supra*, where the loading costs of tort adjudication are discussed.

15. *Id.*

Table of Cases

279

D

E

N

Index

References are to Pages

289

†